Arbuthnot

Atkinson

Bomberg

Coburn

Dismorr

Epstein

Etchells

Gaudier-Brzeska

Hamilton

Hulme

Lewis

Nevinson

Pound

Roberts

Saunders

Shakespear

Wadsworth

# Richard Cork

# VORTICISM

## AND ABSTRACT ART IN THE FIRST MACHINE AGE

Volume 1
Origins and Development

UNIVERSITY OF CALIFORNIA
Berkeley · Los Angeles

UNIVERSITY OF CALIFORNIA PRESS
Berkeley and Los Angeles
Copyright © Richard Cork 1976
ISBN 0–520–03154–7
Library of Congress Catalog Card Number: 75–37227

Set in Monotype Imprint and printed in Great Britain by
Lund Humphries, Bradford and London
Designed by Peter Guy

FOR VENA

WHO DESERVES MUCH MORE THAN THIS

# Contents

(The bibliography appears in Volume 2)

# List of Illustrations in Volume One

To aid conciseness, the word 'lost' is used whenever the whereabouts of an original work is unknown.
Height is stated before width in the measurements listed and they are all given to the nearest half-centimetre.
Where relevant, the number under which a work was listed in the catalogue of *Vorticism and its Allies*, the exhibition held at the Hayward Gallery, London, March–June 1974, has been added in italics at the end of an entry. The number which precedes each entry refers to the page on which the illustration appears.
All the illustrations are reproduced by courtesy of the various museums and other bodies cited in this list to whom the publishers extend grateful thanks.

Frontispiece:
    *Malcolm Arbuthnot*, 1907
        Photograph by Coburn
    *Lawrence Atkinson*, c.1922
    *David Bomberg*, 1914
    *Alvin Langdon Coburn*, c.1917
        Photograph by Craigie
    *Jessica Dismorr*, c.1926
        From a self-portrait
    *Jacob Epstein*, 1914
        Photograph by Coburn
    *Frederick Etchells*, c.1912
        Photograph by Vanessa Bell
    *Henri Gaudier-Brzeska*, c.1914
    *Cuthbert Hamilton*, 1915
        From a painting by Roberts executed in 1961–2
    *T. E. Hulme*, c.1914
    *Wyndham Lewis*, c.1913
    *Christopher Nevinson*, 1915
        From a self-portrait
    *Ezra Pound*, 1913
        Photograph by Coburn
    *William Roberts*, 1918
    *Helen Saunders*, c.1912
    *Dorothy Shakespear*, c.1909
    *Edward Wadsworth*, 1915
        Photograph by Coburn

PAGE:
1. Wyndham Lewis
*Nude Boy Bending Over*, 1900
Chalk, 34·5 × 29 cm
Slade School of Fine Art, London

2. Augustus John
*Moses and the Brazen Serpent*, 1898
Oil on canvas, 170 × 233 cm
Slade School of Fine Art, London

3. Wyndham Lewis
*An Oriental Design* (detail), 1900–05
Ink and wash, 33 × 38 cm
Private collection

6. Augustus John
*Portrait of Wyndham Lewis*, c.1905
Oil on canvas, 80 × 61 cm
Private collection

10. Wyndham Lewis
*The Theatre Manager*, 1909(?)
Ink and watercolour, 29·5 × 32 cm
Victoria and Albert Museum, London. (*1*)

10. Pablo Picasso
*Les Demoiselles d'Avignon*, 1907
Oil on canvas, 244 × 233 cm
Museum of Modern Art, New York
Acquired through the Lillie P. Bliss Bequest

13. Wyndham Lewis
*The Celibate*, 1909–?
Ink, watercolour and gouache, 37·5 × 28·5 cm
Private collection. (*2*)

14. Wyndham Lewis
*Architect with Green Tie*, 1909–?
Ink and gouache, 24 × 13·5 cm
Private collection. (*3*)

16. Wyndham Lewis
*Café*, 1910–11
Ink, chalk, watercolour and gouache, 21 × 13·5 cm
Private collection

17. H. M. Bateman
*Post-Impressions of the Post-Impressionists*, 1910
Lost
Reproduced: *Bystander*, 23/11/10. (*148*)

19. Wyndham Lewis
*Smiling Woman Ascending a Stair*, 1911–12
Charcoal and gouache, 94·5 × 65 cm
Vint Trust, Bradford. (*5*)

20. Augustus John
*The Smiling Woman*, 1909
Oil on canvas, 195·5 × 96·5 cm
Tate Gallery, London

21. Wyndham Lewis
*Indian Dance*, 1912
Chalk and watercolour, 27 × 29 cm
Tate Gallery, London

21. Duncan Grant
*The Tub*, 1912
Oil, wash and wax varnish on paper laid on canvas, 76 × 56 cm
Tate Gallery, London

21. Spencer Gore
*The Beanfield, Letchworth*, 1912
Oil on canvas, 30·5 × 41 cm
Tate Gallery, London

27. C. Harrison
*The New Terror*, 1912
Lost
Reproduced: *Daily Express*, 4/3/12. (*150*)

29. Wyndham Lewis
*Centauress*, 1912
Ink and watercolour, 31 × 37 cm
Cecil Higgins Art Gallery, Bedford. (*13*)

30. Wyndham Lewis
*Two Mechanics*, c.1912
Ink and wash, 56 × 33·5 cm
Tate Gallery, London

30. Wyndham Lewis
*Two Women*, 1912
Pencil, ink, wash, gouache and collage, 47 × 62 cm
Arts Council of Great Britain, London. (*14*)

31. Wyndham Lewis
*The Vorticist*, 1912
Ink, chalk and wash, 42 × 30·5 cm
Southampton City Art Gallery. (*15*)

32. Wyndham Lewis
*The Courtesan*, 1912
Ink and pastel, 27·5 × 18·5 cm
Victoria and Albert Museum, London. (*16*)

33. Pablo Picasso
*Head of a Man*, 1912
Oil on canvas, 61 × 38 cm
Private collection, Paris

34. Wyndham Lewis
*Cabaret Theatre Club Poster*, 1912
Printed paper, 62 × 43 cm
Department of Rare Books, Cornell University

35. Wyndham Lewis
*A Wall Decoration in the Cave of the Golden Calf*, 1912
Pamphlet, 27·5 × 22 cm. Size of drawing: 12·5 × 24 cm
Private collection. (*7*)

35. Wyndham Lewis
*Abstract Design*, 1912
Ink and watercolour, 24 × 38·5 cm
British Council, London

35. Spencer Gore
*Sketch for a Mural Decoration in the Cave of the Golden Calf*, 1912
Oil on paper, 30·5 × 60·5 cm
Tate Gallery, London

37. Cuthbert Hamilton (?)
*Three Dancing Figures*, c.1912–13
Ink, 32·5 × 54 cm
Private collection. (*75*)

38. Wyndham Lewis
*Design for a Programme Cover – Kermesse*, 1912
Ink, 28·5 × 31 cm
Private collection

39. Pablo Picasso
*The Dryad*, 1908
Oil on canvas, 185 × 108 cm
Hermitage Museum, Leningrad

40. Wyndham Lewis
*Kermesse*, 1912
Ink, wash and gouache, 30 × 29 cm
Phillips Family Collection, Montreal. (*9*)

41. Wyndham Lewis
*The Dancers* (*Study for Kermesse?*), 1912
Ink and watercolour, 30 × 29 cm
Phillips Family Collection, Montreal. (*10*)

43. Wyndham Lewis
*Creation*, 1912
Lost
Reproduced: illustrated catalogue of the *Second Post-Impressionist Exhibition* Grafton Galleries, London, October 1912–January 1913. (*17*)

# Acknowledgements

When I first started researching into Vorticism at the end of 1968, for my Cambridge Tripos thesis, the dearth of published information about the entire subject was as shameful as it was acute. Since then, this appalling situation has slowly begun to improve; but I could never have written my book over the intervening period without help provided by a sizable number of generous individuals and institutions. I am grateful to them all for answering my doubtless tiresome queries with such patience, and if space prevents me from specifying how they contributed to the pages which follow, my thanks are no less heartfelt.

Before listing them, however, I must single out Anthony d'Offay for a special tribute. I originally contacted him when he was beginning to prepare for his pioneering *Abstract Art in England 1913-1915* exhibition in 1969, which opened the eyes of many to the true stature of a long-neglected period in English art. Anthony was hearteningly involved, communicated that involvement to me and has always proved ready to be consulted about even the smallest matter. His encouragement and co-operation have been invaluable.

Otherwise, the following fully deserve to be thanked:

Aberdeen Art Gallery and Museum; Ronald Alley; Michael Armstrong; Ashmolean Museum, Oxford; Michael Ayrton; Elizabeth Bailey; Wendy Baron; the Hon. David Bathurst; the late Diana Baum; Olivia Bell; Corinne Bellow; Charlotte Benton; Alexander von Bethmann-Hollweg; Barbara von Bethmann-Hollweg; Birmingham City Museum and Art Gallery; The Bodley Head; Bolton Museum and Art Gallery; Elizabeth Ashby Bolton; Lilian Bomberg; Alan Bowness; Bradford City Art Gallery and Museums; Bristol City Art Gallery; the British Council; British Museum Newspaper Library; Brook Street Gallery; David Brown; L. J. Cadbury; Cambridge University Fine Arts Faculty; Cambridge University Library; National Gallery of Canada, Ottawa; Rodney Capstick-Dale; Victor M. Cassidy; Christie's photographic archives; Mr and Mrs Tobias Clarke; Celia Clayton; Clough, Son & Morton, Cleckheaton; David Coates; Roger Cole; Judith Collins; Department of Rare Books, Cornell University; Stephen Cristea; David Davies; Dinora Davies-Rees; Helen Deleu; Pamela Diamand; Dr Anthony Dismorr; Dr James Dismorr; Christopher Drake; Joanna Drew; David Drey; O. Raymond Drey; Mario Dubsky; Edward H. Dwight; George Eastman House; H. S. Ede; Lady Kathleen Epstein; the late Frederick Etchells; Merlyn Evans; John Farlie; G. M. Forty; Grattan Freyer; Jeremy Friend-Smith; Primrose Friend-Smith; William Gaunt; Helmut Gernsheim; Oscar Ghez; Arthur Gill; Glasgow University Art Collections; Mark Glazebrook; Duncan Grant; Adam Green; Janet Green; Jeremy Green; Simon Green; the late Charles Handley-Read; Elizabeth Harrison; Mark Haworth-Booth; Colin Haycraft; Sir John Heygate; Cecil Higgins Art Gallery, Bedford; Carol Hogben; Holman Brothers, Ltd; Michael Holroyd; Huddersfield Art Gallery; Hull University Library; Professor Sam Hynes; Imperial War Museum; Ingersoll-Rand Company; Israel Museum, Jerusalem; Harry Jonas; Alun R. Jones; Sonia Joslen; Edmond X. Kapp; Keele University Library; Sir Geoffrey Keynes; Lady Lydia Keynes; King's College Library, Cambridge; Katherine Kinnear; James Kirkman; Rex de C. Nan Kivell; Paul Laib; Laing Art Gallery and Museum, Newcastle Upon Tyne; Bonnie Lambert; Kate Lechmere; the Leicester Galleries; Leicester Museum and Art Gallery; Anne Wyndham Lewis; William S. Lieberman; Professor William C. Lipke; Nicholas Lott; Manchester City Art Gallery; Penny Marcus; Marlborough Fine Art Ltd; the late Alice Mayes; the late Frederick Mayor; James Mayor; Nora Meninsky; Walter Michel; Minneapolis Institute of Arts; Molly Mitchell-Smith; Henry Moore; Richard Morphet; Christopher Mullen; Musée National d'Art Moderne, Paris; Museum of Modern Art, New York; Angela Neville; New South Wales Art Gallery, Sydney; Ben Nicholson; Nottingham Museum and Art Gallery; R. H. M. Ody; Sir Roland Penrose; Helen Peppin; Ivan E. Phillips; Phillips Collection, Washington; Clive Phillpot; Godfrey Pilkington; Dorothy Shakespear Pound; Omar Pound; Power Institute of Fine Arts, Sydney University; D. D. Prenn; Punch archives; Princess Mary de Rachewiltz; B. L. Reid; Denis Richardson; Duncan Robinson; Joan Rodker; Sir John Rothenstein; Royal Photographic Society; Edward P. Schinman; Science Museum, London; Scottish National Gallery of Modern Art, Edinburgh; Richard Shone; Francis Sitwell; Reresby Sitwell; Peyton Skipwith; Smithsonian Institution; Sotheby's photographic archives; Southampton Art Gallery; Stoke-on-Trent City Museum and Art Gallery; Charles L. Strong; Denys Sutton; Valentine A. J. Swain; Tate Gallery Library; Sir Richard Temple; Temple Newsam House, Leeds; Robert Tilling; Caroline Tisdall; Towner Art Gallery, Eastbourne; Peter Townsend; Philip Troutman; the Rev. Eric Turnbull; Ulster Museum, Belfast; Victoria and Albert Museum Library; R. W. T. Vint; the late Walter W. Wadsworth; Wadsworth Atheneum, Hartford; National Museum of Wales, Cardiff; Walker Art Gallery, Liverpool; the Rev. John Wall; Kenneth Warr; Simon Watson Taylor; Professor William C. Wees; Robert Wellington; Dame Rebecca West; William Weston; John Wheelwright; Andrew Dickson White Museum of Art, Cornell University; John White; Whitworth Art Gallery, University of Manchester; R. H. Wilenski; A. H. T. Windeler; Miss A. E. Wisdom; the Witt Collection; John Woodeson; Susan Wyatt; York City Art Gallery.

Finally, a special word of gratitude for James Fraser whose enthusiasm for the book has been immensely encouraging at all times.

*The publisher's acknowledgements for quoted sources appear in Volume 2.

# Chronology

1898   Lewis enters the Slade, leaving in 1901.

1899   Hamilton enters the Slade, leaving in 1903.

1902   (Summer) Lewis befriends John.
Dismorr enters the Slade, leaving in 1903.

1904   Lewis exhibits with NEAC.

1905   (January) Durand–Ruel's Impressionist exhibition.
(May) Lewis visits the Whistler exhibition in Paris.
Epstein moves to London.

c.1905   Dismorr studies under Max Bohm at Etaples until c.1908.

1906   Gaudier visits England on a scholarship.

c.1906   Wadsworth studies engineering at Munich and paints at the Knirr School in his spare time, returning in 1907. Bomberg is apprenticed to the lithographer Paul Fischer and studies art at the City and Guilds evening classes. Saunders studies at the Slade.

1907   John sees *Les Demoiselles d'Avignon* in Picasso's studio and probably describes his visit to Lewis.
Epstein's first important commission: eighteen figures for the British Medical Association.

1908   Arbuthnot arouses controversy with a large group of photographs at the London Photographic Salon and befriends Coburn.
Dorothy Shakespear meets Pound.
Wadsworth enters the Slade.
Etchells enters the Royal College of Art.
Gaudier revisits England.
Bomberg attends Sickert's Westminster School evening classes.
Lewis leaves Paris and moves to London.

1909   (March) Arbuthnot holds his first one-man show.
(April) Pound, newly arrived in London, meets Hulme.
Lewis publishes short stories in *The English Review* and meets Pound.
Nevinson enters the Slade.
Roberts is apprenticed to a commercial art firm.
Kandinsky exhibits annually at the AAA Salon until 1911.

1910   (April) Marinetti gives his first London lecture.
Roberts enters the Slade.
(August) Marinetti's Futurist propaganda appears in *The Tramp* along with a short story by Lewis.
(November–January 1911) Fry's Manet and the Post-Impressionists exhibition.

c.1910   Dismorr studies at the Atelier de la Palette until c.1912.

1911   (January) Gaudier settles in London.
(June) The first Camden Town Group exhibition.
(July) Nevinson exhibits in the AAA Salon.
Etchells participates in Fry's Borough Polytechnic mural scheme, leaves the Royal College of Art and rents a studio in Paris where he meets Braque, Modigliani and Picasso.
Bomberg enters the Slade.
(December) The second Camden Town Group exhibition.

1912   Etchells, Nevinson, Saunders and Wadsworth included in the Friday Club exhibition.
(March) Futurists' first London exhibition.
(Spring–Summer) Epstein, Hamilton and Lewis help decorate the Cabaret Theatre Club.
(June–July) Arbuthnot holds his second one-man show.
(Summer) Nevinson and Wadsworth leave the Slade.
(July) Lewis exhibits *Kermesse* in the AAA Salon.
Fry befriends Lewis.
(Autumn) Epstein visits Paris to instal his *Tomb of Oscar Wilde* and befriends Brancusi and Modigliani.
(October–January 1913) Fry's Second Post-Impressionist exhibition.

(Autumn) Lewis meets Kate Lechmere.
(November) Pound announces the birth of Imagism.
(December) The third Camden Town Group exhibition.
(Christmas) Lewis visits Bomberg's Studio.

1913   (January–February) Bomberg, Nevinson and Wadsworth contribute to the Friday Club exhibition.
(February–March) Arbuthnot organizes a Post-Impressionist exhibition in Liverpool.
(c.April) The Omega Workshops founded.
(April) Severini one-man show in London.
(Summer) Bomberg and Roberts leave the Slade. Bomberg visits Paris with Epstein.
(July) AAA Salon exhibition includes Brancusi.
(July) Pound meets and befriends Gaudier.
(Late Summer) Etchells and Lewis stay in Dieppe together.
(Autumn) Dismorr exhibits at the Salon d'Automne.
(October) Etchells, Hamilton, Lewis and Wadsworth leave the Omega Workshops and issue the 'Round Robin'. Lewis invites Nevinson to join the rebel group. Frank Rutter's Post-Impressionist and Futurist exhibition. Coburn holds a one-man show and meets Pound who sits for him.
(November) Dinner at the Florence Restaurant in honour of Marinetti's return to London.
(Winter) Gaudier and Roberts affiliate themselves to the Omega Workshops.
(December) Roberts exhibits with the NEAC.
(December) First recorded reference to 'The Vortex', in Pound's letter to William Carlos Williams.
(December) Lewis begins to discuss *Blast*.
(December–January 1914) Camden Town Group exhibition with 'Cubist Room' section.
(December–January 1914) Epstein's first one-man exhibition which Hulme defends against critical hostility in his first review for *The New Age*.
(December–February 1914) Lewis decorates Lady Drogheda's dining room.

1914   (January) Hulme delivers a lecture on 'Modern Art and its Philosophy'. Gaudier and Roberts exhibit with the Grafton Group. First public announcement of *Blast*.
(February) Clive Bell's *Art* published. Coburn takes Epstein's photograph.
(February–March) Bomberg and Nevinson contribute to the Friday Club exhibition. Modern German Art exhibition held in London.
(March) First London Group exhibition. The Rebel Art Centre opens.
(March–April) Sickert clashes with Lewis and Nevinson in a series of hostile articles in *The New Age*.
(Spring) Pound sits for his *Bust* by Gaudier. Lewis borrows pictures from Roberts to hang in the Rebel Art Centre. Lechmere meets Hulme. Arbuthnot visits Lewis's studio.
(April) Shakespear marries Pound.
(April–May) The Futurists hold their second London exhibition.
(May–June) Twentieth Century Art exhibition at the Whitechapel Art Gallery.
(June) Marinetti and Nevinson publish their 'Futurist Manifesto: Vital English Art' in the *Observer*.
Vorticism's existence is officially announced and the Rebel Art Centre closes down. Pound publishes an article on

Lewis in *The Egoist*.

(July) *Blast No. 1* published. The AAA Salon exhibition includes a special Rebel Art Centre stand. Gaudier previews the Salon in *The Egoist*.

Bomberg holds his first one-man show and Hulme writes a long and admiring review in *The New Age*. Wadsworth visits Rotterdam.

(August) Pound publishes an article on Wadsworth in *The Egoist*.

(August) First World War declared. Gaudier, Hulme and Nevinson join up soon afterwards and go to France.

(September) Pound publishes his 'Vorticism' article in the *Fortnightly Review*.

(November) Lewis decorates Ford's study as a Vorticist Room at South Lodge.

1915   (January–February) Pound publishes a series of 'Affirmations' on Vorticism, Epstein, Gaudier, Imagism and related themes in *The New Age*.

Atkinson publishes a book of poetry called *Aura*.

(March) The second London Group exhibition, includes the first version of *Rock Drill*.

(June) Death of Gaudier in France. The first Vorticist Exhibition.

(July) *Blast No. 2* is published.

(Summer–Winter) Lewis, with Saunders' help, decorates a 'Vorticist Room' at the Restaurant de la Tour Eiffel.

(November) Bomberg enlists in the Royal Engineers.

1916   Hamilton, Lewis, Roberts and Wadsworth enlist. Dismorr spends most of the war in France doing voluntary war-work. Pound publishes his Memoir of Gaudier.

(February) Coburn takes Lewis's photograph.

(March) AAA Salon exhibition.

(June) The fourth London Group exhibition, includes the second version of *Rock Drill*.

(September–October) Nevinson holds his first one-man show.

(November–December) Saunders shows in the fifth London Group exhibition.

(Late 1916) Coburn devises the Vortoscope and takes his first Vortographs with Pound as a model.

1917   (January) The first Vorticist Exhibition outside England is held at the Penguin Club, New York.

(February) Coburn holds the first exhibition of Vortographs.

(February–March) Epstein's second one-man show.

(September) Death of Hulme at the front.

1917–1918 Wadsworth supervises dazzle-camouflage for English war ships and executes work inspired by this theme.

1918   The Canadian War Memorials Fund commissions large war paintings from Bomberg, Etchells, Lewis, Nevinson, Roberts and Wadsworth.

(March) Nevinson's second one-man show.

(May–June) Gaudier's Memorial Exhibition.

(July) Lewis's first novel, *Tarr*, is published in London and New York.

1919   (February) Lewis's first one-man show.

(March) Wadsworth's first one-man show of woodcuts and drawings.

Roberts paints three pictures for the Restaurant de la Tour Eiffel.

(August–September) Dismorr publishes some poems and 'Critical Suggestions' in the *Little Review*.

(September) Bomberg's second one-man show.

Plans for *Blast No. 3* are finally abandoned.

(Autumn) Lewis publishes *The Caliph's Design. Architects! Where Is Your Vortex?*

1920   (January) Wadsworth's second one-man show.

(March–April) Group X exhibition. Lewis writes a catalogue preface, but implies that Vorticism is at an end.

**'Whatever happens, there is a new section that has already justified its existence, which is bound to influence, and mingle with the others, as they do with each other; that is, for want of a better word, the Abstract.'**

WYNDHAM LEWIS
*'A Review of Contemporary Art'*
*Blast No. 2*
July 1915

'Vorticism, especially that part of vorticism having to do with form – to wit, vorticist painting and sculpture – has brought me a new series of apperceptions . . . I have my new and swift perceptions of forms, of possible form-motifs; I have a double or treble or tenfold set of stimulae in going from my home to Piccadilly. What was a dull row of houses is become a magazine of forms. There are new ways of seeing them. There are ways of seeing the shape of the sky as it juts down between the houses. The tangle of telegraph wires is conceivable not merely as a repetition of lines; one sees the shapes defined by the different branches of wire. The lumber yards, the sidings of railways cease to be dreary . . .'

EZRA POUND
'Affirmations. II. Vorticism'
*The New Age*
14 January 1915

**'As far as one can see, the new "tendency towards abstraction" will culminate, not so much in the simple geometrical forms found in archaic art, but in the more complicated ones associated in our minds with the idea of machinery. In this association with machinery will probably be found the specific differentiating quality of the new art . . . It has nothing whatever to do with the superficial notion that one must beautify machinery. It is not a question of dealing with machinery in the spirit, and with the methods of existing art, but of the creation of a new art having an organisation, and governed by principles, which are at present exemplified unintentionally, as it were, in machinery.'**

T. E. HULME
*'Modern Art and its Philosophy'*
delivered as a lecture on
22 January 1914

'An extraordinary political effervescence prevailed in England during the period which lay between the Boer War and the fateful opening years of Armageddon. A spirit of fanaticism invaded a luxurious world which no longer felt itself secure. Pious dissenters broke the law rather than pay the education rate. Well-bred and delicate women smashed windows, scuffled with the police, and by one means and another got themselves sent to prison as a protest against a government which refused them votes. Party spirit ran so high in London over the House of Lords and Ireland that social relations were ruptured. To some Imperialism and tariff reform constituted a religious faith, pressed with sectarian fervour. By others these causes were denounced as synonymous with the exploitation of oppressed peoples by unscrupulous profiteers and the corruption of legislatures by sinister vested interests. The country was full of industrial unrest, the striking habit extending from the mines, the railways, and the factories to the schools.'

H. A. L. FISHER
*A History of Europe*
London, 1936

# Introduction

One of the main reasons why a proper evaluation of Vorticism has been neglected for so long is that it lacks a sense of tightly-knit cohesion. Compared with the other, closely related radical movements which were simultaneously subverting establishment values on the continent, this English uprising seems riddled with dissension and suspiciously short-lived. Whereas the Futurists made a special point of presenting the world with a united front, concealing private differences behind a public display of solidarity, the Vorticists never masked their misgivings about the whole concept of a group endeavour. And while Cubism was granted several uninterrupted years in which to evolve its vocabulary, Vorticism scarcely had a chance to announce itself before the Great War terminated artistic activity in London.

The Vorticist rebellion cannot, therefore, be approached as a neatly self-contained phenomenon. Its very lack of maturity and clear definition means that an attempt must be made to examine all the disparate strands of experiment which helped bring it into being. The network of political manœuvring which dictated the timing of the movement's official inception has to be unravelled before its peculiarly aggressive character becomes fully comprehensible. And work executed by the artists involved needs to be traced back to an earlier, less independent stage, so that the precise nature of their indebtedness to Post-Impressionist and Cubo-Futurist prototypes can be clarified.

If this broader analysis is not carried out, Vorticism will continue to resist accurate description. Many of its participants were extraordinarily young, and they inevitably passed through a whole gamut of influences before managing to develop a final, brief synthesis of all their heterogeneous impulses. The high-spirited iconoclasm which erupted from the pages of *Blast* in the summer of 1914 was caused by many factors, ranging from the Slade to the Omega Workshops, from Fry to Marinetti, from the insular philistinism of English culture to the multi-national character of the rebel group; and all these factors, no less than the hectic ambience of pre-war London, need pinning down. Hence the linear method adopted here, in the hope that Vorticism's essence will become clearer once it has been charted from infancy through to final demise, with as much attention paid to outside forces and the individual motives of the personalities concerned as to the works of art themselves. Vorticist artefacts remain the first priority, and they have never been properly assessed: the loss of about half the movement's most important products, combined with the amount of painstaking and sympathetic research needed to reconstruct its achievements, has successfully impeded this task in the past. But the evidence which it has proved possible to reassemble here, whether from documentary sources of the period or the retrospective memories of surviving witnesses, cannot be fully understood without a concomitant awareness of the peculiar context which produced and indeed shaped its character.

This larger context, as the subtitle of the book implies, embraces the formulation of an indigenously English form of abstraction. The Vorticists may have drawn much of their inspiration from mechanical imagery, and stopped short of believing that a totally non-representational language was either possible or desirable, but their fundamental aim lay in disengaging art from outworn representational conventions. The desire to attain that freedom runs through all the styles they adopted before reaching their goal, and it justifies the inclusion of Bomberg, Epstein and Nevinson, all of whom refused to join the official Vorticist movement even though they shared many of its basic premises. Every one of the rebels, whatever his personal inclinations, felt an overwhelming urge to emancipate his work, so that the advent of a new century would be accompanied by an art that reflected the dramatically changing fabric of life in England. And this ambition, lying beneath everything discussed in the following chapters, is the one unifying force which ensures that Vorticism remains relevant to all those involved in a similar debate today. England, more than most countries, needs to be regularly blasted into an awareness of the importance of renewal, not for its own sake but because the vitality of art works depends on the strength of their organic connections with and relevance to the evolving society which produces them. The Vorticist insurrection deserves to be remembered as a worthy precedent for this continuing enterprise.

*Cambridge, December 1968—London, March 1974.*

# Chapter 1: The First Stirrings of Revolt: Lewis, Pound and the Post-Impressionist Exhibition

If the spirit of cocksure defiance which characterized Vorticism can be said to have originated anywhere, it was at Rugby, that bastion of the English public school system. There, in the last decade of the nineteenth century, a presumptuous teenager named Percy Wyndham Lewis decided one day to flout accepted protocol by transforming his study into a painter's studio. The temerity of this rebellious gesture soon provoked a reaction. 'I remember a very big boy opening the door of the study', Lewis recalled later, 'putting his big red astonished face inside, gazing at me for a while – digesting what he saw, the palette on my thumb, the brush loaded with pigment in the act of dabbing – and then, laconically and contemptuously, remarking, "You frightful artist!" closed the study door: and I could hear his big slouching lazy steps going away down the passage to find some more normal company. The English, I am afraid, are mostly of that stamp.'

Official retribution was swift. This embryonic bohemian was an anomaly: he was always at the bottom of his class, had not moved up a form for four terms and clearly had no business in an institution like Rugby. 'What Public Schools were for', Lewis remembered dismissively, 'was to turn out a stupid but well-behaved executive class to run the Empire Kipling crowed and crooned about.' And his housemaster, disturbed to hear of such a subversive innovation, decreed that the painter's school career was at an end. 'He concluded (quite rightly) that I had got into the wrong school', explained Lewis. 'He thought that an art-school was where I really ought to be; and he wrote to my mother to this effect.'[1] The episode is almost a reflection in miniature of the reception which the adult Lewis and his irreverent friends would be accorded in 1914: but by then, their target had grown from the philistinism of one solitary school to nothing less than the whole of the English art establishment.

Not that Lewis was a fully-fledged rebel on his arrival at the Slade School of Art in 1898. Hubert Wellington, a friend and fellow-student, remembered him being 'surprisingly ignorant about art when he first appeared at the Slade; his favourite painter was a Victorian Academician who specialised in highland landscapes full of sheep grazing in the heather'.[2] The few scraps of drawings that survive from his student days reveal an able but impressionable personality, overawed by the precocity of the Slade's star pupil, Augustus John. Everything about the handling of Lewis's *Nude Boy Bending Over*, which pleased his teachers so much that it helped win him a scholarship competition in 1900, bears witness to the influence of John: the spontaneous outlines and vigorous chiaroscuro directly emulate sketches executed by the older man while he was at the Slade.[3] John had left the Slade in the very same year that Lewis entered it; but Lewis's memoirs testify both to John's frequent return visits, and to the overshadowing legacy which he left behind. 'Fronting the stairs that led upwards where the ladies were learning to be Michelangelos, hung a big painting of Moses and the Brazen Serpent', Lewis recalled, pointing out how John's prize picture of 1898 symbolized the Slade's respect for the past. 'Everything in the place was in the "grand manner": for Professor Tonks . . . had one great canon of draughtsmanship, and that was the giants of the Renaissance. Everyone was attempting to be a giant and please Tonks. None pleased Tonks – none, in their work, bore the least resemblance to Michelangelo. The ladies upstairs wept when he sneered at their efforts to become Giantesses.'[4]

It was all very easy for Lewis to look back at his student experiences, years after the event, and laugh about the academic bias of the Slade, its aesthetic priorities summed up by John's eclectic *Moses* composition. But when Lewis first joined the School, as a callow youth of sixteen, both *Moses* and its creator prompted his admiration. He must have paled beside the glamour of this

Wyndham Lewis
*Nude Boy Bending Over*, 1900

Augustus John
*Moses and the Brazen Serpent*, 1898

swaggering favourite, and later explained that John 'was the most notorious nonconformist England has known for a long time . . . one of those people who always set out to do the thing that "is not done", according to the British canon. He swept aside the social conventions, which was a great success, and he became a public lion practically on the spot . . . He was a legendary "Slade School *ingenious*", to use Campion the doorkeeper's word.'[5] Although John's art could never be called revolutionary, his life-style was already outraging conservative values with the same gusto which the Vorticists would eventually display; but at this stage Lewis remained strangely withdrawn and uncertain about his future direction. William Rothenstein, an early friend who formally introduced him to John in the summer of 1902, remembered this indecision when he described how the student Lewis 'hesitated between writing and painting, meanwhile he made sensitive studies of the nude; I recall no compositions by Lewis – the imaginative and romantic side of his nature he put into his poems and into his daily life'.[6]

Even then Lewis was divided in loyalty between his literary and artistic talents. Apart from his contacts with John, Rothenstein and Spencer Gore – a sympathetic contemporary at the Slade – he struck up an acquaintance with the British Museum set: Sturge Moore, Streatfield and Laurence Binyon. They were impressed by his intellectual ability, and encouraged his interest in poetry so successfully that Lewis later explained how 'to these elders I was known as a "poet" '.[7] He was, therefore, starting to make a name for himself at once as a writer and a draughtsman. And John, who seems rapidly to have become Lewis's father-figure, referred to this duality when reconstructing the advice he gave Lewis soon after the versatile young student left the Slade: 'First of all, for a start, he must drop Ingres. Didn't he, Lewis, have more than a talent for draughtsmanship himself? This Beauty stuff was overdone – no! *Sarcasm*, with daring touches of scurrility, was to be his strong card.'[8] John's understanding of his admirer was shrewd, for his counsel was to prove both constructive and prophetic; but Lewis, perhaps hamstrung by his involvement with the 'sonnets' which John remembered as being 'in the Shakespearian form but of a more than Shakespearian obscurity', was still unable to discover his own individuality as an artist.

In view of the frontal attack he was soon to launch against the timidity of his contemporaries and seniors alike, Lewis's lack of early confidence appears all the

Wyndham Lewis
*An Oriental Design* (detail), 1900–5

more curious. On a purely personal level he was, admittedly, showing signs of that ability to alienate which would later blossom into outright aggression. 'So bitterly do the authorities at the Slade dislike Lewis that anyone going in for a prize or Scholarship is apparently first questioned and his former life examined to find out "whether he is a friend of Lewis",' Spencer Gore wrote to Hubert Wellington in 1902. 'Seems to me that this is nearly as good for him as being great friends with them as they must have a very high opinion of him to consider him dangerous.'[9] But this fascinating glimpse of Lewis's precocious readiness to antagonize his teachers does not mean that he was prepared to translate his restlessness into pictorial terms. An ink drawing of an *Oriental Design*, which may well date from the same year as Gore's letter, is a stumbling exercise, and seems more in love with Rembrandtesque exoticism than innovation. Once again, it squares with his devotion to John, for Lewis recalled his mentor visiting the Slade and surprising everyone by sketching 'a modern Saskia . . . upon the bank-note paper: drawings that followed all came out of the workshop of Rembrandt'.[10]

Small wonder that Lewis himself always did his best to gloss over this awkward period in his life – most of the pictures executed then must have perished at his hands. Possibly he was ashamed of having been a late starter, when so much of the art produced in England at the turn of the century needed an urgent injection of new ideas. Sir Edward Poynter, that arch-exponent of High Victorian banality, held sway over the Royal Academy; Wilson Steer, with his inoffensive brand of diluted Impressionism, taught at the Slade; while Whistler, whose *Nocturnes* and *Symphonies* look gentle enough now, represented all that was most contro-versial in artistic circles of the day. There was room for a radical spirit, but Lewis was simply not ready to provide a fresh lead: it is significant that he left for Europe in 1902, not to escape from a backward-looking environment, but to copy Goya in Madrid with Spencer Gore. Both men were obviously still in awe of the past; and neither could have yet begun to harbour any serious impatience with the nearest approximation Britain then possessed to an avant-garde group of artists, the New English Art Club.

This Janus-headed society, founded in 1886 by Fred Brown – who later be-came a Slade professor and taught Lewis – had originally set itself up to attack everything the Academy stood for. Yet Roger Fry could write of the NEAC's 1902 exhibition that 'the very sincerity of these painters, the absence from their work of the more glaring displays of vulgarity and sentimentality which distinguish the larger shows, bring into more striking relief the poverty of their emotional and intellectual condition . . . It is but their misfortune to have come at a "dead point" in the revolution of our culture'.[11] In 1902 Fry, for all his outspoken impatience, was no rebel himself; but even he damned this self-styled 'advanced' Club as a cul-de-sac. Here, at the very beginning of a new century, English art seemed to have come to a standstill. And Lewis, in the privacy of a letter to Hubert Wellington written the same year, agreed with Fry's strictures: 'The New English is a deplorable display of the degradation of a function, which was originally intended to give delight, but which now extracts delight from all it touches, leaving a formal dullness', he declared with seeming conviction.[12]

Something, however, held him back from acting on these feelings and formulating an independent alternative to New English aesthetics in his own work. Two years later he was still sufficiently infatuated with John's prowess to write to his mother from Paris asking her to send on 'the book of John's torn-up drawings, – the album, you know, with the drawings I found and stuck together . . . I shouldn't like to lose them'.[13] And just as he remained impressed by John's standards of excellence, so he took time off during a 1904 stay in Haarlem copying Frans Hals to tell his mother of his determination to return to London for the NEAC show. 'If I can get in 2 or 3 weeks work before the "New English" in London', he wrote, 'I shall be very glad.'[14] His eagerness was understandable: despite his misgivings about the New English, he sent in a lost *Study of a Girl's Head* to the 1904 annual exhibition and saw it hung there in the 'Non-Members' section.[15]

There is, then, no reason to suppose that Lewis was genuinely dissatisfied with the NEAC's failure to come to grips with the most challenging radical developments in Europe. But he should have been, for England was languishing in a bankrupt form of artistic provincialism. As late as January 1905 Durand-Ruel's magnificent Impressionist exhibition at the Grafton Galleries of more than 300 paintings by men like Degas, Manet and Renoir was received with amazement rather than understanding. 'It is difficult now for anybody to realize that this exhibition excited as much controversy and heated argument as the Post-Impressionist exhibitions did in the same galleries', commented Frank Rutter, the art critic of the *Sunday Times*, who also remembered that 'about this time a fine painting by Degas was offered to the National Gallery, but the gift had been definitely rejected by the Trustees and Director'.[16] It was as much as London could do to swallow the tentative experiments of its native Impressionists, as Lewis afterwards recalled. 'Mr Wilson Steer appeared an outrageous fellow to the critic of the day, in his Prussian-blue pastiches of John Constable', he wrote from the vantage-point of Vorticism in 1915. 'Mr Walter Sickert was a horrifying personage in illustrations of "low life", with its cheap washing-stands and immodest artist's models squatting blankly and listlessly on beds.'[17] The NEAC did not even allow Lewis's work onto its walls after 1904, uncontroversial though his entries must have been at that time. And so he stayed in relative obscurity, moving about between Paris and Munich, wondering how to establish his reputation as an artist and living the permissive life of a student.

Whether his lack of immediate success was due to inability, dilletantism or sheer laziness is hard to determine. Hardly any pictures survive between the *Oriental Design* and a small group of drawings executed in 1909 – a complete gap of about six years – and only the letters written to his mother afford some hint of his progress. When he first joined John in Paris around 1903, he was 'busy trying drawings (caricatures) for the Paris papers', and embarking on 'a series of paintings and drawings of the Creation of the World'.[18] A little later on, he laments indecisively that 'I'm afraid most of my drawings are too serious or not serious enough'.[19] Then, in 1905, a new note of optimism creeps in. 'My drawing has improved a great deal in Paris', he announced, 'and my ideas are taking a certain shape, that is shapeliness, which I hope will be for the best.'[20] In February he reminded his mother to describe the large Whistler Memorial Exhibition at the New Gallery, and Durand-Ruel's Impressionist survey: 'tell me about the "Whistler" show and the French impressionists, if you have read about it in the papers: I dont want to miss them if possible'.[21] Two further letters repeat his desire to see the Whistler exhibition, and then his delight when it moved to Paris in May: 'I shall wait here anyway for the Whistler show, and try and profit by it.'[22] He clearly believed that Whistler, as opposed to his French contemporaries, offered guidance and inspiration; but any supposition that Lewis was excited specifically by Whistler's theoretical insistence on treating a painting as an almost musical arrangement of coloured surfaces is not borne out by the letters.

According to them John was still his hero, and as late as 1907 he wrote joyfully about a new admirer of his drawings, who had 'said they were a million times better than he had ever imagined they could be, as good as John'.[23] His older friend's prowess seems even then to have been the yardstick by which he measured his own art. For there is no reference in his letters to the latest innovations in French painting: Matisse, the Fauves, or the revelation provided by the great Cézanne retrospective exhibition of 1907, which inspired so many nascent Cubists. Instead, he persisted in revering the masters of the past – Duncan Grant remembered meeting him for the very first time in a Paris street and heatedly discussing nothing more advanced than 'the comparative merits of drawings by Ingres and Delacroix'.[24] He persisted, too, in spending much of his time with John, both in Paris and during summers spent in Brittany; and it was there that he wrote most revealingly about their dangerously one-sided relationship. 'I feel that if I were left alone, I could both write and paint just now', he complained in a letter around 1908; 'but near John I can never paint, since his artistic personality is just too strong, and he much more developed, naturally, and this frustrates any effort . . .'[25] To find himself as an independent creative personality, Lewis obviously had to cut the umbilical cord attaching him to the seductive facility of John's talent.

Paris was, nevertheless, an education and a revelation. He rented a studio there, attended Bergson's lectures at the Collège de France, and savoured the pre-war Bohemian life. His contact with Bergson, who believed that intuitive experience was the only means whereby a human could understand reality, and that art was a direct expression of such experience, links Lewis immediately with a philosophy which helped to inspire both Fauvism and Futurism. Vorticism later rejected Bergson because his concept of the continuous flux pervading all material objects came to be identified too closely with the Italian movement.[26] But at this stage, Bergson must have acted as a liberating catalyst on Lewis, encouraging him to move away from the naturalism which still dictated his own art.

It is all the more to be regretted, therefore, that he was in no mood to follow up the implications of this awakening belief in his Parisian pictures. 'It is dangerous to go to heaven when you are too young', he wrote afterwards, looking back on his life in France. 'You do not understand it and I did not learn to work in Paris . . . Indeed, this period in retrospect, responsible for much, is a blank with regard to painting.'[27] The inference is plain. Lewis enjoyed himself too much in a city he remembered as 'expansive and civilised, temperate in climate, beautiful and free'; and John vividly described the way in which his

Augustus John
*Portrait of Wyndham Lewis, c.*1905

young friend dissipated his energies. 'In the cosmopolitan world of Montparnasse, P. Wyndham Lewis played the part of an incarnate Loki, bearing the news and sowing discord with it', John wrote. 'He conceived the world as an arena, where various insurrectionary forces struggled to outwit each other in the game of artistic power politics. Impatient of quietude, star-gazing or woolgathering, our new Machiavelli sought to ginger up his friends, or patients as they might be called, by a whisper here, a dark suggestion there.'[28] And to back up his verbal portrait, John executed a painting around this time showing Lewis as a proud, almost Castilian militant.[29]

John never bothered to explain precisely what kind of thinking lay behind his companion's subversive behaviour in Paris; and neither did Lewis. But as luck would have it, the latter did afterwards reveal one important source of this restlessness to his wife, who remembered Lewis reminiscing about his personal contact with Kropotkin in particular and anarchist theories in general. 'Certainly he knew Prince Kropotkin very well, visiting him constantly, discussing Russia and its authors, learning a smattering of Russian', Mrs Lewis wrote, adding that her husband enjoyed 'joining in Kropotkin discussion groups on Anarchy' and 'always described the Prince as a very gentle man'.[30] At the time Lewis met him,

Kropotkin was in his seventies, an exiled revolutionary propagandist of long standing who was just about to publish *The Russian Revolution and Anarchism* in London.[31] It can hardly be doubted that Lewis was instinctively attracted to this old campaigner's linking of anarchism with a natural human cycle, his insistence that 'evolution and revolution alternate, and the revolutions – that is, the times of accelerated evolution – belong to the unity of nature as much as do the times when evolution takes place more slowly'. Lewis's growing appetite for change would have been as sharpened by such a statement as it would by Kropotkin's assertion in his 1906 book *The Conquest of Bread* that luxury ought to consist, not of material comforts, but of 'the higher delights, the highest within man's reach . . . of art, and especially artistic creation'.

The anarchist émigré surely exerted a potent influence on Lewis, who also found himself 'supporting an Anatole France protest meeting which was endeavouring to get Gorki's release from prison'[32] and afterwards admitted that during this Paris period he was 'for some years spiritually a Russian – a character in some Russian novel'.[33] But the relatively pacific gospel preached by Kropotkin from his sheltered base in England – where Lewis must have met him on one of his 'intermittent visits to England to stay with his mother' – was not enough.[34] As John's description of his friend's Parisian activities suggests, Lewis was already deeply egotistical, and found himself drawn equally strongly towards Nietzsche. Decades later, after declaring that 'Nietzsche was, I believe, the paramount influence' on his early thinking, he countered the confession by insisting that 'I was reasonably immune then to Superman' and the 'titanic nourishment for the ego' to be found in *Zarathustra*. Yet although it is easy to accept Lewis's retrospective claim that 'the impulse to titanism and supernatural afflatus pervading German romanticism has never had any interest for me',[35] he must at the very least have been stirred by Nietzsche's godlike belief in man's ability to overthrow the world.

This supposition is fortified by the knowledge that Lewis probably read one of Nietzsche's mentors, Max Stirner, when his influential book *The Ego and His Own* was first published in an English translation in 1907. Several years afterwards, in 1914, Lewis made his own fictional hero Arghol fling Stirner's book out of the window in disgust;[36] but during the Paris period, he is likely to have been very much in sympathy with the man who could affirm that 'rebellion leads us no longer to let ourselves be arranged, but to arrange ourselves, and sets no glittering hopes on "institutions". It is not a fight against the established, since if it prospers, the established collapses of itself'.[37]

Before long, Lewis would act upon similar, albeit more combative convictions in his attempts to change the course of English art. But so far as Paris was concerned, he succeeded only in displaying a more trivial taste for plots, conspiracies and the occasional dog-fight with a new acquaintance. Duncan Grant, for instance, who was already involved with the budding Bloomsbury circle, wrote about Lewis in 1907 with a disgust that adumbrates the differences in sensibility between Bloomsbury and Vorticism which eventually erupted into conflict a few years later. Referring to his recent encounters with 'a poet-painter called Lewis', Grant told Lytton Strachey that 'my gorge simply rises whenever I see him . . . I simply descend into the depths of gloom . . . and I cannot decide whether my feelings are absurd and silly, but I certainly think all his hopelessly mesquine and putrid'.[38] Lewis's aggressive tactics clearly had a violent effect on those who were antipathetic to him: Grant added that 'it's very odd that anyone should have the power of making one go into' such 'hysterics'. But in the privacy of his own studio, as a would-be artist, Lewis shed this overbearing persona and wrote regretfully to his mother: 'I'm afraid no New English triumphs this autumn: I shall probably have a drawing to send, but that wont do me much good: my triumphs must be subterranean – that is to say not on the gaudy surface of the exhibitions, but rather amongst friends and dealers or "sich" like.'[39] It is improbable, however, that the encouragement of a few casual contacts and the frisson of hostile encounters were any real substitute for the wider acclaim he so eagerly desired.

For the moment, his writing was proving more fruitful, and it now affords further clues about the origins of Lewis's emergent unrest. The summers spent in Brittany, one of which was passed in the company of the relatively traditional artist Henry Lamb, provided him with a whole range of experiences which he was soon to put into short-story form. He was fascinated by the behaviour of the vagrants he saw mouldering away inside humble Breton *pensions*: expatriate Poles, tramps, innkeepers and itinerant clowns all became the raw material for his first attempts at fiction. 'During those days, I began to get a philosophy', he recalled. 'It took the form of a reaction against civilised values. It was militantly vitalist . . . The snobbishness (religion of the domestic) of the English middle-class, their cold philistinism, perpetual silly sports, all violently repudiated by me were the constant object of comparison with anything that stimulated and amused . . . in the clubhouse on an English golf-links I should not have found such exciting animals as I encountered here.'[40] It was in Brittany that Lewis began to formulate his vague dissatisfaction with England into some kind of proto-Vorticist system. Delighted by the crazy antics he came up against and studied so keenly, he selected a range of personalities whose behaviour he could analyse in his stories. 'The characters I chose to celebrate – Bestre, the Cornac and his wife, Brotcotnaz, le père François – were all primitive creatures', he explained, 'immersed in life, as much as birds, or big, obsessed, sun-drunk insects'. These buffoons were the complete antithesis of everything he was growing to loathe in the England of his youth, and he seized on them with alacrity.

There were, moreover, deeply personal motives lying behind his choice of subject-matter. Lewis was often painfully shy, retarded almost, in his dealings with his fellow-men, and the wild strain of madness he detected in Breton people acted as a safety valve for his repressed personality. 'I remained, beyond the usual period, congealed in a kind of cryptic immaturity', he admitted. 'In my social relations the contacts remained, for long, primitive. I recognised dimly this obstruction: was conscious of gaucherie, of wooden responses. . . . It resulted in experience with no natural outlet in conversation collecting in a molten column within. This *trop-plein* would erupt: that was my way of expressing myself – with intensity, and with the density of what had been undiluted by ordinary intercourse.'[41] Imagine the delight with which the desperately inhibited Lewis must have greeted the farcical ways of the Breton peasants! Their antics provided him with an exaggerated reflection of the awkwardness surrounding his own personality and helped to release all his pent-up energy whenever he was given the opportunity. John, who declared that 'Lewis was in favour of over-acting' and considered that 'his view of life was based largely on the Commedia dell'Arte', noticed how he 'revelled in any heaven-sent amateur of the tradition who might from time to time appear on the scene with his bag of tricks! Watching such performances attentively, he would applaud the miming, the postures and the bawdy witticisms, till, overcome with satisfaction, he would drop his mask and howl with laughter like a human being!'[42]

Over the next few years, Lewis would learn to channel this explosion of hilarity into his art by launching an iconoclastic attack on English aesthetics; and a striking prophecy of his attitudes as a Vorticist is contained in an extract from a Brittany short story called 'The Pole', where Lewis explained that 'the practical joker is a degenerate, who is exasperated by the uniformity of life. Or he is one who mystifies people, because only when suddenly perplexed or surprised do they become wildly and startlingly natural. He is a primitive soul, trying to get back to his element. Or it is the sign of a tremendous joy in people, and delight in seeing them put forth their vitality, and in practical joking of a physical nature a joy in the grotesqueness of the human form. Or it is the sadness of the outcast, the spirit outside of life because his nature is fit only for solitude, playing hob-goblin tricks with men that cannot sympathise with him: just as I have no doubt that some anarchist outrages are the work of very violent and extreme snobs, who lie in wait for some potentate, and shoot him, that in the moment of death the august eyes shall become more expressive and show more interest in him than they have ever shown in anybody before. The *farceur* has often many friends and admirers who brave the terrors of his friendship, but he remains peculiarly little understood. He is a lonely hero'.[43] So many aspects of Lewis's own character are outlined here – the man who infuriates his acquaintances, revels in grotesquerie, casts himself as a solitary outsider and plans élitist acts of anarchism – that the entire passage can reasonably be seen as a multi-layered prognosis of the militant energy Lewis went on to deploy in his Vorticist period.

All the elements in Lewis's temperament which eventually made him such an inflammatory rebel were, therefore, latent in the ostensibly quiet years of his continental travels. But finally, around the summer of 1908, he decided he had been abroad long enough. His mother's financial support showed every sign of having come to an end, and he set about renewing contacts with old friends in London, determined to make a success of his life. 'Now I find that I have come to the end of my tether', he wrote from Paris to the faithful Sturge Moore; 'I must hurry back to London in a day or two, and plunge "dans les affaires de nouveau".' But what could this 26-year-old wanderer, a painter who had scarcely exhibited and a writer who had never appeared in print, do for a living? Lewis looked to the novelist Ford Madox Ford – then called Hueffer – for an answer. 'I hope Hueffer will keep to his promise of taking me on as a regular hand', his letter to Sturge Moore continued. 'Troublesome as the monthly article would be, it would be nothing compared to the uncertainties of other work.'[44]

Ford, who also knew Kropotkin and had just started up a lively and in many ways enlightened literary magazine called *The English Review*, was an obvious focus for Lewis's ambitions as a writer. And although the request for a monthly column was not granted, Lewis did pay a surprise visit to Ford's office, dressed – as Ford fondly maintained – in an 'immense steeple-crowned hat. Long black locks fell from it. His coat was one of those Russian-looking coats that have no *revers*. He had also an ample black cape of the type that villains in transpontine melodrama throw over their shoulders when they say "Ha-ha!" He said not a word . . . I have never known anyone else whose silence was a positive rather than a negative quality'.[45] Even when Ford's instinctive tendency to improve on an anecdote is taken into account, it is clear that Lewis was determined to present London with a carefully cultivated persona. His shyness was by now cloaked in theatricality, and he was already eager to indulge in the kind of shock tactics which Vorticism would employ. That, at least, is the inference to be drawn from the account of Lewis's visit which Ford related to his secretary at *The English Review*, Douglas Goldring. Lewis, apparently, managed to surprise the novelist at his toilet, marching by mistake into the bathroom to find Ford 'reclining on his back in the bath, in two feet of hot water, with a large sponge in one hand and a cake of soap in the other'. Undeterred by his faux pas, Lewis announced 'in the most matter-of-fact way that he was a man of genius', and asked Ford if he might read aloud a manuscript for publication. Ford agreed, 'continuing to use his sponge', listened to the stranger's recital and promptly agreed to print it, for 'it was always one of Ford's main ideas to publish the unpublished, to foster budding genius'.[46]

Lewis's bravado had paid off. Ford was sufficiently impressed by the stranger's gifts to publish the Breton stories in no less than three issues of the 1909 *Review*, and the two men soon became friends. But this instantaneous success was not matched by any public showing of Lewis's paintings or drawings. Indeed, only a handful of heterogeneous sketches can be tentatively linked with that year to give any indication of the direction in which he was beginning to move.

△ Pablo Picasso
*Les Demoiselles d'Avignon*, 1907

▷ Wyndham Lewis
*The Theatre Manager*, 1909 (?)

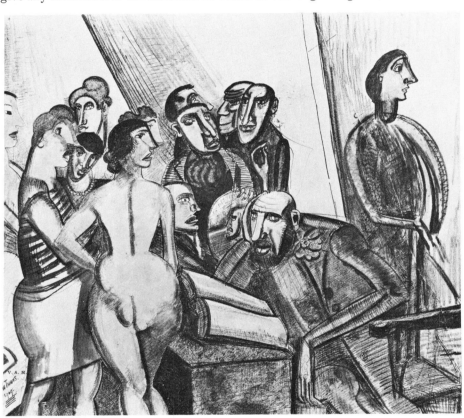

Two of them suggest, however, that he possessed a resiliently individual spirit right from the start of his settled period in England. The first, a small ink and watercolour composition called *The Theatre Manager*, heralds the arrival of a harsh and uncompromising vision. The figures combine archaizing distortions, like tubular arms and phallic noses, with Renaissance references: the heavy nude recalls Dürer's *Four Witches*, while the smirking profile in the middle is close to Leonardo's grotesques. There are faint echoes of the savagery Picasso inflicted on the female form two years earlier in *Les Demoiselles d'Avignon*, painted when Lewis was based in Paris and perhaps even living near Picasso. But the Englishman had probably never seen this first great harbinger of Cubism: although his widow afterwards insisted that 'Lewis was loosely associated with the Apollinaire Group' and 'knew them very well, was interested in their ideas and was on friendly terms with them . . . during the years before he finally returned to England',[47] his contemporary writings nowhere record any contact with the young Cubists. And he categorically stated in 1922 that, although he was well acquainted with Picasso's work, 'I have never actually met him',.[48] If Lewis was involved with early Cubism at all – and *The Theatre Manager* maybe shows his awareness of its existence – it was as an uncommitted outsider who remained wary of applying Cubist ideas to his own work.

Around September 1909, however, when Sturge Moore was staying in France,

Lewis made a special point of asking him if he had managed to 'see any Picasso or Matisse paintings in Paris?'[49] No other artists were mentioned in the letter: these twin leaders of the French vanguard were by then the only two who fired his interest and made him eager to discover what their latest pictures looked like. His curiosity about Picasso might have originally been stirred when he heard about *Les Demoiselles* from John, who in the summer of 1907 visited Picasso's studio and then wrote to Henry Lamb on 5 August that 'I saw a young artist called Picasso whose work is wonderful in Paris'. John did not mention *Les Demoiselles* by name, but he afterwards described the visit in his autobiography and remembered above all that 'a large canvas contained a group of figures which reminded one a little of the strange monoliths of Easter Island'. John's own work remained untouched by this development in Picasso's art, although he was 'at once struck by his unusual gifts' and came close in 1907 to emulating Picasso's pre-Cubist style. But John's enthusiastic reports quite possibly alerted Lewis to the beginnings of Cubism, and it is reasonable to imagine him listening carefully to John's account of Picasso's 'exercises which at first sight disturb or even horrify, but which, on analysis, reveal elements derived from remote antiquity or the art-forms of primitive peoples'.[50] None of Lewis's 1907 pictures survives to show whether his art actually reflected such concerns at that stage: the complete loss of so much early Lewis work means that his dating of *The Theatre Manager* itself has to be taken on trust, and will always remain controversial until either confirmed or denied by the unearthing of further evidence. It is surely safe to assume, however, that even if Lewis did hear about *Les Demoiselles* in 1907 he nevertheless failed to discover for several years how to digest this fascination and harness it satisfactorily to his own pictorial vocabulary.

So much is clear from a comparison between Lewis's muddled drawing and Picasso's seminal masterpiece, for it serves largely to highlight the differences between the two artists. Picasso was here intent on abjuring not only the sentimentality but also the literary nature of his previous work. *Les Demoiselles* represents the moment when he attempted to destroy all his preconceptions about what art should be, and everything is broken down, simplified or flattened out on the surface of the canvas. It is as ungainly as *The Theatre Manager*, and yet every destructive inch is directed towards a formal end: despite hesitations, it suggests a new way of rendering three-dimensional volumes on a two-dimensional surface. Lewis's distortions, by contrast, are inconsistent because they have a far more satirical and literary mind behind them. The creator of *The Theatre Manager* is just as interested in the symbolic meaning of the characters in his confused tableau as he is in their formal properties. He shows a knowledge of the expressive potential of primitive art – an interest that links him once more with the Cubists – but he uses this knowledge in varying ways throughout the picture. Picasso does not pause to linger over the little individual quirks of anatomy or dress which Lewis describes in *The Theatre Manager*. The Englishman was too bound up in the vagaries of external appearance to go as far as *Les Demoiselles*, and too involved with the demands of writing.

He did, in fact, set down his feeling for tortuous, frenetic poses in fiction as well as art. One of his *English Review* stories, 'Les Saltimbanques', describes the posture of the angry Ringmaster's wife with her 'neck strained forward, the face bent down, the eyes glowering upwards at the adversary . . . and one hand thrust out in a remonstrative gesture'. Lewis wrote, with loving attention to externalised detail, that 'the body is generally screwed round to express the impulse of turning away, while the face still confronts whoever is being apostrophised'. Here is the literary equivalent of the distorted configurations delineated in *The Theatre Manager*. And the fact that this story was published in the very same year Lewis may have executed the drawing gives some indication of how closely allied writing and art were in his own mind.

A still more extraordinary demonstration of Lewis's desire to forge his own quirky alternative to the continental avant-garde is provided by a second 1909 design, *The Celibate*. For here he can be seen trying to push all the indecisive strivings of *The Theatre Manager* towards one rigidly schematic conclusion. This eery creature's face has cast off the lingering naturalism of the earlier drawing and become a geometric mask, cold and dehumanised. Further down the body, Lewis becomes rather less resolute and fights a war within himself between curvilinear description and angular abstraction: on the left side of the neck a pentimento shows how an outer curve has afterwards been blocked out and replaced by a straight line, and throughout the figure a network of stiff contours has been scored over the preliminary markings. But Lewis's accelerating need to divest his art of figurative dross reaches a remarkable climax in the background, where huge arcs and segments of form lunge through space to reinforce the celibate's frigid movements. And the acid combination of deep metallic blue, white, mauve and lilac washes succeeds in freezing him even further into a robot-like trance.

So many of Vorticism's most outstanding characteristics are adumbrated here – the insistent diagonal bias of the composition, its steely control and underlying explosiveness – that it would be tempting to suspect that Lewis reworked *The Celibate* at a later date.[51] He may well have done so, but the supposition loses some of its credibility when the fundamentally tentative nature of the drawing is considered. All over the design Lewis's handling is wavering and ruthless by turn, as if he was hiding an inner uncertainty with an outward display of confidence. And despite his restless attempts to transform this figure into a semi-abstract automaton, Lewis persists in clothing him in the statuesque draperies of an older, classical civilisation. He is both a forerunner of the new machine age and a tribute to the dying influence of Greek academicism, a paradox which makes it easier to imagine the entire picture as a product of Lewis's contradictory impulses in 1909. Caught unhappily between the traditionalism of his Slade training, his alliance with John and the growing urge to achieve a revolutionary breakthrough of his own, Lewis could at least have commenced *The Celibate* as early as its inscribed date asserts without grasping the full implications of the style he had evolved.

At any rate, both *The Celibate* and *The Theatre Manager* prove that around then Lewis did begin an individual search for new forms of expression. Possibly the move to England and the need to adopt a more level-headed approach to his activities hastened on this development; possibly the renewed contact with old friends like Gore and Harold Gilman stimulated a fresh spirit of enquiry in his mind; and possibly, too, it was accelerated by a growing disenchantment with John, which Yeats remarked on in April 1909 when he met 'a young poet called Lewis who is an admirer of Augustus John', and found to his surprise that Lewis 'mourned over John's present state, that of much portrait painting for money, and thought his work was falling off'.[52] Lewis must also have changed his mind about the value of the New English Art Club, for he became closely involved with the formation of a more forward-looking splinter group. Many young painters were beginning to agree with Sickert that the N E A C was hopelessly hidebound, and their restlessness came to a head when they found their works rejected by the Club's selection committee. There was an alternative, of course: the Allied Artists' Association, founded in 1908 with the express purpose of replacing the old jury system with a massive annual round-up of talent which was open to all-comers. The attitude of this new Association was summed up by a member of its hanging committee when an elderly woman asked him how he could allow such execrable pictures to be shown. 'My dear lady', he replied,

▷Wyndham Lewis
*The Celibate*, 1909–?

in 'The Pole', published in the May 1909 issue of *The English Review*: 'He seemed to be holding fast and immobilising in his set intensity of expression some forceful mood. In his rigid and absorbed manner, with his smiling mask, he looked as though a camera's recording and unlidded eye were in front of him, and if he stirred or his expression took another tone, the spell would be broken, the plate blurred, his chance lost.' If Lewis was capable of writing such a passage as early as 1909, *Architect with Green Tie* could have been executed then as well, even though his decision to exhibit it in 1911 as a recent work seems strange. Its 'smiling mask' of primitivism is indeed crossed with the stiff correctitude of a Victorian gentleman posing for a daguerreotype, and the *Observer* was justified in declaring on 18 June 1911 that *The Architect*'s 'laboured method of cross-hatching . . . is painfully at variance with the artist's grotesque affectation of archaism'.

The picture has an air of artificiality, of half-understood influences which have yet to be properly worked out, even though Lewis himself later revealed that his interest in primitive art had begun as far back as his student days. 'Polynesian influences . . . occur all along', he told James Thrall Soby in 1947. 'We have here in the British Museum some very fine collections of New Ireland masks, Easter Island monoliths, and other varieties of Pacific and S. America stuff. Even when at the Slade School I was directed to go to the Print Room at the Museum and study the drawings of Raphael and Michaelangelo I had always to pass between cases full of more savage symbols on my way to the shrines of the cinquecento. In an early sketchbook the other day full of Leonardo's old man with the swollen underlip and Michaelangelo's writhing heavyweights I came across Pacific Island masks.'[58] The head in *Architect* is an extension of these early sketchbook copies, which suggests that Lewis's use of primitive prototypes was a development independent of the Cubists' use of similar material. Although he was eager to remain abreast of European experiments, Lewis nevertheless worked at a tangent to the artists he seemed to emulate. Just as he finally infused Vorticism with a stringent critical dislike of rival movements, so now he doggedly pursued a personal, if eccentric, programme rather than aping the pioneers he was beginning to admire. And he was certainly not afraid to formulate a style which inspired hostility even among the Camden Town Group: Sickert's biographer and friend, Robert Emmons, recalled that 'the more extreme post-Impressionist contributions of Wyndham Lewis were passed over, though not condoned, as being out of line with the spirit of the other members'.[59] Lewis was unabashed, telling Sturge Moore soon afterwards in a letter from Dieppe that 'the drawings I showed at Carfax Galleries, which I supposed, naturally, would go unnoticed, caused widespread indignation. The criticism would begin: "Despite the alarming announcements of the character of this 'Group', we find that amongst this band of honest, hard-working & interesting young men (with one exception) that good old English conservatism has saved them from the excesses" etc. Then the next paragraph would begin "*That one exception is Mr. Wyndham Lewis*, whose blackguardly, preposterous, putrid" etc. But invariably! Every notice that came along to our President followed, roughly, this itinerary – I do not know whether any of my old friends saw my drawings: I presume that the Lése Majesté contained in my taking up the brush & pencil again will be resented'.[60] The whole tone of the letter shows how much Lewis enjoyed the thought of notoriety, dramatising himself as a scabrous insurgent at odds with 'good old English conservatism'. It is almost as if he wanted to 'be resented' by older men like Sturge Moore, and went out of his way to plant the idea in his correspondent's mind.

All the same, Lewis gratefully remembered selling 'a largish canvas' of 'two sprawling figures of Normandy fishermen, in mustard yellows and browns' to

Wyndham Lewis
*Café*, 1910–11

the great John himself, 'a circumstance which gave me unusual pleasure'.[61] This painting may well have been the lost *Port de Mer* shown by Lewis at the second Camden Town exhibition of December 1911, and the purchase implies that John was continuing to support and foster his young friend's interests. 'I am glad to possess so interesting an example of your work as "Port de Mer",'[62] he wrote to Lewis, aware perhaps that its theme derived from John's own 1907 studies of Picasso-like French fisher-folk. His forbearance was not, however, shared by the critics. Although Frank Rutter remembered *Port de Mer* as a basically representational painting – 'the figures of his French fishermen were drawn strongly but they were kept flat to take their part in the decorative design, and already a certain squareness in the shapes was observable'[63] – other reviewers dismissed it out of hand. *The Times*' report on the Camden Town show published on 11 December went so far as to declare that 'Mr. Wyndham Lewis exhibits three geometrical experiments which many people will take for bad practical jokes', and most other newspaper reviews did not bother to mention him at all.

The only favourable notice came from Rutter, who did not share *The Times*' view that Lewis's 'geometrical art' was 'merely diagrammatic', and announced in the 3 December issue of the *Sunday Times* that Post-Impressionism 'over-flows into the Carfax Gallery where it finds its most downright and uncompromising exponent in Mr. Wyndham Lewis. For summary expression his "Port de Mer" is the British advance-post, a blaze of yellow for sunlight, three [*sic*] extraordinarily simplified but cunningly placed figures to symbolise the picturesque loafing of fishermen at rest'. Rutter concluded that Lewis should now be labelled 'the extremist', and a drawing called *Café* which is described on its mount as 'one of studies for first exhibited oil . . . bought by Augustus John' suggests why. Although only one of the fishermen is depicted here, Lewis's debt to a Matisse painting like the 1907 *Sailor* is immediately apparent in the flat curvilinear simplification of his face and slouching figure. The deliberately 'careless' execution which Matisse often employed at that time is also used in *Café*, as in Lewis's other contemporaneous works; and it is easy to appreciate how shocking the cursory pen-strokes slanting down the principal woman's dress must have appeared even to Lewis's admirers, who could remember the refined draughtsmanship of *Nude Boy Bending Over*. Lewis was out to shock by disdaining the genteel manners he had been taught at the Slade, but no less important for his future development were the hints of Cubism contained in the angular construction of the female head in *Café*'s foreground, and the severe rectilinearity so evident in the structure of the building behind her – a passage which anticipates the evolution of Lewis's Vorticist phase more directly than any other work of this period. No wonder the critics were aghast when they came across a similarly unsettling amalgam of Matisse and Picasso in *Port de Mer*: Lewis had attempted to exacerbate their sensibilities as raspingly as he knew how, and he succeeded in his task.

The reviewers' anger was inevitable, for the great mass of critical opinion was still inflamed about an exhibition of French painting which had taken England by storm in November 1910. All of a sudden, with scarcely any warning, London was brought face to face with the full reality of recent developments in France. Roger Fry, using his by now formidable influence as a leading critic and connoisseur, managed to persuade the Grafton Galleries to house a survey he called *Manet and the Post-Impressionists*.[64] It ran for three months, until January 1911, and immediately became one of those seminal events, like the first Impressionist exhibitions in Paris, which create the fiercest initial antagonism and yet ultimately mould the taste of a whole generation. Fry's selection focused on the achievements of Gauguin, Van Gogh and Cézanne; and it was to distinguish their work from the Impressionists, who were not included, that he employed the term 'Post-Impressionist'. In order to add some more contemporary spice to the proceedings, he also included a group of younger artists like Picasso, Matisse, Signac, Derain and Vlaminck, who ensured that Neo-Impressionism and Fauvism claimed their share of attention as well.

But he need not have bothered with such distinctions. To the public and most critics, individual differences of style mattered little: the entire exhibition was horrifying, and it caused a furore. Fry's friend Desmond MacCarthy, who helped organize the show and became the exhibition's secretary, explained that it aimed at 'no gradual infiltration, but – bang! an assault along the whole academic front of art'.[65] And despite Fry's diplomatic inclusion of several distinguished names on the committee list – permitted only because of the printed proviso that they were 'not responsible for the choice of the pictures' – the show was denounced as a scandalous disgrace. 'It professes to simplify, and to gain simplicity it throws away all that the long-developed skill of past artists had acquired and perpetuated', cried *The Times*. 'It begins all over again – and stops where a child would stop . . . it is the rejection of all that civilisation has done, the good with the bad.'[66] Newspaper cartoons like H. M. Bateman's dismissive *Post-Impressions of the Post-Impressionists* agreed, and the exhibition secretary had to provide a special book in which the hundreds of outraged visitors streaming through the gallery each day could write down their indignant complaints. One of the most depressing aspects of the controversy was that everyone imagined they were examining wholly up-to-date manifestations of French painting: 'though many people abused the paintings and some praised them', wrote the critic R. H. Wilenski, '*nobody* treated them as what they were – examples of the art produced in Paris a quarter of a century before.'[67]

The reaction of English artists was less straightforwardly hostile, but they too felt out of sympathy with ideas which they should have come to terms with long before. 'The show quite obviously represents a reaction and transition', Eric Gill wrote with a curiously detached air to William Rothenstein, 'and so, if, like Fry, you are a factor in that reaction and transition, then you like the show. . . . If, on the other hand, you are like me and John and McEvoy and Epstein, then, feeling yourself beyond the reaction and beyond the transition, you have a right to feel superior to Mr Henri Matisse (who is typical of the show) . . . and can say you don't like it.'[68] Incredible as it may seem, this was the sterile attitude of all but a handful of young English painters. Fry, himself only a recent convert to the importance of Cézanne, was out on a limb of his own making, with just a few artists like Duncan Grant – who had admired Matisse's *Dance* at the artist's studio in 1909 – the Camden Town Group and Paris-based Fauves such as Fergusson, Rice and Peploe to join him in his enthusiasm for Post-Impressionism. He could not even rely at this stage on the support of Lewis, who seemed equally scornful both of Post-Impressionism's detractors and of Fry when he wrote to Sturge Moore around January 1911. After announcing that 'I see John very rarely. There is nothing more to record as regards him', Lewis asked: 'I suppose the Post-Impressionists' Christmas in London, and the "ahurissement" of the citizens, you will, in one way or another, have heard about? Ricketts of course played a dastardly part in that melodramatic Christmas Press Pantomime. Roger Fry distinguished himself by at once becoming a pupil of Matisse.'[69] Writing from the viewpoint of someone who had long since been converted to Post-Impressionism's importance, Lewis clearly could not stomach Fry's sudden advocacy of the movement any more than he could the hostility which it had aroused in England. Both attitudes were in his eyes reprehensible.

Lewis would therefore have been foremost among the handful of London

H. M. Bateman
*Post-Impressions of the Post-Impressionists*, 1910

artists who responded with genuine admiration to the pictures in this vital exhibition. And judging from the contemporaneous drawings surviving from his hand, he would also have warmed to the unsigned but committed catalogue essay which Desmond MacCarthy wrote with the aid of 'a few notes' from Fry, producing one of the first sustained attempts by an English writer to defend and justify Post-Impressionism. 'There comes a point when the accumulation of an increasing skill in mere representation begins to destroy the expressiveness of the design', MacCarthy declared, arguing from the vantage-point of the artist who wanted to move towards abstraction. 'He begins to try to unload, to simplify the drawing and painting by which natural objects are evoked, in order to recover the lost expressiveness and life. He aims at *synthesis* in design; that is to say, he is prepared to subordinate consciously his power of representing the parts of his picture as plausibly as possible, to the expressiveness of his whole design.' This admirably succinct summary of the problems facing all those English artists who would eventually join the Vorticist cause does not actually suggest that representation might some day be discarded altogether. But the essay's notoriety at the time – MacCarthy remembered that 'this work of mine was far more widely quoted than anything I was ever destined to write, and phrases from it like "A good rocking-horse is more like a horse than the snap-shot of a Derby winner" were quoted and re-quoted with laughter'[70] – means that men like Lewis must have regarded it as an object lesson in stating the avant-garde case with the maximum amount of controversial punch.

Lewis would likewise have approved of the forthright way in which MacCarthy demolished the Impressionists, claiming that their 'receptive, passive attitude towards the appearance of things often hindered them from rendering their real significance'. Leaning heavily on Fry's understanding of Cézanne, MacCarthy maintained that 'Impressionism encouraged an artist to paint a tree as it appeared to him at the moment under particular circumstances. It insisted so much upon the importance of his rendering this exact impression that his work often completely failed to express a tree at all; as transferred to canvas it was just so much shimmer and colour. The "treeness" of the tree was not rendered at all; all the emotion and associations such as trees may be made to convey in poetry were omitted'.[71] Lewis, with his strong literary bias, would surely have agreed with such sentiments: the passively visual art of the Impressionists could never have satisfied the man who told John around 1910 that 'I hope the big present I shall be able to make you soon will be a book of verse. I'm going to do nothing but poetry now this novel's finished'.[72] And so it comes as no surprise to find MacCarthy's same catalogue essay describing Matisse's contribution to the Grafton show in words that could equally well apply to Lewis's work at this period: 'the general effect of his pictures is that of a return to primitive, even perhaps of a return to barbaric art. Primitive art, like the art of children, consists not so much in an attempt to represent what the eye perceives, as to put a line round a mental conception of the object.'[73] Pictures like *The Theatre Manager* and *The Celibate* had likewise courted this 'barbaric' quality, and their brusque distortions were the product of an acutely intelligent 'mental conception' around which Lewis had 'put a line'.

During the course of 1911 and 1912, the linear nature of his style became at once more pronounced and more refined. The *Smiling Woman Ascending a Stair*, an accomplished study for a lost painting of *The Laughing Woman*, displays an admirable new command over technical resources. Lewis's construction of this towering figure is stripped to its essential ingredients and then built up again in boldly schematized planes that reveal the growing influence of Cubism. But the face itself still clings to naturalism, a sharp summary of the woman's features

Wyndham Lewis
*Smiling Woman Ascending a Stair*, 1911–12

which borders on caricature. Lewis is far too interested, naturally, in the satirical meaning of his creation; and a direct parallel to the mood of the drawing is to be found once more in his Breton stories. 'One sees in the Breton peasant a constant tendency to sarcasm', Lewis wrote in 'Les Saltimbanques', published by Ford in 1909. 'Their hysterical and monotonous voices are always pitched in a strain of fierce raillery and abuse. But this does not affect their mirth. Their laughter is forced and meant to be wounding, and with their grins and quips they are like armed men who never meet without clashing their swords together.'[74] Lewis's leering harpy is just such a creature, and her 'raillery' may be specifically directed against John: his famous *Smiling Woman*, painted around 1909, was exactly the kind of academic picture Lewis now abhorred. And so the strong Cubist bias of this alternative *Smiling Woman* could well have been intended, on one level at least, as a pictorial slap in the face for his former hero, averring in no uncertain terms that John's frames of reference were now irrevocably redundant.

Augustus John
*The Smiling Woman*, 1909

Cubism was not actually represented in Fry's exhibition: Picasso's work was culled from the pink and blue periods, with paintings as undemanding as the 1905 *Girl with a Basket of Flowers*. But Lewis, with his extensive cosmopolitan experience, was not tied down to the pictures on view in London galleries. He continued to make annual trips to Paris even after he settled in England, and he could not fail to have been impressed by the Cubist works he saw on show there. The *Smiling Woman* makes these preoccupations plain; and yet it adheres to the facts of a posed model, and does not dare join the Cubists in their endeavour to transform the figure into a near-autonomous structure of shapes and colours. Lewis persists in copying, whereas Picasso was recreating images with their own independent terms of reference. It is even possible to detect the ghost of John's robed women lingering beneath the framework of this smirking puppet; and Lewis virtually admitted the *Smiling Woman's* dependence on observed facts when he discussed the drawing three years later. 'That picture is a Laugh, though rather a staid and traditional explosion', he told a newspaper interviewer in 1914. 'The body is a pedestal for the laugh. Although the forms of the figure and head perhaps look rather unlikely to you, they are more or less accurate, as representation. It was done from life.'[75]

For all his temerity, therefore, Lewis had some way to go in his search for a truly emancipated formal vocabulary. He struck out in a number of contradictory directions, by no means exclusively centred on the sober geometry of Cubism, and for a while looked as if he might become nothing more than a clever eclectic. But it was, in reality, his own way of asserting that he intended to be no-one's disciple, and the almost alarming diversity of several drawings dating from 1912 prove rather that he wanted to assess the potential of various conflicting ideas by putting them down on paper. Many are patently half-digested and inconclusive, yet Lewis's determination to liberate his art from the bondage of description and imitation which enslaved the majority of his sluggish compatriots is apparent throughout.

Even *Indian Dance*, a study that seems to be riddled with conflicting inspirations, contains discernible seeds of this ambition within its hybrid organization. Most of the background shapes are inconsequential, but Lewis is clearly interested in their force as abstract components in the design: perspectival recession is flouted, and in its place a freewheeling enjoyment of lines and washes for their own sake is allowed to develop. The contours of the primitive figures reinforce this element, too, as Lewis plays around with a number of alternatives in articulating the slope of a thigh, the movement of an arm. At one point, indeed, he lets the line describing the breasts of the woman on the right shoot up past her shoulder into the air, thereby discarding its naturalistic role and becoming an independent force in the composition. Lewis is beginning to escape from the duty to represent, and his imagination is gradually being set free to roam around the surface of his picture at will. The strangely undefined landscape shows another step forward as well, away from the narrative connotations of a drawing like *The Theatre Manager* towards a more timeless locale. In 1909 Lewis had placed his characters in a scene as theatrical as a staged tableau; but now, three years later, the figures have become more aloof and their world is left unspecified and mysterious.

The bleakness and uncompromising severity of Lewis's vision is made plain if *Indian Dance* is compared with Duncan Grant's painting of *The Tub*, executed in exactly the same year. For although the nude in Grant's picture is inspired by the same kind of primitive sculpture that lies behind Lewis's figures – Grant met Picasso in Gertrude Stein's studio around the time that *The Tub* was painted – she is the product of a gentle, domestic, Bloomsbury sensibility. Despite the extreme simplification which Grant has inflicted on his woman,

△ Duncan Grant
*The Tub*, 1912

◁ Wyndham Lewis
*Indian Dance*, 1912

the picture remains warm and playful; whereas Lewis's drawing is stark, un-relieved by any hint of reassuring prettiness or caprice. *Indian Dance* may be uncertain and diffuse in effect, but its willingness to experiment with dissonant ideas marks Lewis out as the most adventurous English artist of his generation. In her autobiography Gertrude Stein certainly remembered the keenness of his desire to learn from and test himself against the Parisian vanguard when he visited her studio, 'tall and thin . . . rather like a young frenchman on the rise', in order to 'sit and measure pictures. I cannot say that he actually measured with a measuring-rod but he gave all the effect of being in the act of taking very careful measurement of the canvas, the lines within the canvas and everything else that might be of use. Gertrude Stein rather liked him'.

Grant had joined him in the ranks of the Camden Town Group at their second exhibition in December 1911, and yet his presence did little to alleviate the loneliness of Lewis's artistic position. He had embarked on an experimental journey which was bound to be full of false starts, pitfalls and second thoughts at the outset; and an enormous act of will was required for him to break away from his cautious English environment and come to terms with the Cubist challenge he encountered on his trips to Paris. John was a patron and friend, but hardly likely to be enthusiastic about such radicalism; Gore, despite isolated departures like *The Beanfield, Letchworth*, did not feel temperamentally inclined towards extremism; Fergusson's Fauve circle, abandoning themselves to an un-inhibited enjoyment of colour over in Paris, were far too sensuous and emotional in their approach; and Sickert, although he possessed a wide knowledge of what was happening on the continent, was in the end too deeply entrenched in his Camden Town stronghold ever to sympathize with the direction taken by Cubism. 'The modern cult of post-Impressionism is localised mainly in the pockets of one or two dealers holding large remainders of incompetent work', he growled in an article published in January 1912. 'They have conceived the genial idea that if the values of criticism could be reversed – if efficiency could be

Spencer Gore
*The Beanfield, Letchworth*, 1912

considered a fault, and incompetence alone sublime – a roaring and easy trade could be driven . . . Picassos and Matisses could be painted by all the coachmen that the rise of motor traffic has thrown out of employment.'[76] Lewis could find no real sympathy in that quarter, yet who else could he turn to as a source of inspiration? Was there anyone in England who would not only be an encouraging listener, but also match his impatient intelligence concept for concept?

The answer for the moment lay not, as might be expected, with Lewis's painter friends, but rather among his expanding literary contacts. After Ford had printed his stories in *The English Review*, Douglas Goldring took up the young writer and in 1910 published some more of Lewis's stories and a poem in his own new magazine called *The Tramp*. Goldring's venture was to prove as short-lived as the *Review*, but he was at least willing to give a hearing to some of the startling ideas being propounded by the European avant-garde. As early as August 1910 he was, for example, sufficiently enlightened to carry Marinetti's swingeing attack on Italian culture in an open letter entitled 'Futurist Venice'. 'Burn the gondolas, those swings for fools', declaimed the Futurist leader with unabashed rhetoric, 'and erect up to the sky the rigid geometry of large metallic bridges and manufactories with waving hair of smoke, abolish everywhere the languishing curves of the old architecture.'

Such impassioned prose introduced a mood of iconoclasm entirely foreign to the English art world, and yet literary men like Goldring warmed to Marinetti's sentiments with remarkable ease. The editor of *The Tramp* declared that the Futurist polemic was 'courageously worded, in its quaint English', and that it 'deserves a wide publicity'. He even went so far as to print extracts from the 1909 Futurist Manifesto, commenting rather breathlessly: 'Is it not thrilling?'[77] As chance would have it, Lewis's story 'A Breton Innkeeper' was published in the selfsame issue as Marinetti's broadside, and it is therefore certain that he read Futurist propaganda when it first made its debut in England. He might well have warmed to it immediately, for here was a boldness and a rejection of the past that could hardly fail to strike a responsive chord in Lewis's heart. And even if he was not yet ready to follow Marinetti's lead and hit out verbally against the sterile traditionalism of his own English past, these Futurist clarion-calls may have succeeded in awakening him to the need for a full-scale rebellion.

But there was, too, an American poet three years younger than himself, moving about in the same literary circles and making the kind of outspoken noises which he was beginning to consider necessary. In June 1909, one month after Lewis's 'The Pole' was printed in *The English Review*, another of Ford's protégés called Ezra Pound published 'Sestina, Altaforte' in the same magazine alongside a Lewis story, 'Some Innkeepers and Bestre'. It was inevitable that these two precocious egotists, who shared a weakness for exhibitionism and aggressive displays of erudition, should eventually meet. And it was equally predictable that they would regard each other at first with a suspicion bordering on jealousy. 'It was with a complete passivity on my side', recalled Lewis, 'tinctured with a certain mild surliness, that acquaintance with Ezra Pound was gradually effected.' The introduction, at the Vienna Café in New Oxford Street – a rendezvous for the British Museum group who had encouraged Lewis's writing talents a decade before – definitely occurred in 1909, and probably through the aegis of Laurence Binyon, then an assistant keeper at the British Museum.[78] 'When Pound appeared I was mildly surprised to see an unmistakable "nordic blond", with fierce blue eyes and a reddishly hirsute jaw, thrust out with a thoroughly Aryan determination', Lewis remembered. 'But this moment of disillusion past, I took no further interest in this cowboy songster . . . I "sensed" that there was little enthusiasm . . . And when I rose to go back to the Museum he had whirled off – bitterness in his heart, if I know my Ezra.'[79]

Clearly, a clash of temperaments had taken place. Pound, for all his interest in the troubadours and other literatures of the past, had started to commit himself to the renewal of poetry ever since he joined a new, radical offshoot from the Poet's Club in April 1909, a few months after arriving in London with only £3 in his pocket and some copies of *A Lume Spento* tucked away among his belongings.[80] He probably felt that Lewis was trying to steal his thunder; and Lewis, for his part, regarded the Yankee as an absurdity, all outward show and no inner depth. But their differences can be exaggerated. It is surely significant, for instance, that both men were able to view English culture from the impatient vantage-point of a foreign invader: Lewis, despite his public school background, had in fact been born on a ship in the Bay of Fundy, a comfortable distance from the country in which he was to settle. Moreover, the truth of the matter was that Lewis loved to show off and broadcast his individuality as loudly as his American counterpart. 'Both of them, at that period, in clothes, hairdressing and manner, made no secret of their calling', wrote Goldring. 'Pound contrived to look "every inch a poet", while I have never seen anyone so obviously a "genius", as Wyndham Lewis.'[81]

Small wonder, then, that even their second meeting was a tense affair, full of antagonism and mutual distrust. Lewis recalled that 'there had been some question of the whereabouts of a kidnapped or absconding prostitute', and Pound took this topic of conversation as the cue for a sally against his rival. 'This young man could probably tell you!' he said, gesturing in Lewis's direction 'with a great archness, narrowing his eyes and regarding me with mischievous good-will . . . Ezra was already attributing to those he liked proclivities which he was persuaded must accompany the revolutionary intellect'.[82] Lewis, apparently, refused to rise to the bait and did not deign to reply. But when he finally did strike up a relationship with Pound, he felt as if he were boarding a 'bombastic galleon' – even though he soon 'discovered beneath its skull and cross-bones, intertwined with *fleurs de lys* and spattered with preposterous starspangled oddities, a heart of gold'.[83]

The friendship was established, and it must have been beneficial for both parties involved. Pound, as much as Lewis, was acquiring a taste for battle, and possessed an unholy impatience with the staleness and conventionality of post-Victorian verse. Indeed, the similarities between the two men were unconsciously pointed out as early as January 1911, when an American critic linked a poem of Pound's called 'Provenca' with Fry's Post-Impressionist Exhibition. 'Mr Pound is a very new kind of poet', he declared. 'Thinking of the art exhibition just held in London, one might, for want of a better figure, call him a Neo-Impressionist poet. Like the Neo-Impressionist painters, like the Impressionists in their day, Mr Pound is open to misunderstanding, even to ridicule . . . But though these poems have often an unconventional form, bizarre phraseology, catalectic or involved sentence structure and recondite meanings, yet it is always apparent that the poet knows what he is doing.'[84] The same could almost have been said about Lewis's art at this stage, even if the critic confuses Neo-Impressionism with Post-Impressionism.

But Pound actually ran ahead of his artist friend when it came to inaugurating an avant-garde movement, for he and two poetic colleagues – Richard Aldington and Hilda Doolittle – decided around April 1912 that they were agreed upon three principles of good writing: a direct treatment of the subject, a rejection of any word which was not absolutely essential to the presentation, and a determination to follow the musical phrase of a poem rather than strict regularity. This trio of beliefs became the cornerstone of Imagism, a movement which was officially launched some months later in Pound's book of poems called *Ripostes*, and dedicated to the overhauling and concentration of poetic language.[85] Just as Lewis wanted to escape from all the existing English pictorial formulae, to clear the decks and start all over again, so Pound yearned for a poetry that would isolate an impression or emotion, freed from comment or verbiage and emancipated from an imposed metrical form. 'I believe in technique as the test of a man's sincerity . . . in the trampling down of every convention that impedes or obscures the determination of the law, or the precise rendering of the impulse', he wrote in a 1912 poetic credo entitled 'Prologomena'. And in the same essay he prophesied that the best poetry of the coming decade 'will be harder and saner . . . It will be as much like granite as it can be . . . We will have fewer painted adjectives impeding the shock and stroke of it. At least for myself, I want it so, austere, direct, free from emotional slither'.[86]

Pound's words could easily have been uttered, without any sense of contradiction, by Lewis: for he was likewise working towards an art which exploited 'shock and stroke' by stripping his pictorial vocabulary of every 'convention' preventing it from becoming as tough as 'granite'. And Pound himself clinched the connection between the two men's preoccupations when he described the creation of an outstanding early poem called 'In a Station of the Metro'. 'Three years ago in Paris I got out of a "metro" train at La Concorde, and saw suddenly a beautiful face, and then another and another . . . and I tried all that day to find words for what this had meant to me, and I could not find any words that seemed to me worthy, or as lovely as that sudden emotion', he wrote in 1914. 'And that evening, as I went home along the Rue Raynouard, I was still trying and I found, suddenly, the expression. I do not mean that I found words, but there came an equation . . . not in speech, but in little splotches of colour. It was just that – a "pattern", or hardly a pattern, if by "pattern" you mean something with a "repeat" in it. But it was a word, the beginning, for me, of a language in colour . . . I realized quite vividly that if I were a painter, or if I had, often, *that kind* of emotion, or even if I had the energy to get paints and brushes and keep at it, I might found a new school of painting, of "non-representative" painting, a painting that would speak only by arrangements in colour.'[87]

If Pound really did think of his poetry in those visual terms as early as 1911, then he and Lewis must have found their friendship particularly stimulating. For while Lewis was gradually returning to a basic formal language by learning from primitive art and Cubism, Pound was taking an intensive look at the Japanese *haiku* tradition and teaching himself to pare his poems down to their fundamental constituents. The first version of the 'Metro' poem ran to thirty lines, but he destroyed it and made a second version of half the length six months later. Then, determined to rid himself of everything except the essential experience and approach more nearly to his original idea about the non-representative colour patches, he settled for two lines a year later:

The apparition   of the faces   in the crowd:
Petals   on a wet, black   bough.

The tension between these two lines, the statement and its corresponding image, is the core of the poem: their juxtaposition seems unexpected at first, but it finally assumes a rightness and an inevitability which belongs to the finest poetry. The extraordinary isolation obtained by the splitting up of the words within each line – a technique which was only printed in the version of the poem published by *Poetry* in April 1913 – parallels Lewis's growing desire to regard a picture as the sum of a series of formal components. And the abruptness of the pauses serves likewise to reinforce the semi-abstract image of the petals, in themselves the verbal counterpart of an almost non-figurative painting. 'In the "Metro" hokku, I was careful, I think, to indicate spaces between the rhythmic units', Pound wrote to the editor of *Poetry*, 'and I want them observed.'[88]

Although some of Pound's other contemporaneous poems like 'The Garret' took this idea of poetry as a visual design even further, by no means all of his Imagist experiments were as disciplined or successful as 'In a Station of the Metro'. Pound was, in his own encyclopaedic way, as deeply attached to the past as Lewis had been when he copied Goya and Hals in Europe; and it was difficult for both of them to forget the achievements of previous centuries. But they were eager to try, and Pound again showed himself to be in sympathy with Lewis's pictorial standpoint when he attacked Impressionism in his *Ripostes* book. He was united with Lewis in his opposition to its principles, claiming that the Impressionists had 'brought forth: "Pink pigs blossoming on the hillside",' and he laughed too at the kind of Post-Impressionists 'who beseech their ladies to let down slate-blue hair over their raspberry-coloured flanks'.[89]

Pound's resolve to see poetry and painting as related parts of the same innovatory enterprise was, moreover, fortified by a visit to Whistler's 1912 Tate Gallery exhibition. Like Lewis, who had declared his readiness to 'profit by' the Paris Whistler show back in 1905, Pound now composed a poem dedicated 'To Whistler, American' and chose him as a mentor for his own literary insurrection. 'I count him our only great artist', he told a fellow-American in August 1912, 'and even this informal salute, drastic as it is, may not be out of place at the threshold of what I hope is an endeavor to carry into our American poetry the same sort of life and intensity which he infused into modern painting.'[90] The admiration was entirely comprehensible, for Whistler – an American expatriate, like Pound – had always been at pains to stress that a picture relied primarily on the orchestration of its painted surface. Pound responded to that viewpoint, and he also attempted to emulate Whistler's deliberately iconoclastic behaviour as well. Richard Aldington, who described Pound in 1912 as 'great fun, a small but persistent volcano in the dim levels of London literary society', remembered that 'unluckily, Ezra had read Whistler's *Gentle Art of Making Enemies*, and practised it without the "gentle".'[91]

Within little more than a year, however, Lewis was to take the place of Whistler as Pound's artistic hero, and the two men would join together to help formulate a new movement which satisfied their desire for absolute revolution.

# Chapter 2: The Impact of the Futurist and Cubist Invasions on the English Rebels

It would be difficult to exaggerate the impetus which Lewis's yearning for revolt must now have been given by Futurism's first concerted onslaught on London. Until the *Exhibition of Works by the Italian Futurist Painters* arrived at the Sackville Gallery in March 1912, his experience of the European avant-garde had been based almost exclusively upon works of art alone; but the Italians' activities proved to him that controversial new ideas could be effectively disseminated in other ways as well. For Futurist art was, from the outset, so inextricably tied up with a concerted polemical onslaught that the paintings themselves were overshadowed by the inflammatory manifestos and public demonstrations launched by the movement. Even its exhibition catalogue was armed with verbal exhortations which were calculated to outrage: the very first words, 'we shall sing the love of danger, the habit of energy and boldness', struck a note of hectoring bravado entirely lacking in Fry's promotion of Post-Impressionism. They came from Marinetti's *Initial Manifesto of Futurism*, a headlong poetic tirade that set out to denigrate 'passéist' institutions. 'Set fire to the shelves of the libraries!' it screamed. 'Deviate the course of canals to flood the cellars of the museums! Oh! May the glorious canvases drift helplessly! Seize pickaxes and hammers! Sap the foundations of the venerable cities!' And this exclamatory plea for the destruction of the intimidating past led on to an open advocacy of aggression, even more alien to Fry. 'We wish to glorify War – the only health giver of the world – militarism, patriotism, the destructive arm of the Anarchist, the beautiful Ideas that kill, the contempt for woman.'[1]

Marinetti was providing perfect copy for the London press, and he knew it. 'We shall sing of the great crowds in the excitement of labour, pleasure and rebellion', the Futurist leader proclaimed, 'of the multi-coloured and polyphonic surf of revolutions in modern capital cities; of the nocturnal vibration of arsenals and workshops beneath their violent electric moons; of the greedy stations swallowing smoking snakes; of factories suspended from the clouds by their strings of smoke; of bridges leaping like gymnasts over the diabolical cutlery of sunbathed rivers'.[2] The old studio motifs still favoured by Cubism must be pushed aside, he insisted, in favour of a style and subject-matter which would bring art into closer contact with the mechanized environment of a new century. And the abandoned extravagance of Marinetti's prose reflected the enthusiasm with which he evoked the wealth of fresh visual material awaiting the artist ambitious enough to take it on. He succeeded in communicating a genuine love of industrialized life which counteracted the manifestos' senseless delight in physical destruction; and this combination of positive vitality and subversion would have appealed to Lewis, hungry as he was for new directions, new answers to old problems. Whether or not he ever sympathized with the Futurist ideal of 'universal dynamism' is more open to doubt: while he continued to cultivate clarity, precision and linear definition, the Italians aimed to destroy 'the materiality of bodies' and discard outlines so that objects could merge into their backgrounds with frenetic force. 'How often', they cried, 'have we not seen upon the cheek of the person with whom we were talking the horse which passes at the end of the street?' And whereas Lewis was concerned with the solidity of a single image, Futurism wanted to bring together a multitude of different images, culled from various simultaneous events, or the additive constituents of one single movement. 'All things move, all things run, all things are rapidly changing', declared the Italians, asserting with disarming confidence that 'a running horse has not four legs, but twenty, and their movements are triangular.'[3]

The Futurists revelled in the sensationalist bite of such brash statements: they knew that modern art was news to the English Press, and the critics had a field day. 'Nightmare Exhibition at the Sackville Gallery', ran the headline for P. G. Konody's review in the *Pall Mall Gazette*; and even though he admitted that the Italians were 'not only sincere, but endowed with overabundant imagination', two days later he changed his mind and damned them in the *Observer* as 'the outcome of a new and thoroughly objectionable literary tendency'.[4] The *Evening News* was far more brusque and dismissive, claiming that Futurism 'has fallen flat as a breathless pancake',[5] while Sir Philip Burne-Jones wrote a furious letter attacking the Italians as the creators of 'ludicrous productions' which were 'outside the pale of Art altogether, and in no way concerned with it'.[6] In vain did Max Rothschild, who purchased a number of paintings from the show, come to Futurism's aid and declare that 'when from one mansion there bursts forth a song of youth and originality, even though harsh and discordant, it should be received, not with howls of fury, but with reasonable attention and criticism'.[7] Fleet Street was out for blood, and while the *Bystander's* cartoonist showed a Commons' debate reduced to chaos by a 'Futurist Eye', the *Daily Express* summarized London's dismissive reaction to the Futurists in a cartoon called *The New Terror*, which seized on the movement's superficial characteristics and made merciless comic capital out of them all.

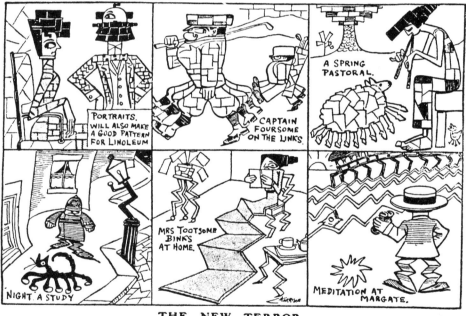

THE NEW TERROR.

C. Harrison
*The New Terror*, 1912

But the apotheosis of official condemnation was reached when the *Morning Post* decided not to print Robert Ross's review of the show. 'In the exercise of his duty, it seems that Mr Ross prepared an article on the Futurist Exhibition', reported Sickert in *The English Review*. 'I am told that this could not be published on the plea that the Futurist Exhibition was in itself an immorality, and must not be chronicled!'[8]

The whole furore prompted the irrepressible Marinetti to consider the show a 'colossal success', for over 350 articles were written about it, and picture sales brought in more than 11,000 francs.[9] Despite the surfeit of viciously slanted criticism, the Futurist leader continued to have faith in England as a potential convert to the movement: he had, after all, been fired by the reception his lectures had previously been accorded there, right back to the time when he first gave a public talk in London at the Lyceum Club for Women in April 1910. Perhaps his personal charisma had something to do with his tremendous impact on Anglo-Saxon audiences – Goldring admiringly described him as a 'flamboyant person, adorned with diamond rings, gold chains and hundreds of flashing white teeth'.[10] Such theatricality was a relatively novel phenomenon in the discreet literary circles of London, and although he delivered his lecture in French the response was overwhelming.

He was, needless to say, receiving the same delighted response two years later, when he organized a lecture at the Bechstein Hall on 19 March 1912 to coincide with the Sackville Gallery exhibition. The Italian propagandist was in his element, beginning by congratulating Britain on its material success, 'its brutality and arrogance', and then berating it 'as a nation of sycophants and snobs, enslaved by old worm-eaten traditions, social conventions, and romanticism'.[11] The accusation of romanticism was somewhat misplaced, coming as it did from one of the most unrepentant romantics in the history of art, but he quickly made up for his inconsistency by reciting a number of his poems. The performance was spectacular enough for *The Times* to gasp at his 'impassioned torrent of words', so startling that 'some of his audience begged for mercy'. Predictably, *The Times* went on to decree that the 'anarchical extravagance of the Futurists must deprive their movement of the sympathy of all reasonable men', but Marinetti's listeners once again pampered him with their 'laughter and applause'.[12]

He knew exactly how to handle inquisitive reporters as well as the literary world, and played cunningly to the public in an interview with the *Evening News*. 'Why, London itself is a Futurist city!' he exclaimed, determined to seduce the English into becoming apostles of his movement. And to that end he rhapsodized about the capital's 'coloured electric lights that flash advertisements in the night', the 'enormous glaring posters' and 'brilliant hued motor buses'. But it was, ultimately, in the Underground that Marinetti claimed 'I got what I wanted – not enjoyment, but a totally new idea of motion, of speed'. And then he at last broached the subject most dear to his megalomaniac heart: the young English painters, all of whom he imagined could be initiated into the Futurist faith and start the movement off on a world-wide basis. He was careful to stress that English artists had not even begun to exploit the fresh themes thrown up by the twentieth century cityscape, and castigated them for failing to reflect their own time in their work. 'The fact is', he announced emphatically, 'that your painters live on a nostalgic feeling, longing for a past that is beyond recall, imagining that they live in the pastoral age.'[13] Marinetti had finally thrown down the gauntlet in public, and confidently expected at least some London artists to pick it up.

But even Lewis, anxious though he was to learn both from the propagandist techniques and the spirit of modernity heralded by Futurism, could not force himself to adopt more progressive attitudes. Many years later, David Bomberg accused him of raiding on the Futurist style in a flagrantly opportunist way: 'Lewis had seen the illustrated Milan advance copy of reproductions with the Italian 1909 Futurist Manifesto written by F. T. Marinetti to support the Futurist Exhibition at Sackville Galleries 1912. Freehand without a tracing, [he] adapted the figures [of] Boccioni . . . from [the] 1912 London Exhibition.'[14] But Bomberg had not at this stage met Lewis; and although the Futurists had an undeniable influence on his work, the truth was that he had to reach a synthesis of his own, through an internal development of a more genuine kind. On the evidence of his 1912 drawings, Lewis did experience a painful period of trial and error, testing all the maddeningly diverse impulses which appealed to his gadfly imagination. John recalled visiting his friend at his studio, 'in his usual squalor', and finding there some drawings of elephants with beards. He promptly accused Lewis of inconsistency, but the latter 'answered rather sharply, "You may be right, but I happen to *like* beards". This was unanswerable, and I made no further cavil, zoological or otherwise, for I knew it was not a bit of good arguing with P.W.L. over questions of fact during one of his creative moods'.[15] The elephant drawings have since disappeared, but plenty of others survive to

Wyndham Lewis
*Centauress*, 1912

demonstrate how Lewis, hampered by the need to write as well as paint, persisted in introducing blatant literary references to pictures which attempted to
move towards abstraction. His schizophrenia is, for instance, particularly acute
in the drawing of a *Centauress*, where a mythological creature rears up in front
of a rigidly organized arrangement of non-representational forms. The result ends
up, of course, as stylistic mayhem. It is as if Lewis had chosen to dramatize his
predicament by juxtaposing a symbol of an older form of art with the forces of
abstraction, and the two elements war with each other at the expense of formal
singlemindedness. The centauress starts back, horrified to realize that her
abstract surroundings threaten to overwhelm and terminate her very existence.

In order to resolve these conflicting elements, Lewis seems to have decided
to move still nearer to the view of man presented in his early stories. For 'A
Breton Innkeeper' had, as far back as 1910, outlined a tentative conception of
human beings as automatons, mere machines. Its detailed portrait of Roland,
the innkeeper himself, concentrated with characteristic precision on the external
movements of the man. Time and again Lewis equated Roland with a mechanism:
'You are afraid with Roland to pose him any questions; there is a feeling that he
is not to be approached with impunity, as with the wheels of a machine in
motion.'[16] Lewis's satirical vision saw these Breton peasants essentially as puppets
who have only one function: subservience to a ritual. And gradually, this very
ritual is presented as some immense, grinding, mechanical process which runs
on monotonously and controls every single movement.

Two years after he put forward this concept in print, Lewis at last managed
to translate it from literary terms into some of his most convincing 1912 pictures.
The large watercolour of *Two Women*, for instance, takes an analytical Cubist
nude and uses its faceted structure to evolve something entirely personal: attenuated, energetic and fantastic. It was originally called *The Starry Sky*, and
such a poetic title emphasizes the freedom with which Lewis departs from his
French prototype.[17] For Picasso and Braque split their figures up into a series
of austere planes in order to arrive at a more comprehensive way of presenting
their experience of a human being, and their formal priorities ensured that the
background areas became an integral part of this structure. But Lewis seized on

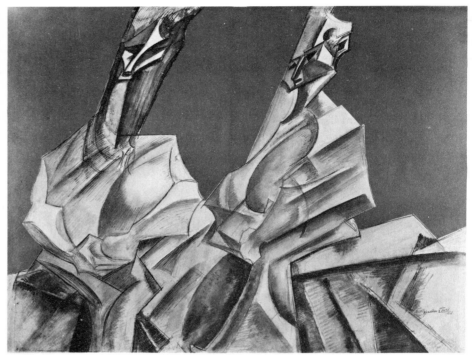

△ Wyndham Lewis
*Two Mechanics*, 1912

▷ Wyndham Lewis
*Two Women*, 1912

the mannerism alone, rather than the autonomous way of seeing it implied. Using Cubism as his tool, a springboard for his own fertile imagination, he makes his *Two Women* into a pair of seraphic, rock-like creatures; and stresses their sculptural solidity by cutting them out and pasting them onto a warm brown backdrop. They were later described, more than a little ridiculously, as 'two plastic Watteauesque figures',[18] but the term does serve to point out the high-flown, unashamedly capricious strain in Lewis's art.

The fancifulness only pays dividends here because *Two Women* shows an increased willingness to introduce a mechanical element into its figures: these other-wordly beings are inflexibly built up, rooted in their jagged base with an almost armour-plated inviolability. And the implications contained in this water-colour receive open expression in a closely related drawing of *Two Mechanics*, where the new machine-like style finally succeeds in merging with a new subject-matter. Lewis does not even need to specify any drills, so overt is their action in the taut, straining poses of the workers themselves. At some stage, Lewis enlarged his study of the mechanics alone to incorporate an evocative environment of industrial shapes.[19] They dominate the figures, suggesting perhaps that these depersonalized robots are surrendering their humanity to the new automated life-style of the twentieth century. Here are the first mature signs of Lewis's emergent sensibility, now attuning itself to the idea of an urban, industrial art which would interpret through its form and content the changing conditions to be witnessed everywhere. Marinetti's challenge was being taken up, but in a spirit entirely foreign to the soaring optimism of Futurist romance. For *Two Mechanics* is a stark, utterly unsentimental step forward towards the concerns of Vorticism.

All the same, it must be admitted that *Two Mechanics* is still a relatively crude work, full of hesitation and unresolved passages. The hatching of the pen is everywhere dry and niggling, and the figures do not really relate to their added surroundings. Pictorial discovery was for Lewis a painful business; but once he had hit upon his new direction, he did not fail to capitalize on it. Suddenly he found himself able to throw off a consummate study like *The Vorticist*, where every single part of the robot-like figure is defined with a whiplash elegance of contour.[20] The full force of mechanical man is expressed in a staccato vocabu-

Wyndham Lewis
*The Vorticist*, 1912

lary of driving shapes, flexible enough to contain figuration and abstraction in
one fiercely commanding image. The ambiguity exploited in this new style
ensures that every part of the drawing can be read either as a section of anatomy,
a fragment of some streamlined machine, or an amalgam of both at the same
time. Lewis has developed a rich language which gathers together a myriad of
conflicting references into one coherent whole. He has digested the influence
of Cubism so thoroughly, now, that he can afford to harness its formal potential
to his own ends. *The Vorticist* dodges between representation and non-representation with as much assurance as the best analytical Cubist paintings, but it
simultaneously escapes from the Parisian obsession with the studio and plunges
wholeheartedly into the mainstream of twentieth century dynamism recommended by Futurism. The drawing suggests, too, how much of a secondary debt
Lewis owed at this period to Japanese prints: *The Vorticist's* body is flung across
the paper with much of the taut linear energy, frenzied diagonal movement and
grimacing exaggeration of a Japanese actor-warrior in full battle-cry.

By this time Lewis had become so much at home with his new-found freedom
that he was able to take a theme as time-honoured as that of a procuress whispering in a prostitute's ear and make of it something entirely fresh and relevant.

Wyndham Lewis
*The Courtesan*, 1912

*The Courtesan* manages to transform a subject heavy with Old Master associations into a stern agglomeration of mask-like faces, elongated arms as straight as connecting rods, and purely abstract forms arranged together with great precision on the paper. An element of doodling, of playing with shapes for their own sake, is present here, too: another pair of heads is swiftly sketched, upside down on the bottom of the sheet, to serve as a shorthand guide to the far less clarified scene above. The overall meaning of that scene is explicit enough, however. Just as *The Vorticist* shows modern man at once enhanced and imprisoned by his mechanistic attributes – he could, in fact, be opening his mouth in a scream of anguish at the twentieth-century condition – so *The Courtesan* presents a dehumanisation which Lewis was obviously in no mood to greet with unqualified enthusiasm. Even at this stage in the evolution of Vorticism, he was fully aware of industrial civilisation's capacity for emotional brutality; and instead of celebrating it, *The Courtesan* suggests how fearsome and implacable it could become. A steadfast refusal to be merely intoxicated by modern technological advance, along with an awareness of its darker forces, characterised Vorticism from the beginning. And *The Courtesan*'s clear-eyed realisation that twentieth-century change did not automatically herald the dawn of a mechanised golden age stands it in good stead from the disenchanted perspective of today.

A cruel world populated by creatures devoid of passion or sympathy is created here, light years away from the relative humanism of the Cubists. And yet only the most advanced analytical works produced by the French movement could have lain behind the sophisticated stylistic juggling employed by Lewis in *The Courtesan*. Such pictures were readily to hand in London during 1912, too: Picasso's roughly contemporaneous *Head of a Man* was only one of many comparable paintings shown at the Grafton Galleries from October right through to the end of the year.[21] A Cubist work like *Head of a Man* sets off a near-abstract fragmentation of the subject against totally abstract surroundings, and reshuffles them all so subtly that it is never quite clear where the one ends and the other begins. Lewis deployed precisely the same technique in *The Courtesan*, and he added descriptive clues such as the inverted pair of heads in much the same spirit as Picasso uses a button, a moustache or numerals in his composition. But the gap separating the two artists consists of the difference between a formal and a literary painter. Picasso reduces his motif to a geometrical scaffolding because he wants to simplify the syntax of painting as far as he can without losing sight of its starting-point in visible reality. Yet Lewis espouses a similar method of construction to articulate his vision of a mechanistic universe, a concept which was inspired more by philosophical speculation than by purely pictorial research.

Works as articulate as *The Courtesan* probably date from the closing months of 1912, but the experience they draw upon was gained earlier in the year through Lewis's first important commission. Improbably enough, it was for a nightclub. But no ordinary one: its owner was none other than the notorious Madame Frida Strindberg, whom one acquaintance wickedly described as 'the origin, or shall we say one of the inspirations, of Strindberg's tirades against women in general and married women in particular'.[22] This amorous, theatrical and terrifyingly persuasive woman promised, in her grandiose *Preliminary Prospectus* for the club issued in April 1912, that the interior would be 'entirely and exclusively' decorated by 'leading young British artists'. For Madame Strindberg had cultural pretensions. The visitor would see, she announced in her uneasy English, 'a varied programme, with the tendency of a return of art to intuition and simplicity . . . On one hand such art as we owe to the genius of the people, the dance, folk lore – on the other offering free development to the youngest and best of our contemporaries and – "Futurists" '.[23]

Determinedly up to date – the reference to Futurism was penned only a month after the Sackville Gallery exhibition had burst upon London – the patroness who promised all these exotic delights managed to procure the best creative talent for her venture. And she did so by dint of sheer personality. Even a robust woman-eater like John confessed that she 'unnerved' him, and he testified to her extraordinary energy by wryly remembering that 'Madame frequently "committed suicide" but as often recovered: for a woman of her constitution, no amount of veronal had any permanent effect: it merely upset her stomach for a week or two'.[24] It was this same 'constitution' which enabled her to assemble an impressive array of artists for the establishment she proposed to christen – with a characteristic touch of the absurd – 'The Cave of the Golden Calf'. Lewis, as one of the most controversial painters of the day, was a predictable choice, as were the Camden Town luminaries Ginner and Gore. But Madame Strindberg was not content to stop there, and insisted on asking Epstein, the perpetrator of the derided Strand statues and the equally infamous Wilde tomb in Père La Chaise, to model a new sculpture for her club.

How did this Swedish expatriate succeed in enlisting the services of such a promising group of men? The answer is simple: she invited them out to an

Pablo Picasso
*Head of a Man*, 1912

Wyndham Lewis
*Cabaret Theatre Club Poster*, 1912

expensive restaurant dinner. 'The meal was sumptuous', recalled Epstein, 'the champagne lavish.' The fêted artists had, however, been enjoying a fraudulent feast, for 'when the management presented the bill Madame Strindberg took it in her hand, and turning to the assembled company said: "Who will be my knight, tonight?".'[25] Nobody, it seems, was chivalrous enough to rise to the bait; but despite the vagaries of its owner's income, the 'low-ceilinged night-club' which Osbert Sitwell remembered as 'appropriately sunk below the pavement' in the heart of the West End at 9 Heddon Street was duly launched, adorned with the most provocative decorations.[26] With Lewis's specially designed poster offering unlimited delights in the form of a brusquely simplified nude siren, the Cave seemed assured of a *succès de scandale*.

The decorations must have been completed rapidly, for during the course of 1912 the Cabaret Theatre Club – as it was more familiarly known – became the haunt of the cognoscenti, a fashionable nocturnal equivalent of the Café Royal. 'The lesser artistes of the theatre, as well as the greater, mixed with painters, writers and their opposite, officers in the Brigade of Guards', wrote Sitwell, who claimed that the club 'appeared in the small hours to be a super-heated Vorticist garden of gesticulating figures, dancing and talking, while the rhythm of the primitive forms of ragtime throbbed through the wide room.'[27] Pound relished watching Madame Strindberg 'wave a customer away from her table, saying as she did so that sleep with him she would, but talk to him, never: "One must draw the line *somewhere*".'[28] And he found himself exhilarated by the hectic *ambience* of a club which seemed to mirror the increasingly feverish and uninhibited mood of London as a whole. 'We want a place given up to gaiety, to a gaiety stimulating thought, rather than crushing it', cried a rhetorical Cabaret brochure. 'We want a gaiety that does not have to count with midnight. We want surroundings, which after the reality of daily life, reveal the reality of the unreal.'[29] And can it be doubted that the club, with its unique *mélange* of Veil Dances, Jester Songs, Breton Wakes, 'Playing with Fire', Margaret Morris with her Greek Children Dancers, shadow-plays written and performed by Ford, 'Exultations' and Russian stories recounted 'in a very melodramatic fashion'[30] by Frank Harris, fully lived up to the heady promises of its advertisements? The pre-war *zeitgeist*, which contributed so much to the emergent style of Vorticism, must here have received a wonderfully defiant and unconventional expression.

Nothing now survives of the paintings and sculpture which once helped to create the Cabaret's unforgettable atmosphere, but descriptions of Lewis's share have been recorded. Sitwell considered the walls to be 'hideously but relevantly frescoed', even though an official club prospectus specifically stated that the paintings were executed on 'large panels';[31] and Ford's mistress, Violet Hunt, was reminded of 'raw meat' when she gazed at the 'Bismarckian images, severings, disembowellings, mixed pell-mell with the iron shards that did it, splashed with the pale blood of exhausted heroes'.[32] Her outrageous hyperbole evokes an art of total iconoclasm, but a drawing which Lewis contributed to Madame Strindberg's illustrated prospectus gives a more sane idea of his efforts.[33] Here primitive figures lunge and wheel across a dramatically lit background of abstract segments; and another, closely related 1912 drawing – the first nonrepresentational design in Lewis's entire *œuvre* – suggests that at least one of his decorations may have dispensed with figuration entirely.[34] It will never be known for certain, just as the precise extent of Lewis's handiwork at the Cabaret remains unclear: a note, probably written to him by Madame Strindberg, offers payment for no less than two paintings, two screens and the arrangement and decoration of the walls.[35] But one eye-witness has been able to remember that Lewis's contributions included 'a backcloth for the stage, containing figures in a frieze. It was almost abstract, painted in very bright colours, and Madame

Wyndham Lewis
*A Wall Decoration in the Cave of the Golden Calf*, 1912

Wyndham Lewis
*Abstract Design*, 1912

Spencer Gore
*Sketch for a Mural Decoration in the Cave of the Golden Calf*, 1912

Strindberg used to tell me it was the product, "not of talent, but of genius!" '[36]

However sparse the evidence concerning Lewis's supposedly radical contributions, it is possible to assert that they were infinitely more forward-looking than the other artists' compositions. Although two oil-sketches by Gore are preserved to show that he abandoned his normally reticent subject-matter in favour of an extravagant mythical theme, their stylistic ineptitude simply does not measure up to Lewis's daring assurance.[37] They are vividly coloured exercises, handled with a painterly freedom reminiscent of Kandinsky's early work, and Lewis's regard for Gore's final decorations is implicit in an obituary written after his friend's untimely death two years later. 'The memorial exhibition of his work shortly to be held', Lewis declared, 'should, if possible, since the Cabaret Club has closed, contain the large paintings he did for that place.'[38] Lewis's respect was understandable, in that the oil sketches by both Gore and Ginner – who likewise devised a lurid jungle scene with bizarre animals – represented a bold departure from their previous work.[39] Yet they still resisted Lewis's skilful use of Cubism and Futurism, and set beside his dithyrambic designs their studies appear playful and utterly inoffensive.

Epstein's part in the decorative scheme, on the other hand, may well have been as spectacular as Lewis's. His ambitious plan was to surround the 'two massive iron pillars' which 'supported the ceiling' with sculptured reliefs: he later recounted how he 'proceeded directly in plaster and made a very elaborate decoration which I painted in brilliant colours'.[40] His tantalisingly brief description suggests a pair of psychedelic totem poles, worthy successors to the Assyrian inspiration so evident in the flying figure he had created for the Wilde tomb. Violet Hunt, who remembered them as 'white wooden pillars like caryatids', was also able to testify that 'all had scarlet details, the heads of hawks, cats, camels'; and this barbaric cornucopia of animal imagery would have made, together with the paintings, a startling visual environment for the Cabaret's visitors. They, in their turn, probably discussed the disturbing new forms of art with a wider public than Lewis had ever contacted before, and helped to spread the fame of everyone involved in the venture. 'With the Epstein figures appearing to hold up the threateningly low ceiling, the somewhat abstract hieroglyphics I had painted round the walls, the impassioned orchestra, it must have provided a kick or two for the young man about town of the moment', Lewis wrote afterwards. 'It was my first job: and if I had acquired the taste for alcohol (as I had not) I might have got a kick or two myself.'[41]

The whole exercise earned him a welcome total of £60, and introduced him to the London circles most likely to give him further commissions – he even confessed later that he 'would have done them for nothing'.[42] But as important as the publicity which the Cabaret gave to his blossoming reputation was the opportunity it afforded to bring the young radical artists of England together. From his earliest days in London, Epstein had been friends with men like John and McEvoy, who belonged to the milieu of the New English Art Club. And yet now, by working alongside Ginner, Gore and Lewis, Epstein came into direct contact with some of London's most experimental artists. The experience indubitably helped him, wavering as he was between the challenge of abstraction and the equally compelling demands of representational portrait busts, to formulate a more forward-looking direction.

It was also of immense value to a relatively unknown 28-year-old artist named Cuthbert Hamilton, who came in to aid Lewis with his decorations, collaborated with him on a shadow-play project for the Cabaret and may even have executed a design of his own.[43] Hamilton's presence was in one sense entirely understandable, for he had known Lewis ever since they were student contemporaries at the Slade. He was gifted enough to win a scholarship there, but immediately afterwards lapsed into temporary obscurity while teaching at Clifton College between 1907 and 1910. By the time he came to the Cabaret, however, he must have been active and – more vital still – advanced enough to stand comparison with the other artists at work there, or else Lewis would certainly not have accepted him as an ally during the implementation of the decorative projects. A drawing does in fact survive, reputed to be by Hamilton, which displays an obvious sympathy for Lewis's precepts.[44] Its theme of dancing figures may even mean that it is a working sketch for a Cabaret painting, and Hamilton's trans-

Cuthbert Hamilton (?)
*Three Dancing Figures, c.* 1912–13

lation of their gyrating bodies into a Lewisian amalgam of puppets, automatons and warriors does imply a stylistic debt to his older friend. Even though the execution is summary to the point of outright crudity, Lewis would have warmed to the spirit of brash adventure which the drawing evinces. And he took the trouble of writing to Hamilton after the Cabaret commission had been completed, in order to implore him to keep their new friendship alive. 'I hope that beastly Cabaret, that has been the cause of so many ridiculous vexations to me, is not going to add lessening of our good camaraderie to the number of its senseless misdeeds', Lewis wrote. 'See that it doesn't, for Heaven's sake.'[45] Valuable associations had been formed under the aegis of Madame Strindberg's patronage, and Lewis – always a politician as well as an artist – was naturally determined not to lose hold of them. If common interests really were being discovered, then he need remain isolated no longer, and it was vital that these points of agreement should be shared, discussed and developed.

At the same time, moreover, Lewis continued to fortify his growing claim to be considered as the spearhead of the English avant-garde by exhibiting a monumental and audacious canvas at the Allied Artists' summer salon. Virtually nine feet square in size, this vast painting proved to be far and away the most extreme work he had ever executed; and Frank Rutter of the *Sunday Times* was so impressed that he was still emphasizing its seminal importance in the history of contemporary British art over twenty years later. 'Here for the first time', he declared in 1933, 'London saw by an English artist a painting altogether in sympathy with the later developments in Paris.'[46] Unfortunately, it is no longer possible to judge the accuracy of Rutter's evaluation: the painting has disappeared completely, and even its title is a matter of some controversy. Although the only exhibit by Lewis listed in the AAA's catalogue is called *Creation*, Roger Fry's review of the show described the picture as a 'design of a Kermesse, originally intended for the Cave of the Calf, the new Cabaret Theatre'.[47] Furthermore, a contract still exists concerning the renting of a Lewis painting called *Kermesse* to Madame Strindberg, who hung it on the stairway of the Cabaret leading down from the street; and the picture which caused such a sensation at the AAA's salon did subsequently become known by that same title.[48]

What did this canvas, which Sickert thought 'magnificent' but which the bewildered Press variously referred to as 'a delirious octopus', 'a rather disunited family of Mr Wells' Martians', 'an aeroplane disaster', 'The Battle of the Angles',

Wyndham Lewis
*Design for a Programme Cover – Kermesse*, 1912

'crabs in anguish', 'the famous tournament scene in Ivanhoe' and 'some terrible battle of extermination between murderous insects', actually look like?[49] One conclusion can be drawn from this extraordinary outburst of conflicting reactions: the subject-matter was by no means clear, and must have been almost lost in a welter of explosively abstract fragments. But the few miscellaneous sketches which would appear to give some indication of the painting's appearance are, curiously, quite open about their figurative intentions. One of them, an ink study called *Design for a Programme Cover – Kermesse*, combines a degree of representation with a savagery of execution unmatched by any other Lewis drawing of 1912.[50] Clearly no more than a slight work dashed off in haste – the title suggests that Madame Strindberg commissioned it as an illustration for one of her brochures – the composition is considerably less advanced and sophisticated than a picture like *The Courtesan*.

The number of protagonists in this sketch contradicts the most authoritative record concerning *Kermesse*, which described it in 1927 as a 'cubistic rendering of three festive figures, the central in rich yellow, the others in varying shades of red and purple'.[51] But the rawness of the *Programme Cover* study does nevertheless tally with Lewis's only comment on the final painting. 'Now, the Kermesse is in its primitive state', he wrote disparagingly to Pound, '. . . even for a wall painting it is too uncouth and its unfinished state would not recommend it to the very discriminating, *with which ideal audience we must always suppose we are dealing.*'[52] By 1916, when this letter was written, Lewis's ideas about what was 'uncouth' had doubtless changed considerably; but it can be inferred that *Kermesse* was originally a wildly handled work, headlong enough in its urgency to disregard conventional shibboleths about 'finish' or 'discrimination'. And yet it probably did not possess the mad tonal oppositions of yellow, red and purple mentioned in the 1927 description, either. Before Lewis repainted the canvas in 1916, *The Times* had declared that *Kermesse* 'would be better in

have been eager to; Fry was, after all, the most influential as well as the most enlightened critic in England, and contact with such a man could only be to Lewis's advantage. Although ultimately they proved to be temperamentally incompatible, both of them must have derived considerable benefits from their relationship at this formative stage. Fry's ideas about the direction art should take were undergoing an intense reappraisal, and Lewis's practical example can only have confirmed beliefs which Cubism had already forced the older man to adopt. There is a sense of excitement in Fry's comments on *Kermesse*, as if the sight of that picture had made him realize that English artists were capable of the radicalism he had previously found in French painting; and so it comes as no surprise to find Lewis's work hung alongside masterpieces by Picasso, Matisse and Braque in the *Second Post-Impressionist Exhibition* which Fry organized at the Grafton Galleries in October 1912. For Lewis had clearly earned his place in a show that aimed, as Fry wrote in the catalogue introduction, to survey Post-Impressionism 'in its contemporary development not only in France, its native place, but in England, where it is of very recent growth'.[60] And to make his respect for Lewis's achievement doubly plain, Fry even reproduced one of the former's exhibits, *Creation*, as an illustration in the lavish catalogue.[61]

Wyndham Lewis
*Creation*, 1912

But the impact of this confident marshalling of nude figures, standing erect in a whirl of colliding segments which almost succeed in taking over the composition and establishing their own abstract autonomy, was overshadowed by an outstanding group of Lewis's watercolours and drawings, originally intended for a special edition of Shakespeare's *Timon of Athens*. So impressive did this series appear, even among the superb Cubist works which the show also contained, that *The Athenaeum*'s critic called it 'one of the most noteworthy features of the exhibition', and contrasted it favourably with Lewis's earlier contributions to the Camden Town shows, where 'he seemed to hover between a flat linear convention and the plastic vision on which he has now happily decided'. The success of the drawings did not, however, ensure their publication in book form: Douglas Goldring explained that his partner in Max Goschen, the short-lived publishing house for which he worked around then, 'unfortunately had the text printed off without the blocks being fitted into the places designed for them, so these, much to Lewis's justifiable wrath, had to be issued as a separate portfolio. The whole venture was thus rather a fiasco'.[62] The portfolio was not ultimately published until the following year, by which time it contained twenty separate drawings on sixteen sheets of paper. But the Timon series that Goldring remembered was 'well hung and attracted a great deal of attention' at Fry's exhibition only consisted of six items.[63] To make matters even more confusing, none of the drawings reproduced in the final portfolio bears a title or a date, so it is hard to speculate about which of the series were actually hung at the Grafton Galleries. And it is equally difficult to understand why the complete suite was not included in the show, for Lewis's passing reference in a 1917 letter from France to the effect that 'I am now not so far from the part where I did my Timon drawings one summer'[64] suggests they were all executed together, presumably in the summer of 1912.

Lewis never stated, either, why he chose this particular play as his theme; but Pound, who eventually donated his copy of the portfolio to the Victoria and Albert Museum, asserted that 'if you ask me what his "Timon" means, I can reply by asking you what the old play means. For me his designs are a creation on the same *motif*. That *motif* is the fury of intelligence baffled and shut in by circumjacent stupidity. It is an emotional *motif*. Mr Lewis's painting is nearly always emotional'.[65] While agreeing with the broad meaning of Pound's interpretation, it is surely possible to go further: for the story of Timon, a nobleman turned misanthrope who is driven into the wilderness by an alien

Wyndham Lewis
*Timon of Athens: The Creditors*, 1912–13

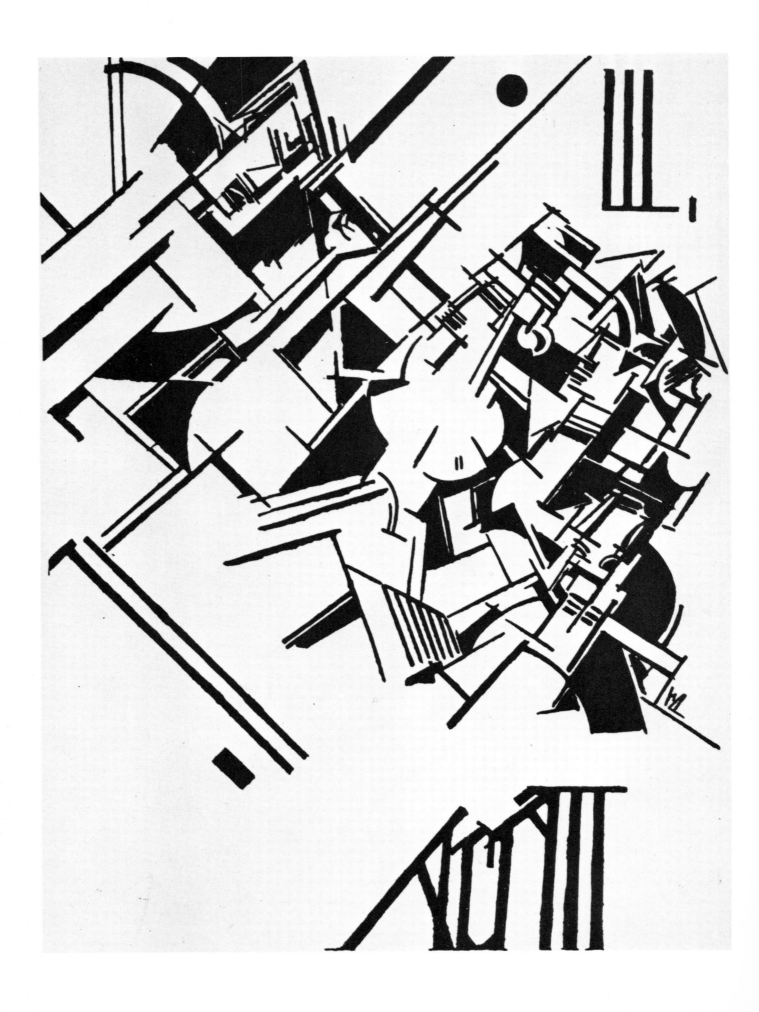

and totally materialist society, could easily have been seen by Lewis as an appropriate parallel to his own situation in the English art world. Just as Timon turns on his former friends and offers them water instead of a banquet, so Lewis might have seen *Kermesse* or this very portfolio as a brutal slap in the face for his timid contemporaries. Indeed, he must have revelled in the excoriating abuse Timon hurls at his fellow humans by the end of the play, and found in Shakespeare's unbuttoned rhetoric a source of inspiration for the attack he was soon to mount against an establishment which refused to recognize his own pioneering achievements.

The drawings themselves certainly bear out this supposition. Lewis's by now familiar mechanistic figures, often armed and warlike in appearance, are in sheet after sheet caught up in an impressively co-ordinated maelstrom of abstract shapes. Lewis seems to have seized on the climactic banquet scene for his vision of an apocalypse of destructive fury: the moment when Timon's guests realize that the feast they have been served consists of nothing but water provides the catalyst for the mood of the whole portfolio. The guests recoil in horror, Timon throws the water into their faces, and his declamation,

△Wyndham Lewis
*Timon of Athens: Composition*, 1912–13

◁Wyndham Lewis
*Timon of Athens: Act III*, 1912–13

> Burn house, sink Athens, henceforth hated be
> Of Timon man and all humanity

ignites the chaotic storm of line and wash which Lewis proceeds to unleash in succeeding designs. Some of them are virtually devoid of representational content, and bear out *The Athenaeum*'s perceptive comments on the abstract force of the series as a whole: 'the furious and violent contrast of interpenetrated forms is always his theme, and to maintain the dominance of the main planes against the exaggeration of his details, he conceives them as continued into surrounding space, there to spend their force or set up reactionary curves in the void.'[66]

Technically, too, they are by far the most accomplished of Lewis's works to date. He often plays off dark sweeps of colour against untouched areas of plain white paper, which thereby shine through with increased brilliance. The once incoherent rebel is now in full command of his resources, switching from descriptive passages over to total abstraction with the swaggering dexterity of a virtuoso. In some of the sheets, the numbers of the play's acts are built into the composition with such a feeling for schematic organization that they almost become formal elements in their own right, deriving their impact solely from their pictorial arrangement on the page. And such drawings imply that Lewis had been looking intently at the way Boccioni incorporated the numerals I and III into his hectic *States of Mind: Those Who Go* painting, which had been on view in London at the Futurist Exhibition in March 1912. Boccioni's picture, in fact, may have been a vital source of inspiration to Lewis when he was at work on the Timon drawings, for its mask-like heads are caught up in a holocaust comparable to the one afflicting the figures throughout Lewis's portfolio. Futurism, as well as Cubism, was now consistently feeding the imagination of the alert young Englishman, and they both fortified the already fruitful interest in Japanese art which Pound pinpointed when he wrote in *The Egoist* on 15 June 1914 that 'I have here also the design out of "Timon", marked act III, and a Japanese print which is curiously cubist. Plenty of people admire the latter and I am at a loss to know why they cannot admire the former'.

But the masterpiece of the whole series, and one of the most consummate works produced by English art at this time, is the scene where an army of soldiers stand poised for aggression in sharply beaked helmets and glinting armour. This superb watercolour, carried out in washes of brown and purple, may well represent the moment when Alcibiades, at the head of his forces, encounters the mad Timon in the woods outside Athens. The howling man

Umberto Boccioni
*States of Mind: Those Who Go*, 1911

Wyndham Lewis
*Timon of Athens:
Alcibiades*, 1912–13

rushing in from the far right of the design could be Timon himself, bellowing imprecations at the warrior as he stands four-square in the centre, accompanied by the Amazonian forms of his mistresses, Phrygia and Timandra. These speculations cannot be proved for certain, of course, but the tenacious control which Lewis exerts over every tiny detail of an immensely complex composition is indisputable. The arcs and straight lines describing limbs, landscape and clumps of spears are carried right through into the background, so that hillside, clouds and sky are equally solid, all of a piece with the protagonists down below. Every single facet of this picture is crystallized by the brittle action of the pen, and the overall effect is curiously reminiscent of the quality which Lewis himself admired in a celebrated quattrocento painting he wrote about three years later: 'Uccello in his picture at the National Gallery formularised the spears and aggressive prancing of the fighting men of his time till every drop of reality is frozen out of them.'[67]

Alongside this immobility is a fierce spatial recession, driving back through the tunnel of glancing planes towards the top of the design. But the space is nevertheless represented with cunning ambiguity. It is never made apparent, at any given point, where exactly the figures are placed in this maze of bristling shapes, or how far back they stand. Lewis reserves the right to startle and disorientate, as he darts from a comparatively realistic area over to a constellation of jagged forms which do not describe anything except the stern emotions of the artist himself. And in this sense, the picture suggests a knowledge of another Futurist painting Lewis had the opportunity to study at the Sackville Gallery exhibition: Carrà's *Funeral of the Anarchist Galli*, which uses lines of force and bold contrasts of complementary colours to break up its forms into a haze of blurred confusion. The similarity between the two artists' aims reaches its most acute point in Carrà's sky, where plane after brightly tinted plane crash into each other with the forceful interpenetration so evident in Lewis's Alcibiades watercolour. Carrà was implementing the celebrated Futurist dictum which vowed to 'put the spectator in the centre of the painting', and Lewis's spatial conundrums echo this resolve.

Carlo Carrà
*Funeral of the Anarchist Galli*, 1910–11

But in the end, the English artist remains temperamentally averse to the dizzy speed of Futurism. Although he enjoys ambiguity, each shape in his design is enclosed in a crisp network of lines to make for greater stability and overall clarity. The stand taken up by the Alcibiades picture would assume great importance when the Vorticists went into battle against the principles of Futurism, and it occupies a position roughly halfway between Carrà's *Funeral* and a Cubist painting like Léger's *The Wedding*. Lewis may or may not have seen this work on one of his regular trips to Paris, but it is immediately clear that Léger has likewise arranged here a number of rigidly angular figures within a spatially confused setting. On the lower right of *The Wedding* a road leads down to a diminutive group of distant houses, and yet the rest of the composition entirely denies the perspectival recession established by that view. Léger, like Lewis, makes up his own rules as he roams around inside his picture-space, assembling the painting out of several disparate elements. Both *The Wedding* and *Alcibiades* exploit a carefully premeditated interplay between figuration and abstraction, Lewis's thin shafts and arcs being a more energetic counterpart to Léger's slow-moving blocks of colour. The comparison is a fascinating one, and shows how involved Lewis had become with the preoccupations of the European avant-garde. For the Timon series, through its originality no less than its executant panache, now established him as one of the most advanced artists at work anywhere in the world.

It also inspired Pound to write a passionate exposition of the younger generation's need to revolt against the standards cherished by its elders. Over a year

Fernand Léger
*The Wedding*, 1911

after the Timon drawings were first displayed in the Grafton Galleries exhibition, he was still celebrating the central meaning of the portfolio in prose as uninhibited and martial as Lewis's pictorial onslaught. 'Mr Lewis has in his "Timon" gathered together his age, or at least our age, our generation, the youth-spirit, or what you will, that moves in the men who are now between their twenty-fifth and thirty-fifth years', he proclaimed in *The Egoist*, equating Timon's radicalism with a wide-ranging insurrection against the taste and prejudices of the English public in general. Pound's impatience with his adopted country's conservatism had by now hardened into unrepentant antagonism, and this hatred was ideally dramatized for him in Lewis's new style. 'It is no easy matter to express the Zeitgeist nor even immediately to comprehend it when we find it laid forth before us in word or in diagram', he continued. 'The "man in the street" cannot be expected to understand the "Timon" at first sight. Damn the man in the street, once and for all, damn the man in the street who is only in the street because he hasn't intelligence enough to be let in to anywhere else, and who does not in the least respect himself for being in the street, any more than an artist would respect himself for being hung in the Royal Academy. But the man whose profoundest needs cannot be satisfied by Collier or by Mr Sargent's society pretties, the man who has some sort of hunger for life, some restlessness for a meaning, is willing to spend six months, any six months, in a wilderness of doubt if he may thereby come to some deeper understanding; to some emotion more intense than his own; to some handling of life more competent than his own fumbling about the surface. So it is amply worth while taking half a year to get at the "Timon", fumbling about, looking at Matisse and Cézanne and Picasso, and Gauguin and Kandinski, and spoiling sheet after sheet of paper in learning just how difficult it is to bring forth a new unit of design.'[68]

Pound had mounted a deeply-felt plea for complete personal renewal, triggered off no doubt by his own unrelenting efforts to clear his mind of its preconceptions about art and fully respond to the Timon series. He must have found it a formidable task at first, for the selection of Timon drawings displayed in Fry's exhibition would have appeared almost as daunting as the most hermetic Cubist works on show in the same gallery. Fry, however, did not fail to justify the complexity of the paintings he had chosen for his second onslaught on the visual sensibilities of London, and he outlined in the catalogue a theory of abstraction which embraced Lewis's work as well. The Cubists, he wrote, aimed 'to arouse the conviction of a new and definite reality. They do not seek to imitate form, but to create form; not to imitate life, but find an equivalent for life. By that I mean that they wish to make images which by the clearness of their logical structure, and by their closely-knit unity of texture, shall appeal to our disinterested and contemplative imagination with something of the same vividness as the things of actual life appeal to our practical activities. The logical extreme of such a method would undoubtedly be the attempt to give up all resemblance to natural form – a visual music; and the later works of Picasso show this clearly enough'.[69] So do some of the designs in the Timon portfolio, as they progressively play down the importance of recognizable references in favour of an autonomous arrangement of abstract components. Small wonder that John, who had for so many years cast a powerful and approving shadow over Lewis's artistic personality, wrote to him in November 1912 with utter bewilderment. 'As for your recent drawings of which you send me photos', he grumbled, 'I must at once admit my inability to discover their merits.' And he widened out his complaint to include the contents of Fry's exhibition, claiming that 'Picasso and Cie. have become . . . metaphysicized or God knows what. Have they lost all *joie de vivre*?'[70] John's querulous letter marks the effective termination of any influence he might have exerted over his friend in preceding years, and Lewis now had to face the fact that he could no longer expect whole-hearted praise or encouragement from his former hero.

For the moment, he was receiving far more sympathy and understanding from his new Bloomsbury associates: especially Clive Bell, who in his introduction to the English section of Fry's show drew 'an important distinction' between 'the treatment of form as an object of emotion and the treatment of form as a means of description'. Bell declared that 'the art of Mr Wyndham Lewis, whatever else may be said of it, is certainly not descriptive. Hardly at all does it depend for its effect on association or suggestion'. And he insisted that 'there is no reason why a mind sensitive to form and colour, though it inhabit another solar system, and a body altogether unlike our own, should fail to appreciate' Lewis's work. But he countered that statement by adding that to 'fully appreciate some pictures by Mr Fry or Mr Duncan Grant it is necessary to be a human being, perhaps, even, an educated European of the twentieth century'.[71] Lewis's iconoclastic style was being ranged – with a discernible hint of Bloomsbury disapproval – against the more civilized and cultivated art of Fry and Grant. Distinctions which would become vitally important in the course of the following year, and ultimately be the cause of dissension in the ranks of the English avant-garde, were being committed to print already.

The ambivalent attitude to Lewis which was beginning to grow in Bloomsbury circles was also voiced by Lytton Strachey, who discovered one of the Breton stories in a back number of *The English Review*. 'It was cleverly done', he told Lady Ottoline Morrell in October 1912; 'I could no more have written it than flown – fiendish observation, and very original ideas. Yet the whole thing was most disagreeable; the subtlety was curiously crude, and the tone all through more mesquin than can be described . . . Ugh! the total effect was affreux. Living in the company of such a person would certainly have a deleterious influence on one's moral being. All the same I should like to see more of his work – though not his paintings . . .'[72] Strachey did not, of course, share the enthusiasm with which Fry and Bell greeted the latest developments in art, but the blend of fascination and distaste expressed in this letter foreshadows the profound disagreements which were soon to spring up between Lewis and the Bloomsbury faction.

Another leading contributor to the English section of Fry's exhibition, Frederick Etchells, was already wavering between these two camps. Almost four years younger than Lewis, and a product not of the Slade but the Royal College of Art where he studied between 1908 and 1911, he was a high-spirited and irreverent student right from the start. 'I was taught by Lethaby, who was good but only interested in the early Italians', he remembered later, 'and the College itself was very corrupt, rather like the Church of England in the 1830s. The principal was not the slightest bit interested in art, and all the other students seemed to have been there for forty years. I was a very bad pupil: the prevailing standards seemed to me awfully dreary and dull, so I used to do things like ringing the College's alarm bell, just to stir things up a bit.'[73] Although a large group of respectable, academic watercolour studies after mediaeval stained-glass windows survives from 1910 to prove Etchells' orthodoxy as a student artist, his temperamental discontent soon led him to study the continental avant-garde with avid interest.[74] 'I divided my time almost equally between London and Paris', he recalled, 'where I got to know Modigliani very well, met Picasso at Gertrude Stein's and then came across Braque in the South of France.' He taught part of the time at the Central School and various polytechnics after leaving the Royal College, but a 'very small allowance' from his father enabled him to rent 'a magnificent studio in Paris with a marble floor' as well. And his French contacts ensured that he now chose his friends in England among the most advanced forces: particularly Ginner, who 'was a great chum and probably introduced me to Lewis'.[75]

Etchells and Lewis warmed to each other, and often travelled over to Paris together; but for the moment Etchells' own painting remained more closely attuned to the Bloomsbury group. 'I became very friendly with Fry, Duncan Grant, the Bells and Virginia Woolf', he stated, 'and I used to rent a house at West Horsley in Surrey which was quite near Fry's Guildford home. We dropped in on each other quite a lot.'[76] For his part, Fry demonstrated his confidence in the young man's talent by inviting him to join other artists in an ambitious decorative scheme for the students' dining-room at the Borough Polytechnic. The project had been organized by Fry himself, who was eager to put his new theories about the function of art in the modern state into practice. By selecting this site, he hoped to show how ordinary halls and refectories could be made attractive at a comparatively low cost, and six artists – including Grant and Etchells – agreed to help him by executing a design each.[77] The series was carried out in 1911, centering on the theme of Londoners on holiday, and stylistic unity was imposed by a diaper motif running around each contribution. But Grant, who remembered that 'Etchells and I both liked to experiment at that stage, and were very much in sympathy with each other', wanted to unify the scheme more fully than that: 'rather self-consciously, I decided with Etchells on a particular "mural style" for the paintings – specific colours for flesh-tones and shadows, that sort of thing. And this is why our contributions look so similar'.[78]

Frederick Etchells
*The Fair* (fragment: right-hand part), 1911

They do indeed, but it is a similarity which extends beyond procedural methods. Etchells' *The Fair*, like Grant's *Bathing* and *Football*, has a pronounced curvilinear bias that immediately suggests a debt to Matisse. It is an unhappy work, however, full of an ill-understood mixture of abstract patterning and naturalistic detail. Etchells simply has not permitted himself to go far enough with his stylization: the three cloth-capped men dancing with the gypsy women appear laughably wooden, the victims of a desire for schematic symmetry which has not been taken as far as it should. Etchells has been caught between the old traditions and the new, vaguely realizing the need for a radical approach and yet producing a sum of contradictory influences which fail to cohere. The Romany subject-matter used in *The Fair* recalls a large John decoration like *The Mumpers*; but even though Etchells has managed to simplify his composition more drastically than John ever did, the older man always possessed a far greater command over rhythmical organization. *The Fair* is in every sense a callow work, infected by hot-headed ideas which still need time to mature.

An air of irresolution likewise hangs over a picture called *The Hip Bath*, which Etchells exhibited at the Bloomsbury orientated Friday Club in February 1912. For despite the fact that the paint is laid on in delicate dabs in the background, and the figure inclines her head gently downwards in a wistful attitude, the design is remarkable for its toughness. This is a positively muscular nude, with powerful shoulders, sinewy arms and angular buttocks. Etchells enjoys tracing the irregular lines round the edges of her body, letting them swell outwards and then suddenly make inroads into the flesh. And this clash between painterly docility and linear harshness ensures that the painting is, at heart, schizophrenic in feeling. The tin bath motif, firmly within the tradition of Degas, and the fine web of brushstrokes enveloping the model contain nothing which would have contravened Bloomsbury taste: Fry, in fact, purchased *The Hip Bath* for his own collection. But co-existing with this sensibility is an altogether more anarchic love of arbitrary distortion, already foreshadowing the time when Etchells would lose patience with the gentility of his present artistic allies. The

Frederick Etchells
*The Hip Bath*, 1911–12

critics of the Friday Club show seem to have sensed this aspect of his temperament, too: one reviewer damned *The Hip Bath* as 'a downright insult to visitors to the Gallery', and the *Observer* accused Etchells of setting out to 'merely play the clown and lose all sense of responsibility'.[79]

At this stage, however, critical abuse was more than outweighed by the continuing support of Fry, who had great faith in Etchells' potential and actually rated him above Lewis. Writing to Charles Vildrac in April 1912, the critic described how he had included both men in a forthcoming Paris exhibition of 'my little group of English artists' and declared that 'Duncan Grant will exhibit and certainly he has genius, perhaps Etchells also; the others like myself have but a little talent and at least goodwill'.[80] Fry's opinion must have been shared by Adrian Stephen and his sister Virginia (Woolf), for they asked Grant and Etchells to execute a mural in 'the big ground-floor dining-room' of their house in Brunswick Square. David Garnett, who was invited there for tea in the autumn of 1912, recalled that the artists had 'painted its walls with a continuous London street scene, in which the centre of dramatic interest was a fallen cab-horse with the driver of the hansom still perched precariously aloft though the cab was tilted forward with the shafts touching the pavement'.[81] And around the same time, Fry again showed his respect for Etchells by asking him to help Grant design the poster for the impending Post-Impressionist exhibition. 'Will you do it on cartridge paper, thirty by twenty inches, and leave the largest space possible for the lettering', he wrote to Grant, 'and send it here as soon as possible for Etchells to put in the lettering?'[82] Fry was obviously doing his best to foster a spirit of communal co-operation among the artists he considered most capable of sustaining an adventurous group endeavour; and another Bloomsbury painter, Vanessa Bell, commemorated Etchells' place within this exclusive circle by executing a sensitive portrait of him at work with his sister Jessie in Asheham, Virginia Woolf's Sussex home.[83]

It was inevitable, therefore, that Etchells should be granted a strong showing of no less than six pictures at the Post-Impressionist exhibition. And one of them, a large painting called *The Dead Mole* which Fry singled out and illustrated in the catalogue, again revealed the streak of wilful eccentricity so evident in *The Fair*. The elongation and wayward distortion of the two figures, posturing like amateur ballet dancers around the animal they have discovered, here reaches fanciful proportions. There is a strong vein of Mannerism in this composition, of stylistic caprice acted out in a holiday mood for the artist's own clique of friends. And Etchells himself bore out this interpretation many years later, when he explained how the idea was conceived in his garden at West Horsley. His youngest sister lived there as well, 'to housekeep for me', and the two of them felt free to indulge their love of inconsequential pranks. 'We were young and foolish', he admitted, and 'I took on a sort of tramp, and dressed him in a sort of corduroy (theatrical) suit. We also had a boy to stay, and the incident of the "Dead Mole" occurred between these two'.[84] The frivolity of this charade-like motif also affected the formal quality of the painting, for the meandering lines which trace the contours of the tramp and his companion contradict the inspiration of Cézanne proclaimed in the tall trees behind. But Etchells' readiness to play around with a pot-pourri of disparate conventions reaches its apogee in his handling and tonal orchestration: the foreground, a riot of semi-Pointillist spots and slabs which mix green, pink and ochre with purple shadows cast by the figures, is succeeded in the sky above by an abandoned swirl of lime and yellow worthy of Van Gogh. The trees, on the other hand, are treated in an altogether more solidly modelled combination of puce and green, as are the vivid blue mountains; and their colours swear openly both with the tramp's strawberry sleeves and the predominantly maroon zigzags of the painted frame.

Frederick Etchells
*The Dead Mole, c.* 1912

It is as if Etchells, still operating within idioms which held sway before the arrival of Cubism and Futurism, wanted to mount a spectacular attack on the more discreet harmonies of English Post-Impressionists like Ginner. He knew Fergusson very well over in Paris, and the Scotsman's flamboyant example may well have helped him plunge into this orgy of colour. But in the final analysis, his own idiosyncratic temperament contributed most to *The Dead Mole's* vagaries. Although comparisons could be drawn with the equally wayward distortions and brushwork of Grant's *Queen of Sheba*, which was also shown at Fry's 1912 exhibition, Etchells' other paintings of the period do likewise make plain his penchant for playful excursions. A similar collection of masqueraders – this time dressed up in elaborate eighteenth century costumes –

trip their way across the loosely handled surface of a picture called *Group of Figures*; and an openly whimsical version of *The Entry into Jerusalem* shows a caricatured Christ riding a pale blue and mauve donkey past a frieze of spectators equipped with tiny heads and fantastically elongated bodies.[85] Etchells seems to have enjoyed performing stylistic tricks for their own sake, too: he even painted a pastiche of an English sporting print, with huntsmen leaping over a fence and one rider already sprawling on the ground, in a flagrantly Post-Impressionist manner.[86] The result, with its absurd clash between traditionalist theme and avant-garde treatment, clearly gratified his anarchic temperament.

The only other painting which can now be confidently identified as one of Etchells' contributions to Fry's exhibition, however, turns away from these artistic in-jokes. No subversive escapades have been allowed to disturb the unruffled gentility of *On the Grass*, where two women relax and quietly enjoy the sunshine in an impeccably middle-class setting.[87] 'Both my youngest sister, who is the figure on the left, and the other woman posed for me out-of-doors

Frederick Etchells
*From an English Sporting Print, c.* 1912–13

Frederick Etchells  *On the Grass, c.* 1912

Frederick Etchells
*The Entry into Jerusalem, c.* 1912

in the orchard at West Horsley',[88] declared Etchells, and this experiment in *plein-airisme* possesses in abundance those civilized qualities which Clive Bell admired in the paintings of Fry and Grant. But if it seems more poised and assured than the ungainly ambition of *The Dead Mole*, *On the Grass* fails to give any hint of the forcefulness Etchells was to display in his Vorticist work. A far more prophetic picture, in this context, is his portrait of *The Big Girl*, which did not appear in the Post-Impressionist survey but was probably executed in the same year and shown at the Friday Club.[89] For this is a notably tough painting, its irregular structure heightened by the broad outlines that stress the unruly contours of armchair, cushion and body as they travel in edgy, unexpected directions across the picture-surface. And alongside the crude linear strength, Etchells adopted a Pointillist technique which dapples and softens the harshness of the draughtsmanship, castrating its attempt to fill the portrait with restless linear rhythms. He had not yet learned how to master his desire for more aggressive forms of expression, and only when he rejected the patronage of Bloomsbury in favour of Lewis's more militant cause did his art manage to fulfil its most uncompromising leanings.

Frederick Etchells
*The Big Girl*, c. 1912

That volte-face was not to occur for several months; and in the autumn of 1912 most critics of the Second Post-Impressionist Exhibition ignored these stirrings of a new English vanguard in order to concentrate, quite naturally, on the comprehensive selection of pictures by Matisse, Picasso, Braque, Derain, Vlaminck and others who could be considered either as Fauves or Cubists. Many reviewers resorted to outright vituperation and invective to voice their disgust with the works on display, and Leonard Woolf, who as exhibition secretary 'sat at my table in the large second room prepared to deal with enquiries from possible purchasers or answer any questions about the pictures', found himself 'kept busy all the time'. The experience gave him 'a lamentable view of human nature, its rank stupidity and uncharitableness', for hardly any of the visitors 'made the slightest attempt to look at, let alone understand, the pictures, and the same inane questions or remarks were repeated to me all day long'. He was particularly horrified by the arrival of 'some well-groomed, red faced gentleman, oozing the undercut of best beef and the most succulent of chops, carrying his top hat and grey suede gloves, [who] would come up to my table and abuse the pictures and me with the greatest rudeness'.[90]

But Arnold Bennett, writing in his Journal on 8 October, noticed a subtler form of hostility. One reason, he decided, for 'the popularity of these shows is that they give the grossly inartistic leisured class an opportunity to feel superior'. He described in particular 'one large woman of ruling classes, with a large voice and *face-à-main*, in front of a mediocre picture: "Now no one will ever persuade me that the man who painted that was serious. He was just pulling our legs." Self-satisfied smiles all over the place all the time'.[91] Nor were enemies of Post-Impressionism exclusively concentrated among Bennett's 'leisured' classes. Clive Bell later remembered 'walking through the Grafton Galleries with a man who is certainly one of the ablest, and is reputed one of the most enlightened, of contemporary men of science. Looking at the picture of a young girl with a cat by Henri-Matisse, he exclaimed – "I see how it is, the fellow's astigmatic".' By the end of the tour, Bell's companion had concluded that 'no picture in the gallery was beyond the reach of optical diagnostic'; and when Bell suggested that the distortions were intentional, the professor 'became passionately serious – "Do you mean to tell me", he bawled, "that there has ever been a painter who did not try to make his objects as lifelike as possible? Dismiss such silly nonsense from your head." '[92] His opinion was seconded in a still more dramatic way by Sir Claude Phillips, art critic of the *Daily Telegraph* and Keeper of the Wallace Collection, who was so incensed by the exhibition that he 'threw his catalogue upon the threshold of the Grafton Galleries and stamped on it'.[93] And Sickert, perhaps inspired by Sir Claude's intemperate gesture, claimed that 'the cubical, cylindrical, rhomboidal invasion' had been rebuffed, while 'the only lady-fauviste in the country is reported to have taken the night boat to Montmartre, disguised in a thick blue outline, and students are back on their stools continuing to study drawing'.[94]

Despite the inflamed controversy aroused by the show, Bell felt able flatly to contradict Sickert's pessimistic sarcasm and proclaim in his catalogue preface that 'the battle is won. We all agree, now, that any form in which an artist can express himself is legitimate ... We have ceased to ask, "What does this picture represent?" and ask instead, "What does it make us feel?" We expect a work of plastic art to have more in common with a piece of music than with a coloured photograph'.[95] Bell was jubilantly supporting the artist's right to experiment, but his brave words appear less convincing when juxtaposed with the works of his wife Vanessa or his friends Fry and Grant. If in theory they all welcomed the advent of Cubism, in practice they tended to cling to the example of Cézanne or Matisse and at this stage avoid anything which led down the heretical path towards total abstraction. Unlike Lewis, who had already begun to digest the influence of Futurism in his Timon series and warm to their brash polemics, the Bloomsbury group ranged themselves in opposition to the noisy Italians. In his preface to the Second Post-Impressionist Exhibition catalogue, Fry set down his reason for deciding to exclude the movement from his show when he wrote that 'the Futurists have succeeded in developing a whole system of aesthetics out of a misapprehension of some of Picasso's difficult and recondite works'.[96] And Bell, casting aside his role as an open-minded champion of pictorial renewal, was soon to declare that 'as works of art, the Futurist pictures are negligible'.[97]

Both men undoubtedly feared that the Futurist onslaught launched in the spring would supersede the influence which they hoped their own French heroes would exert on English painters. But Lewis, more and more hungry for an art capable of the iconoclastic vigour commanded by Futurism, was not prepared simply to uphold Cubism at the expense of the Italian insurgents. And an unpleasant row blew up between him and Fry at the end of the exhibition, petty in itself yet marking the inception of a rift which would rapidly divorce the Bloomsbury faction from those who yearned for a truly revolutionary movement in England. 'When the time came to pay artists their share of the purchase amounts of pictures sold', recounted Leonard Woolf, 'Roger insisted upon deducting a higher commission without any explanation or apology to the painters. Most of them meekly accepted what they were given, but Wyndham Lewis, at best of times a bilious and cantankerous man, protested violently. Roger was adamant in ignoring him and his demands, Lewis never forgave Roger.'[98] The wound was, in fact, patched up temporarily; and yet a few months later it was to split open once more, widening into a public dispute which helped to rally a whole range of younger artists around Lewis's discontented initiative.

# Chapter 3: Student Unrest at the Slade

By a strange and highly appropriate coincidence, most of the painters who would soon commit themselves to Lewis's fast-maturing cause came from his old art school, the Slade. An unusual constellation of talent, restless and impatient enough to be susceptible to avant-garde ideas which more senior spirits condemned, trained there between 1908 and 1913, including David Bomberg, Christopher Nevinson, William Roberts and Edward Wadsworth.[1] They were by all accounts part of a very rash, self-confident generation, who took a delight in rebellion and were not afraid to contest traditional principles with exclamatory delight. Marinetti would have warmed to the combative spirit evident in the clique of Slade students, including Nevinson and Wadsworth, who 'had become a gang, sometimes known in correct Kensington circles as the Slade coster gang'. Nevinson, who was one of the most aggressive members of the gang, remembered with some pride that 'we were the terror of Soho and violent participants, for the mere love of a row, at such places as the anti-vivisectionist demonstrations... We also fought with the medical students of other hospitals ... This often entailed visits to Tottenham Court Road police station, Bow Street, and Vine Street. There is no doubt we behaved abominably and were no examples for placid modern youth'.[2]

This warlike group was flatly opposed to the aestheticism of earlier Slade students, and Nevinson made clear just how daring and outspoken they considered themselves to be. 'We represented a reaction against the priggishness, posturing, and posing, which had been left as a legacy to the Slade from John's generation', he declared later, 'and we must have been a sore trial to poor virgin Tonks.'[3] Something of this determined pugnacity is captured by a photograph of the Slade picnic, probably taken in 1912, where a roughly dressed Bomberg assumes a fighting stance among his more respectable professors in the back row while the other male students all crowd together at the front, carefully segregated from their female counterparts and staring brazenly towards the camera.[4]

It is easy to believe that this defiant assembly's most immediate objective was to overthrow the reactionary standards of a Royal Academy still ruled over by the obsolescent Sir Edward Poynter, and several of them went so far as to steal through the august portals of Burlington House to take unsuspecting

Photograph of the Slade picnic, *c.* 1912. Back row: 2nd from right, C. Koe Child, Slade Secretary; 3rd from right, Prof. Fred Brown; 4th from right, Bomberg. Kneeling on left: Isaac Rosenberg. Front row: left, Dora Carrington; 3rd from left, Nevinson; 4th from left, Mark Gertler; 4th from right, Roberts; 3rd from right, Adrian Allinson; 2nd from right, Stanley Spencer

visitors on lecture tours. Bomberg, indeed, after gathering a party of spectators around him and making a harmless little speech in praise of the Academy, proceeded to launch into a fierce tirade against everything it stood for. He was duly ejected from the premises, and angry letters were exchanged between the Academy and the authorities at the Slade.[5] Meanwhile Nevinson, as a true child of Marinetti's machine age, gave himself up 'to my new toy, the motor-bike, and went all over the country', provoking a 'look of icy disdain when I turned up on my mount, most un-aesthetic, to a general meeting of the New English'.[6]

To such a provocative generation, the Futurist and Post-Impressionist exhibitions which followed each other so quickly during the course of 1912 must have been enormously stimulating. Roberts later recalled how he grew up in 'an age of impacts, and English artists were experiencing the combined impact of Cézanne, Van Gogh, Gauguin, Picasso and the rest of the French Cubists, besides the Italian Futurists with their manifestos. The Art Clubs were filled with the disputes of the Ancients versus the Moderns; and the thrust and parry of contending aesthetic opinions packed the correspondence columns of the newspapers'.[7] Paul Nash, himself a Slade student but at that stage least likely to be affected by the new ideas, likewise confirmed that 'the Slade was then seething under the influence of Post-Impressionism. Roger Fry had brought about the second exhibition of modern continental art in London, and now all the cats were out of the bag'. So widespread was the furore that Nash remembered it as 'a national upheaval', and he was sure that 'all this had a disturbing effect at the Slade. The professors did not like it at all. The students were by no means a docile crowd and the virus of the new art was working in them uncomfortably. Suppose they all began to draw like Matisse? Eventually, Tonks made one of his speeches and appealed, in so many words, to our sporting instincts. He could not, he pointed out, prevent our visiting the Grafton Galleries; he could only warn us and say how very much better pleased he would be if we did not risk contamination but stayed away'.[8] His warning went unheeded, for Roberts later testified to the fact that 'at the Slade we were all familiar with the work of the French Cubists', and the students would have been more ready to respond to the series of lectures Fry delivered to them than listen to Tonks' panic-stricken advice.[9]

Fry was a natural mentor for the students, committed as he was to the idea of pictorial innovation and the need to encourage original young English artists. His lectures, entitled 'The Appreciation of Design in the History of Art', stressed the vital importance of Cézanne's contribution as well as the early Italian masters. And to give some notion of the range of his sympathies, alongside the attempts he made to relate past art to the upheavals of contemporary painting, it is revealing to list the kind of topics he gave talks on between 1913 and 1914: 'The Problem of Representation and Abstract Form', 'Palaeolithic and Children's Drawing' and 'Elements of Abstract Design'.[10] How much more congenial these subjects must have appeared to the students than the academic instruction offered at the Slade, which insisted that 'the first year men should draw from the plaster cast before being permitted to work in the life room'![11] With typical adventurousness, Fry was eager to discuss the issues raised by his exhibitions with the painters most likely to have been inspired by them. He was never at a loss for words when the opportunity arose for aesthetic debate, for he displayed his brilliance most impressively in conversation; and the students, in their turn, were only too pleased when he asked them to exhibit with him at the Friday Club. This small, exclusive society, led by Fry, Vanessa Bell and Grant, would have appealed to their appetite for revolt: one critic described its February 1911 exhibition as 'chiefly composed of pictures almost certain to be labelled as post-impressionist', and the February 1912 show caused the *Observer* to report that 'the members of the Friday Club are celebrating their Mardi Gras at the Alpine Gallery, and behave as if the notoriety gained by the Futurists in Paris had aroused their jealousy. It is a very Witches' Sabbath of fauvism or post-impressionism'.[12]

Unfortunately, very few paintings survive from this vital, formative period by any of the Slade students to show how far they were willing to admit their radical impulses into works of art. It seems clear that Nevinson, who came to the Slade in 1909 from the St John's Wood School of Art, remained at first relatively unaffected by Post-Impressionist developments, even though he was taken up by the Friday Club as early as 1911. Frank Rutter actually singled out the 'limpid studies of "Liverpool Street" and "Gasometers"' he displayed there, and commended him in the *Sunday Times* for being 'obviously in love with his selected subjects, feeling the charm of form and colour in unexpected industrial situations'.[13] Already, then, Nevinson was beginning to seek out the mechanized, urban motifs favoured by Marinetti: Rutter prophetically described him as 'a painter who sees beauty in what the world condemns as ugly', and his kind words were soon echoed by Sickert, who welcomed the student into the Camden Town circle and introduced him to fellow artists. 'I had become a visitor to the Camden Town Group', Nevinson recalled; 'Sickert had encouraged me in my work, which I was selling; I had formed with Gilman and Gore a friendship which was to last till their deaths; and I had made the acquaintance of Percy Wyndham Lewis. It seemed I was making progress.'[14]

But despite these precocious connections – Lewis talked to him 'a great deal about the African mask and the curious earth colours and brick-reds of the early Derains'[15] – Nevinson's student paintings were in no sense revolutionary. On the contrary: Rutter remembered him as 'an impressionist' when he exhibited three works at the 1911 AAA Salon, and noted that 'only a few discerned traces of an inquiring mind in his *Cement Works* and *Carting Manure*'.[16] To judge from these titles, the pictures he sent in to the AAA must have been close to the feeling of *A View of Bradford*, a lost painting which probably dates from the same period.[17] In the surviving photograph, the Bradford landscape appears an orthodox exercise in English Impressionism, sensitive and able but closer to Maximilien Luce than Steer or Fisher. The composition is entirely traditional: for all its industrial bias, it still belongs spiritually to the 'pastoral age' which Marinetti despised; and its concern with subtle atmospheric effects links it immediately with another landscape, *The Railway Bridge, Charenton*, which was shown at the Friday Club in 1912.[18] The French light appears to have confirmed Nevinson's stylistic preferences. He went to Paris later in 1912, working at 'Julian's in the Rue de Dragon', in the evenings at 'the other Julian's, in Montmartre', and sometimes at the *Cercle Russe* where Matisse himself taught; but the Charenton view, presumably the product of an earlier French visit, shows him still perfectly content to work within an Impressionist idiom. And Rutter pinpointed this conservatism in his review of the painting by declaring that 'instead of trying to be clever and original, we feel that Mr Nevinson has put every ounce of his knowledge of paint and colour into the endeavour to give a true impression of what he saw'.[19]

Nevinson could have made a successful career for himself simply by continuing to paint in this acclaimed style, defined so neatly by one critic as 'a half-way house of his very own between the colour and technique of Boudin and Claude Monet'.[20] He was not yet ready to follow up the implications of the Futurist and Post-Impressionist exhibitions, although his suffragette mother had praised Marinetti's Lyceum Club lecture in *The Vote* as early as December 1910. Mrs Nevinson reported in excited language on the Futurist leader's vision of 'a

Christopher Nevinson
*A View of Bradford, c.* 1911–12

△ Christopher Nevinson
*Self-Portrait,* 1911

◁ Christopher Nevinson
*The Railway Bridge, Charenton,* 1911–12

world in which even the human race may be governed by mechanism, and where everybody will be of masculine gender'.[21] But her son, whose outward behaviour at the Slade seemed so patently affected by Marinetti's teachings, continued to paint as if the avant-garde did not exist. Adrian Allinson, a student contemporary at the Slade, claimed that the spectacle of Nevinson's 'progressive enthusiasms for the works of Turner, Whistler, Monet, the Post-Impressionists, and finally the Italian Futurists was for me a liberal education'.[22] And yet when Nevinson stopped theorizing and sat down to execute his *Self-Portrait* in 1911, his obstinate 22-year-old features were couched in a dry, meticulous realism that would have appealed to Holman Hunt. There is no trace in this carefully drawn but crabbed painting of the Impressionist language employed in his contemporaneous landscapes; and the explanation for Nevinson's excursion into an academic style he was never again to espouse is to be found, as he himself suggested, in the quattrocento affiliations of his fellow-student Mark Gertler. 'By this time I was largely under the influence of Gertler and was doing highly finished heads in the Botticelli manner',[23] Nevinson explained later, omitting to add that he was wise to exchange such an archaising impasse for the Futurism which fully captivated him after his departure from the Slade in 1912.

The *Self-Portrait*'s straightforward naturalism contains as little hint of the rebel Nevinson would become as Wadsworth's *Self-Portrait*, likewise executed in 1911 at the age of 22. His head is swathed in a turquoise turban – an exotic, Rembrandtesque motif which he may well have borrowed from Grant's 1911 *Self-Portrait*, where the turban conceit is also adopted. But the comparison only points up Wadsworth's limitations: although his handling is more assured than Nevinson's, Grant uses paint with far more spontaneity and zest. The dogged construction of this *Self-Portrait* contains nothing that Wadsworth's tutors at the Slade could possibly have disapproved of, and it remains an undemanding display of craftsmanship rather than an assertion of artistic individuality. The *Yorkshire Post*, however, praised its 'genuine power' when Wadsworth – who had trained at the Knirr School of Art in Munich and the Bradford School of Art before winning a Slade scholarship in 1908 – exhibited the painting at the Bradford Arts Club. 'The influence of Whistler is felt in the obvious endeavour to secure a sense of design by a carefully planned silhouette',[24] wrote the *Post*'s critic, who compared Wadsworth's other exhibit, an untraced portrait of *Cuthbert Kelly*, with Whistler's celebrated *Carlyle*. It was a curious connection to make, for there is very little of Whistler's understated delicacy in the emphatic chiaroscuro of Wadsworth's brooding features.

He did, nevertheless, succeed in breaking away from the literal description of the *Self-Portrait* when he tackled the problems of landscape. Just as Nevinson became noticeably more free when he escaped from portraiture and set out to evoke the atmosphere of a given scene, so Wadsworth loosened up in his lost painting of *Harrogate Corporation Brick-Works*, depicting the strong skeleton of the railway tracks and the encrusted layer of snow with considerable verve.[25] According to Wadsworth himself it was painted at Harrogate in December 1908, when he was only 19, and the sadly inadequate photograph which has survived suggests a form of mild Impressionism which would not have displeased the New English Art Club. It comes as no surprise, therefore, to find Wadsworth exhibiting his landscape at the Club in 1911, along with another untraced *Portrait of John Hope-Johnstone*; and the Slade authorities thought it accomplished enough to merit first prize in a landscape competition in 1910. The conclusion is inescapable: Wadsworth was at this stage sufficiently conventional in his aspirations to aim at pleasing his seniors, and a 1911 *Nude in the Life Room* is preserved at the Slade to prove that he was even prepared to paint an unashamedly academic showpiece.

If the fluid treatment of its background heralds a more painterly approach than had been evident in the *Self-Portrait*, the monumental life-class nude conforms to all the traditional pictorial canons. Faultlessly proportioned and modelled with a slick eye for the play of light on a buttock or a shoulder-blade, the figure stands astride the canvas with a four-square assurance. It is a resolutely Victorian image, worthy of the good Sir Edward Poynter himself; and although it earned Wadsworth the first prize for figure painting in 1911, he must have executed it more out of a perverse sense of duty than pleasure. For

Edward Wadsworth
*Self-Portrait*, 1911

Edward Wadsworth
*Harrogate Corporation Brick-Works*, 1908

Edward Wadsworth
*Nude in the Life Room*, 1911

Edward Wadsworth
*Portrait of Miss Sylvia Meyer* (later Mrs Harold
Gilman), 1911

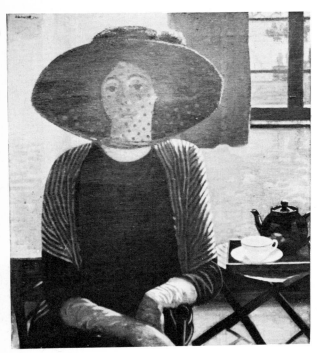

Edward Wadsworth
*Portrait of Mrs Violet Wallis*, 1911

it contains none of the irreverent high spirits which Adrian Allinson remembered him possessing. Both of them, apparently, 'shared a common enthusiasm for music, and were at that time suffering from a chronic attack of Wagneritis; we drove the entire life room to distraction by our humming or whistling of "leit-motifs" from Tristan or the Ring'.[26] If Wadsworth had managed to inject a little of this energy into his *Nude* painting, he might have prevented it from becoming such an obedient exercise, just as a contemporaneous portrait of Gilman's future wife Sylvia Meyer needed a more independent approach to cut through its limiting ties with Wilson Steer and even Velazquez.

Another 1911 painting, the *Portrait of Mrs Violet Wallis*, shows Wadsworth trying to escape from this conservatism and embrace the precepts of the Camden Town Group. The whole mood of this seductive picture, with its wistful, genteel sitter posed contre-jour against a faintly shabby background, recalls the interiors of Sickert or Gore. Even the teapot and cup look as if they have strayed from a Gilman painting, and an air of afternoon ennui pervades the room. But Wadsworth has only gone halfway towards Camden Town: the painting's tonal range is a predominantly Whistlerian blend of black, grey and silvery white, scarcely affected by the broken palette which Sickert exploited so thoroughly. And so, despite the assurance with which this sensitive portrait is constructed, it is as timid in its attitude towards innovatory ideas as Mrs Wallis would appear to be, hiding behind the enormous spotted veil of her Edwardian hat. Only the severe frontality of the composition, combined with the emphatic treatment of the striped shawl and the hat's spectacularly flattened oval geometry, contain any hints of Wadsworth's future interest in structural abstraction.

Like Nevinson, he still had to channel his restless impulses into adventurous works of art, and the process only began during a trip to Le Havre in the same year. Photographs have luckily survived of two spirited little beach scenes he executed then, and they show him escaping from academicism in order to embrace the spirit of Fauvism.[27] Every form in these charming compositions, which are both taken from the same motif, is simplified into broad strokes of paint; and if a first-hand description of *Plage au Havre* is to be believed, they were conspicuously bright in their colours. The mood is now far sunnier than the gloomy sobriety of the Slade pictures, more relaxed and informal. Wadsworth's visit to Le Havre seems to have had a liberating effect, bringing him closer to the French intimiste tradition of flat, decorative patterning. But perhaps the most convincing source for these beach studies is to be found in the work of Marquet, which Wadsworth would have seen in abundance at the first Post-Impressionist exhibition. For a picture like *Sainte-Adresse*, executed by Marquet in 1906, parallels *Plage au Havre* in an extraordinary number of ways – not only through the shared subject-matter of striped bathing tents, elaborately dressed women and long pier-heads, but also in terms of style.[28] If Wadsworth's frieze-like designs are less ambitious than the coursing diagonals of Marquet's composition, the two men do handle paint in the same bold manner, translating the scene in front of them to a few spare strokes of high-pitched colour.

Wadsworth may, on the other hand, have come under the influence of Marquet at secondhand, through a British Fauve like Anne Estelle Rice who also painted comparable beach studies at Etretat. But at least one critic actually suggested a debt to Marquet: Rutter, reviewing Wadsworth's lost contributions to the 1912 Friday Club show, declared that 'when Mr Edward Wadsworth paints Long Acre, from an aeroplane presumably, we can entertain no hope till he gets at least as much out of this bird's-eye-view business as Marquet and others have done in Paris'.[29] Rutter's strictures may seem rather unfair up against the modest élan of the 1911 Le Havre pictures, and yet it must be admitted that Wadsworth was erratic enough to swing back in 1912 to an

Edward Wadsworth
*Plage au Havre*, 1911

Edward Wadsworth
*Still Life with Fruit*, 1912

unaccountably traditional *Nature-Morte* painting.[30] The composition, with its statutory napkin, chest of drawers, wine bottle and dish of peaches, is a painfully straightforward pastiche of Cézanne, whose inspiration is evident even in the hatched brushwork on the skin of the fruit. And through Cézanne, Wadsworth still shows himself susceptible to the British Fauves, for the heavily Cézannesque still lifes of Peploe could well lurk behind this painting. It lacks Peploe's crisp precision, however, and comes as a leaden disappointment after the freedom of the Le Havre studies, even if the two vertical stripes at the top of the design and the structure of the reflections on the table hint at an incipient involvement with more abstract ideas.

If Wadsworth had to wait until he left the Slade in 1912 before he was able to branch out into more challenging forms of expression, both Roberts and Bomberg did succeed in meeting the demands of the avant-garde during their student days. Roberts, by far the youngest of the group, joined the Slade at the precocious age of 15 in 1910, after proving himself with such accomplished drawings as *The Girl with the Red Nose*. Modelled on the artist's sister, and executed a year before he won the LCC scholarship which enabled him to give up studying commercial art, this sketch seems to look back to the achievements of High Renaissance Florentine draughtsmanship. The red-chalk drawings of Andrea del Sarto, in particular, are evoked in the sensuous treatment of this Cockney face – a connection that Tonks, with his love of the 'giants of the Renaissance' would undoubtedly have cherished. Other studies from the same period pay more explicit homage to Tintoretto and Michelangelo; but by 1912, when Roberts tackled *The Resurrection* as a Slade Sketch Club subject, the seeds of abstraction had already been planted in his work.

A lingering debt to the Pre-Raphaelites is evident in the drooping Burne-Jones figure kneeling on the left of this impeccably organized composition, no less than in the detailed fretwork of shadows spread out across the foreground. Roberts probably derived this influence directly from the teachings of Brown and Tonks: as Andrew Forge has pointed out, they 'had been brought up on Ruskin and the Pre-Raphaelites. This, far more than Courbet and Monet, was the source of

William Roberts
*The Girl with the Red Nose* (detail), 1909

William Roberts
*The Resurrection*, 1912

their reverence for nature'.[31] But alongside this link with the previous century, Roberts possessed an equally apparent urge to simplify his figures into massive, schematic units; and although some of the shading is still painstakingly naturalistic, Roberts obviously enjoys banishing irrelevant curves from his bodies. As a result, Christ's figure has become a series of right-angles, shooting up out of the coffin until his outstretched arms cut through the geometrical arc of the rainbow. And the coffin lid, flying back through the air away from the impact of this supernatural explosion, carries the abstract force of the vocabulary Roberts was to employ in his Vorticist work.

In another 1912 drawing, a strange conglomeration of styles called *David Choosing the Three Days' Pestilence*, Roberts shows himself still more rigorous in his approach to the problems of simplification. And the diverse impulses jostling for attention in this work make it at once more puzzling and full of fascination. The gesticulating Rabbis in the foreground introduce a strain of overt caricature into Roberts' personality which was to become an integral part of his mature work; the tree leaning to the left is a direct quotation from the kind of summary of form Derain derived from Cézanne; and the gigantic nude figure of David climbing over a fence represents a note of fantasy that may well have been inspired by Roberts' fellow-pupil at the Slade, Stanley Spencer. The most significant area of the drawing, however, lies in the group of people dancing on a platform in the centre of the composition. Their attention seems to be concentrated on a pair of sacrificial cows waving their tails in the middle of the platform: both men and women have formed themselves into a tight cluster of activity around the animals, and they are throwing their arms and legs about in a frenzy of religious emotion. The feeling of hysteria reaches its climax on the far right of the platform, where a man beats himself with a whip while his companions fall to the ground. But more exciting than the meaning

William Roberts
*David Choosing the Three Days' Pestilence*, 1912

of these gestures is the way in which Roberts has shorn his participants of superfluous detail, so that the vitality of their physical movement takes on the rhythm of a semi-abstract design. Despite the clutter of influences that threatens to choke the whole picture, he was moving steadily forward, feeling his way towards a new bareness and economy.

Similar conclusions were being reached by his friend Bomberg, who came to the Slade in 1911 after studying under Sickert at Westminster School evening classes. So tenaciously independent was this small Jewish artist from a poverty-stricken quarter of Whitechapel – he was the fifth child of a Polish immigrant leather-worker – that when he executed a large watercolour of *Sleeping Men* in his first year at the Slade no trace of Sickert's influence could be discerned.[32] He had, in fact, amused himself at the Westminster by turning Sickert designs upside-down 'to form a non-figurative composition',[33] and *Sleeping Men* is handled in broad washes of dark colour which contain nothing of Sickert's broken palette. Three years earlier he applied for the Slade with a portfolio of ballet drawings 'showing strong Degas-Sickert affinities';[34] but now his figures' limbs are as monumental as those of the recumbent soldier in Roberts' *Resurrection*, and the uninhibited freedom of brushwork goes beyond Roberts already. Bomberg's use of foreshortening is extreme enough to flatten the boulder-like masses of these men up against the picture-surface; and this search for a single plane, combined with the painterly abandon, serves to announce his incipient

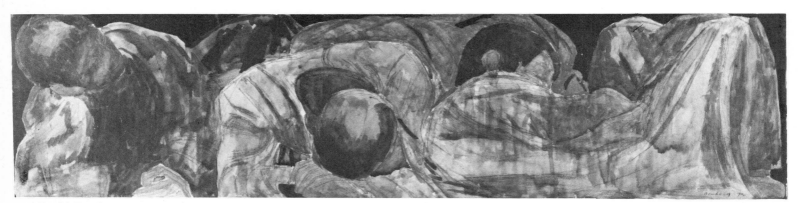

David Bomberg
*Sleeping Men*, 1911

interest in form and colour for their own sake. Bomberg admitted as much later, when he told Cliff Holden that *Sleeping Men* 'was drawn not from sleeping men but from a row of pillows. During the process of drawing the elements that have hitherto been identified as pillows reassemble and are invested with a new identity'.[35]

The interest had intensified by the following year, when he started the large and ambitious *Island of Joy*, probably as a Slade competition subject.[36] And although the unfinished nature of the canvas suggests that Bomberg felt his way forward as he painted it, never managing to resolve his evolving ideas in one cohesive work of art, the design does show a progressive process of simplification from the descriptive detail of the foreground figures through to the minimal outlines in the background. There, the men fighting with the centaurs have been reduced to one-dimensional slabs of paint: everything has been suppressed in favour of a geometrical network of struggling limbs, and their constantly intersecting diagonal movement is all that Bomberg really cares about. He attempts to structure this jostling, almost kinetic rhythm by juxtaposing a light triangle at the top of the painting with a dark triangle at the bottom, but the improvisatory nature of the composition prevents him from making this device fully effective. There is, too, a confused air about the wall running along the base, containing as it does the only passive figure in the picture reclining in a shallow pool of water. The motif of an indoor bath would eventually become the starting-point for Bomberg's most outstanding painting; and yet here it appears inconsequential, an area so spatially ambiguous that it may or may not be raised above the struggle raging elsewhere in the canvas.

*Island of Joy* remains, nevertheless, an impressive demonstration of Bomberg's pictorial ambitions, a battlefield of formal problems which he chose to work out in the painting itself so that the tension between the rival demands of representation and near-abstraction could be publicly displayed. The mythological fight being conducted so vigorously by the lapiths and centaurs is paralleled by the artist's own fight for creative renewal, and Bomberg must have thought hard about those background figures, realizing that in their reductive simplicity lay the direction he ought to pursue. He might easily have received some encouragement, not only from the exhibitions promoted by Fry and the sight of Lewis's *Kermesse* on view at the AAA salon, but also from John Fothergill, the elegant editor of the Slade Magazine, whom Nevinson remembered as 'an exquisite in dark blue velvet suiting, pale-yellow silk shirt and stock, with a silver pin as large as an egg, and patent court shoes with silver buckles. It was possible in those days, of course, to be a dandy without being thought a pansy as well'.[37] Fothergill's provocative essay on 'Drawing', published in the 1910–11 edition of the *Encyclopaedia Britannica*, was of special interest to Slade students who were trying to come to terms with the issues it raised. As a committed formalist, Fothergill used his wide knowledge of theoreticians like Wundt, Loewy and

David Bomberg
*Island of Joy, c.* 1912

Berkeley to criticize artists who took 'literary content' into account when they judged a picture. 'As the immediate purpose and content of drawing', insisted Fothergill, 'there remains the reproduction of forms only'; and this flat declaration of principles was soon followed by a discussion of the importance of pure form – a concept championed so controversially three years later in Clive Bell's treatise on *Art*. Towards the end of his essay, Fothergill concluded that 'it is, then, by the combination of the ideas derived from pure vision and the ideas derived from touch that we know the length, breadth and depth of a solid form', and Bomberg would have warmed to this obsession with the viability of abstract volumes.[38] He shared Fothergill's concerns, but instead of writing about them he proceeded in the later months of 1912 to put them down in a painting which broke entirely fresh ground in the evolution of English art: *Vision of Ezekiel*.[39]

In the lamentable absence of any surviving paintings by Lewis before 1914, this astonishing work can be seen as the first canvas to broach a specifically British form of abstraction. And more than three elaborate preliminary drawings exist to testify to the prolonged deliberation which preceded its execution. One of them, the least like the final painting and therefore the first of the group, takes the rectangular platform used by Roberts in his roughly contemporaneous *David Choosing the Three Days' Pestilence* and places upon it the same kind of gesticulating bodies. It even introduces a similar, presumably sacred, animal to the scene; but whereas Roberts made his pair of cows into the centre of agitated attention, Bomberg's towering fetish acts merely as a backdrop for the complex interplay of limbs disposed on the platform in front. They thrust, jerk, grovel and sway according to the dictates of a ritual that defies all ordinary analysis. The focal point of the design – if such a notably decentralized composition could be said to possess a focal point – is surely to be found in the protagonist seated more or less in the centre foreground of the drawing. He wears a tall hat, reminiscent of the elongated head-dresses portrayed by Piero in the Arezzo frescoes, and his is the only face to be characterized with any degree of completeness. Bomberg makes him smile as he acknowledges the frantic homage of the figure genuflecting before him, and the sadistic glee with which he rests himself on a body writhing in pain beneath injects a sinister meaning into the drama. It is impossible to make out a coherent interpretation of his precise significance, however, for the ostensibly Biblical theme is swamped by a plethora of tangled arms and legs, where wrestlers perform beside acrobats and dancers mingle with mothers holding babies in their hands.

David Bomberg
*Struggling Figures: Study for
Vision of Ezekiel, c.* 1912

David Bomberg
*Study for Vision of Ezekiel,
c.* 1912

points and reinforces them: the topmost corner of the platform is now accentuated by the addition of a standing figure, who is cut off summarily above the buttocks as if to prove that he functions as a formal device alone. And if the man standing in the lower left corner is compared with his counterpart in the previous drawing, it immediately becomes clear how Bomberg is reducing all the components in his design to the same linear rigidity that already defines the platform. Even the carefully ruled lines drawn across the surface of the study seem to play their part in the overall structure, slicing it up into a series of neatly regularized sections which each play an equal part in the almost mathematical sequence of the whole.

Now that most of the little inconsistencies and hesitations were ruthlessly corrected, and the picture moved from the localized environment of the first drawing to a more unspecific and timeless setting, Bomberg was ready to tackle the painting. He was not, however, willing to rest satisfied with his last sketch; and, ever more doggedly scrupulous, set about composing a starker equation of essential form and colour. The platform, lopped off at three of its corners with a resourceful skill that prevents any symmetrical monotony, is contrasted dramatically with a strip of deep maroon traversing its perimeter. And another pair of bands spreading outwards to the edges of the painting also ensures that the outlying figures are as subject to the geometry controlling the composition as the people in the centre. For Bomberg knew he could afford to dispense with anything which disturbed the abstracted equilibrium he had created, including the facial features of the seated figure who had been so dominant in all the preparatory drawings. Each person in the picture is now accorded equal value, and none is allowed to detract from the patterns created by the participants as they exercise themselves in a strenuous parade of strutting limbs across the canvas. Bomberg was intent upon making each separate gesture tell with the utmost force, and so he continued to prune the composition of its extraneous elements: the kneeling figure who struggled with his companion at the top centre of the final drawing has been taken away altogether, leaving the strong line of a wide stripe to travel unobscured right up to the edge of the painting.

The outcome of all this sifting and refinement might have been a somewhat arid, purist affair if Bomberg had not decided to let colour work as cogently as form, and cast the majority of his protagonists in a brilliant combination of pale yellow flesh set off against the lightest of pink shadows. This head-on clash of tones produces a potent sense of movement on its own, quite independent of the rhythm set up by the stabbing complex of legs and arms. Even at this early date, he was beginning to explore the ability of flat colour to set a picture in motion, and much of *Vision of Ezekiel*'s vitality derives from the unlikely contrast between physical movement and the infinitely more ethereal movement of yellow on pink. In order to ensure that his design did not fall apart under the strain of such an unnerving spectacle, he placed a number of darkly modelled figures in among their pale neighbours, and used them as anchoring devices at all four corners of the painting. They succeed in making the lighter people appear by comparison even more ghostly and insubstantial, while at the same time helping to root them in a relatively solid reality. And their presence serves as a reminder of the risks Bomberg was taking: there is nothing slick or facile about this disconcerting jumble of toppling forms and hard-edge colour contrasts, nothing simple-minded in the way he plays off the thrust of a torso against the angle of a thigh. Although he was attempting to create something without precedent, this stubborn 22-year-old student refused to comfort himself with easy harmonies and predictable solutions.

Small wonder that Sir Claude Phillips, when he first saw *Ezekiel* exhibited, should have been moved to describe it as 'really a very pretty pattern, but one

Francis Picabia
*Procession in Seville*, 1912

in which we can distinguish nothing of the prophet or his sublime vision. We should have been inclined to name it *Symphony in Pink'*.[42] How could the critics of the day be expected to understand such a revolutionary vision, except by referring it back rather flippantly to the musical terminology of Whistler? There was virtually nothing in English art to which it could be related, and neither do any Cubist works offer themselves as obvious source material for Bomberg's markedly independent investigations. It has connections with Léger's use of Cubism in a painting like the 1909–11 *Nudes in a Landscape*, since both pictures employ a faceted subdivision of the human body to infect their compositions with emphatic motion. But Bomberg probably never saw Léger's first masterpiece, and *Ezekiel*'s reliance on high-pitched colour and flamboyant gesture differs greatly from the low-keyed concentration on volume displayed in *Nudes in a Landscape*. An apparently more pertinent parallel is provided by Picabia, whose *Procession in Seville* – painted in the very same year as *Ezekiel* – likewise reduces the whole picture-surface to an intricate and kinetic pattern of coloured segments. Picabia's mourners have the same sculptural quality as Bomberg's figures as they tumble down the canvas in a blend of bright blue, orange, white and grey; and they are integrated still further with their background to establish an overall kaleidoscope of geometry and colour.

It would be unwise to push the resemblances between the two works too far, of course: Bomberg only paid his first visit to Paris in the summer of 1913, some months after he had completed *Ezekiel*. But, though he never actually mentioned Bomberg by name, Lewis himself later pointed out the plausibility of the links binding the two men when he wrote that 'Picabia, in France, reducing things to empty but very clean and precise mathematical blocks, coldly and wittily tinted like a milliner's shop-front . . . is on a par with a tendency in the work of several excellent painters in England, following the general Continental movement. Only in their case it is sculpturesque groups of lay figures, rather than more supple and chic mannequins'. In this respect, Bomberg's adherence to a large figure composition format was still attuned to the precepts of Tonks: as Lewis went on to explain, 'the grandiose and sentimental traditionalism inculcated at the Slade is largely responsible for this variety'.[43]

The power of the Slade was still strong enough to persuade Bomberg momentarily to retreat from the stand taken up in *Ezekiel* and execute a more orthodox, realistic drawing of a *Jewish Theatre*.[44] It was entered for a Slade competition in January 1913, and the requirements stipulated in the contest presumably dictated the profusion of descriptive detail that comes as such a surprise after the abstraction of *Ezekiel*. Tonks, after all, remained unyielding in his opposition to the influence of Post-Impressionism: when George Moore suggested that he modify his position, and officially allow the principles of Cubism to penetrate the hallowed precincts of the Slade, the professor stood firm. 'My dear Moore', he replied, 'you're untroubled by a conscience, and will never understand a certain side of life. I cannot teach what I don't believe in. I shall resign if this talk about Cubism doesn't cease; it is killing me.'[45] But despite pressures from the school authorities, *Jewish Theatre* persists in employing grotesquely heightened gestures, and the audience shrinks away from the play because Bomberg can use such movements formally, as shapes which almost become the exclusive content of the drawing. It could not be more opposed to the theatre pictures of his old teacher, Sickert, who concentrated in his music-hall scenes on an evocation of momentary atmosphere rather than the architecture of spectators' bodies. And if Bomberg was originally encouraged to look to the theatre for raw material by Sickert, there was no trace of the latter's influence left by the time he drew *Jewish Theatre*. He was a faithful supporter of his local Pavilion Theatre in Whitechapel, which appealed to the whole of London's Jewish colony, and the

David Bomberg
*Jewish Theatre*, 1913

intensely dramatic offerings staged there might well have helped inspire the rhetorical poses in Bomberg's paintings.

Roberts shared his friend's interest, for he recalled a typical evening with Bomberg when they arranged to 'have dinner together in a Jewish restaurant in Whitechapel, opposite the Pavilion Theatre, and go to a Yiddish play afterwards', accompanied of course by some 'beautiful brunettes'.[46] But the latest works to survive from Roberts' Slade period show that he was not yet as radical as his companion: two drawings from a projected series of London street market scenes, commissioned by Sir Cyril Butler early in 1913, are conspicuously less advanced than Bomberg's experiments with *Ezekiel*.[47] One of them, an ink and chalk study of *Billingsgate*, looks at first like a thoroughly traditional and even anecdotal essay in realism. And only later does it become apparent that Roberts has counterbalanced the meticulous detail of the fish, the gushing water pump and the portrait heads with an austere collection of cubic packing cases, which rise up into the air above the porters' hats in a monumental, proto-abstract progression. Both *Billingsgate* and its pair, *Leadenhall Market*, seem to owe more to the sprightly urban reportage of a Camden Town painter like Robert Bevan than Bomberg; and yet, for all that, the second drawing has very little documentary impulse behind it. Roberts has included only the most skeletal topographical information, and accentuated instead the gaunt outlines of ware-houses, evenly shaded, which dwarf the crowd below. These figures, despite their carefully characterized faces and clothing, are emphasized as a flat mass by the strong ink line running around their contours and generalizing overall rhythms. Roberts enjoys seeing them as so many darting patterns, just as he seizes on the crane platform in the upper right corner of the design and makes it into a zig-zagging silhouette. But he also views the people satirically, as a gaggle of frantic automatons reminiscent of Lewis's Breton peasants. They are embodiments rather than individuals, caricatures like the two bowler-hatted traders who lean towards each other in the centre and create a neatly

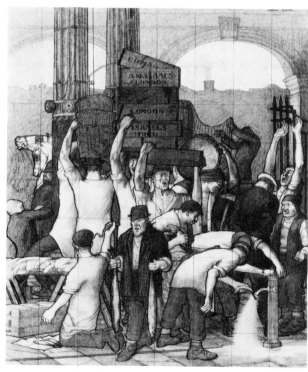

William Roberts
*Billingsgate*, 1913

William Roberts
*Leadenhall Market*, 1913

symmetrical pyramid of argument. Everywhere humans are embroiled in energetic activity, often of the most melodramatic kind, yet subservient all the time to the massive industrial impersonality of their environment.

*Leadenhall Market* represents, however, a very temporary phase in Roberts' development; and it was not long before he found himself able to embrace the language of the European avant-garde. 'I became an abstract painter through the influence of the French Cubists', he affirmed later, adding that 'this influence was further strengthened by a stay in France and Italy during the summer of 1913.'[48] It would be idle to speculate on particular paintings which he might have seen during this vitally formative journey, but the results were palpable enough when he returned home. Setting to work on some studies for a *Nativity* as a projected entry for the 1913 Prix de Rome, he executed two drawings which mark a clear advance on his previous work.[49] One, a large and elaborate pen, pencil and watercolour design which reinterprets a classic Renaissance motif through an eye affected as much by the self-conscious distortions of Mannerist altarpieces as by the angularities of Cubism, is now willing to discard the heavy modelling still so evident in *Leadenhall Market*. A freely applied series of muted washes perform that function instead, letting Roberts' always confident command over line run a brittle, frenetic course through the entire composition. At the same time, however, it adheres very strongly to a naturalistic idiom,

William Roberts
*Study for The Return of Ulysses*, 1913

William Roberts
*The Return of Ulysses*, 1913

corner; and Ulysses kicks over a vessel of liquid with his elongated leg. It is fair to say that none of these extra devices actually improves on the watercolour's subtle balance between areas of thickly populated activity and stretches of empty space: rather does the drawing drain away the uncluttered vitality of the original study. And if the actions of the figures are now more comprehensible, this clarity has been won by adopting a degree of naturalistic elaboration which borders on the academic.

The painting, which retains the same dimensions as the studies, fortunately discards some of this descriptive excess.[50] Although Roberts exhibited it at the New English Art Club in December 1913, he did not let the Club's reactionary standards affect his desire to win back a measure of the watercolour's exemplary freshness. The niggling pedantry has all but disappeared again; and a welcome dynamism is created both by the lengthening of the central table's downward thrust into the picture-space, and by the introduction of another table shooting in diagonally from the top right corner. Certain shapes register themselves with a new, almost autonomous force, too: the aggressive funnel of the wine bottle which has been placed on the central table, and the startling black of Penelope's dress. But to set against these improvements, Roberts has abandoned the lively orchestration of the watercolour and opted instead for a more discreet, terracotta tonality. He has, likewise, muted the strength of those all-important shadows by making them at once paler and more complex, so that they spread across most of the floor in a relatively undistinguished mass. Compared with the ruthless geometry of *Ezekiel*, *Ulysses* betrays an unwillingness to drive Roberts' new-found Cubist allegiance to its ultimate conclusion.

Bomberg, on the other hand, insisted on bringing his Slade studentship to an unforgettably challenging close. One small oil, which seems to be based on the orthodox motif of a male model sitting astride a life-class drawing 'horse', reduces its contents to an even more drastic equation than *Ezekiel*. Both the figure and his seat have been relieved of all unnecessary detail, and they are presented simply as crude strips of light or dark paint. The 'horse' and the mysterious architectural shapes on the left stand out clearly in a forthright combination of whites and blues; but the model's body is painted in the same range of warm reds as the background, indicating that Bomberg had decided to stress the integrity of his picture-plane by flattening his figure up against it. The result is a brash, unresolved and yet immensely bracing image, which shows how ready Bomberg was to court ungainliness for the sake of formal purity.

▷David Bomberg
*Interior, c.* 1913

▽David Bomberg
*Figure Study, c.* 1912

△ David Bomberg
*Racehorses*, 1912–13

△ David Bomberg
*Cubist Composition, c.* 1913

And around the same time, he attempted to impose the same kind of solution on a watercolour of an *Interior*, where the functional structure of a staircase is transformed into a one-dimensional pattern of remarkable ambiguity. Other contemporaneous drawings, like *Racehorses* and *Cubist Composition*, were equally adventurous, but they represent only the most radical fraction of the work Bomberg executed at the Slade: his first wife recalled that in 1915 'many evenings were spent going through his old "Slade" drawings and the grate every night was filled with old drawings which, after thoroughly studying, he decided to discard . . . He said in his Jewish way he had of summing up a situation, "There – in flames, goes three years' work of sitting on a low donkey stool from ten to four drawing worm's eye views of the nude".'[51]

But Bomberg was not content to rest with these minor statements. Applying their abrasive logic and discipline to the demands of a fully considered painting, he executed a confident *tour de force* which carried the discoveries of *Ezekiel* through to a still more daring stage – *Ju-Jitsu*. A vigorous working drawing for the picture makes clear that the idea originated in the familiar theme of gesticulating figures; and yet this time they are shown, not on an open platform, but enclosed within the bleak confines of a bare room. The setting – more complex spatially than *Ezekiel* – is probably inspired by Schevzik's Steam Baths in Brick Lane, situated close to Bomberg's Whitechapel family home at Tenter Buildings where he had his first studio. The Baths, which still exist to confirm the similarity with the room portrayed in this drawing, were to become the starting-point for an outright masterpiece Bomberg painted more than a year later, and he would have enjoyed their clean symmetry and geometrically tiled walls.[52] Perhaps it was the pattern formed by those very tiles that made him think about the technique of dividing up drawings and canvases into a neat grid of squares, a classic Slade tradition which he doubtless first learned when studying under Sickert. The grid system was endemic in Sickert's whole approach to the business of transforming a given scene: sometimes he even left them visible in the finished painting as a reminder of the tight underlying structure. But Bomberg now realized the full abstract potential of this grid technique. Instead of hiding it in his final picture as he had previously done, with an overlay of paint, he decided to exploit it for his own expressive purposes, and in *Ju-Jitsu* the surface of the entire composition is dominated by an heraldic scaffolding of sixty-four neatly drawn squares.[53]

▽ Photograph of a tiled wall in the former
Schevzik's Steam Baths, Brick Lane,
London E.1

David Bomberg
*Study for Ju-Jitsu*, c. 1913

The real subject of the painting is not, as it was in the drawing, the relation between the figures and their confused, ambiguous surroundings. Now it is the tension set up by the jerking puppets and the grid which contains them, at once defining and confining their every movement. In order to lend an additional complexity to the picture and further remove it from its representational origins, Bomberg subdivided his squares into triangles as well, so that when he passed his figures through the grid they were sliced up into a splinter of glittering fragments. Occasionally a recognizable head, leg or arm peeps through the tortuous maze, fighting to establish its figurative identity against the geometry threatening to overwhelm it. The contest is evenly waged on the left of the painting, where the men's movements can be reconstructed without too much difficulty. But over on the far right the battle has been resolved in favour of abstraction, and the ladder described so clearly in the drawing disintegrates altogether into a tiny shower of ochre particles. The formal polyphony created by the whole design could have become merely cerebral, and yet Bomberg alleviates the severity by using a singing series of colours, ranging from ultra-marine and crimson through to seductive shades of coffee brown and pale grey. The colours at the top of the picture stand out independent of any interference, a relatively straightforward sequence of patterns which manage to convey the guide-lines of the walls without unduly compromising the grid's structure. Down below, however, they are penetrated by the figures and caught up in a frenetic jigsaw puzzle of staccato motion that ends up affecting the colours, changing their hue from one square to the next. *Ju-Jitsu* is alive with intense abstract activity: even the squares seem to change into triangles and back again in a state of perpetual optical flux, and the painting darts and jumps with a kinetic restlessness which looks as vital now as it must have done when Bomberg first dared to put it into pictorial action.

is impossible for Wyndham Lewis, – Bomberg! I have come to see what you are doing." He expressed admiration of the Jewish Theatre and a number of things – I was courteous to a man who inverted conceptual precepts in imitation of G.B.S. such as "It's too true to be good".' Although obviously wary of each other, these two dedicated pioneers revelled in this chance to exchange views, discuss each other's work and agree about the need for an uprising in the staid world of English art. Bomberg later admitted 'there was a gap to breach of a decade' in their ages, but he 'regarded Lewis [as] very well informed' and re-membered that 'we had talked ourselves silly when he left, – dawn, the next morning. I recognised in the conversation, a Slade man honouring the same pledge to which I was staking my life – namely, a Partizan'. The only problem was that Bomberg became uncomfortably aware that Lewis 'had spent six years mingling with the group of reputations known as the pioneers of the advance movement of the visual arts and literature in Paris'. Lewis may well have shown off too much, and friction soon resulted: Bomberg remembered 'the clashes that followed from his repeated unsolicited visits to the East End to keep himself in touch with what I was doing and thinking'.[55]

Such an independent pair of personalities could never have succeeded in striking up a lasting friendship, but their contact with each other was still momentously significant. Bomberg's respect for his visitor, whose *Kermesse* and *Timon* series he would already have seen and appreciated in public exhibitions, had probably risen to a height during the month when their first meeting took place. For Lewis was then showing, in the December 1912 Camden Town Group exhibition at the Carfax Gallery, a large painting called *Danse* which must undoubtedly have appealed to the creator of *Ezekiel*.[56] The picture is now unfortunately lost, but *The Athenaeum*'s critic devoted a considerable amount of his review to its merits. 'This design has the momentary, precarious balance of a kaleidoscope pattern, and we feel that the raising or depression of the poised toe of one of the figures would induce an immediate shifting of all the other angles of the structure,' he wrote, describing Lewis's exhibit in terms that could equally well be applied to a work like *Ju-Jitsu*. 'Much, no doubt, has been sacrificed to the violence of the play of these angles – greater elasticity of movement, for example, might easily have been secured without departing from the chosen convention, had the artist consented to the notation of the slight tilt of a pelvis, the slight bending of a supporting limb, whereby the weight of a figure poised on one leg is distributed and the balance maintained. The imagina-tive interest of the dance is somewhat lessened by the formal starring of the figure from a centre, which makes it a rather obviously mechanical marionette.'[57]

*The Athenaeum*'s reviewer obviously felt that *Danse* was altogether too geo-metrical and rigidly constructed; but the young man who was in the process of conceiving *Ju-Jitsu* would not have demurred at Lewis's insistence on a 'mechanical marionette'. And Bomberg's admiration was almost certainly reci-procated by Lewis, amazed to find such progressive pictures painted by someone still at college. The very fact that an individualist as imperious as Lewis bothered to make the journey to Whitechapel at all argues that he was anxious to discover fellow rebels and gather them under his own discontented banner. Bomberg, so responsive in this first conversation, always resisted propositions of a political nature; but it does seem clear that Lewis, already beginning to find fault with Fry as his new mentor, was thinking about rallying prospective troops. Having established his mature artistic identity, he must by now have suspected that the only way to persuade London of the potency of his beliefs was to set about forming a movement, as Marinetti had done so spectacularly with the Futurists. There was creative ferment at the Slade, and Lewis wanted to contact the individuals involved, talk with them and impress them with his own hopes and ambitions. For he had tasted a measure of critical notoriety, his appetite was whetted and the expression on the face of his incisive *Self-Portrait*, drawn about this time, is above all alert – watchful and waiting. Now, surely, it was only a question of time.

Wyndham Lewis
*Self-Portrait*, 1911–12

# Chapter 4: Dissension at the Omega

Ostensibly, Lewis still chose to hide his mounting recalcitrance and follow Fry's lead in finding a solution to the most perplexing problem which now confronted the English avant-garde: how to join forces and come together on a more permanent and rewarding basis. It had, after all, been clear for some months that Fry was turning over an idea in his mind, and Lewis was not yet in sufficiently strong a position to disregard proposals from such a powerful quarter. Ever since the beginning of 1912, when Fry invited Grant to lunch at his Guildford home to meet some potentially useful dealers, the dilemma had become pressingly apparent. Grant did not arrive: he had barely scraped together the money for the journey, stored it away somewhere for safe keeping and then lost it completely. So it was hardly surprising that Fry viewed the incident as a symbol of the general plight afflicting the impoverished artists he admired, and decided that a constructive scheme should be implemented to aid their experiments with Post-Impressionism. He was optimistic, brimming with energy and determined that the interest his exhibitions had aroused be put to good practical use. And as early as February 1912 he wrote Lewis a letter, inviting him to a meeting 'to settle the nature of the group of artists which Duncan Grant, Etchells and I propose to start'.[1]

The plans put forward by this team – basically a nucleus of the men who had worked together on the Borough Polytechnic murals – may already have centred on the formation of an artists' workshop. But it was a difficult operation to organize. Then as now, England was notorious for its philistine attitude towards contemporary art, and Richard Aldington recalled how a visit to Italy around this time had convinced him that 'on the Continent the arts were taken far more seriously, were much more widely and sincerely practised and enjoyed than in England, where sport usurped their place in all classes. Certainly there was in England no respect for the artist such as existed in France or Italy. On the contrary, the artist in England was an object of suspicion, dislike and contempt – unless he happened to make money'.[2] Moreover, any advanced institution modelled along the lines Fry was eager to propose immediately came up against the uncomprehending hostility not only of senior British artists, but also of the small band of collectors and patrons whose support was essential for the survival of a group concern. 'In the spring of 1913', wrote Paul Nash, 'in spite of the many signs of unrest, in spite of Roger Fry's Post-Impressionist Exhibitions . . . the doctrine and practice of the New English Art Club represented all that was most typical of modern art in England, Augustus John's being still the most conspicuous talent.'[3] And, quite apart from the establishment, there was even antagonism to be encountered among the Slade students: Mark Gertler, by no means a diehard conservative in his views, told Dora Carrington in September 1912 about his contemptuous feelings when he 'went out and saw more unfortunate artists. I looked at them talking art, Ancient art, Modern art, Impressionism, Post-Impressionism, Neo-Impressionism, Cubists, Spottists, Futurists, Cave-dwelling, Wyndham Lewis, Duncan Grant, Etchells, Roger Fry! I looked on and laughed to myself . . .'.[4]

The plethora of strange impulses and loudly championed new movements which were being bandied around in London art circles was bound to provoke cynicism and mistrust among those who had no taste for theoretical controversy. But Fry had long since learned how to thrive in adversity, and by December the chorus of debate surrounding his Grafton Galleries show had infected him with renewed faith. Once again he wrote to Lewis, declaring that he was 'working very hard trying to raise capital for our decorative scheme. So far the only help promised comes from Bernard Shaw. But I am still full of hope and shall call a meeting to discuss the situation soon'. Significantly, Fry referred to the project as 'our scheme', a joint venture with which Lewis must by now have been actively associated; and Fry's letter displayed an added respect for Lewis by asking him 'to let us have something of yours to help fill up gaps' in the 1912 Grafton Group show. 'Also tell me of any other painters or draughtsmen you recommend', Fry continued. 'Where, for instance, can I see this man's work (I forget his name) who has a show now? Also what other Frenchmen do you suggest? I shall be up on Tuesday; will you come round and talk to me?'[5] Such a barrage of requests for help must have been highly flattering to Lewis, and there can be no doubt that the two men spent a considerable amount of time with each other: in August 1912, Eric Gill noted in his diary that he had 'met Wyndham Lewis with Roger Fry at Guildford'.[6] But the months went past, and no outward signs of progress appeared until April 1913, when an announcement was published in the *Art Chronicle* informing the public of a new organization called the Omega Workshops – 'a new movement in decorative art', ready to 'embrace the making of "character" furniture which will reflect the artistic feeling of the age'.[7]

The declaration seems to imply that a group had finally been formed, one that was willing and able to take on commissions for any kind of decorative work for clients who wanted something in the most advanced style. And in the same month Lewis received another letter from Fry, declaring that 'I'm very much interested by what you say about the need of some big belief outside of art. I must talk it over with you. The situation of the artist becomes more hopelessly paradoxical the more one gets to some idea of what art is. We must talk it over. I've taken 33 Fitzroy Square. We'll meet there soon'.[8] Fry's anxiously repeated desire to discuss the ideology behind the Workshops points to his growing respect for Lewis's articulate intelligence, and suggests that the latter played an active part in formulating the Omega's aesthetic position. As Fry's letter indicates, Lewis went along to enlist at the large house in Fitzroy Square containing design studios, a showroom and artists' workshops long before it was officially opened in July 1913. He needed money desperately; the Omega aimed to provide a minimum weekly payment in return for part-time work in applied art; and besides, Fry was virtually the only critic to praise his latest paintings with enthusiasm. When his lost *Group* was shown at the AAA's Summer Salon, for instance, Fry pronounced it to be a 'remarkable' work which was 'more completely realised than anything [Lewis] has shown yet. His power of reflecting those lines of movement and those sequences of mass which express his personal feeling is increasing visibly. Mr Lewis is no primitive'.[9]

Given the partisan support of a man as influential as Fry, the Omega could in theory have blossomed into a vital communal centre for the avant-garde, where they could all meet, exchange views and earn a guaranteed thirty shillings a week to subsidize their own experimental work. 'I only went to the Omega for one or two days a week',[10] Lewis wrote later, explaining how the arrangement left him time to pursue his private ends as well; and he was soon joined by a whole array of radicals who had already been associated with Fry through exhibitions at the Bloomsbury oriented Friday Club or the Grafton Group. Fry's name acted as a cynosure for artists like Wadsworth, Hamilton, Etchells, Bomberg and Roberts, all of whom joined the Omega at various times during the course of 1913. And Lewis, of course, lost no time in making friends with the men he had not previously had a chance to meet: Wadsworth, returning home after a day at the Workshops, told his wife that 'I've met an interesting man; he's coming to see us',[11] and within days Lewis visited their house – just as he had called on Bomberg at Tenter Buildings some months before.

But despite the financial attractions of the Omega, and the opportunity it afforded Lewis to confirm his alliances with old colleagues like Etchells and Hamilton, Fitzroy Square was from the outset riddled with dissension. Lewis, involved as he was with the dynamic ideas of Marinetti and the creation of pictures as deliberately exacerbating as *Kermesse*, the *Timon* series and the Cabaret murals, could never have been wholeheartedly in sympathy with the ideals of Workshops standing in a direct line of descent from the Arts and Crafts movement and the precepts of Ashbee, whom Fry had known in his youth. The Omega's Morris-like programme was hardly calculated to appeal to a man who would have preferred to form his own movement rather than concur with a prospectus which undertook, in Fry's words, 'almost all kinds of decorative design, more particularly those in which the artist can engage without specialised training in craftsmanship . . . Substituting wherever possible the directly expressive quality of the artist's handling for the deadness of mechanical reproduction, they have turned their attention to hand-dyeing and have produced a number of dyed curtains, bedspreads, cushion covers, etc.'[12] Instead of rebellion, and an art that would measure up to the achievements of Cubism and Futurism, Lewis was being offered a gentle affair, full of good intentions and fresh ideas but far too inoffensive to satisfy his imperious longings. Where Fry believed that the machine could be made subservient to the artist, Lewis wanted to acknowledge the machine and incorporate its power into his own pictorial vocabulary.

Wyndham Lewis
*Three Figures: Study for a Screen*, 1913

As a result of the Omega's complete lack of technical expertise, its first products suffered from Fry's courageous belief in the hand-made. 'With no preliminary workshop training it was idle to suppose that half a dozen artists could cope with all – or indeed any – of the problems of waxing, lacquering, polishing, painting and varnishing of furniture . . . or the hand-painting of textiles which the plan involved', Lewis explained afterwards, ridiculing the Workshops' shaky beginnings. 'Naturally the chairs we sold stuck to the seats of people's trousers; when they took up an Omega candlestick they could not put it down again, they held it in an involuntary vice-like grip. It was glued to them and they to it.'[13] Sarcasm, however, was always Lewis's métier, and there is no evidence to suppose that when he and his new comrades first joined the Omega they poured scorn on the growing pains attending its inception. Their hostility only manifested itself later; and Lewis's few identifiable contributions to the Workshops show him attempting to suppress his own inveterate harshness in favour of a playful charm that would have gratified Bloomsbury taste. His study of *Three Figures*, probably a sketch for a folding screen, looks back to Picasso's pre-Cubist work, and it strikes a note of appealing wistfulness quite uncharacteristic of his previous productions.[14] Its indeterminate stylization proves that Lewis was forcing himself to work in an uncomfortable, even half-hearted vein, sufficiently removed from his central preoccupations to be comparable with Grant's screen, which was displayed alongside a Lewis screen in the inaugural show.[15] Indeed, a *Design Representing a Couple Dancing* has survived as a testimony to a close initial collaboration between the two men: it is a study for one of the two painted panels by Lewis and Grant which were placed on either side of a window as shop signs on the first floor, but Grant later found it impossible to 'state certainly which was his work'.[16]

Duncan Grant
*Design Representing a Couple Dancing*, 1913

Lewis, therefore, appears momentarily to have conformed to the principles laid down in another Omega prospectus, where Fry claimed that his artists 'refuse to spoil the expressive quality of their work by sand-papering it down to a shop finish, in the belief that the public has at last seen through the humbug of the machine-made imitation of works of art'.[17] Lewis's series of *Designs for Candle Shades*, which were painted in by other Omega hands and represented subjects as sardonic as 'stages in the bargaining between a roué and a procuress for the purchase of a young woman',[18] go along with this belief by moving right away from his austere vision of mechanical man towards a far milder form of

Wyndham Lewis
*Design for Candle Shade*, 1913

slight, light-hearted caricature. And his colleagues likewise found themselves resorting to whimsicality when Fry set them to work. 'Cuthbert Hamilton and I had to design carpets and got awfully bored with it all', recalled Etchells; 'so we used to amuse each other by drawing obscene figures, and then hiding the pornographic details with abstract shapes because Fry was rather proper – Quaker upbringing, you know. We disguised the suggestive areas so successfully that we could still see the sexual organs even though no-one else was able to. Fry would come along to examine our work and say: "Oh, what admirable designs!" '[19]

There was, however, another side to the Omega's activities: one that was much more concerned with the potential of total abstraction. 'At the Omega Workshops we thought and spoke only of modern French art, Derain, Picasso, Matisse and others', wrote Nina Hamnett, one of the founder members; and one of the practical results of this obsession was Fry's genuine attempt, for a time at least, to come to terms with the challenge of Synthetic Cubism.[20] Never content to stand still in one fixed theoretical position, he told his confidant Lowes Dickinson in a 1913 letter that 'I'm continuing my aesthetic theories and have been attacking poetry to understand painting. I want to find out what the function of content is, and am developing a theory which you will hate very much, *viz.*, that it is merely directive of form and that all the essential aesthetic quality has to do with pure form'. The concept which had already fascinated

Vanessa Bell
*Folding Screen*, 1913–14

Square, and Etchells' *Design for a Rug* is remarkable for its complete repudiation of the impulses so evident in his previous work. In this rough gouache sketch he has managed to banish the quixotic blend of influences which informed an earlier painting like *The Dead Mole*, in favour of a severely simplified mass of primary shapes which are intermingled in a crude, almost architectural structure. And Lewis also achieved a comparable austerity in his related *Design for a Rug*, where a swift series of lines zigzag around the edges and then dart across the middle of a central area of dark wash. Both these *Designs* are undistinguished works in themselves, mere scraps dashed off in haste and preserved by some fluke of fate; but they do symbolize an interest in the potential of complete abstraction which was to prove prophetic of Vorticism's future course. The uneasy combination of asymmetrical diamonds and symmetrical background squares which fights openly in the large *Omega Rug* executed from Etchells' sketch can be seen as a first statement of ideas he would follow up as a Vorticist,

▽ Frederick Etchells
  *Design for a Rug*, 1913

△ Wyndham Lewis *Design for a Rug*, 1913

▽ Frederick Etchells *Omega Rug*, 1913–14

Anon
*Desk with Inlaid Design, c.* 1913

and Fry was sufficiently pleased with the *Rug* to illustrate it in an Omega brochure. For even if the Workshops' leader would never acknowledge Vorticism as a movement worthy of the name, he must at this stage have delighted in the proto-Vorticist forms deployed in perhaps the most elegant and professional of all Omega products – the *Desk with Inlaid Design*.

Its precise authorship is unknown, like so many of the Workshops' surviving items; but the spirited wood panel rising up out of its back is an outstanding example of Fry's 'pure design'. It is a sophisticated piece of craftsmanship, blending serrated forms suggestive of dancing limbs with occasional passages – diagonal lines, the familiar zigzag – which were to become an integral part of Vorticist abstractions executed the following year. The *Desk* could have been created by any member of the radical group: either Etchells – whom Lewis remembered as 'I think the most technologically minded of us'[24] – Hamilton, Wadsworth, Bomberg, Roberts or Lewis himself. And it can stand as a symbol of all the most positive aspects of the Omega, for its clean lines and stark simplicity look forward to the innovations of the Bauhaus while at the same time meeting the strictures laid down in the *Burlington Magazine* as long ago as 1903. 'Where commonsense dictates that our furniture shall be flat, we are to find it bulge', ran the *Burlington's* angry editorial, probably written by Fry himself; 'where structure and convenience demand a straight line, "originality" insists on flaccid curves; where beauty and the operations of the craft required an edge, we are to have a veiled contour.'[25] In the best designs excuted at Fitzroy Square, the *Burlington's* complaints were finally satisfied; and the non-representational experiments conducted there were soon to be translated by the Vorticists into the more demanding mediums of oil on canvas, graphics, stone and bronze. It can reasonably be claimed, in fact, that the Omega period gave Lewis and his friends the confidence to employ in the field of applied art a degree of abstraction which they were not yet ready to use elsewhere. In this sense Fitzroy Square was a vital precedent, perhaps even a catalyst, for the birth of the Vorticists' own movement.

But the period of time allotted to them at the Omega was doomed to be abruptly terminated. Soon after the Workshops officially opened in July, Lewis finally lost all patience with Fry, whom he had viewed with partial suspicion ever since the Omega leader decided to take a bigger cut out of the 1912 Post-Impressionist Exhibition sales than had originally been agreed. Even Leonard Woolf, a close friend of Fry's, remarked in his account of this earlier incident that 'I was more than once surprised by [Fry's] ruthlessness and what seemed to be almost unscrupulousness in business',[26] and Lewis's congenital paranoia seized on this aspect of Fry's many-sided personality. It had grown into a deep resentment by August 1913, when he wrote to Fry complaining that he had not been invited to exhibit at Liverpool with other Post-Impressionist artists. 'The implication is obvious', Lewis's letter stated bitterly. 'I am animated by most cordial sentiments as regards yourself and your activities. But to continue in an atmosphere of special criticism and ill-will, if such exist, would have manifest disadvantages, as well as being distasteful, to me.'[27]

The threat implied in this painfully courteous letter burst out into open hostility when Lewis's old friend Spencer Gore discovered that Fry had unfairly appropriated a commission given by the *Daily Mail* to design a 'Post-Impressionist Room' at the October 1913 Ideal Home Exhibition. Gore, an honest and supremely apolitical man who would never have dreamed of fabricating the story, claimed that the *Mail's* agent – in a July interview at their Fleet Street office – had invited Lewis, Fry and himself to plan the 'Room' as an artistic triumvirate. Gore naturally lost no time in hurrying round to the Omega where, failing to locate either Fry or Lewis, he told Grant to inform them both of the good news and left behind a *Daily Mail* booklet about the previous year's Ideal Home rooms.[28] Then, unaccountably, the confusion began. Gore heard nothing more about the commission until Lewis one day told him an incredible story: that Fry had asked Lewis merely to carve a mantelpiece for an Ideal Home Room which the *Mail* had commissioned from the Omega alone. When Lewis heard Gore's indignant version of the story, all his suspicions about Fry seemed to be dramatically confirmed. His reaction was both immediate and explosive. Without even bothering to verify the matter with the *Mail* itself, he marched out of the Omega on 5 October after a heated argument with Fry on the staircase. And three other members of the Workshops accompanied him, too: Etchells, Hamilton and Wadsworth, all of whom were by now so disenchanted with the running of the Omega that they believed Lewis's sinister interpretation of the episode implicitly. '*Ça c'est trop fort*',[29] cried Fry as the four insurrectionaries stormed off down the stairs and out of the front door, slamming it hard behind them.

At long last, Lewis had the perfect opportunity to expand his dissatisfaction with Bloomsbury into a full-scale public revolt. Gathering his allies around him, he hurriedly composed an excoriating attack on Fry and everything he stood for in the form of an open letter. This 'Round Robin', as Lewis dubbed it, was then circulated among the Omega shareholders, and a revised copy sent to the Press to ensure that the whole of London knew about the rift.[30] Ostensibly addressed to all interested parties at the Workshops and signed jointly by Etchells, Lewis, Hamilton and Wadsworth, it brusquely announced that 'we the undersigned have given up our work' at the Omega, since they were 'no longer willing to form part of this unfortunate institution'. Their reasons were made abundantly, even sensationally clear in the rest of the letter, which alleged with lofty authority that 'it was the idea of those who recommended these artists to the Daily Mail authorities that a room should be decorated on the lines of their joint decorations in the Cabaret Theatre Club'. Their statement was convincing enough, in view of the widespread comment that the Cabaret murals had aroused: any up to date *Mail* editor would have warmed to the idea of using the talents behind the Cabaret decorations for the artistic side of his Ideal Home show. The combined flair of Gore and Lewis would have ensured that the 'Post-Impressionist Room' was the talk of London; and proof still exists that Madame Strindberg actually recommended Gore for the job. 'The Ideal Home Exhibition asked Konody for an eminent Futurist painter, to decorate a room for them', she told Gore in a note. 'I told Konody to give them your name and addresse. He has done so. For God's sake don't recommend another man *but make the money YOURSELF*.'[31] This, at any rate, was the commission Lewis would have liked to secure, with Fry – who had nothing to do with the success of the Cabaret, anyway – relegated to a subordinate position. As the 'Round Robin' curtly asserted, 'Mr Fry, as head of the Omega Workshops, should supply the furniture'.

The truth of this claim will never be confirmed for certain, but the letter afterwards went on to outline the real source of dissatisfaction: not political squabbles so much as an irreconcilably opposed view of art. In a passage of brilliantly sustained invective which could only have come from Lewis's uninhibited pen – 'I don't think I helped write the "Round Robin",' Etchells recalled; 'I simply thought it great fun signing it to give one in the eye to Fry'[32] – the letter made plain exactly what its signatories thought of Fitzroy Square aesthetics. 'As to its tendencies in Art, they alone would be sufficient to make it very difficult for any vigorous art-instinct to long remain under that roof', declared the 'Round Robin'. 'The Idol is still Prettiness, with its mid-Victorian languish of the neck, and its skin is "greenery-yallery", despite the Post-What-Not fashionableness of its draperies. This family party of strayed and Dissenting

Aesthetes, however, were compelled to call in as much modern talent as they could find, to do the rough and masculine work without which they knew their efforts would not rise above the level of a pleasant tea-party, or command more attention.'

The real origin of the grievance, then, was not the Ideal Home commission. That had only acted as a fuse to ignite the gunpowder of dissent accumulating beneath the Omega's foundations. Lewis and his friends had grown to despise Fry's ideas, which they saw as a fatal compromise, an attempt to dress up nineteenth-century concepts in the surface glitter of Post-Impressionism. And the strict rule of anonymity Fry imposed on his artists was resented, too: the rebels considered that they were making all the important stylistic innovations, while Fry was getting the credit for their daring. He was unbearable in their eyes, a leech and a crafty exploiter of other people's talent, and in the most vicious part of the 'Round Robin' Fry was impaled on the spikes of Lewis's rhetoric. 'This enterprise seemed to promise, in the opportunities afforded it by support from the most intellectual quarters, emancipation from the middle-man-shark. But a new form of fish in the troubled waters of Art has been revealed in the meantime, the Pecksniff-shark, a timid but voracious journalistic monster, unscrupulous, smooth-tongued and, owing chiefly to its weakness, mischievous.' To those who knew Fry best, this Dickensian portrait was a scandalous libel that bore no relation to reality. But behind its satirical self-indulgence – a speciality Lewis was increasingly to exploit as his rebellion gathered impetus – lay one undeniable fact: the total incompatibility of the two men's personalities and ambitions.

Fry, undoubtedly with wisdom, calmly continued a continental holiday and maintained a steady silence as the abuse mounted around him, refusing to be drawn into the fray. Maybe he viewed the whole affair with the same patronizing disdain as Lytton Strachey, who told Etchells in a drily tongue-in-cheek letter that he 'sympathised deeply and it must indeed be terrible for Lewis to have lost the chance of making an Ideal Home'.[33] This Bloomsbury coolness paid its own dividends, for an observer like Edward Marsh – Churchill's private secretary and a keen patron of young artists – interpreted Fry's silence as a mark of integrity. 'There's a terrific row about the Omega Workshop', he told Michael Sadleir in a letter. 'Wyndham Lewis, Etchells and Wadsworth are sending round a circular accusing Fry of the blackest conduct, intercepting their letters, jockeying them out of commissions, preventing them from exhibiting, etc. I hear they are disappointed because Fry hasn't come posting back from the S. of France to meet their murderous attack. I haven't heard his side yet. Of course it must be a misunderstanding, he has probably been very unbusinesslike, but he is certainly quite honest.'[34]

For some maddening reason, Fry never did make 'his side' entirely clear, but Marsh was being far too optimistic when he attributed the 'row' to a simple matter of 'misunderstanding'. If the Ideal Home commission had never been mooted, the split would still have occurred before very long; and the 'Round Robin' merely succeeded in raising passions so high as to obscure the true source of the dispute. For a long time there was utter confusion over who was in the wrong, but in 1964 Quentin Bell and Stephen Chaplin helped to clarify the whole tortuous story in a detailed account entitled 'The Ideal Home Rumpus'.[35] And they reproduced Gore's vitally important letters to Fry, particularly one written on 7 October, to prove that Gore did actually leave a message at the Omega. 'Unfortunately Lewis & you were both away', Gore explained. 'But I saw Duncan Grant, explained the offer to him, asked him to ask you to communicate with the agent, left the aforementioned booklet, and have since been rather surprised to have heard nothing from you whether or not you were going to do it, and still more surprised when I saw Lewis the other day and he told me the room was being done & found he did not know he was one of the people who had been asked to do it.' This letter appears to constitute a damning indictment of Fry's behaviour; and the latter's failure to give Gore any explanation in his reply beyond the rather tame invitation to 'come round to the Omega' because 'I can explain it easier than in writing'[36] would seem to compound Fry's guilt.

But it is not as simple as that. Grant, for one, was later prepared to concede that 'it may have been my fault – I was supposed to have received the message from Gore but I really can't remember now'.[37] And none of the surviving letters explains why Gore himself failed to obtain written confirmation of the commission from the *Mail* with which to denounce Fry. Vanessa Bell, who had taken over the Omega in Fry's absence, did precisely that immediately she heard of the situation, and the *Mail*'s reply has been preserved to prove that 'the commission to furnish and decorate a room at Olympia was given by the *Daily Mail* to Mr Roger Fry without any conditions as to the artists he would employ'.[38] This letter, written by the Secretary of the Ideal Home exhibition on 22 October, would accord with the anonymous nature of all the work produced at the Omega; but Gore's assurance that he, Lewis and Fry were asked to share the commission cannot be doubted. Perhaps there was some administrative confusion at the *Mail* whereby its art critic, Konody, set two officials to work who acted independently of each other. Or possibly the *Mail* itself changed its mind after giving a promise to Gore.

The truth will never be known now, for the *Mail*'s archives were completely destroyed in 1940. It seems ridiculous to imagine that Fry consciously plotted to exclude the other two: they could so easily have exposed him, if their story was correct, by asking the *Mail* for proof. But Lewis's persecution mania ensured that nothing half so sensible was done. The two rivals never had a reasoned discussion about the controversy; instead, Lewis preferred to snatch up the pretext afforded by Gore's testimony and stage a vituperative demonstration against everything Fry stood for. 'You will hardly expect me to be amused at these tricks and contrivances, or wish to remain longer in the vicinity of a bad shit', Lewis snapped in an October letter to Clive Bell, adding in another letter soon afterwards that Fry 'has some vulgar nasty, mean crookedness in his nature, that has left a trail of particular unsavouriness in his life'.[39] Faced with such overheated calumny, Fry maintained a studied calm. 'I have tried to treat Lewis with every consideration', he told Gore in a letter on 5 October, 'but I fear nothing I can do comes up to his ideal of what is due to him. He has left saying he will never come back which I knew must happen sooner or later.'[40] The Ideal Home crisis made it happen sooner than either of them had expected.

The final form of the 'Room' created for the exhibition, which ran from 9 to 25 October, served to widen the rift between the two parties even further. In a letter to the Press issued by Gore and Lewis along with the 'Round Robin', they hotly affirmed that 'the artists signing this letter wish to repudiate the pallid Charivari of what they should have done to be found among other Idealities at Olympia, and in defence of their own work, wish to publicly state that they had no hand in the decoration of this room'.[41] Their emphatic denial of any responsibility for the 'Room' was scarcely surprising, for the official Ideal Home catalogue described it simply as a 'sitting room decorated and furnished by the Omega Workshops Ltd. The walls are decorated in distemper by various artists working together on the general theme of designs based on the movements of the dance'.[42] No wonder Lewis and his friends did not wish to be involved in a project so curtly referred to as the work of 'various artists'! The only name mentioned in the catalogue was Fry's, and the rebels no longer had any patience with an organization that shrouded their identity under the blanket of another man's fame.

The rift was made even more unbridgeable by a subsidiary accusation in the 'Round Robin', which claimed that Fry had also withheld from Etchells and Lewis some letters from Frank Rutter inviting them to show at an important West End mixed exhibition. 'A second unpleasant fact is the suppression of information in order to prevent a member from exhibiting in a Show of Pictures *not* organised by the Direction of the Omega', the circular declared. 'Mr Rutter, the Curator of the Leeds Art Gallery, in organising a Post-Impressionist Exhibition in Bond Street, wrote to Mr Fry some weeks ago. In this letter he asked for Mr Etchells' address, wanting some of his work for the Exhibition. He was given to understand that Mr Etchells had no pictures ready and would have none till 1914. This statement of Mr Fry's was not only unauthorised but untrue. It is curious that a letter from Mr Rutter to Mr Lewis on the same subject, and addressed to the Omega Workshops, should never have reached him.' Heady allegations indeed, and this time it seems that Fry's practical incompetence was to blame, for he wrote to Lewis on 10 October apologising for his mistake. 'I find this afternoon in packing up to go away the letter from Mr Rutter of which you spoke', he confessed. 'I never saw it till now (can only suppose that you left it about and that it got put away by things). If this was due to my carelessness and want of method, I am extremely sorry.'[43] His frank admission was by this time too late to repair the damage: in fact, it probably confirmed the rebels' deep mistrust of Fry and all his activities.

Even Etchells, who of all the malcontents had once been the closest to Fry and the Bloomsbury circle, was now adamant in his opposition. 'I decided that we had better see Etchells', Vanessa Bell wrote to Fry around 12 October, '& try to get him to see that whether they were right or not they had behaved monstrously in writing this letter without first accusing you to your face. We went to see him this afternoon & talked for nearly 2 hours. He . . . could hardly be made to see our point at all. When he did see it he simply said that he didn't agree. He brought up a long tale of grievances of how he had gradually become convinced against his will of your meanness. Evidently he had been storing up small things which had at last been brought to a point by this. It is all such a muddle that one couldn't convince him of anything. But I don't think either he or the others will give in at all, or that there is any use in trying to get them to.'[44] She was right: Etchells and his fellow protesters had made their final decision weeks before, and nothing would now divert them from their commitment to a course drastically at odds with the one pursued by the Omega Workshops.

The 'rumpus' was inevitable, since both Lewis and Fry wanted to use their natural talent for leadership to place themselves at the head of the English avant-garde. 'It was generally admitted that Roger Fry was without doubt *the* high priest of art of the day', recalled Paul Nash, 'and could and did make artistic reputations overnight.'[45] Lewis was not prepared to accept this hegemony indefinitely, and acquaintanceship with Fry must have made him realize that their respective outlooks would never coincide. While Fry's aesthetic ideal was based on the legacy of Cézanne, resisting total abstraction as a practical ideal and abhorring any form of deliberately self-seeking publicity, Lewis and his friends were attracted by extremism and shared the Futurists' determination to furnish themselves with radical reputations by any means they could devise. A sense of tradition was pitched against a need for iconoclasm; a regard for sensibility and cultivation clashed with the desire for virility and action; and a preference for pacific insights was flatly in contradiction with a thirst for aggressive discordance. On all three counts Fry's world diverged from Lewis's, and as soon as they realized the full extent of their differences it was obvious that war would have to be declared. Both men wanted their own particular viewpoint to triumph, and they were prepared to brook the fiercest hostility to achieve that end. They even visited Gertrude Stein, on separate occasions, to justify their own behaviour in the affair: she recalled in her autobiography how she had 'particularly liked [Lewis] one day when he came in and told all about his quarrel with Roger Fry. Roger Fry had come in not many days before and had already told all about it. They told exactly the same story only it was different, very different'.

Although the Bloomsbury faction chose not to retaliate with the weapons Lewis had employed, Clive Bell did nevertheless pen a letter that was in its own haughty way just as devastating as anything Lewis had concocted. 'There may be plenty that's irritating, or at any rate vexatious in Roger Fry', he wrote to Lewis sometime in October, 'but he's not that sort: you're wrong. And anyway', he continued, warming to his theme, 'whatever you think of him and his doing you ought not to bombard the town with pages of suburban rhetoric. The vulgarity of the thing! And the provincialism! That's what I mind. You don't belong to the suburbs, so what the devil are you doing there?'[46] This withering disapproval seems to have had its effect on the unstable part of Lewis's personality, for Vanessa Bell reported on an extraordinary encounter between him and her husband in a letter written to Fry on 13 October. 'Clive went out this afternoon & in Bond Street whom should he run into but Lewis, who came forward and said "I hope you're not very much upset!" ' she wrote, and proceeded to describe an interview that makes Lewis out to be little more than a charlatan. 'They then had a long talk walking about Bond St. & Piccadilly. Lewis explained that he had had to use politics to defend himself, that he had his way to make etc. . . . Lewis then tried to put all the blame of the letter on the others & said it wasn't the sort of thing he liked doing. "I hope my colleagues were not hurt by any remarks about Prettiness", he said. *He* had not wished to put in that sort of thing.'

How can it be believed that Lewis would ever have retracted his criticisms of the Omega with such miserable dishonesty? Either Vanessa Bell enjoyed herself by embroidering on the facts, or else Lewis must be judged nothing less than a schizophrenic, a turncoat who did not possess the courage of his own convictions. 'Clive seems to have made him feel rather foolish', she continued, '& found out that they are all longing for you to reply. Lewis was very much disappointed that you had not rushed back from France at once! What they would really like would be an action for libel. It seems quite clear now that the best thing is to do nothing.'[47] Whether or not this letter stands as an accurate account of Lewis's behaviour – and even Vanessa Bell admits later on that 'Clive wants me to say that you musn't think that Lewis was really in at all a conciliatory mood to start with' – it does represent the kind of tactics Bloomsbury could employ when they found themselves threatened. In public, they all heeded Vanessa Bell's advice and remained silent; but in private, Grant felt able to tell Fry that 'I'm perfectly sure the whole thing was engineered by Lewis simply to advertise himself and that he made use of the others to bring about a general strike'.[48] There was no question of asking themselves whether or not the criticisms in the 'Round Robin' possessed the smallest atom of truth. Instead, Fry replied to Grant in a similar vein, declaring his suspicion 'that Lewis has never been in the Omega except for what he could get out of it, and that even before we came back from Italy he had formed a "cave". I quite agree with you about Etchells; I always thought he would act on rather romantic impulses. The only thing is that I personally find it a little hard to think that he could turn so completely against me after having been so very friendly, and without ever listening to me. But I really want to help him and I quite expect that when he's seen the thing in a more reasonable way we shall be able to'.[49]

Fry's hopes were unfounded: he did not seem to understand that the main purpose of the 'Round Robin' lay in enabling Lewis and his allies to assert their control over events rather than taking orders from a paternalistic authority in Fitzroy Square. 'Fry bossed the show there', Etchells remembered. 'It was his money and his enterprise, but as far as Lewis was concerned there could only be one real boss. He persuaded me to walk out: I didn't care very much, but it was true that Fry paid very little. He came from a rich family and we were all broke – his complacency wasn't always very palatable to an impecunious artist.'[50] Neither was his insistence on the Omega's communal anonymity. Only Fry could possibly become generally known through such a system, and Lewis's group was by now certain enough of its own ability to resent this ruling. Despite the determined attempt of the 'Round Robin' to make London understand that the rebels considered themselves superior to the Omega, the Press persisted in thinking of them as minions of the Workshops even in December 1913, when Wadsworth wrote a furious postcard to Lewis complaining that 'a disgraceful paragraph has appeared in a Yorkshire paper saying that we are the "disciples" of Mr. Roger F. It refers to us as the "Omega group", if you please'.[51] Such misplaced aspersions were an unbearable torment to the rebels, who were struggling to break away from Bloomsbury and establish their own alternative movement in its stead.

What they needed in order to assert their own corporate identity was an English Marinetti: someone who could publicize their work on the grand scale and shout into the ears of London a rousing proclamation of their artistic ideals. Roberts, looking back on the events of that year, stated the situation with waspish precision. 'It was the impact of the manifestos of the Italian Futurist poet Marinetti upon him, that made Lewis realise how valuable a manifesto of his own would be to himself', he wrote. 'Fry was the first to feel the force of this new weapon; it was inevitable that sooner or later he would be served with a manifesto; as an ally he was too powerful for the comfort of someone aiming at a leading role in the English revolutionary art movement.'[52] If Lewis's activities cannot in fairness be viewed – despite Roberts' retrospective accusations – as one long political machination, it is still possible to watch him training himself for the role he desired. Winifred Gill, one of his colleagues at the Omega, considered that 'at this time Wyndham Lewis was building up what would now be called a public "image"', and she remembered someone telling her that Lewis ' "had all the airs of a maître d'école without being one". He took great pains over the business'.

Just how great can be gauged from Miss Gill's description of Lewis at the Omega, 'wearing a large black sombrero and his great coat and jacket were open showing the very first royal blue shirt I had seen', bragging about the number of letters he received 'every day . . . mostly from women', and talking to friends like Wadsworth and Etchells about the latest exhibitions, his conversation punctuated frequently by 'a portentous intake of breath issuing in a rich deliberate speech'. Most extraordinary of all, however, is her memory of an incident which shows Lewis preparing like a meticulous and irredeemably self-conscious actor for the part he now wanted to play. Miss Gill was resting alone one afternoon on a bed in the back showroom when Lewis suddenly burst in and, without noticing her, drew 'an outsize cloth cap, at least a foot across and made of a large black and white check material', out of a paper bag. Trying it on in front of the mirror over the mantelpiece, 'he cocked it slightly to one side to his satisfaction, then, taking a few steps backward, raised his hand as though to shake hands with someone and approached the mirror with an ingratiating smile. He backed again and tried the effect of a sudden recognition with a look of surprised pleasure. Then cocking the cap at a more dashing angle his face froze and he turned and glanced over his shoulder as if at someone standing there with a look of scorn and disgust. As you may imagine I was in a state of petrifaction lest he should see me. I felt sure that he would strangle me. I pretended to be asleep but I couldn't help peeping'.[53] Eventually, to her 'great relief', Lewis left the room; but only after having convincingly demonstrated how he viewed himself, in his most private moments, as a fully rehearsed tactician ready to participate in the arena of London art politics.

One of his first manoeuvres following the Omega rumpus was to approach yet another ex-student of the Slade: Nevinson, a self-confessed Marinetti admirer who had not so far been officially approached by Lewis, remembered receiving a letter from the English rebel leader asking him 'to join [Lewis's] party against Fry and the Omega workshop. To quote his letter, he felt that Fry was a "shark in aesthetic waters and in any case only a survival of the greenery-yallery nineties". I found Lewis the most brilliant theorist I had ever met. He was charming, and I shall always look back with gratitude to the enchanted time I spent with him'.[54]

This fulsome tribute, from the man who was eventually to find himself attacked with the savagery already inflicted on Fry, is a remarkable testimony to a quality in Lewis's character which is all too easily forgotten. Alongside his seemingly unlimited capacity for hostility, Lewis possessed a talent for friendship that rarely failed to impress and win over people with whom he wished to ally himself. He had immense personal charm, and Nevinson was sufficiently captivated by it to become for a time one of his staunchest admirers. The young ex-student of the Slade was by now alienated from Fry, anyway: Grant recalled that 'Nevinson was violently against Fry because of some phrase Fry had used when criticising his paintings – "literary", or something like that'.[55] And so it was logical that in October 1913, the very same month in which Lewis's cohorts had deserted the Omega, Nevinson should conspire to invite Marinetti over to London for another triumphal round of lectures and demonstrations. 'Marinetti . . . thought of coming to England', Nevinson recounted later, 'and told Severini, who wrote to me about him. I asked Severini to persuade him to come.'[56]

The Futurist leader had plenty of incentive for a return visit. There were distinct signs that a group of young English artists were prepared to espouse his cause, and support for the movement was rapidly growing among London's literati as well. The September 1913 issue of *Poetry and Drama* magazine was devoted exclusively to a discussion of the merits of Futurism, and its editor, Harold Monro, boldly declared that 'our motives are two fold. Firstly, a movement which has obtained such wide notoriety legitimately demands study and consideration – secondly, we claim ourselves, also, to be Futurist'.[57] After such a startling display of loyalty, this special issue proceeded to examine Futurist poetry, review Marinetti's ceaseless activities and reproduce the complete text of his new manifesto, 'Wireless Imagination and Words in Liberty'. The Italian propagandist wanted to return to London so urgently that Monro was able to announce proudly to his readers that 'on the eve of going to press, unfortunately too late to report in this number, the Editor had an interview . . . with Signor Marinetti in Milan. The leader of the Italian Futurist movement expressed his intention of visiting England on a campaign of Active Propaganda next November'.[58]

Small wonder, after such a rousing accolade, that Marinetti did indeed fulfil his promise and hurry over to London in November. The excitement among the rebel artists was intense. 'Nevinson wants to get up a dinner for Marinetti who is coming to London [on] November 14th for six days', Wadsworth's wife wrote to

Lewis on 4 November. 'I think it would be a good thing to do – if you think so, communicate with him.'[59] Lewis obviously agreed with Nevinson's plan, for Marinetti found himself fêted at a dinner organized in his honour at the Florence Restaurant on 18 November.[60] The banquet, organized by a committee consisting of Etchells, Hamilton, Lewis, Nevinson and Wadsworth, was a sensation. 'It was an extraordinary affair', Nevinson remembered fondly. 'Marinetti recited a poem about the siege of Adrianople, with various kinds of onomatopoeic noises and crashes in free verse, while all the time a band downstairs played, "You made me love you. I didn't want to do it".' And once this unforgettable performance had been completed, Marinetti went on to impress the company with his ideas and prodigious energy. 'Most people had come to laugh', admitted Nevinson, 'but there were few who were not overwhelmed by the dynamic personality and declamatory gifts of the Italian propagandist.' The rest of the evening did not, however, proceed according to the original plan. 'I made a short speech in French', Nevinson recalled, 'and Lewis followed, then jealousy began to show its head. Marinetti knew of me through Severini and he understood my French better, so he paid more attention to me. He did not know, poor fellow, that he was wrecking a friendship that promised well.'[61]

Marinetti's partiality for Nevinson must have been particularly galling to Lewis, in view of his burgeoning ambitions to lead the English avant-garde. And he would have been stung still further by a note from Nevinson the day after the Florence dinner, which revealed that 'I had quite a great deal of difficulty in preventing Marinetti from again expounding and proposing his philanthropic desire to present us to Europe and be our continental guide, etc.'[62] He, Lewis, should be the one to whom Marinetti addressed such overtures, even if it was unlikely that the majority of English rebels were ever seriously tempted by the prospect of becoming affiliated with the Futurists. They had, after all, recently been at pains to dissociate themselves from Fry's discipleship, and to run under Marinetti's protective wings might be too much like exchanging one form of paternalism for another. Their hard-won independence had to be maintained, and from that safe distance Lewis felt free to admire the Futurist leader's ebullience. Around the time of the Florence dinner, he was moved to confess to a friend that 'I was sorry you did not come to the Cabaret Club last night, as Marinetti declaimed some peculiarly bloodthirsty concoctions with great dramatic force'. Patently excited by the unabashed violence of Marinetti's onslaught upon English sensibilities, he even went so far as to advertise for the Italian in a fairly insistent manner, urging his correspondent to attend Marinetti's lecture 'at the Doré Galleries at 8.45 on Thursday evening next. He will not, there, enter into direct rivalry with the Grand Guignol, I imagine; but will no doubt be worth hearing. I enclose you a handbill of the affair'.[63]

Lewis probably regarded Marinetti's performances with the same delight he had earlier reserved for the antics of itinerant Breton clowns. 'When I first was present at a lecture of his', Lewis remembered, 'I accompanied him afterwards in a taxicab to the Café Royal. "Il faut une force de poumon épouvantable pour faire ça!" he explained to me, wiping the perspiration off his neck, and striking himself upon the chest-wall.'[64] Here was somebody essentially larger than life, who escaped from what Lewis considered to be Fry's enfeebled backwater and glorified the new mechanical century. 'Marinetti, when reciting his own poems, used an amount of energy that was astonishing', wrote Epstein, 'pouring with perspiration, and the veins swelling, almost to bursting point, on his forehead. Altogether an unpleasant sight.'[65] It was a true case of the medium being the message: the poems were themselves the verbal equivalent of their author's bodily exertions.

[145]

verde   sangue   **tza . tzu   tatatatatata**   la
gomena   puzzare   fumare   **errrr   prac-prac**
troppo   tardi   inferno   al   diavolo   il   ponte
angolo   ottuso   arco   teso   gonfiare   il   suo
ventre   **apriiiiirsi   aaaaahi   patapum-**
**patatraack**   maledizione   cana-
glia   canaglia   gridare   gridare   urlare   muggire
**scoppio   di   cuori   turchi**   squar-
ciagola   sfrangiarsi   scapigliamento   di   **hurr-**
**rrrrraaah**   **tatatatatata   hurrrrrraaah**
**tatatatata   PUUM   PAMPAM   PLUFF**
**zang-tumb-tumb**   **hurrrrraaah   ta-**
**tatatatata   hurrrraaah**

ran one of the most spectacular items in Marinetti's volume of poetry entitled *Zang Tumb Tuuum*[66], using *parole in libertà* with an uninhibited verve which Vorticism would soon employ, and in performance it must have had a shattering effect upon his audience. 'A day of attack upon the Western Front', Lewis insisted later, 'with all the "heavies" hammering together, right back to the horizon, was nothing' in comparison with Marinetti's 'unaided voice.'[67] And if one man could achieve so much with his vocal chords, what could a properly organized rebel army not do to awaken English art from its insular slumbers? This was the challenge which Lewis, freed from the restraining influence of the Omega, now had to meet.

# Chapter 5: The Formulation of a Rebel Group at the October 1913 Exhibition

The autumn of 1913 was, in many different ways, a decisive period for the evolution of the Vorticist movement. Not only had Fry been ousted from the rebels' affections and Marinetti honoured as a rival worthy of the name: Frank Rutter also proceeded to launch his *Post-Impressionist and Futurist Exhibition* at the Doré Galleries in October.[1] His letters inviting Lewis and Etchells to partake in the show had, of course, been mislaid in the Omega debacle; but both artists were duly represented in a survey that pinpointed for the first time a concerted group of Englishmen reacting to Cubism and Futurism. Rutter, who as curator of Leeds Art Gallery, editor of the periodical *Art News* and author of an outspoken 1910 book on *Revolutionary Art* was one of the more enlightened critics of his day, stated quite factually in his catalogue foreword that 'this exhibition is an attempt to set forth in a coherent and so far as possible in a chronological order examples of various schools of painting which have made some noise in the world during the last quarter of a century'. More significantly, he called attention to the young rebels as some kind of putative group, probably the first time they had been so acknowledged in the public world of gallery exhibitions. 'That "cubism" and "futurism" have already stirred English artists', he wrote, 'is shown by the contributions of Mr Wyndham Lewis, Mr Wadsworth, Mr Nevinson and others.'[2]

Those 'others' were Epstein, Etchells and Hamilton; and although pitifully few of their exhibits can be traced today, it has proved possible to reconstruct some of their contributions by piecing together the evidence contained in fugitive press reviews and illustrations. One of Wadsworth's most intriguing exhibits, for instance, now exists only as a small reproduction in *The Graphic*, and the article accompanying it was typical of the flippant response these paintings received from the critics. After branding them as 'English imitators of the Futurists', it went on to declare that 'the gallery is stacked with them; and we are rather sorry for the British public which is trying to take them in. It is the painters who are doing that'.[3] Even more scornful was the attitude of the *Daily Sketch*, which reproduced a selection of the pictures under a screaming banner headline. 'You Wouldn't Think These Were Paintings, Would You?' it asked, so confident of its readers' response that it juggled the illustrations around on the page to add to the fun. 'In order to show that it doesn't matter', ran the gleeful caption, 'we have used one of these photographs sideways and the other two upside down.'[4]

As it happened, *The Graphic* was perfectly correct in assuming that Wadsworth had fallen under the influence of Futurism. After leaving the Slade in 1912, he married and travelled on the continent for six months, going first to Madeira and Las Palmas – where he painted a number of small panels – and then moving on to Paris, addressing himself there to the execution of landscapes on the outskirts of the city. As luck would have it, two paintings from this period still exist: a crude but fiercely coloured Fauvist study of *La Baule* and the *Landscape, Grand Canary*, which was inspired by the scenery he and his wife enjoyed on their honeymoon in April and May. The style of the Canary picture inaugurates a notable shift away from the Gilmanesque preoccupations of the *Violet Wallis* portrait, the latest of his extant Slade works. Working out of doors made his brushwork become notably more free in the foreground, interspersed as it is with a scattering of irregular coloured dabs. But this gives way in its turn to the more solidly modelled forms of the hills behind, where a sensitive feeling for the play of light is revealed in the subtly gradated areas of sunshine and shadow. There is still very little that can be pinned down as an individual artistic personality; the allegiance to Gilman has been replaced by an equally overt debt to a lyrical landscapist like Innes, many of whose studies were carried out in a similarly romantic range of mauves and purples. Only the structural

Edward Wadsworth
*La Baule, Brittany*, 1912

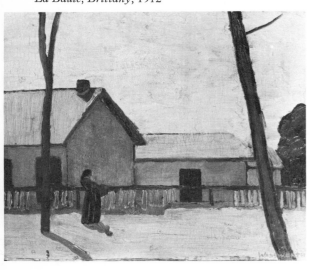

austerity and the flatness of the design as a whole suggest that Wadsworth was capable of trying out ideas which Innes would never have wanted to attempt; but he does not seem to have moved any further towards an avant-garde standpoint by the end of 1912. Even when Fry decided to honour him by showing two of his pictures in the final month of the Post-Impressionist Exhibition in January 1913, Wadsworth's offerings appear to have been relatively straightforward and undemanding.[5] *The Times*, noting that 'a number of pictures have been added to the Post-Impressionist Exhibition', singled out his lost *Viaduct* as 'novel only in [its] unaffected simplicity'[6] – suggesting a painting comparable with the pleasing modesty of the *Canary* landscape.

Inclusion in the Post-Impressionist show meant that Wadsworth, for the time being, went out of his way to support Fry. When the critic found himself under attack in January 1913 for a merciless review of Alma-Tadema's memorial exhibition, in which he had asked how long it would take 'to disinfect the Order of Merit of Tadema's scented soap', Wadsworth wrote to *The Nation* and protested that 'everyone who is sincerely interested in the aims and spirit of modern art will have thanked Mr Fry for having so vigorously and lucidly defined Sir Alma Tadema's position'.[7] But the 'aims and spirit of modern art' defended in this letter only began to enter Wadsworth's own work a little later that year, when he based a series of watercolours on a woodland setting near Lewes in Sussex.[8] One of them, which has here been entitled *Pool in Forest*, is clearly inscribed '1913', and thereby gives an authoritative date for the others as well.[9] All the watercolours show Wadsworth exploring the language of early Cubism, using Cézanne in much the same way as Picasso and Braque had done several years before to simplify the components of his chosen landscape into schematic forms.

*Pool with Trees and Punt*, the most assured and elaborate of the entire group, can probably be related to the watercolour listed as *The River* in Rutter's exhibition.[10] It summarizes the avenue of trees overhanging the water with crisp precision, forcing them to merge with their reflections into an overall pattern of thrusting poles. Arcs created by the branches are everywhere deftly contrasted with these severe diagonals so that a sophisticated geometrical interplay results; but Wadsworth is still too fond of incidental detail to eliminate the moored punt and the latticed window of the house in the background from his architectonic

Edward Wadsworth
*Landscape, Grand Canary*, 1912

◁ Edward Wadsworth
*Pool with Trees and Punt*, 1913

▽ Edward Wadsworth
*Pool in Forest*, 1913

△ Edward Wadsworth
*The Farmyard, c.* 1913

▷ Edward Wadsworth
*Trees Beside River,* 1913

design. Another extant watercolour called *Trees Beside River*, which must also have been included in Rutter's show, repeats this balance between representation and abstraction so slavishly that Wadsworth might have been tempted to slip into a stylistic formula.[11] These fears are quickly allayed, however, when a watercolour of *The Farmyard* is examined.[12] For the main elements in this composition have now been allowed to stand on their own, uninterrupted by any extraneous description: the foreground tree-trunk, its branches and the ground on which it stands are treated as one solid mass of dark blue, while the buildings grouped around the pool beyond are pared down to a minimal combination of outlines and pale washes.

Yet it must be said that a picture like *The Farmyard* represents a provincial attempt by a young English artist to catch up with principles established in Paris long ago. And the critic of *The New Age* seemed to realize this in his comment on *The Farmyard*, describing it as 'a drawing made before an actual landscape, in which the planes which interested the artist are given *in* the objects in which they occurred. But it is easy to see how this emphasis on the relation between planes inevitably developed into later cubism, where the planes are given without any representation of the objects which suggested them'.[13] It took Wadsworth some time to progress along the path laid out by *The New Age*'s critic: a lost painting which can perhaps be entitled *Sussex Farm* still clings to the type of Cubist landscape which Picasso was executing at Horta de Ebro as early as 1909.[14] There is, all the same, an incipient sense of movement in this composition which implies that Wadsworth had decided to introduce Futurist dynamics into his pastoral Cubist language. Dark lines and wedges of paint suddenly isolate themselves from their context within the scene they help to construct and dart off on anarchic journeys, filling the picture with restless abstract rhythms which threaten to leave the ostensible subject far behind. Wadsworth's subscription during the latter half of 1913 to *Les Soirées de Paris* – which included many illustrations of Picabia's work – may have helped him understand the latest developments in Europe more fully; but there can be little doubt that his contact with Lewis at the Omega must also have encouraged him to become more daring. Progress is even more clearly evident in his lost painting of a *Sandpit*, where the familiar early Cubist forms of roofs and walls

Edward Wadsworth
*Sussex Farm* (?), *c.* 1913

are incorporated into a spatially ambiguous environment.[15] A railway track curves past the buildings in the foreground with scant regard for perspectival recession, and this hint of a one-dimensional pattern is confirmed in the treatment of the trucks. The whole composition, with its tilted, swaying angles and mysterious aerial viewpoint, moves away from external appearances towards a reliance on the vitality of shapes in their own right. Nowhere is this more evident than in the complex of diagonal planes at the top of the picture, carrying the rocking rhythms of trucks and houses through into an area of intense abstract activity. *The Sandpit* is a transitional work, where Wadsworth is seen escaping from the stability and uncomplicated angles of vision employed in his previous landscapes in order to exploit a freewheeling form of semi-abstraction.

Whether the painting of *Adam and Eve* he exhibited at Rutter's show took this process any further is impossible to tell: it has been lost, and the sarcastic descriptions recorded by press reviews do not really help to ascertain its appearance. 'Our Irreverent Critic', writing in one daily newspaper, considered that Wadsworth 'really ought not to take such liberties when he goes in for ancestral portraiture. Adam looks like a negro boxer, and Eve's figure is so bad that no intelligent serpent would have noticed her at all. He would just have thought that she was a piece of gate-post that had blown off in a gale'.[16] Although the reference to a gate-post surely implies an advanced degree of abstraction, *Adam and Eve* must remain a matter for conjecture alone; but luckily enough a contemporary photograph does still exist to record the appearance of *L'Omnibus*, perhaps Wadsworth's most ambitious contribution to Rutter's exhibition.[17] And it reveals that he here finally departed altogether from the rural lyricism of his earlier landscapes to embrace the mechanical life of the city recommended by the Futurists.

The urban involvement of *L'Omnibus* coincides wholeheartedly with the sentiments expressed by Severini when he held a London one-man show the previous April at the Marlborough Gallery. In an interview with the *Daily Express* which Wadsworth may well have read and sympathized with, Severini described the experience of his first train-ride in England. 'And then the hideous prettiness of the panorama (the delight of landscape painters) has been replaced at the end of my journey by the city, the violent affirmation of human activity,' declared the Italian, usefully outlining Wadsworth's progress from the forest scenes to *L'Omnibus*. 'The elements of nature are being overtaken by inevitable destruction', he continued in a dogmatic, Marinettian vein, 'and must give place to the mechanical ingenuity of man'. Severini even went on to appeal to British painters, claiming that 'the essentially masculine spirit of the English people ought to understand our exhaltation of strength and energy, and also the inexplicable inner force that drives us to the study of the phenomena of human activity in the modern world'. And he concluded with a command which Wadsworth was to follow up in his 1913 paintings, ordering artists to 'put away your knowledge of the exterior appearance of things, for that knowledge is very far from the ideal and complex truths towards which our efforts tend'.[18]

Wadsworth might not have entirely agreed with Severini's extremist desire for iconoclasm, but he was sufficiently impressed by Futurist theories to select a subject that directly reflected the preoccupations of the Italian's London one-man show. The first painting listed in the catalogue of Severini's Marlborough Gallery exhibition was likewise entitled *The Motor Bus*, and Wadsworth's choice of a similar theme was surely more than a coincidence. Indeed, Severini's description of *The Motor Bus* in his catalogue provides a much more accurate summary of *L'Omnibus* than his own picture: 'it has been my endeavour to produce by means of lines and planes the rhythmic sensation of speed, of spasmodic motion, and of deafening noise', he wrote. 'The heavy vehicle pursues

Edward Wadsworth
*The Sandpit, c.* 1913

Edward Wadsworth
*L'Omnibus,* 1913

Adrian Allinson
*The Futurist Wadsworth, c.* 1913–14

its headlong career from Montmartre to Montrouge along the crowded streets of Paris, dashing across the path of other motors, grazing their very wheels and hurling itself in the direction of the houses.'

But if *L'Omnibus* places its engine and coaches in a welter of confused, colliding planes that possess a brutality and violence foreign to Severini's more orderly *Motor Bus*, it is nevertheless directly comparable with another Futurist painting shown in London the previous year. At the great Sackville Gallery exhibition, Carrà displayed a hectic picture called *What I Was Told by the Tramcar*, and its dislocated kaleidoscope of urban bustle has exactly the same intention and effect as *L'Omnibus*.[19] Carrà's sharp angles and blocklike forms betray a link with Cubism, as does *L'Omnibus* itself, but the central feeling of both paintings – jerky, discordant, syncopated – corresponds well with a celebrated Futurist manifesto edict: 'the motor-bus rushes into the houses which it passes, and in their turn the houses throw themselves upon the motor-bus and are blended with it.'[20] Wadsworth appears to have aimed at providing nothing less than a literal illustration of this passage. If his forms are not as blurred as the figures in Carrà's painting, he still ensures that every element in his design hurtles into its neighbours with such force that the omnibus itself is barely distinguishable from its turbulent surroundings. The change of sensibility within the space of one year, from the Canary Islands landscape to this clangorous celebration of twentieth century speed and force, had been as swift as it was dramatic. *L'Omnibus* signified Wadsworth's espousal of a truly modern pictorial vocabulary, and his friend Adrian Allinson marked this artistic coming-of-age by caricaturing him in a witty cartoon called *The Futurist Wadsworth*.

Nevinson, similarly, did his best to make his work adhere to the Futurist cause which had first attracted him at the Slade. Soon after departing from the School in 1912, he returned to Paris until the following spring, studying hard both at *Julian*'s and the *Cercle Russe*. His admiration for Severini's exhibits at the Sackville Gallery show had already led to a meeting with the Italian painter over lunch with Fry and Clive Bell; and the acquaintance was cemented in Paris.[21] 'Through Titi, the clown, I had formed a friendship with Severini', he wrote, and this new contact enabled him to be introduced to a whole range of Cubists and Futurists.[22] 'Severini had painted his "Danse de Pompom" [*sic*] at the Monico', he remembered, 'and through him I came to know Boccioni, Soffici, and, later, Modigliani. I was also on nodding terms with Kisling. Most of these painters were desperately poor, but I was certainly in the *milieu*, and we used to sit and listen to Appolinaire [*sic*].'[23] He got to know advanced Parisian circles so intimately that 'for some time I shared a studio with Modigliani. He was a quiet man of charming manners and I knew him as well as, if not better than, most men'.[24]

But it was Cubism that first succeeded in arousing his interest, and he found it in retrospect 'impossible to describe the worry, the doubts, which this form of technique gave rise to. I felt the power of this first phase of Cubism and there was a desire in me to reach that dignity which can be conveyed pictorially by the abstract rather than by the particular. So often I had spoiled pictures by elaborating them'.[25] His words virtually echoed Desmond MacCarthy's earlier advocacy of an ideal 'synthesis in design' in the 1910 Post-Impressionist Exhibition catalogue, and the bracing aesthetic challenge posed by his experiences in Paris prompted Nevinson to rethink his entire standpoint. 'It was a period of intense study', he explained, 'and I must have examined literally hundreds and hundreds of pictures. I was like a man in any other walk in life who is struck suddenly by a truth which he has always known to be at the back of his mind, and I was altering my standards accordingly.'[26]

Christopher Nevinson
*Les Fortifications de Paris*, 1912–13

The 22-year-old artist was undergoing a formative crisis, and the first fruits of his new stylistic experiments were necessarily tentative and uneasy. A painting like *Les Fortifications de Paris* shows him discarding his cherished Impressionism in favour of a far less beguiling form of simplification.[27] The shimmering effects of light so characteristic of his earlier *Charenton* landscape have now given way to a crude emphasis on the structure of the scene. Its main compositional outlines following roads, embankments, trees and houses are stressed earnestly, even clumsily; and all sense of atmosphere has been banished in favour of a dry, flat indication of the essential pattern. Impressionism lingers on in the brush-work of the pathways straggling across the foreground slope, but Nevinson is trying hard to counteract spatial recession and bring his entire design flush with the surface of the canvas. Naïve, toy-like windows stand out of the houses with a complete lack of regard for the haze or distance he had dwelt on so lovingly before, and they give the painting something of the clear-eyed innocence of the Douanier Rousseau. Nevinson, in fact, recalled seeing 'the strange land-scapes of Rousseau' on his first trip to Paris – he also attended a number of 'the Saturday Salons of Gertrude Stein, where I first heard the name of Picasso'[28] – but the resemblance is in reality a superficial one. Far more germane are the contemporaneous landscapes of a minor Cubist like Jean Marchand: Nevinson later revealed that a Marchand painting, 'of the roofs of Montmartre with an Indian-red factory chimney, made an astonishing impression on me'.[29] If *Les Fortifications de Paris* appears hopelessly immature beside Marchand's brisk organization of form, it still possesses a brashness that hints at the more ad-venturous experiments to follow.

Nevinson was as prolific as he was gregarious, and *Les Fortifications* was probably only one of a great number of similar studies finished with great speed in Paris. As he himself recorded, 'a great deal of my time was spent on the Fortifications, in La Villette, and on the Buttes Chaumont'.[30] And something of his hasty impatience can be discerned in Nevinson's own description of his professional method when he recorded that 'I did not paint much from nature then, but hung round the Gare St. Lazare, the Gare du Nord, the Seine, and the outskirts of Paris, working on quick sketches and inventing a new formula for myself'.[31] His choice of the word 'formula' is oddly appropriate, for Nevin-

Christopher Nevinson
*The Viaduct, Issy les Moulineaux*, 1912–13

Christopher Nevinson
*Waiting for the Robert E. Lee, c.* 1913

son's way was always to seize on a convention and make it more immediately comprehensible to a wider cross-section of the public. In one sense, he was following in the footsteps of his famous journalist father, who 'had reacted against the purely literary coteries of London and worshipped the Man of Action. I myself have this hereditary trait, and the conflict is always within me'.[32] *Les Fortifications* suffers from that conflict, torn as it is between a desire for comprehensible description and an equally strong wish to assimilate the lessons of early Cubism. The product is an embarrassing compromise, just as another surviving painting of *The Viaduct*[33] is an almost academic travesty of Cubist principles; but Nevinson was soon to probe deeper into the implications of the new theories with which he was confronted in Paris.

The friendship with Severini and other Paris-based Futurists he met in France began to bear fruit. In the Friday Club Exhibition of January 1913 he displayed an untraced picture entitled *The Rising City*; and its link with Boccioni's celebrated canvas, shown at the Sackville Gallery as *The Rising City*, must have been more than merely coincidental.[34] Nevinson doubtless intended it as an overt act of homage to the precepts of a movement he was now increasingly willing to accept, for a newspaper photograph of another of his lost exhibits at Rutter's show, *Waiting for the Robert E. Lee*, shows him trying to translate Severini's work into his own terms. 'It certainly is rag-time art' was the *Daily Sketch*'s sarcastic response to this painting, but it is clear from the poor reproduction which survives that Nevinson has attempted to set up a complex rhythm of intercutting diagonals and burgeoning arcs to express the boisterous vitality of a dance hall. The lunging figure of the bowler-hatted man who dominates the centre of the composition establishes the mood of the whole picture; and yet the entire design, with its hasty outlines and blatant dissonances, is a ham-fisted attempt to combine representation with abstraction.

It is reasonable to assume that Nevinson was striving for the kind of urbane stylistic juggling displayed by Severini in his *Spanish Dancers at the Monico*, exhibited in his Marlborough Gallery one-man show. And the Italian artist's description of his painting in the exhibition catalogue – 'musical rhythm accompanies the arabesque of lines and planes, the harmony of tones and values. Light, translated through abstract forms, now and then breaks into the rhythm'[35]

△ Christopher Nevinson
*The Departure of the Train de Luxe, c.* 1913

◁ Gino Severini
*Spanish Dancers at the Monico*, 1913

– can serve as a summary of the ambitions contained within the slapdash orchestration of *Waiting for the Robert E. Lee.* Nevinson's painting was effective enough in its aim to inspire the acid critic of one newspaper to remark that '*Waiting for the Robert E. Lee* perfectly expresses the feeling aroused by five barrel organs in succession playing that inescapable tune under one's windows'.[36]

But the influence of Futurism only came resolutely to the fore in another of the lost paintings Nevinson exhibited at the Doré Galleries show: *The Departure of the Train de Luxe.*[37] Rutter, who himself liked the painting so much that he reproduced it on the Private View invitation card, remembered it in retrospect as 'the first English Futurist picture'.[38] And it certainly does seem to mark a significant watershed in Nevinson's own career. Here, for the first ascertainable time, he abolishes the traditional pictorial canons so evident in all his previous work and accepts the teaching of his new-found Futurist friends. Just as Wadsworth took up Marinetti's recommendation and chose the theme of an omnibus, so Nevinson decided to explore the potential of a locomotive in motion. It was a subject he would have witnessed many times on his visits to Gare St. Lazare and the Gare du Nord; and the titles of his other untraced exhibits at Rutter's show, *The Iron Bridge* and *The Circular Railway*, testify to his increasing interest in mechanical motifs. The fascination had been with him since his school days at Uppingham: he later remembered that 'I had little interest in the classics, but was enthralled by modern mechanics, and above all by the internal-combustion engine',[39] and two months later he was to display no less than two lost versions of the *Gare St. Lazare* theme in a rebel exhibition.[40] But he must have been encouraged, too, by the seminal example of Severini, who had shown *The 'North-South' Metro* in his London exhibition the previous April.

Both painters convey the experience of a journey on urban transport by bringing together different locales and moments in time. Severini's use of this Futurist belief in simultaneity is far more advanced than Nevinson's: his composition is full of sudden changes of gear, distant vistas juxtaposed with glaring signs and flashing lights penetrating the forms of the seated passengers. *The 'North-South' Metro* is a harsh, abrupt, infinitely ambiguous affair, whereas *The*

Gino Severini
*The 'North-South' Metro*, 1912

*Departure of the Train de Luxe* appears by contrast disconcertingly simple-minded. Nevinson has not really understood the true meaning of simultaneity, and concentrates instead on splitting up the contents on one particular scene into a series of broken facets. Yet there is no evidence of a genuine vision. Where Severini evolves, Nevinson borrows, applying a watered-down version of Futurism to his own, fundamentally conventional outlook. The Italian would never have treated the train itself in such a jarringly illustrative manner: Nevinson has failed to stylize its shape in accordance with the rest of his painting, and it remains an archaic anomaly in surroundings that are notably forward-looking. Even the unsympathetic critic of *The Times* pointed out this mistake in his own derogatory way when he wrote that 'Nevinson precipitates himself on public notice with his "Departure of the Train de Luxe", a glaring defect of which is the close resemblance that a splash in the middle of the canvas bears to a railway engine'.

Not that the young ex-student hung back from involving himself with enthusiasm in the avant-garde: he recorded that 'I was able to be of some use to Frank Rutter ... by writing personally to artists of the various movements'.[41] And a postcard which he sent to Severini in December 1913 survives as proof of the young Englishman's admiration for his Futurist friend's work. 'I very much regret that it is impossible for you to come to London' it begins, and goes on to disclose that 'I am delighted that you will write soon about your latest ideas, because they interest me enormously'.[42] Nevinson's circle of painter-friends was becoming impressively comprehensive; but he was still worldly enough to build up a useful group of aristocratic connections as well. 'Rutter lectured in the evenings on Modern Art', he remembered, looking back on the Doré Galleries Exhibition, 'and here I met Lady Muriel Paget, Lady Grosvenor, Lady Lavery, and through them pre-War Society.'[43] The *Train de Luxe* may have been regarded by its viewers as a revolutionary absurdity, but it did not prevent its creator from making his name known in the most fashionable London circles.

Etchells, on the other hand, who also figured prominently in Rutter's show, was still hovering uneasily between the legacy of his erstwhile Bloomsbury associates and the more aggressive alternative offered by Lewis, whose side he had finally taken in the Omega affair. Duncan Grant remembered 'Etchells telling me at a party soon after the Omega rumpus that Lewis wasn't an artist at all';[44] but around the same time, Etchells executed a large painting called *Woman at a Mirror* as a trial run for his adoption of Lewisian principles.[45] Like many preliminary ventures into a previously unknown area, the experiment founders. The leering face of the woman immediately evokes Lewis's grinning brood of harpies. But this one is clumsily executed, entirely lacking Lewis's talent for linear precision; and the body, divided up into an awkward conglomeration of sculptural planes, fails to come alive. *The Athenaeum*'s review of the exhibition was too kind when it declared that Etchells' contributions were 'rugged fantasies not without power in a vein akin to that of Mr Lewis'.[46] For Etchells was still groping, torn between Lewis's emphatic need for abstraction and his own weird penchant for grotesque forms.

Etchells was never entirely happy about succumbing to Lewis's artistic beliefs. 'I liked Lewis enormously', he explained, 'but he was an uncomfortable man to be with. He was a tremendous bully who wanted to be top dog all the time, and I used to get ratty with him: sometimes, I just thought he was all theory.' This overweening urge to dominate and enslave could reach farcical proportions, for Etchells laughingly remembered how Lewis 'imbibed a lot of nonsense from Stendhal, and used to delight in stopping me when we were

Frederick Etchells
*Woman at a Mirror, c.* 1913

walking down the street in Paris. "See that little seamstress over there?" he
would say. "I'm going to do a Stendhal on her!" Crossing the road, he would
proceed to walk parallel with her for a time, then put on the pace to get well
ahead and finally swing round to stand in her path, so that he could give her a
push with his body. The girl would get terribly annoyed, naturally enough, and
the method never worked. I thought it was all tosh, but Lewis had a certain kind
of inferiority complex which insisted that he came, saw and conquered.'[47] Half
willingly and half reluctantly, Etchells likewise found himself a target for Lewis's
tactical manoeuvrings, and the effect on his art was at first deleterious.

*Woman at a Mirror* suggests how unhappy he might initially have felt about
the closeness of his new relationship with Lewis, and perhaps the painting
falls down simply because Etchells could not bring himself to go along wholeheartedly with his friend's combative opinions. But this reservation did not

△ Frederick Etchells
*Head, c.* 1913

▷ Frederick Etchells
*Head, c.* 1913

prevent him from pursuing the direction he had taken, and exhibiting at Rutter's show a brace of drawings of *Heads* that lean far more heavily on the precedent established by analytical Cubism.[48] With their sharply pointed mouths, slit eyes and disjointed features, they are as blatantly ugly as *Woman at a Mirror*; but they do at least go further towards an understanding of Cubist stylization. Now Etchells feels able to transform the line of the cheekbone into a triangular shape in its own right, and enjoy the fragments incorporated into foreheads and jaws for their abstract force as well as their figurative connotations. The smaller and less impressive of the *Heads* insists on clinging to a representational framework, thereby laying itself open to the kind of deflating comment made by Sir Claude Phillips in his review of the exhibition. 'Etchells is the dullest and least accomplished of the group', he wrote sternly in the *Daily Telegraph*, 'but even he manages to be humorous in the "Drawing of a Head", of more or less Egyptian character, which we should like to rename "Rameses with a Gumboil".'

The small *Head*, with its swollen jawline, could be the drawing to which Phillips so irreverently refers, but in a sense it only has itself to blame for such remarks. If Etchells had departed more drastically from a recognizable image, the critics would not have been able to poke fun at him quite so freely. But because he wavers rather indecisively between a study from life and a Cubist exercise the result is inevitably open to censure. The other *Head* uses the Cubist language with a greater degree of liberation – its energetic mass of planes and fluid use of watercolour wash succeed in constructing a design of undeniable grandeur.[49] But even here, he has failed to treat the hand propping up the troubled head with the same degree of schematization as the rest of the composition. It obtrudes, a naturalistic exception in the otherwise ruthless collection of formal segments, and a distinct stylistic clash results. The verdict on such a drawing can only be unfavourable: it looks dangerously like an English attempt to catch up with stylistic experiments pioneered in France several years before. Picasso's *Head of a Woman*, for instance, which was included in Fry's 1912 Post-Impressionist show, attempts the same kind of analytical examination and succeeds so much more impressively. Etchells may have leaned on his memory of Picasso's picture when executing his *Heads*, but he was still too uncertain of the direction in which they were moving to carry them through to a more convincing extreme.

The same dilemma affects his lost view of *Patchopolis*, where he broaches Futurism without really accepting its underlying premises.[50] The destructive fury of the Italian movement has only just seeped through into the style of the picture: it ripples like a gentle wave through the undulating lines of the tiled roof, tips the sheds on the upper left into a slight inclination and then descends into murky incoherence towards the bottom left corner. *Patchopolis* is a naïve, unsatisfactory work which retains the framework of a traditionally picturesque landscape even as it seeks to question the viability of this very convention. Hence the crudity of its execution, reflecting Etchells' doubts as he struggled to digest the discoveries of Futurism and harness them to his own personality. And he was equally unsure of himself in a closely related composition based on the theme of *Dieppe*.[51] Unlike *Patchopolis*, which Etchells later admitted was an imaginary title 'because I sometimes liked to give my pictures fancy names', *Dieppe* arose from an intimate knowledge of the town itself. 'I stayed with Lewis at Dieppe for some time in the working class quarter, which must have inspired this drawing',[52] Etchells recalled; and although he could not remember exactly when this sojourn took place, it is known that Adrian Stephen returned to England in the first week of September 1913 'from Dieppe, where he had been staying with Wyndham Lewis and Frederick Etchells.'[53] The visit presumably took the form of a summer holiday, for both rebels were certainly back in England by the time the Omega split took place at the beginning of October. And Etchells' picture is a reconstruction of memories rather than an observant account of the town itself. Taking as his model a Futurist townscape like

Pablo Picasso
*Head of a Woman*, 1909

Frederick Etchells
*Patchopolis*, c. 1913

△ Umberto Boccioni
*The Street Enters the House*, 1911

▷ Frederick Etchells
*Dieppe*, c. 1913

Boccioni's *The Street Enters the House* – which he would have seen at the 1912 Sackville Gallery show – Etchells tries to express the dynamism informing such a busy port. Boccioni reflected the intense energy of his town by making the walls of the houses give way before the torrent of noise and activity issuing from the harbour below. But Etchells produces a far more generalized earthquake, which hurls windows, roofs, chimneys and bricks into an undisciplined mess of miscellaneous masonry. *Dieppe* is no less crude a picture than *Patchopolis*, and the comparison with Boccioni only accentuates its lack of finesse.

It could be that Hamilton's three exhibits at Rutter's show suffered from the same complaint, but it is impossible to tell. Unfortunately a minimal amount of his pre-war work, either paintings, watercolours or slight drawings, appears to have survived the passage of time. It is known, however, that he was taken up by Fry when the second Post-Impressionist show was rearranged for its final month in January 1913; and if the titles of the lost pictures he displayed there – *Head of a Woman*, *Portrait Study*, *Head of a Man* and *Composition* – give little clue as to their character, it can be presumed that they were at least as advanced in style as Grant's exhibits.[54] Fry would otherwise hardly have wished to include them, and Lewis would certainly not have accepted him as an artistic ally during the Omega period. Indeed, Hamilton's friendship with Lewis argues that his paintings would, by the autumn of 1913, have begun to display as much of the latter's influence as Etchells' work had imbibed. He had, at any rate, shifted his standpoint far enough away from Bloomsbury to earn the displeasure of Clive Bell at the Doré exhibition.

In a review of the show for *The Nation*, which was otherwise the most sympathetic and perceptive notice of any in the Press, Bell roundly condemned Hamilton's *Portrait*.[55] 'Ugliness is just as irrelevant as prettiness', he asserted, 'and the painter who goes out of his way to be ugly is being as inartistic and silly as the man who makes his angels simper. That is what is wrong with Hamilton's portrait in the big room – to take an instance at random. Hamilton has plenty of talent, and this picture is well enough, pleasant in colour and tastefully planned; but his talent would be seen to greater advantage if it did did not strut in borrowed and inappropriate plumes.' Bell does not, regrettably, describe the kind of stylistic 'plumes' he considers the *Portrait* to have 'borrowed': he merely implies that they offended his own stated preference for a 'pleasant' and 'tasteful' work of art. But the abuse he proceeds to heap on the picture suggests that Hamilton was employing a degree of arbitrary distortion similar to Etchells' *Woman at a Mirror*. 'The simplifications and distortions of the head perform, so far as I can see, no aesthetic function whatever', Bell stormed; 'they are not essential to the design, and are at odds with the general rhythm of the picture. Had the painter scribbled across his canvas "To hell with everything", it seems to me he would have done what he wanted to do, and done it better.'[56] Even if, as seems possible, Hamilton was as guilty in this painting of as much inconsistency as Etchells, Bell's denunciation still indicates that a species of abstraction had been used which flouted the standards upheld by Fitzroy Square. Hamilton must, therefore, have decided to extend the loyalty he showed Lewis when the Omega walk-out occurred: now it was his own painting that succumbed to the charisma of the would-be rebel leader.

Needless to say, there was never any possibility of Epstein's contributions to Rutter's exhibition falling under the dominance of Lewis's ideas. Although this New York-born sculptor had been associated with New English Art Club members like John and Muirhead Bone when he first settled in London around 1905, his dissatisfaction with traditional styles and willingness to experiment soon became a byword.[57] The completion of the Strand Statues in 1908 catapulted him into a premature notoriety, but these figures, with their uncomfortable vein of melancholy symbolism, did not break away from the sculptural past. They belonged to the old century rather than the new, and bore witness to Epstein's determination to learn from the rich collections housed at the British Museum. He was at this stage 'tremendously interested in the Elgin Marbles and Greek sculpture',[58] and only half-heartedly considered abandoning his attempts to emulate the great achievements of classical sculpture. The first sign of an active concern with more primitive cultures appeared in 1910, when he momentarily rejected his involvement with the European tradition and carved an imposing *Sunflower* head in San Stefano stone. At the age of 30, Epstein had at last succeeded in making a foray into a startlingly simplified formal language. The *Sunflower*'s face is an emphatic circle of stone, its abstract shape disturbed only by a bare summary of features which Brancusi, whom Epstein had yet to meet, would surely have admired. The emphasis is on essential form, freed from superfluous details and aggressively austere; but more astonishing still is the double row of stark triangles exploding outwards from the circumference of the face. They are as brazen as the dog-tooth carvings on Romanesque arches which Epstein might have admired on visits to English cathedrals, and yet it is more probable that they reflect his budding interest in 'the Egyptian rooms and the vast and wonderful collections from Polynesia and Africa'[59] in the British Museum. Several years before, during his first visit to Paris, he had been impressed by the Louvre's holdings of 'early Greek work, Cyclades sculpture, the bust known as the Lady of Elche, and the limestone bust of Akhenaton';[60] and the memory of those works doubtless helped him when he decided to turn his back on Victorian realism and carve the *Sunflower*. Balanced serenely on its elongated neck, the face stares ahead with an utterly impersonal pride, its symbolic overtones subservient to a declaration of the power contained in geometrical shapes.

It was, however, an isolated phenomenon in Epstein's œuvre at this stage: none of his contemporaneous drawings echoes the minimal structure of *Sunflower*, apart from an uncharacteristically brutal wash study of a *Head* which retains much of the carving's mesmeric presence. And it is significant that the

Jacob Epstein
*Head, c.* 1910

Jacob Epstein
*Sunflower, c.* 1910

only other 1910 work to employ primitive distortion was a collaborative, open-air project with Eric Gill which was never realized. Described by Gill as 'a great scheme of doing some colossal figures together (as a contribution to the world), a sort of twentieth-century Stonehenge',[61] the plan centred on a plot of about six acres attached to Asheham House in Sussex. An Epstein drawing inscribed *One of the Hundred Pillars of the Secret Temple* is probably connected with this soon-abandoned scheme – Augustus John excitedly told Gill that 'the Temple must be built'[62] – and it is symptomatic of Epstein's uncertainty that the style of the 'colossal figures' themselves is markedly more orthodox than that used in the surrounding pillars, where his budding involvement with primitive art has resulted in some abstracted, strikingly angular hieroglyphics. Only in the more decorative and incidental part of the Temple, therefore, could he permit his already avid interest in Africa and Polynesia to exert a palpable effect, just as *Sunflower* may owe much of its radicalism to the fact that it was originally intended to be a *Garden Carving*.[63]

Simultaneously engaged in the production of naturalistic portrait busts which upheld the Classical and Renaissance conventions of the nineteenth century, Epstein never followed up the implications of *Sunflower* until 1912 when – having 'shared with Lewis the honours of opprobrious attention' at the AAA summer salon with his eclectic and unresolved marble carving called *Maternity* (*Unfinished*) – the completion of his commission for the *Tomb of Oscar Wilde*

△ Photograph of Epstein carving *Maternity*, c. 1911–12

△ Jacob Epstein
*One of the Hundred Pillars of the Secret Temple*, c. 1910

◁ Jacob Epstein
*Tomb of Oscar Wilde*, installed 1912

once again enabled him to draw inspiration from primitive sources. Compared with the ruthless simplification of *Sunflower*, the 'flying demon-angel' he carved into the face of this twenty-ton slab of Hopton Wood stone seems cluttered with literary detail: in his own words, 'a symbolic work of combined simplicity and ornate decoration, and no doubt influenced by antique carving'. Pound, who found it 'over-ornate', decided that it was a sculpture 'which one, on the whole, rather dislikes';[64] but despite the hotch-potch of allegorical appendages that threaten to counteract the fine sweeping lines of the figure's Assyrian wings, the *Tomb* nevertheless represents Epstein's renewed desire to strip away descriptive excess and remain true to the intrinsic character of the monumental stone with which he was working.

The *Evening Standard*'s critic realized the importance of Epstein's consciousness of materials when he first saw the *Tomb* exhibited in the sculptor's Cheyne Walk studio. In an enthusiastic article, he pointed out that 'the muscular divisions are suggested by linear treatment rather than by aggressive modelling, and a vertical plane would enclose the carved surface of the monument. Thus there is nothing to destroy the effect of a rectangular block of stone that has felt itself into expression'.[65] The same was true of Brancusi's 1910 version of *The Kiss*, which was also executed as a Paris cemetery memorial; and the powerful presence of the *Tomb* seems to have galvanized English critics into appreciating the need for fresh ideas in sculpture. The *Pall Mall Gazette* wrote three days later that 'Mr Epstein is not only a real sculptor – a carver, not a modeller – but he is also a Sculptor in Revolt, who is in deadly conflict with the ideas of current sculpture, and who believes that it is on the wrong tack altogether. And one would be bold in denying that he may be right. Imitation of Nature, either in bronze or marble, becomes mere futility and ape-work unless it be illuminated by a plastic idea, not only closely associated with and deriving all its beauty from the medium in which it is worked, but suggested by it'.[66] Despite the brutal outburst of philistinism which the *Tomb* engendered when it was erected in Père Lachaise cemetery, therefore, Epstein was being encouraged by enlightened pockets of the London press to carry his experiments further.

His visit to Paris in the summer and autumn of 1912 succeeded in fortifying his resolve. 'I made the acquaintance of Picasso, Modigliani, Ortiz de Zarate, Brancusi, and other Montparnasse artists',[67] he recalled, and this first direct contact with some of his most revolutionary European counterparts made him realize the importance of a radical approach. It was a crucial moment in his career: he saw Modigliani 'for a period of six months daily', attempted to find a 'shed' they could share on the Butte Montmartre to 'work together in the open air', and was forcibly impressed by the sight of 'nine or ten of those long heads which were suggested by African masks'[68] in Modigliani's studio. Brancusi likewise provided an inspiring example. Epstein visited his studio as well, with its neat rows of 'bottles of milk "maturing" ... in the passage,'[69] and took careful note of the great pioneer's opinions. 'African sculpture, no doubt, influenced Brancusi, but to me he exclaimed against its influence', Epstein recalled. 'One must not imitate Africans, he often said. Another of his sayings was directed against Michelangelo, for his realism. He would pluck at the back of his hand and pinch the flesh, "Michelangelo", he would say, "beef steak!" '[70]

Perhaps it was the heady diet of new concepts which Epstein fed upon in Paris that prevented him from executing any important sculpture during his stay. His head was full of challenging ideas, and he must have needed time to digest them all, mull them over in his mind and decide which of them he was going to pursue. 'For one reason or another I did little work, and in the end got very exasperated with Paris', he wrote, 'and determined to go back to England – if possible get into some solitary place to work.'[71] He desperately

Jacob Epstein
*Flenite Relief, c.* 1913

needed isolation in order to collect his thoughts and embark on a series of works he knew would elicit an angry response from his friends in London. Possibly his involvement with the Cabaret Club decorations helped to strengthen his desire for experiment: the presence of Lewis, Hamilton and Bomberg would have made him realize he was not alone in his questioning of accepted precepts. Lewis may even have tried to draw him into the group of radicals he was so busily attempting to create, for Pound later testified to Epstein's admiration for Lewis's work. 'Years ago, three I suppose it is, or four', wrote Pound in 1916, 'I said to Epstein (not having seen these things of Lewis, or indeed more than a few things he had then exhibited), "The sculpture seems to be so much more interesting . . . than the painting". Jacob said, "But Lewis' drawing has the qualities of sculpture" . . . that set me off looking at Lewis.'[72]

But if Epstein was being partially drawn into Lewis's magnetic orbit, he resisted the possibility of an open political alliance by retreating from London in 1913 and renting 'a bungalow on the Sussex coast at a solitary place called Pett Level, where I could look out to sea and carve away to my heart's content without troubling a soul'.[73] Here it was, in congenial surroundings where he embarked on 'a period of intense activity' and became 'very happy', that Epstein produced a group of carvings which placed him for a few brief years in the forefront of the European avant-garde. Although it is difficult and perhaps unnecessary to establish a firmly chronological sequence of events, he seems first to have acquired some pieces of serpentine – which he nicknamed 'flenite'[74] – and decided to explore its possibilities in three separate sculptures. The least ambitious of this group is a tiny *Flenite Relief*, which appears little more than a technical experiment carried out to discover how amenable the new substance was to his chisels. The limbs of this archaistic doll have been scored out of the stone so brusquely as to constitute a rejection of conventional sculptural skill, as if Epstein wanted to start all over again, forgetting all the clichés and sophisticated techniques he had worked so hard to acquire during the previous decade, in order to return to the fundamental principles of sculpture. And it must have been an enormously refreshing exercise for him, tired as he was of stale recipes and traditional solutions. Sequestered in a remote district of southern England, he could afford to dismiss the towering achievements of the European past and enter into the spirit of his primeval ancestors, who would have hacked out just such a hieratic image as a cult-object to fear or worship. If the *Flenite Relief* seems now like a rather self-conscious attempt to identify with the remote beginnings of sculpture – the very choice of the title 'flenite' indicates how much he wanted to stress the primitive origins of his inspiration – it did enable Epstein to clear the ground, establish his true priorities so that he could move on to more complex and ambitious carvings.

Turning to another lump of the same material, he proceeded to fashion a slightly larger *Figure in Flenite* which exchanged the irregular surfaces of the *Relief* for a smoother, more highly polished finish. This time, the creature is definitely identifiable as a woman, for her legs have been cloaked in a full length robe that was probably conceived to emphasize the original character of the serpentine. Nothing is specified: this dress is nothing more nor less than a solid block of stone, an abstracted support for the hunched upper section of the figure. The rising belly suggests the woman is pregnant, which accounts for her cramped attitude as she strains forward to protect the swelling held so tenaciously in her paws. This cringing, somewhat vulnerable figure is on the defence, and stares out of huge, almond-like eyes which recall those outlined on the face on the earlier *Sunflower*. But compared with the bristling confidence of that earlier carving, this figure seems to belong to another, darker era, when terror of the unknown rather than aggressive pride was the norm.

Jacob Epstein
*Figure in Flenite, c.* 1913

Jacob Epstein
*Study for Female Figure in Flenite* (?), *c.* 1913

Jacob Epstein
*Female Figure in Flenite*, 1913 (1st view)

Jacob Epstein
*Female Figure in Flenite*, 1913 (2nd view)

It would be easy to assume that Epstein, dissatisfied with her undeniably awkward posture, sketched a schematic black crayon study of the same motif and then executed *Female Figure in Flenite*, which constitutes a more serene variation on the same theme of incipient childbirth. However, Pound noted that this carving was 'earlier'[75] than *Figure in Flenite*, and so perhaps Epstein finally wanted a more brutal and monumental image than *Female Figure in Flenite* offered him. But *Figure in Flenite* seems far more dependent on aping Polynesian and African models than its predecessor, which could not possibly be accused of slavishly copying any prototype. Instead of the ineloquent block of stone which served as a base for *Figure in Flenite*, two robust legs now rise up like columns from the rectangular slabs of the feet. Their slightly diagonal axis lends a far subtler rhythm to the composition: the angle of the legs tilts up towards the vital focus of the belly, and the upper half of the figure sways back and then curves over the top of the pregnant swelling in a sweeping semicircle of protective movement. Every element in the mother's body is concentrated on her womb, which she holds with far more compassion than her successor. In place of the harsh transitions and deliberate primitivism so evident in the *Figure in Flenite*, Epstein has injected his own psychological insight into *Female Figure*, so that its archaic qualities are married to the sculptor's twentieth-century knowledge of the condition of motherhood. Possibly remembering Brancusi's counsel not to 'imitate Africans', he realized in this case that a revival of primitive art for its own sake was not enough. *Female Figure in Flenite* is affecting because of its poised interplay between contrasting rhythms, all conspiring to emanate a feeling of human tenderness and warmth. These are qualities which rarely touched the concerns of true prehistoric sculpture; and Epstein was perfectly correct in borrowing only the formal simplification of primitive art rather than

Photograph of Epstein with *Granite Mother and Child*, c. 1913–15

pretending to be an emotional primitive as well. Hence the precise measure of the difference between the *Relief* and the *Female Figure*: where the former tried to pass itself off as a straightforward essay in sculptural innocence, the latter manages to couch a potentially sentimental theme in a vocabulary of pared-down shapes that do not try pedantically to copy African sources.

Epstein finally decided to exhibit this most successful of the three sculptures in the 1913 AAA Salon: it was listed as *Carving in Flenite*, but a visitor's sketch of the carving in a catalogue margin[76] identifies it as *Female Figure in Flenite*. He probably thought that a small flenite piece would be more acceptable to his London audience than the most monumental version of the themes incorporated in the carvings: *Granite Mother and Child*. The final appearance of this gargantuan sculpture, which brought together the child of *Flenite Relief* and the mother of the other two figures in one grand union, is unknown – the only surviving photograph shows Epstein standing proudly beside the half-finished block. But enough of its titanic structure is visible to indicate that he proposed to dispense with the pregnancy theme and show the mother balancing a squatting baby on her knees. It must have been one of his

Constantin Brancusi
*Three Penguins, c.* 1912

Jacob Epstein
*Sketch of Doves, c.* 1913

most commanding images. The outlines of the child, firmer and more rigid than the uncertain silhouette hewn into the style of the earlier relief, suggest that the group would have been more hieratic and geometrically defined than the flenite carving. In other words, a work that might have shocked and disturbed the plentiful admirers of Epstein's more conventional portrait busts. Perhaps he was wise to save himself such consternation; for even though he did eventually exhibit the still 'unfinished' sculpture in a 1917 one-man show, the American collector John Quinn spurned the work after it had been shipped over to New York for his collection. Infuriated by Quinn's behaviour, Epstein seems to have ordered his American brother to jettison the entire granite block into the obscurity of the East River.[77] Its loss is to be deplored, for he obviously meant it to be the first major statement of the style he had begun to evolve at Pett Level.

Despite his new-found confidence, Epstein was still wary of displaying his latest work in October, when Rutter invited him to exhibit two pieces in the Doré show. As a tactful compromise, Epstein chose to send in a relatively naturalistic *Baby's Head* executed in 1907; and then he cast all caution aside by accompanying it with the finest of his new series of marble dove carvings. It was a decisive step, for this sculpture definitely placed him in the same broad stylistic camp as Lewis and his rebel cohorts, as well as linking him, in choice of subject at least, with Duchamp-Villon's decision to execute a lost concrete carving of *The Doves* in 1913. The extended series of dove sculptures must have been started after Epstein had completed his flenite carvings, for they move away from primitive art towards a direct emulation of the work he would have seen and admired in Brancusi's Paris studio. One particular carving which he might well have watched the Rumanian executing – the 1912 *Three Penguins* – seems to have inspired Epstein in his search for an even more simplified formal vocabulary.[78] Its translucent white marble medium, no less than its bare equation of geometrical shapes, was carried over more or less wholesale into the *First Marble Doves* created at Pett Level. They appear more naturalistic than Brancusi's *Penguins*, for Epstein – involved as he was in the characteristically sexual motif of two coupling birds – wanted to specify every facet of their bodies. Where Brancusi was more concerned with building up an abstract polyphony of pure contours and incised outlines, Epstein remained obsessed with the more literary notion of animal intercourse.

He may have obtained the idea from his observation of the birds he kept in his Pett Level studio, for a slight *Sketch of Doves* shows him seizing on the moment when two birds start nuzzling together amorously on their perch.[79] And underneath this study, he rapidly sketched in two more birds, one poised aggressively above its companion as if in contemplation of the sexual act. Throughout his career, Epstein was never afraid of dealing with such themes in the frankest manner, but with the dove carvings it is difficult at first to appreciate that copulation is being represented. In *First Marble Doves* the male has alighted on the back of his partner, but he has not yet gone further: Epstein wanted to explore the muscular tension of the bird's pose as he balances momentarily, claws splayed out on his female companion while he contemplates the next move. It is this feeling of transitory movement that makes this group the least resolved of the dove carvings: the simplified forms of the birds lend them a timeless quality which directly contradicts the temporary nature of the action Epstein has depicted.

Although the *Doves'* chronological order is unknown, Epstein may now have moved on to *Second Marble Doves*, where intercourse is openly represented and the male has settled in comfortably along the entire length of his partner.[80] The new pose works with conspicuous success: now the feeling of extreme stasis produced by the rigidly defined components of the birds' bodies is echoed in the

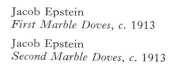

Jacob Epstein
*First Marble Doves, c.* 1913

Jacob Epstein
*Second Marble Doves, c.* 1913

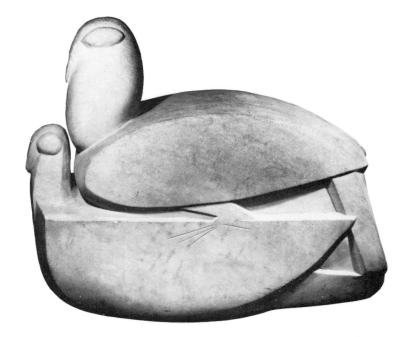

serenity of their pose, slotted together in one compact mass of interlocking forms. Epstein has calculated his composition so carefully that each detail fits into its neighbour with a satisfying sense of inevitability. The female's tail, for example, is stretched out along the base of the group to provide a ledge for the downward thrust of her mate's tail; while her wings curve up at their ends to carry the rhythm in a circular motion towards the sloping rump of the male's wings. The contours of both doves are treated as one coherent whole, whereas the two birds in the 'first' version had remained separate entities, awkward and disunited. The obvious difference in quality was pointed out by Pound, a great admirer of the dove carvings, when he wrote to John Quinn recommending him to purchase one of them for his collection. 'For God's sake get the two that are stuck together,' the poet warned, 'not the pair in which one is standing up on its legs.'[81] His advice prompted Quinn to write hurriedly to Epstein himself for reassurance; and the sculptor tetchily replied that his patron was indeed to receive the *Second Marble Doves*, but 'wondered by what right Pound was commenting on his work with such vehemence: Pound might mind his own business'.[82]

Jacob Epstein
*Third Marble Doves*, 1913

The most successful of the entire series, however, was undoubtedly the *Third Marble Doves* which Epstein exhibited at Rutter's show. The catalogue vaguely listed it as *Group of Birds*, but a photograph of its side view reproduced by the *Daily Mirror* in an article on the exhibition proves that this masterpiece of the whole group did indeed go on display.[83] Its superiority is manifested in many different ways. Most outstanding of all is Epstein's decision to space the male dove back from his companion so that the feeling of restriction apparent in *Second Marble Doves* is avoided. Instead of cramming the male's neck up behind the female's head so that their virtually identical shapes are reiterated in a rather monotonous way one above the other, he has decided to vary the two poses. And whereas the male's front section is separated from his body by a sharply defined division in the marble, the female's front quarters flow smoothly back towards her rear in one uninterrupted expanse of white stone. More subtle, but equally vital, is the change of emphasis at the back of the carving, where the rather abrupt transition from upper to lower tail favoured in *Second Marble Doves* becomes an eloquent, gradual slope. The result is an access of sensuality: for the doves' bodies, plumper and less tightly partitioned into planes than the 'second' version, gain in organic credibility. They are no less abstract than the other pair, but seem by contrast far more alive.

The *Third Marble Doves* can now be seen as one of the most tranquil and beautiful of all Epstein's works, but it received a savage mauling from those critics who deigned to acknowledge its presence in Rutter's show. 'About Mr Jacob Epstein's "Group of Birds" the less said the better', chortled one reviewer. 'One good thing is that he hasn't messed the marble up much, so that it will come in nicely to make something else.'[84] It was the degree of abstraction which infuriated the press: to them, Epstein's consummate refinement was a cheat, a short cut which by passed all the hard work academic sculpture required before it could be considered finished. They did not know, or refused to let themselves realize, that the seeming facility of the dove carving had only been attained after

considerable heart-searching on Epstein's part. And when its formal qualities
were not being attacked, the doves were abused for their subject-matter: the
Countess of Drogheda included them in an exhibition of Epstein's work held at
her house in 1914, until Lord Drogheda stalked in and exclaimed: 'I won't
have those fucking doves in here – I'll throw them out of the window!'[85] Pound,
however, stood apart from this abuse and recognized the true quality of the
series, praising them in some of his most elevated prose. 'These things are
great art because they are sufficient in themselves', he declared in *The Egoist*.
'They exist apart, unperturbed by the pettiness and the daily irritation of a
world full of Claude Phillipses and Saintsburys and of the constant bickerings
of uncomprehending minds. They infuriate the denizens of this superficial world
because they ignore it. Its impotences and its importances do not affect them.
Representing, as they do, the immutable, the calm thoroughness of unchanging
relations, they are as the gods of the Epicureans, apart, unconcerned, unrelenting.'[86] What Pound was attempting to express, in his own high-flown manner,
was the universal quality Epstein had achieved in the dove carvings: the cool
way in which they rode over the chicanery of an uncomprehending public.

Committed to the same aims in his own poetry, Pound delighted in his fellow-
countryman's ability to create images which lorded it over the philistine masses
and created an exclusive art form out of near-abstractions. It appealed to the
strong streak of élitism in Pound, and he rapidly became one of Epstein's
staunchest admirers. 'Epstein is a great sculptor', he announced categorically
to Isabel Pound in November 1913. 'I wish he would wash, but I believe Michel
Angelo *never* did, so I suppose it is part of the tradition.'[87] It seems, in fact, to
have been Epstein rather than Lewis who gradually awakened the poet to a
new, polemical involvement in modern English art during 1913. Two years later
he declared that 'so far as I am concerned, Jacob Epstein was the first person
who came talking about "form, not the *form of anything*"',[88] and at first he showed
more enthusiasm for the sculptor's work than for Lewis's. He especially admired a fourth dove carving entitled *Bird Pluming Itself* – of which no trace
now remains – likening it to 'a cloud bent back upon itself – not a woolly cloud,
but one of those clouds that are blown smooth by the wind. It is gracious and
aerial'. And the greatest compliment Pound ever paid Epstein came when he
claimed that the dove groups had altered his way of looking at the world. 'Last
evening I watched a friend's parrot outlined against a hard grey-silver twilight',
his article in *The Egoist* concluded. 'That is a stupid way of saying that I had
found a new detail or a new correlation with Mr Epstein's stone birds. I saw
anew that something masterful had been done. I got a closer idea of a particular
kind of decision.'[89] Such an impassioned appreciation would have been a huge
comfort to Epstein, bedevilled by admirers of his earlier work who were now
retracting their support. Pound was hardly a great art critic: he never properly
analysed the works which excited his attention, or submitted them to a rigorous
formal examination. But then, he did not want to. Rather did he aim at dissemi-
nating the spirit of modernism in his journalistic activities, just as Apollinaire
boosted the efforts of his Cubist painter friends with poetic celebrations of their
work and Marinetti promulgated Futurist art through his inspired propaganda.

Lewis, however, seemed in no need of critical adulation by the time he exhibited
in Rutter's show. A total of no less than seven works ensured that he was represented in force: *Creation* was on display once more and so was the formidable
*Kermesse*, which Clive Bell greeted with approval. 'I do not grumble at the
reappearance of Wyndham Lewis's "Kermesse", which has been altered and
greatly improved since its last appearance at the London Salon', he wrote.
'Lewis promises to become that rare thing, a real academic artist. He is academic

△Wyndham Lewis
*At the Seaside*, 1913

in the good sense of the word, that is to say, he uses a formula of which he is the master and not the slave.' But Bell could not quite make up his mind about the quality of Lewis's work. By the time he reviewed the Doré exhibition in *The Nation*, the Omega row had confirmed the doubts he had always harboured about the rebel leader; and yet he was by now engaged in completing the theories about 'significant form' which would be propagated in his book on *Art* the following year. Lewis's struggle towards abstraction seemed to accord with those theories, and so Bell's criticisms of his exhibits centred on their literary content, a quality that warred with their abstract elements. 'The enemy that dogs him in all his works is an excessive taste for life', Bell warned. 'He is inclined to modify his forms in the interests of drama and psychology to the detriment of pure design. At times his simplifications and rhythms seem to be determined by a literary rather than a plastic conception.'

The failing which annoyed Bell had been apparent in Lewis's work as far back as 1909, when *The Theatre Manager* was executed; and Bell was right to encourage Lewis to escape from the literary streak that seemed positively to prevent him from taking the vital step forward into formal abstraction. Lewis, he implied, ought to rid himself of a weakness for the kind of allegorical themes which could, in a picture like *At the Seaside*, destroy the stylistic consistency of an entire composition. He simply could not afford to confront the mechanistic creature in the foreground with the relatively naturalistic figure of the bowler-hatted man who stands behind. The presence of alternative conventions almost negates the credibility of both sets of images, and Lewis obviously had to learn to opt for a single stylistic direction, one that would eliminate symbolic content in favour of a self-sufficient abstract language. Bell realized this, and counselled the artist to abandon the incidental pleasures of representation. 'He who is working by formula towards the realisation of a minutely definite intellectual plan must be willing, on occasions, to sacrifice the really valuable qualities of sensibility and hand-writing as well as the adventitious charm that springs from happy flukes', insisted Bell. And although he appeared to disapprove of such an 'intellectual plan' – Bell, after all, cherished 'sensibility and hand-writing' – he went on to exhort Lewis to create 'vast organisations of form, designed, I imagine to have something of the austere and impressive unity of great architecture'.[90] He was being uncannily accurate: for Lewis produced, probably later than 1913, drawings that accorded almost exactly with Bell's prescription.

The overriding quality of Lewis's Vigorous watercolour entitled *Composition* is, as Bell so rightly prophesied, architectural. And it represents the definitive break with figurative references which Bell wanted him to achieve. Now all ostensible subject-matter has been banished from a design concerned exclusively with the mechanistic forms which were to become the hallmark of Vorticism. If *Composition* has a definite theme at all, it lies in the iconoclastic spirit of the *Timon* portfolio, for Lewis himself afterwards dubbed it a 'later drawing of the Timon series'.[91] But no hint of human, least of all Shakespearean, content remains. The feeling of violence is so pervasive that the forms seem to be in the process of breaking up into splintered fragments, destroyed either by some cosmic cataclysm or their own internal dynamics, with a frenzy that recalls the hectic abandon of Wadsworth's *L'Omnibus*. And just as Wadsworth's painting represented his Futurist-inspired reaction to the frenetic quality of modern urban life, so the skyscraper structure at the bottom of the *Composition* suggests Lewis's similar response to the new industrial environment. The evocation of an urban city-scape is irresistible, and yet tangential. Lewis presents a metaphor rather than a recognisable skyscraper, and his newly emancipated language is all the richer because of this indirect relationship with the visible world.

To limit it to such an emphatic area of reference is misleading, however:

▷Wyndham Lewis
*Composition*, 1913–14

Gino Severini
*Spherical Expansion of Light (Centrifugal)*, 1914

Apart from this intriguing connection with an artist whose work he probably did not see in 1913, what else might have inspired Lewis to produce his abstractions? The only other stylistic influence which can be proposed with any feasibility is Severini, who exhibited among the more representational works in his London one-man show of April 1913 a group of 'Drawings with Indications of Colour'. He described them in the catalogue as the products of 'an overpowering need for abstraction', which had 'driven me to put on one side all realisation of form in the sense of pictural [*sic*] relief. By the simple indication of values and of mass I have arrived at arabesque. The indication of form and colour should give us the total reality. These drawings are plastic rhythms'.[96] So were Lewis's, even if he would never have sympathized with Severini's desire for 'arabesque'; and a painting like *Spherical Expansion of Light* (*Centrifugal*), included in the Futurists' second London exhibition in 1914, shows just how far the Italian was now prepared to push himself towards complete abstraction. He believed in what he termed the 'Plastic Absolute', which he considered to be 'the communion, the sympathy which exists between ourselves [and] the centre of things'.[97]

Lewis admired Severini's work, and admitted a few months later that he was 'the most important' Futurist, who 'with his little blocks, strips and triangles of colour, "zones" of movement, etc., made many excellent plastic discoveries'.[98] But the Englishman was, even so, totally unsympathetic towards the Italian's romantic ideas about an empathy with the natural world, and his abstraction firmly rejects Severini's lyricism in favour of tough geometrical oppositions. Severini delighted in the figurative analogies – 'the plastic analogies of dynamism' – which he hoped his designs would conjure up in the imagination, and he pointed them out in typical 1913 picture-titles such as *Dancer = Sea + Vase of Flowers*. Lewis, by contrast, finally abandoned all figurative references in his *Composition*. It is true that, on another level altogether, the Italian had formulated the concept of a basic energy activating all matter and either pushing forcefully outwards from its centre or drawing inwards to a dynamic vortex. The notion immediately becomes a possible source for the fundamental impulse behind Vorticism, but Severini was still working inside the premise of the divisionist tradition: the source of energy in his abstract images is that of light. And here once again Lewis would have disagreed, for his abstraction is inspired by mechanical artefacts rather than natural phenomena. If the Italian's non-figurative experiments were on view in London at a time when Lewis would have been most receptive to their impact, and provided a valuable spur for the latter's own move towards abstraction, profound differences separated the two artists which were to become still more marked when Vorticism established itself in 1914 as an independent movement.

Bell's comments on the 'unity of great architecture' in Lewis's Doré exhibits suggest that he had begun to formulate the mature Vorticist style. His abstractions may have been included in Rutter's show, since one of his exhibits there was simply listed as *Design* in the catalogue; and it is safe to assume that his contributions compared favourably with the work displayed by Wadsworth, Nevinson, Etchells and Hamilton. There seems, moreover, to have been an element of internecine rivalry or jealousy among the rebel company, for Sir Claude Phillips reported with some relish that 'within the group of British extremists, though they present an individual front to the enemy, there is just at present civil war; a most terrific thwacking of shields, a splintering of swords, and cleaving of helmets is going on – and, alas! not exactly with closed doors. For not even Cubism seems to bring with it equanimity; these valiant knights of the new movement, these geometers of the brush, are as quarrelsome, as little in agreement among themselves, as were the irascible doctors and no less aggressive philosophers of Molière.'[99] Allowing for the fact that Phillips may have been referring in the main to the Omega dispute, there may well have been other squabbles centering on Lewis's determination to take command; and possibly some of the group were already balking at Nevinson's unqualified espousal of Marinettian aesthetics. There might, too, have been long and heated arguments in the Café Royal about the viability or otherwise of completely abstract works of art. Speculation alone is possible, but what seems certain is the unprecedented vitality of the London art world, its willingness to listen to fresh ideas and its open-ended desire to attempt something entirely new.

All Lewis's colleagues were supremely conscious of the need to evolve an original style, a language that would prove English artists to be as independent as the Cubists or Futurists. They would even have understood the strictures with which Bell concluded his review of the Doré exhibition, since he censured them for having 'swallowed, more or less whole, the formulas which French masters invented'. The criticism would have been acceptable to them because Bell, refusing to be merely destructive, ended with a rousing plea for creative originality. 'If I were older', he wrote, 'I would advise Nevinson and the more intelligent of this company to shut themselves up for six months, and paint pictures that no-one is ever going to see. They might catch themselves doing something more personal if less astonishing than what they are showing at the Doré Galleries. Artistic courage, that is what is wanted – courage to create the forms that express oneself instead of imitating those that express the people for whom one would gladly be mistaken.'[100] His sentiments coincided with the feelings and ambitions of the artists at which they were aimed, even if Bell's review originated in a Bloomsbury outlook which had just been brutally dismissed. For within a year, these Doré exhibitors were to produce an autonomous national movement based upon the undoubted originality of achievements like Lewis's *Composition*. And this movement, paradoxically, was not destined to be one that Bell himself would have liked to foresee.

# Chapter 6: The Cubist Room and the Theories of Hulme

Although the rebel contributors to the Doré Galleries exhibition had been attacked by most of the critics, they soon began to be looked upon with favour by those wealthy and enterprising enough to commission their services. Nevinson, whose *Train de Luxe* had attracted a great deal of attention at the show, found himself so much in demand that 'I had more on my hands than I knew how to cope with'; and he even claimed that he 'was at the same time able to put work in [Lewis's] way'. A curious reversal of roles must have taken place for Lewis to find himself less popular than his young student friend, but the two men managed to collaborate quite happily together 'designing a tableau for the Albert Hall Picture Ball of the Futurists'.[1]

At the moment, Lewis was prepared to shelter under the label of the Italian movement: Futurism was becoming fashionable, and he had been slighted for so long that any popularity which gave him the chance to work was welcome. Mrs Percy Harris, wife of the Deputy Chairman of the London County Council and a friend of Ford's, proposed at one stage to commission some decorations from him for her Sloane Street home.[2] And he began positively to revel in this new notoriety, cultivating a theatrical, egocentric façade which was greeted with a mixture of awe and disapproval by those he came across. 'Another new light whom I met today is Wyndham Lewis (I am going to the Picture Ball, if you please, as a futurist picture designed by him!)', Edward Marsh wrote gaily to Elliott Seabrooke in November 1913. 'He is very magnificent to look at, but I don't think he liked me, and I suspected him of pose, so we shan't make friends. Hoping to strike a chord, I told him I had spent the day with Stanley Spencer, and he said, "I don't know him, is he a painter?" Which *must* have been put on.'[3] The letter vividly evokes the essential dichotomy in Lewis's character: Marsh cannot contain his delight at dressing up in a costume designed by such a handsome and controversial figure, but at the same time he is repelled by Lewis's self-conscious hauteur. For Lewis occasionally delighted in affronting the sensibilities of the fashionable people who lavished their hospitality upon him. Nevinson recalled a dinner 'at Lady Constance Hatch's', where 'for reasons best known to himself, P. Wyndham Lewis turned up . . . in ordinary clothes. This embarrassed nobody except himself, but my inoffensive white tie did much to increase his enmity towards me'.[4]

The 31-year-old artist could now afford not to care about alienating those he had no wish to befriend, for by the end of the year he found himself courted by someone who wanted to enlist his services alone. Around 30 November he was at once gratified and surprised to receive a flattering note from 40 Wilton Crescent, the London residence of Kathleen, Countess of Drogheda. 'I adored your *Norwegian Dance* at the Doré Gallery', she enthused, referring to *Kermesse* by the nickname it had somehow acquired, 'and gazed at it for ages – it moved before me – and I am gradually having my stupid old brain taught to appreciate the great cleverness of futurism.' The adventurous Lady Drogheda was eager to see her dining-room transformed by a young blood daring enough to create an interior that would be the talk of Belgravia, and her choice had fallen on Lewis. '*Do* please come and see me', her note urged, 'I should so love you to do a frieze for me – and I will get the Decorator here at the same time.'[5] Lewis had received another commission: but this time, unlike the Cabaret decorations, the Ideal Home or the Picture Ball he was not being asked as one of a whole group of artists. He was out on his own, even if the machinations behind Lady Drogheda's request puzzled his former partner, Nevinson. For whereas the latter recorded that he 'went fifty-fifty with Lewis' over a project 'Lady Cunard had arranged' to 'decorate the drawing-room of Mr Moore, who was giving a dance to General Sir John French', the alliance broke down when it came to the dining-room and 'somehow or other [Lewis] got the job entirely'.[6] Lady

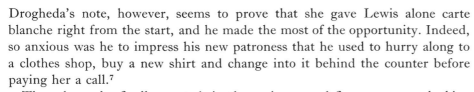

△ Wyndham Lewis
Back wall of Lady Drogheda's dining-room at
40 Wilton Crescent, 1913–14

◁ Wyndham Lewis
*The Dancing Ladies*, 1913–14

Drogheda's note, however, seems to prove that she gave Lewis alone carte blanche right from the start, and he made the most of the opportunity. Indeed, so anxious was he to impress his new patroness that he used to hurry along to a clothes shop, buy a new shirt and change into it behind the counter before paying her a call.[7]

The scheme he finally created, in the main ground-floor room overlooking the street, no longer exists; but extensive photographic coverage by *The Sketch* – reproduced under the ironic title of 'Lady Drogheda's Futurist Dining Room Decorations' – demonstrates how Lewis refused to compromise himself in any way, and produced an environment that in no sense side-stepped from the path along which his art was moving.[8] Perhaps the most radical feature of the scheme was the large, near-abstract painting of *The Dancing Ladies* placed above the doorway.[9] Its severe, angular design was more extreme than the drawing of dancing figures which Lewis had contributed to Madame Strindberg's prospectus the previous year: now geometry triumphs over representation of the human body, and a group of barely distinguishable mechanistic forms crank their way across the surface of the picture. Both they and the totally non-figurative background, which spurns any need to place these jerking women in a recognizable setting, make no concessions to contemporary taste; and the painting as a whole shows Lewis preparing himself to proclaim the viability of near-abstraction on a grand scale.

Most visitors, however, would have been far more startled by the extraordinary colour which Lady Drogheda had permitted Lewis to use elsewhere in her dining-room. All four walls and, it seems, the ceiling as well were covered in sheer black, and a breathless reporter from *Vanity Fair* magazine revealed just how shocking this choice must have appeared at the time. 'As it were in protest against the dazzling whiteness of the conventional decoration of the period which seems to have invaded every piece of architecture from the Savoy rooms down to the meanest provincial cinema palace, [Lady Drogheda] had the walls painted jet black', he wrote; and just in case his readers thought he was affronted by such a colour, the article insisted that the result was 'pleasing to a degree, especially to those nauseated with the nauseating uniformity of the average drawing-room, as tyrannical in its decorum as a court function or a church ceremony'.[10] Lewis had flouted this convention in the most dramatic manner, and a photograph reproduced in *Vanity Fair* shows how he used the colour as a foil for his own decorations, deliberately playing off the walls' unrelieved darkness against the strident orchestration of the painted frieze above.[11] Unlike *The Dancing Ladies*, this long panel running beneath the cornice right around the room was completely abstract, and *Vanity Fair* gasped at its 'rioting mass of colours, each vying with each other in brilliance, quite irrespective of form,

Wyndham Lewis
Overmantel in Lady Drogheda's dining-room,
1913–14

Omega Workshops
Interior decoration scheme, London, 1914

meaning, or design – colour for colour's sake, so to speak'.[12] And as if this orgiastic display was not enough in itself, bevelled glass was also installed in the corners of the room to provide sudden, unexpected glimpses of Lewis's frieze.

The Countess herself must have revelled in it all, for one wicked contemporary remembered how she approved of the way the black walls contrived to 'show off her bare shoulders at dinner parties'.[13] But even Lady Drogheda's beauty would have been overshadowed by the climax of the room: an enormous overmantel situated opposite *The Dancing Ladies*, where Lewis executed another frieze of *Fish, Flesh and Fowl* all the way round an imposing chimney glass.[14] The stark geometry of this black-beaded mirror echoes the structure of the two elongated figures who stand guard at either side like two primitive fetishes. They seem to be composed of the same jagged, linear vocabulary as the surrounding zigzag pattern which ultimately runs up beside the tiny standing forms placed at each end of the frieze above. And no trace of *Fish* or *Fowl*, let alone *Flesh*, has been allowed to exist there; instead, Lewis indulges his preference for a cluster of non-representational circles, diagonals, diamonds and other fragments of a proto-Vorticist language. They look positively barbaric even in the surviving photograph, and when in situ – combined with the totemic figures, the unadorned severity of the chimney glass and the ghostly illumination of two red glass vases lit from their insides – they might well have disconcerted any society lady who wandered over to adjust her hair in the mirror.

The entire room occupied little more than two months of Lewis's time, for Lady Drogheda invited a select circle of friends including artists like John and Epstein to view the finished product on 26 February the following year.[15] She also arranged an exhibition of Lewis's drawings in the house, to coincide with the unveiling of her new décor, and his name was thereby circulated widely among the aristocratic patrons of London. They would have been shocked as much by the drawings as by the dining-room, for John remembered that 'among the exhibits, hung a picture described as a portrait. Although taken from the back, the artist had included an attractive pair of breasts, apparently attached to the subject's shoulder-blades! . . . I thought it was going too far myself but, wisely, I think, made no comment. After all, I might have been mistaken. What I took to be the lady's back hair might have been her face in shadow or something; you never can tell'.[16] John's bemused incomprehension must have been seconded by most of the guests at the private view: Pound, who privately thought the decorations 'weren't very good', nonetheless recorded that they 'caused such a stir',[17] and helped to promote discussion about the room by announcing to the readers of *The Egoist* that 'one can only pause to compliment the Countess of Drogheda that she has set a good example to London'.[18]

It is worth realizing, too, just how much of an unmistakable break with the decorative standards of the Omega the Wilton Crescent commission represented. Anyone who had studied the 'Round Robin' and wondered what kind of aesthetic ideals Lewis wanted to substitute for the work executed at Fitzroy Square had only to visit the dining-room; for its overall effect would have been bleak and forbidding, a defiantly personal creation which stood in adamant opposition to a typical Omega interior of the period.[19] Here, although the prevailing language is as uninhibited and spectacular as Lewis's, a spirit of wayward fancy and charm counts for everything. And compared with the stylistic consistency of the Drogheda scheme, the Omega's decorations are marred by wilful eclecticism. Lewis's decorations appear more singleminded and original, yet the Bloomsbury-oriented *Athenaeum* decided that they were carried out 'for purposes of immediate sensationalism' rather than 'in a serious monumental spirit'. *The Athenaeum*'s critic did admit his admiration for Lewis's 'great cleverness in utilizing . . . a gold cornice of flagrantly Renaissance design and other existing

features', but the degree of abstraction employed in the dining-room scheme
alienated his sympathies. 'The exiguous surfaces open for treatment by painting
are so dealt with as to be sufficient as colour for the decoration of the room',
he continued, 'yet (combined, perhaps, with the doctrinaire hatred of "representation" current among Mr Lewis's supporters) they induce a use of scarcely
legible hieroglyphics, and this hardly gives full scope to the power of sustained
draughtsmanship which makes Mr Lewis, in our opinion, the leader of the
English Cubists.'[20]

It was possible by then for a critic to refer with all confidence to such a group,
since Lewis and his friends had achieved official recognition in December 1913
with an exhibition at Brighton. Ostensibly it was a Camden Town Group show,
but the vital corollary 'and Others' was added to the title in the catalogue to
remind all the contributing artists that the Camden Town Group had in reality
ceased to exist. None of its three exhibitions had been a financial success, and
after the director of the Carfax Gallery refused to house any more, some of the
members asked William Marchant of the Goupil Gallery whether they could
transfer the Group's shows to his premises. Marchant was willing to help, but
shied at the unpleasant associations that the scandalous Camden Town murders
had given the Group's name. He therefore suggested that it be enlarged, so that
his far bigger gallery-space would be properly filled.

His proposals acted as a catalyst on the profusion of societies that had come
into existence in London by 1913, all of which were too small and lacked the
finances to operate with any real success. Lengthy discussions took place, during
which the Camden Town Group merged with the so-called 19 Fitzroy Street
Group, and then Sickert eventually presided over a grand meeting of all interested parties on 15 November 1913 at 19 Fitzroy Street. The outcome of this
historic conference was far-reaching in its implications: Lewis's group agreed
to join up with Sickert and the Cumberland Market Group – led by Gilman and
Bevan – to form a coalition of English radicals who would all exhibit together
under the tactful, non-committal name of the London Group. 'Gilman was the
motive force', wrote Nevinson, who attended the fateful meeting. 'Slowly but
surely . . . he gathered all the warring elements of Impressionists, Post-
Impressionists, Neo-Primitives . . . Cubists, and Futurists. At the first general
meeting we had Sickert in the chair, and Marchant consented to let us have the
Goupil Gallery on the usual commission basis, provided that he dissociated
himself from the Group . . . I was elected secretary, Gore treasurer, and Gilman
eventually accepted the presidency because Sickert, with his usual modesty,
refused the honour.'[21]

For one extraordinarily harmonious moment, it really did look as if all the
internal rivalries, the petty jealousies and political disputes among those artists
who rejected the ethos of the New English Art Club were at an end. But anoma-
lies remained. Where, for instance, did the impatient Lewis stand, subordinated
as he was to the authority of a youth like Nevinson? The London Group was
the last umbrella under which he desired to hide his fierce individuality, and so
he plotted to ensure that the first exhibition bore the imprint of his own strongly
expressed views. Accordingly, the catalogue of *The Camden Town Group and
Others* show, which opened at Brighton Public Art Galleries on 16 December
and continued until 14 January the following year, ended up with an entirely
independent foreword to 'Gallery III' specially written by Lewis. He dubbed it
'The Cubist Room', which seemed to contradict the principles laid down by
the English Impressionist J. B. Manson in the catalogue's main introduction. 'In
the London Group, which is to be the latest development of the original Fitzroy
Street Group, all modern methods may find a home', Manson optimistically

declared. 'Cubism meets Impressionism, Futurism and Sickertism join hands and are not ashamed, the motto of the Group being that sincerity of conviction has a right of expression. . . It is well, perhaps, that the vital qualities in modern art should be concentrated in one definite group, instead of being scattered in the medley of modern exhibitions.'

Noble sentiments indeed; but Lewis had been busy undermining them by arranging that the nucleus of Doré Galleries rebels – Epstein, Hamilton, Wadsworth, Etchells and Nevinson – should shut themselves off in one single room with a special name to highlight their autonomy. And a new adherent joined this exclusive clique of five painters and one sculptor: Bomberg, who had by now likewise broken off his tenuous connections with the Omega and displayed no less than six works in 'The Cubist Room'. At first, apparently, Lewis had tried to prevent Bomberg's election to the London Group. 'Not only did he insult me in public', recalled Bomberg, 'but went so far in December 1913 as to cause my character to be cleaved by an imputation wrapped up in buffoonery – that I was not a fit person to be elected a Foundation Member of the London Group – the onus was upon Harold Gilman the first President who insisted . . . that I had been elected – Harold Gilman obtained the evidence that Lewis's information was groundless.'[22]

Lewis's hostile attitude did not stop him from marking Bomberg's arrival with a special paragraph in his catalogue foreword, asserting that 'David Bomberg's painting of a platform announces a colourist's temperament, something between the cold blond of Severini's earlier paintings and Vallotton'. He countered this favourable mention by insisting that Bomberg's 'form and subject matter are academic', but then concluded that 'the structure of the criss-cross pattern [is] new and extremely interesting'. The passage appears to describe *Vision of Ezekiel*; but it was not actually listed in the catalogue, and only years afterwards did Bomberg explain why. 'This painting would not have gone to Brighton had Lewis been permitted to have his way', he recalled grimly. 'Spencer Gore, Lewis and myself were engaged in the exhibition and stacking this painting – Lewis had hidden "The Dream [*sic*] of Ezekiel". Spencer Gore – the secretary – a painter and person holding the reputation for uncovering truth rescued my painting from Oblivion & himself ran it down to the van already moving off to Brighton with the collection of paintings for exhibition.'[23] In view of Lewis's spiteful action, it was strange that he made a point of describing *Ezekiel* in the foreword at all; but he then proceeded to hang the painting badly in the exhibition itself. 'David told me that Lewis placed *Ezekiel* behind a door so that it could hardly be seen', Lilian Bomberg recalled. 'So David angrily took the painting away with him on the roof of a taxi during the exhibition.'[24]

Despite this unpleasant incident, 'The Cubist Room' succeeded in making the impact Lewis so eagerly desired. His foreword made it clear that by the time the Drogheda commission was being executed, he was no longer willing to restrict the spirit of rebellion implicit in the decorations to works of art alone. Marinetti had shown that proclamations and manifestos were an integral part of an artistic revolution, and Lewis was determined to follow suit. In Rutter's exhibition, his group had been scattered at random in amongst Ginner, Gilman and Gore; but now – for the very first time – they had the chance to stand alone. Lewis's prose rose to the occasion. 'These painters are not accidentally associated here, but form a vertiginous, but not exotic, island in the placid and respectable archipelago of English art', he began, full of the importance of the event he wanted to celebrate. 'This formation is undeniably of volcanic matter and even origin; for it appeared suddenly above the waves following certain seismic shakings beneath the surface. It is very closely knit and admirably adapted to withstand the imperturbable Britannic breakers which roll pleasantly against its sides.'

The foreword shows Lewis actively seizing his opportunity to announce the formation of a fully-fledged group, shrewdly selecting words like 'island', 'formation', 'volcanic' and 'closely knit' to convince the rest of the London Group – as well as the artists so presumptuously spoken for – that a rebel army had indeed been created. It was an exaggeration, of course. Most of the 'Cubist Room' contributors were allies only in the negative sense that they were opposed to the principles both of Sickert and Fry; and Lewis had no right to force them into a political pigeon-hole of his own making. But he was ruthlessly ambitious, and in the rest of the foreword constructed his own movement around theories partially inspired by Futurist polemics. 'A man who passes his days amid the rigid lines of houses, a plague of cheap ornamentation, noisy street locomotion, the Bedlam of the press, will evidently possess a different habit of vision to a man living amongst the lines of a landscape', he declared, regurgitating views already outlined in the Futurists' Sackville Gallery catalogue well over a year before. Lewis knew full well that the one factor genuinely unifying him with his fellow exhibitors was an antipathy to Fry, and so he lashed out at the Omega leader without actually mentioning his name. 'To be done with terms and tags, Post Impressionism is an insipid and pointless name invented by a journalist', he declared dismissively. '[It] has been naturally ousted by the better word "Futurism" in public debate on modern art.' The recent shift in his sympathies was thereby openly defined; but Lewis was far too intelligent not to anticipate accusations of plagiarism, and neatly forestalled criticism by ridiculing Italian Futurism as 'the Present, with the Past rigidly excluded, and flavoured strongly with H. G. Wells' dreams of the dance of monstrous and arrogant machinery, to the frenzied clapping of men's hands'.

Paradoxically enough, Lewis's satire could have been applied to many of his own contemporaneous drawings, except that there was nothing frenzied about them. Compared with the blurred, riotous compositions favoured by the Futurists, a sketch like *The Enemy of the Stars* opts firmly for one static, clearly defined geometrical image.[25] For Lewis was still torn between the invigorating theories of Futurism, the dynamic personality of Marinetti and his earlier respect for Cubist art. He even felt the need to describe Cubism in the foreword as 'chiefly, the art, superbly severe and so far morose, of those who have taken the genius of Cézanne as a starting point, and organised the character of the works he threw up in his indiscriminate and grand labour. It is the reconstruction of a simpler earth, left as choked and muddy fragments by him. Cubism includes much more than this, but the "cube" is implicit in that master's painting'. For himself, Lewis was working towards a unique synthesis of Futurist vitality and the 'morose' austerity of the Cubists, and his ideal is confirmed and developed in the most convincing, prophetic part of the foreword, where he insisted that 'the work of this group of artists for the most part underlines such geometric bases and structure of life, and they would spend their energies rather in showing a different skeleton and abstraction than formerly could exist, than a different degree of hairiness or dress'.

The convoluted grammar of the sentence only serves to underline Lewis's excitement, as he verbally trips over himself in the struggle to enunciate his radical theories for the first time in public. 'All revolutionary painting today has in common the rigid reflections of steel and stone in the spirit of the artist', he continued, introducing the all-important concept of a 'revolutionary' art; 'that desire for stability as though a machine were being built to fly or kill with; an alienation from the traditional photographer's trade and realisation of the value of colour and form as such independently of what recognisable form it covers or encloses'. Apart from the enigmatic phrase about a machine 'to fly or kill

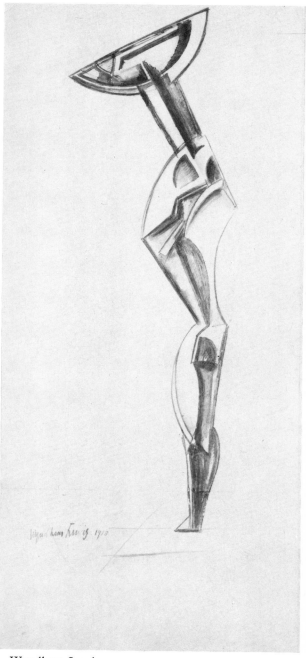

Wyndham Lewis
*The Enemy of the Stars*, 1913

with', the statement is remarkable for its independence of Futurist dogma: Lewis proposes an art of stability and rigidity, of steel and geometry. Already an alternative, specifically English, set of aesthetic principles is beginning to be articulated – even if Lewis had not yet expressed it satisfactorily. 'People are invited, in short', he summed up, 'to entirely change their idea of the painter's mission, and penetrate, deferentially, with him into a transposed universe, as abstract as, though different to, the musician's.'[26] The stated ambition was there for all to see, either in the Brighton catalogue or in the pages of the first issue of a new magazine called *The Egoist*, where the foreword was reprinted on 1 January. It was a symbolic date: for Lewis's ungainly prose was struggling to establish an abstract art within the philistine boundaries of his own adopted country.

Apart from Pound, who had not yet committed himself to a programme of consistent support for the new movement, there was only one other writer in England advocating the kind of art that Lewis so ambitiously envisaged. That man was the former poet and philosopher T. E. Hulme; but the fact that he propounded his ideas most effectively in conversation, combined with Lewis's unwillingness to publish anything substantial on his aesthetic theories before the summer of 1914, makes it virtually impossible to ascertain the true nature of their intellectual relationship. What does remain certain is the strong similarity between the personalities of the two men, stretching right back to the time in 1904 when Hulme echoed Lewis's departure from Rugby by being sent down from Cambridge University with the 'longest mock funeral ever seen in the town',[27] riding on a hearse 'astride the coffin with his friends in deep mourning grieving beside him'.[28] Although he might well have met Lewis soon after the young artist returned from the continent in 1908, Hulme's early career in London was exclusively devoted to the twin problems of philosophy and poetry, and he exerted at that stage a far more palpable influence over Pound.

On 22 April 1909, the American expatriate was introduced to a newly-established group of poets who with Hulme at their head had just broken away from the aegis of the more traditional Poet's Club. Their avowed aim was the renewal of English poetry, and they tirelessly read and corrected each other's poems, argued about imagery, *vers libre* and the desirability of transposing foreign verse-forms into English, as well as debating how poetry could be bullied into reflecting the modern world. Hulme, who already realized the relevance of modern French poetry and had – like Lewis – attended Bergson's lectures in Paris, was the most vigorous champion of the new movement; and his talent for synthesizing the ideas of others was already apparent in the 'Lecture on Modern Poetry' he delivered to the Poet's Club around the beginning of 1909. 'Verse forms, like manners, and like individuals, develop and die', he told his older colleagues. 'They evolve from their initial freedom to decay and finally to virtuosity. They disappear before the new man, burdened with the thought more complex and more difficult to express by the old name. After being too much used, their primitive effect is lost.'[29] While Lewis was at the same time attempting to return to just such a 'primitive effect' in drawings like *The Theatre Manager*, Hulme wanted to revolutionize post-Victorian verse in a comparable manner.

Pound, by contrast, was still in love with the poetic achievements of the past. He had much to learn; and in August 1909, only four months after he had joined the new group, he was able to read Hulme's article in *The New Age* declaring that 'images in verse are not mere decoration, but the very essence of an intuitive language'.[30] The importance of such a declaration for Pound's future theories is obvious, just as Hulme's handful of poems were courageous enough to try out the principles that Pound would take further in his linguistic experiments. Almost three years were to pass before Pound composed his own poems according to similar theories, but in the winter of 1911 he was impressed by some lectures Hulme delivered on Bergson at the home of Mrs Franz Liebich. Having attended a philosophical congress in Bologna the previous April at which Bergson expounded on 'the image', Hulme was able to tell his London audiences about the Frenchman's theory of artistic creation. The original artist, he insisted, immerses himself in the inner flux of life and re-emerges with 'a new shape', which he then attempts to consolidate in a work of art. He is only able to make this act of discovery because his individuality makes him realize that old conventions will not suffice to express what he perceives in the world around him.

Pound was excited by the lectures, told his mother in a letter how good they were, and informed Hulme that his own researches into Guido Cavalcanti had revealed a similar preoccupation with the new means of expression. 'I spoke to [Hulme] one day of the difference between Guido's precise interpretative metaphor, and the Petrarchian fustian and ornament.' Pound recalled later, 'pointing out that Guido thought in accurate terms; that the phrases correspond to definite sensations undergone ... Hulme took some time over it and then finally said: "That is very interesting"; and after a pause: "That is more interesting than anything I ever read in a book." '[31] The two pioneers consolidated their relationship, and Pound's first announcement of Imagism in fact appeared in his introduction to 'The Complete Poetical Works of T. E. Hulme', printed alongside his own poems in *Ripostes*. Hulme duly returned the compliment when he was reinstated at St John's College, Cambridge in the same year – on the strength of an enthusiastic recommendation from Bergson – by inviting Pound to read a paper at Cambridge in the autumn. Both he and Edward Marsh attended the American poet's lecture; and by this time, the three of them would have been willing to discuss their views on modern art as well as modern poetry, for during the previous year Hulme had been thinking about the relevance of contemporary painting and sculpture to his constantly evolving theories.

Quite by accident, the Bologna Philosophical Congress of April 1911 had marked a watershed in the progress of his thoughts and interests. The members of the Congress were entertained for a day at Ravenna as guests of the Italian government, and Hulme had his first chance to see the famous Byzantine mosaics. Their full significance did not occur to him immediately: it was only later that he began to reconsider the implications of the Ravenna mosaics and realize that there was a definite link between their stiff, formalized geometry and the work being produced by the two artists he had befriended through Pound in 1912 – Epstein and Lewis. For Hulme's way of working was always to use other men's ideas to supply the answers to the questions thrown up by his own, deeply felt experiences. The ideas that first drew his attention away from philosophy and poetry towards the visual arts were those of the German art historian Wilhelm Worringer, who in 1908 published what proved to be a highly influential book entitled *Abstraction and Empathy*. During the winter of 1911 Hulme heard Worringer lecture on art at the Berlin Aesthetic Congress, where he 'had an opportunity of talking with him'.[32] And he later admitted that his central distinction between 'geometric' and 'vital' art was 'practically an abstract of Worringer's views'.[33] The attraction was a natural one: Hulme was not concerned with the aesthetic delights of looking at pictures so much as with the philosophy of art, and in Worringer 'I found an extraordinarily clear statement, founded on an extensive knowledge of the history of art, of a view very like the one I had tried to formulate'.[34]

Worringer's statement amounted to nothing less than a renunciation of the writers who saw the art of the past largely as a history of technical ability. Worringer, and the aesthetician Riegl before him, rejected the theory of empathy formulated by Lipps, whereby primitive geometrical art was seen as an inferior formula concocted by artists who lacked the talent to convey the organic lines of realistic forms. The new approach proposed by Riegl in such books as *Stilfragen* (1893), and relied upon by Worringer, insisted that the stylistic peculiarities of archaic art arose not from a lack of ability but from a different kind of spiritual need. Primitive artists, argued Riegl, did not want to create the sensuous empathy of Greek art: their expressive urge, or 'absolute artistic volition', was directed towards totally opposite ends. How else could it be explained that the Egyptians were able, when they so desired, to achieve realism of the most astonishingly proficient kind in relatively minor forms of their art?

Hulme seized on this important if overgeneralized distinction – he was the first Englishman and one of the first anywhere to realize its value – and connected it both with the works of Epstein and Lewis and with his own previous thinking. He saw the opposition between geometrical and 'vital' art as identical with the opposition he had already formulated between religious and humanist, classical and romantic. Just as he had prophesied the downfall of humanism and the death of romantic poetry, so now he announced the end of naturalistic art and the rebirth of the older geometrical art. 'I started with the conviction that the Renaissance attitude is breaking up and then illustrated it by the change in art, not vice versa', he explained. 'First came the reaction against Renaissance philosophy and the adoption of the attitude which I said went with the geometrical art.'[35] Nothing could have been more logical. The new art was the first reflection of man's reawakening sense of Original Sin – of the fact that humanity once more felt divorced from nature, alone and apart. Art was the first medium of expression to register this new situation because 'so thoroughly are we soaked in the spirit of the period we live in, so strong is its influence over us, that we can only escape from it in an unexpected way, as it were, a side direction like art'.[36]

The artist, therefore, was the intuitively inspired prophet of the defeat of the Renaissance tradition, and Hulme's over-simplified but clear-cut theory could confer philosophical respectability on the creative work of his new artist friends. He was able, also, to attack representational art as the enfeebled 'sloppy dregs' of a dying romanticism, and was quick to outline his new ideas in an absorbing lecture on 'Modern Art and its Philosophy' delivered to the Quest Society at Kensington Town Hall on 22 January 1914.[37] Here, only eight days after the 'Cubist Room' exhibition closed in Brighton, he elaborated on the distinction between the 'soft and vital' lines of 'Greek art and modern art since the Renaissance', and the 'other arts like Egyptian, Indian and Byzantine, where everything tends to be angular, where curves tend to be hard and geometrical, where the representation of the human body . . . is . . . distorted to fit into stiff lines and cubical shapes of various kinds'.[38] It is at once apparent that Hulme was angling his description of primitive art to fit in with the characteristics of the new English painting and sculpture. He claimed that a 'positive proof' of the 'certain change of sensibility' he foresaw in the world was to be found 'in the actual creation of a new modern geometrical art'. But this movement, he added hurriedly, must not be confused with the 'complete breaking away from tradition' to be witnessed in art 'at the present moment in Europe'. Hulme firmly refuted any supposition that he was 'speaking of futurism which is, in its logical form, the exact opposite of the art I am describing, being the deification of the flux, the last efflorescence of impressionism'. Neither did he support 'certain elements of cubism, what I might call analytical cubism – the theories about interpenetration which you get in Metzinger for example'. He dismissed the innovations of the continental avant-garde, and claimed that he was thinking only of 'one element which seems to be gradually hardening out, and separating itself from the others'.[39]

Hulme's description of the form he imagined the new art would take was an astonishingly accurate forecast of the movement that would emerge in a few months' time as Vorticism. 'The new "tendency towards abstraction" will culminate', his lecture continued, 'not so much in the simple geometrical forms found in archaic art, but in the more complicated ones associated in our minds with the idea of machinery.' And this mechanistic element would, he maintained, probably be 'the specific differentiating quality of the new art', for artists would favour 'lines which are clean, clear-cut and mechanical'. Admiration would grow for the qualities contained in 'engineer's drawings, where the lines are clean, the curves all geometrical, and the colour, laid on to show the shape of a cylinder for example, gradated absolutely mechanically'. The description immediately recalls the diagrammatic impersonality of Lewis's *Composition*, but Hulme incorporated sculpture in his challenging thesis as well by advocating 'admiration for the hard clean surface of a piston rod'. He even went so far as to ask himself 'what will be the relation to the artist and the engineer?' and complained that 'at present the artist is merely receptive in regard to machinery'. His anti-Omega sympathies suddenly became overt when he castigated Fry as 'a mere verbose sentimentalist' for talking 'as he did lately, of "machinery being as beautiful as a rose"'; and Hulme called instead for the evolution of an art 'having an organisation, and governed by principles, which are at present exemplified unintentionally, as it were, in machinery'. He was flatly opposed to the Futurists' literal use of the machine as a subject in their pictures, insisting instead on the influence of machinery on form alone; but that did not mean he was proposing an exclusively abstract art. 'One might be pardoned', he declared drily, 'if one felt no particular interest in the eternity of a cube.' What really excited him was a marriage of abstraction and figuration. 'Put man into some geometrical shape', he argued, 'which lifts him out of the transience of the organic'. And after this vitally prophetic prescription, it was inevitable that he should record some specific praise for Lewis, who had already paved the way with paintings and drawings in which the 'only interest in the human body was in a few abstract mechanical relations perceived in it, the arm as a lever and so on'. Epstein, too, was commended for his 'drawings for sculpture', where the theme of birth and generation was transformed 'into something as hard and durable as a geometrical figure itself'.[40]

The new art was aiming, Hulme concluded, at turning 'the organic into something not organic', and trying 'to translate the changing and limited, into something unlimited and necessary'. He utterly discounted 'the materialist explanation' of the geometrical movement, and emphasized that 'the use of mechanical lines in the new art is in no sense merely a reflection of mechanical environment'. Naturally enough, he was prepared to admit that the artist 'passively admires' the 'superb steel structures which form the skeletons of modern buildings, and whose gradual envelopment in a parasitic covering of stone is one of the daily tragedies to be witnessed in London streets'. But materials like steel 'can only be used when the inclination and taste to which they are appropriate already exist'; and this 'inclination' is a deep-seated urge, not something that comes merely from a prolonged observation of the industrial environment. The argument contradicted Lewis, of course, who had explained in his 'Cubist Room' foreword that 'a man who passes his days among the rigid lines of houses . . . will eventually possess a different habit of vision to a man living amongst the lines of a landscape'. Such a hypothesis was incurably superficial to Hulme, who sought out the impulse towards abstraction rather in the inward spiritual condition of the artist's soul. 'Pure geometrical regularity gives a certain pleasure to men troubled by the obscurity of outside appearance', he insisted. 'The geometrical line is something absolutely distinct from the messiness, the confusion, and the accidental details of existing things.'[41]

A complete philosophical justification of the art which Lewis and his compatriots were formulating had, then, been publicly announced at the Quest Society as early as January 1914. Hulme succeeded in adding a potentially powerful new weapon to the artists' armoury; and Pound, who attended the lecture, granted in an *Egoist* article in February that Hulme had been 'quite right' in declaring that the difference between the new art and the old was not a difference in degree but a difference in kind. He complained, perhaps out of simple cheekiness, that Hulme's theories had been 'almost wholly unintelligible', but then went on to develop an argument almost synonymous with that of his old friend and mentor. 'My generation is not the generation of the romanticists', he proclaimed. 'To the present condition of things we have nothing to say but "merde" and this wild new sculpture says it.'[42] Hulme's theories obviously coincided with the opinions of artists and writers active in his own immediate circle, for Bomberg declared years later that 'there had only been journalistic criticism of painting in this country – with the exception of Walter Sickert, George Moore, Roger Fry and Clive Bell, these, though the most eminent, had not the remotest idea of what we were doing. Hulme had and wrote about it, and in this way he became the spokesman for the innovators in the first exhibition of the London Group'.[43] Leaving aside Pound, no other writer championed their work with such infectious zeal, or with the certainty which enabled Hulme to affirm at the end of his Quest lecture that the 'association with the idea of machinery takes away any kind of dilettante character from the movement and makes it seem more solid and more inevitable. It seems to me beyond doubt that this, whether you like it or not, is the character of the art that is coming. I speak of it myself with enthusiasm, not only because I appreciate it for itself, but because I believe it to be the precursor of a much wider change in philosophy and general outlook on the world'.

The philosopher rapidly became accepted among the artistic circles where his theories received most approbation. He was an enormously sociable man as well as a fairly formidable intellectual, and the 'Cubist Room' artists realized for their part that he would present their work to the public sympathetically and without literary pretensions. Epstein, to whom Hulme was temperamentally most closely attached, remembered that 'he was of a generous and singularly likeable character, and with artists he was humble and always willing to learn'.[44] And Hulme made a point of showing his admiration for his friends in the most positive way: he bought two of Epstein's flenite carvings, paying him a pound a week and carefully recording each separate instalment in a little black notebook. Indeed, he even wrote that 'the only absolutely honest and direct and straightforward word expression of what I think as I go round . . . an exhibition would be a monotonous repetition of the words "This is good or fairly good. How much does that cost?" for I would certainly rather buy a picture than write about it. It seems a much more appropriate gesture'.[45] The disarming honesty of such an attitude endeared him to the artists he championed in print, and goes a long way towards explaining the quite phenomenal success of the celebrated weekly salon he held at a beautiful seventeenth-century house at 67 Frith Street.

The house was owned by Mrs Kibblewhite, whose marriage had been foundering so badly before she met Hulme that her husband had on more than one occasion threatened to kill her.[46] She became an intimate of the philosopher and delighted in opening the doors of her house every Tuesday to his wide circle of friends and acquaintances, playing the hostess with her sister Dora and even her old father, a designer of stained-glass windows. Her home had been, according to D. L. Murray, 'the Venetian Embassy in the eighteenth century, and something of the traditions of the Serene Republic seemed still to linger on in the superb first-floor salon'[47] where Hulme always held court. Here, among the 'First Empire mirrors and chandeliers', the cream of London's artists and intellectuals gathered regularly, and the most widely opposed factions mixed freely with each other in the general euphoria. Ford, Rupert Brooke and the Georgian poets were to be seen in the same company as Pound, Aldington, John Cournos and A. R. Orage, the enlightened editor of *The New Age*. On the artistic side Sickert, Gore, Ginner and Gilman rubbed shoulders with Lewis and his allies, an unlikely consortium that would have been impossible to imagine without the 'genially aggressive' personality of their host. 'Hulme had the most wonderful gift of knowing everyone and mixing everyone', testified Nevinson, one of his most frequent guests. 'There were journalists, writers, poets, painters, politicians of all sorts, from Conservatives to New Age Socialists, Fabians, Irish yaps, American bums, and Labour leaders.'[48] The salon had its detractors, of course: David Garnett, whose sympathies lay more with the ambience of Bloomsbury, considered that 'there was in that company an atmosphere of swashbuckling, a tendency to talk for display in order to impress or score off others, an anxiety to be among the first to *épater les bourgeois* with fashionably outrageous ideas'.[49] Women must have been equally opposed to the Frith Street evenings, too, for Hulme refused to admit them on the grounds that 'the sex element interfered with intellectual talk'. Such discrimination was, Epstein insisted, simply 'a confession of his own weakness'.[50]

It is impossible to determine the precise degree of influence Hulme exerted over his contemporaries. Lewis claimed many years later that 'it was mainly as a theorist in the criticism of the fine arts that Hulme would have distinguished himself, had he lived. And I should undoubtedly have played Turner to his Ruskin. All the best things Hulme said about the theory of art were said about my art . . . We happened, that is all, to be made for each other, as critic and "creator". What he said should be done, I *did*. Or it would be more exact to say that I did it, and he said it'.[51] Such an unbearably pompous account merely emphasizes that theirs was not a straightforward relationship, and there is plenty of evidence to suggest that Hulme preferred Epstein to Lewis. The sculptor's work seems to have been the first to spark off his interest in art, for in the Quest lecture he stated that 'finally I recognised this geometrical character re-emerging in modern art. I am thinking particularly of certain pieces of sculpture I saw some years ago, of Mr Epstein's'.[52] And Hulme devoted much of his energy to the planning of a monograph on Epstein's work, which unfortunately disappeared without trace in the trenches of the First World War. Both Lewis and Epstein, however, must in their own ways have appealed to Hulme, who combined a restless intelligence with a personality that was equally iconoclastic.

He was deeply impressed by the ideas of Georges Sorel, whose 1908 book *Reflections on Violence* he was translating and whose approval of the class struggle was based on the view that proletarian upheavals like a general strike were beneficial to the vitality of society. Sorel thought that true social emancipation was a myth – he later followed Pound into an involvement with Italian Fascism – but he did believe in violent action's ability to foster a productive enthusiasm among the workers. And Hulme, who considered 'there are many who begin to be disillusioned with liberal and pacifist *democracy*, while shrinking from the opposed *ideology* on account of its reactionary associations', thought it likely that 'to these people Sorel, a revolutionary in economics, but classical in ethics, may prove an emancipator'.[53] He must have discussed Sorel, and *Reflections on Violence* in particular, with Lewis, and both men would have been especially attracted to Sorel's conviction that man's potential moment of real liberation could be attained through violence, 'when we make an effort to create a new man within ourselves'. Such an ideal linked up at once with Lewis's earlier interest in Kropotkin's anarchism and with his growing desire for an extremist, unashamedly violent rebellion in art. Even if he did not by this time share Hulme's other great passion for Bergson, who had himself influenced Sorel, Lewis probably drew considerable inspiration from *Reflections on Violence* and its revolutionary yet classical creed. As for Hulme, it can be seen impregnating not only his philosophy and personal hopes for art, but also his subversive and aggressive behaviour in daily life.

He always took an impish delight in any opportunity to outrage middle-class sensibilities, and amused himself by impressing his friends with colourful accounts of his sexual prowess. 'Hulme would suddenly pull out his watch while a group of his acquaintance sat talking with him at a table in the Café Royal', recalled David Garnett. ' "I've a pressing engagement in five minutes' time", he would say and stride out of the building. Twenty minutes later he would return, wipe his brow, and complain that the steel staircase of the emergency exit at Piccadilly Circus Tube Station was the most uncomfortable place in which he had ever copulated.' As might be expected, Garnett added that the episode 'rather offended my youthful idealism.'[54] But can it be doubted that Lewis and all Hulme's other friends savoured these antics just as much as they enjoyed Marinetti's physical exertions on the lecture platform? They were all a part of the high-spirited belief in rebellion which increasingly infected London's artistic milieu during these memorable pre-war months. Aesthetic dissent was coming to a head and Hulme, who reminded one acquaintance of 'a farmer at a fair', contributed to the general excitement through his personal life no less than his courageously independent theories of art.

# Chapter 7: The Rebel Art Centre and Gaudier-Brzeska's Emergence

With the advent of the new year, a fresh rash of schisms broke out between the rival artistic coteries. This time it was the indomitable Sickert, alienated by the extremity of the 'Cubist Room' artists, who decided to join the fray. He had made a short speech at the Brighton exhibition after the Mayor declared it open to the public and, as his biographer recorded, 'stressed the fact that the group would not be associated with any one society or academy. Art should not be made into a party question. Such a course was both illogical and insincere. Even the New English Art Club, to which he belonged, was found shaking one fist at the Academy while it held on to the frock coat of Mr Sargent with the other. He dissociated himself personally from the extremist views of Post-Impressionism, but insisted on the healthful influence on art of free speech'.[1]

Sickert was trying to have it both ways, declaring his belief in the value of an aesthetic democracy while openly disapproving of the work produced by its most advanced members. But by February 1914, the preparations for the first London Group exhibition brought his mounting antagonism to a head. 'Like the lady in bridal attire who bolts at the church door the Epstein-Lewis marriage is too much for me & I have bolted', he wrote in a heated letter to Nan Hudson. 'I have resigned both Fitzroy Street and the London Group. You who have watched the stages will not think me merely frivolous . . . First Gilman forced Epstein on me, as you know against my will. But I was in a minority. At Brighton the Epstein-Lewis-Etchells room made me sick & I publicly disengaged my responsibility. On Saturday Epstein's so-called drawings were put up on easels & Lewis's big Brighton picture. The Epsteins are pure pornography – of the most joyless kind soit-dit & the Lewis is pure impudence. Then I left, once and for all, but *never again for an hour* could I be responsible or associated in any way with showing such things. I dont believe in them, and, further, I think they render any consideration of serious painting impossible.'[2]

It was scarcely unexpected, therefore, when he took it upon himself to usher in the spring of 1914 with a series of open assaults upon Lewis and his allies. As a dry run for the first attack, he used his combative column-space in *The New Age* of 5 March to assert that no artist had ever been 'more shamelessly exploited than Cézanne when his respectable name was made to cover the impudent theories of Matisse and Picasso, who, talented themselves, have invented an academic formula which is the salvation of all *arrivistes* without talent'. His generalized remarks were slanted enough to trigger off a flurry of letters in the *Pall Mall Gazette*, where he took part in a running skirmish with Nevinson about the ability of the 'Cubist Room' rebels. And little more than a fortnight after Sickert had published a particularly vitriolic letter about their 'meaningless patterns', he let fly with his heaviest artillery in a prolonged tour de force of abuse in *The New Age* of 26 March. His article was ironically entitled 'On Swiftness' and it denounced the 'English Cubists', declaring that they were not only without talent but pornographers to boot. 'While the faces of the persons suggested are frequently nil', he wrote of their work, 'non-representation is forgotten when it comes to the sexual organs. Witness Mr Wyndham Lewis's "Creation", exhibited at Brighton . . . and several of Mr Epstein's later drawings.'

The slander hit home and Lewis, continuing his self-appointed role as group spokesman, was quick to reply. The following week, in *The New Age* of 2 April, he refuted the allegations and enjoyed himself hugely in an uninhibited, satirical survey of Sickert's own career. After claiming that Sickert had once been a 'Bohemian plague-spot on clean English life', Lewis's letter followed this accusation of decadence by charging its victim with senility. 'But now he has survived his sins, and has sunk into the bandit's mellow and peaceful maturity', Lewis crowed. 'He sits at his open front door and invents little squibs and contrivances to discomfort the young brigands he hears tales of, and of whose exploits

PROGRESS.

Post-Elliptical Rhomboidist: "Him a modern! Bah! He paints in the old-fashioned manner of last Thursday!"

BY WILL DYSON.

Will Dyson
*Progress*, 1914. Seated, left Epstein (?) and right Augustus John (?) Background, in hat, Lewis (?)

he is rather jealous.' Then Lewis became rather more constructive and serious, discounting his allies' supposed delight in the description of salacious anatomical details. ' "Cubism", as a matter of fact, would tend quite in the contrary direction', he protested, 'as it is a movement largely occupied in banishing extraneous or literary stimulus, concentrating on forms and colours for their own sake; essentially inhuman and pure.' The argument was logically convincing, and Lewis claimed with reason that Sickert's interpretation of 'my painting "Creation" ' amounted to 'a deliberate misstatement and invention. I have always found pornography extremely boring and regarded it as the hallmark of the second-rate. As for Phallic aesthetics, I have no quarrel with them, only I don't happen to participate myself, that is all'. He had mounted a resilient counter-attack, but the wily Sickert was not to be silenced. Old journalistic campaigner that he was, he struck back again in *The New Age*, this time alleging that the 'Cubists' were the worst kind of fraudulent poseurs. 'The sense of advertisement has created the intentional, we may almost say the professional *refusé*, the type of the *douanier* Rousseau in Paris',[3] he maintained, totally dismissing the genius of the great Frenchman.

Sickert's mockery was well wide of the mark. Deliberate naïvety was never a part of the 'Cubist Room' group's programme, and the cartoonist Will Dyson was far better informed when he drew a spirited little barb called *Progress* for *The New Age* in which the rebels were shrewdly christened 'Post-Elliptical Rhomboidists'. But this light-hearted badinage was not echoed by Professor Tonks, who was stolidly maintaining his traditional teaching-methods at the Slade and often ruefully observed: 'What an unholy brood I have raised up.'[4]

Lewis and his allies were consequently out on their own, having disassociated themselves first from the Slade, then the Omega and now Sickert, the leader of the old avant-garde. All they needed now was a rallying-point and a central identity, for they were growing impatient with the arbitrary labels of 'Cubist' and 'Futurist' which bewildered critics showered on them more or less at random. The stigma of Fry's earlier domination rankled still, and Lewis continued to pen bitter notes objecting to the Omega leader's tendency to suggest that 'his personal friends – Duncan Grant and Mrs Bell – were very rare spirits and peculiarly fine artists'.[5] Fry, in his own detached fashion, occasionally noticed the continuance of ill feeling in the authors of the 'Round Robin'. 'It is really sad that these young artists understand their common interests so little', he complained to Simon Bussy in December 1913. 'I think Lewis's vanity touches on insanity, and it is he who has lead the others, who are not bad but only ignorant and romantic, astray. In any case the Omega carries on quite well without them.'[6] And three months later, he was still sufficiently disturbed to tell Grant that 'the Lewis gang do nothing else even now but abuse me', at the same time wondering 'why I inspire such intense dislike' and expressing surprise at such a long-lasting 'display of vindictive jealousy among artists'.[7]

By the time Fry wrote this puzzled letter, however, the 'Lewis gang' were busily forming their own practical alternative to the Bloomsbury Workshops. Lewis himself was delighted to receive one day an offer of help from Kate Lechmere, a painter friend whom he had first met in 1912 at a dinner party given by Mrs Bevan. During the course of the evening Miss Lechmere, not knowing the authorship of the *Timon* drawings then to be seen at the Grafton Galleries, admitted that she 'did not care for them'. Mrs Bevan was quick to inform her that the artist in question was of the company, but Lewis reassured the embarrassed guest by telling her that he 'didn't mind at all'. Moreover, he asked Miss Lechmere out to dinner soon afterwards, and a friendship was rapidly established.[8] Apart from their mutual liking for each other, Miss Lechmere also sympathized with Lewis's aesthetic standpoint: she afterwards described herself as a 'Cubist painter at that time', and the three works she exhibited at the 1913 AAA Salon – *Study (Man)*, *Lady in Furs* and *Buntem Vogel* – were indeed described by one visitor as the work of a 'Cubist lady'.[9] They have all been lost, but two photographs of *Buntem Vogel* taken in 1914 clearly show the Cubist influence. She was extremely fond of Lewis, whom she nicknamed 'Gollywog' because of his 'untidy long hair'; and was so eager to support his interests that early in 1914 she wrote him a letter from Nice not only proposing the formation of an atelier based on the French system, but also offering her services as a financial backer for the scheme.

In other words, she gave Lewis the chance to realise the ideal he had failed to discover in the Omega: an artists' commune, united by similar underlying ideas, yet at the same time flexible enough for each individual member to express himself freely. 'After I wrote to Lewis about the atelier, I came back to London', Miss Lechmere recalled. 'Lewis told me firmly that "we are not going to have it in Chelsea", so I looked around elsewhere; but I think Etchells found the eventual site because he had a flat directly opposite it.'[10] The large, now demolished Georgian house finally selected at 38 Great Ormond Street was only a few minutes' walk away from its older rival at Fitzroy Square; but Lewis made the atelier's separate identity abundantly clear when he chose its stirring name: the Rebel Art Centre. This insurrectionary title was printed in bold capitals on the official stationery letterhead, while the totally abstract design which appeared above it affirmed the central preoccupation of the place.[11] Lewis's headquarters was to be dedicated to aesthetic revolution, and he wanted its official designation – no less than its pictorial insignia – to make that aim clear right from the start.

The Centre, which was formally inaugurated in the spring of 1914, consisted of the first floor alone; and Miss Lechmere, who paid the rent out of her own funds, demolished 'the whole of one large wall' so that it consisted of 'two big rooms in one, with a little room at the end for Lewis to store his canvases and another small space which was used as an office'.[12] According to the *Daily News and Leader*, the result was 'a room obviously designed for the destruction of melancholy. Curtains of crocus gold falling in long laughing lines transmuted the abysmal darkness of a March afternoon into something luminous and radiant. Doors of lawless scarlet amicably agreed to differ with decorous carpets of dreamy blue'.[13] The walls were painted pale lemon, Nevinson decorated a table and Miss Lechmere herself, who insisted on painting a 9 ft long divan red and covering it with red, white and blue striped material from Liberty's 'to hide its stupid little floral covering', created an independent flat for herself on the top floor, complete with roof garden and window boxes painted in strident abstract patterns.[14] It was duly celebrated by a *Vanity Fair* correspondent, who described in an ecstatic article called 'The Futurist Note in Interior Decoration' how 'Miss Lechmere, one of the directors, has gone further and has decorated a whole flat – her own – in Futurism (the only one in London), in order to show the possibilities of the new decoration. It is situated above the Cubist salons, and contains black doors in cream walls, and black curtains in addition to the usual orgies of colour. I am told she is engaged in planning a Cubist rock garden, with strange, stunted trees from Japan'.[15]

The Press obviously could not make up its mind whether the Rebel Art Centre represented Cubism, Futurism, or some mysterious amalgam of the two, and Lewis did not help matters by asking membership cheques to be made out to 'The Cubist Art Centre, Ltd.' Fleet Street was puzzled still further by the rebels' determination to deny themselves all hint of the traditional image of artistic bohemianism personified by John. One newspaper, according to Kate

Kate Lechmere
*Buntem Vogel*, 1913

Photograph of Kate Lechmere with *Buntem Vogel* (detail), 1914

Wyndham Lewis (?)
Letterhead for the Rebel Art Centre, 1914

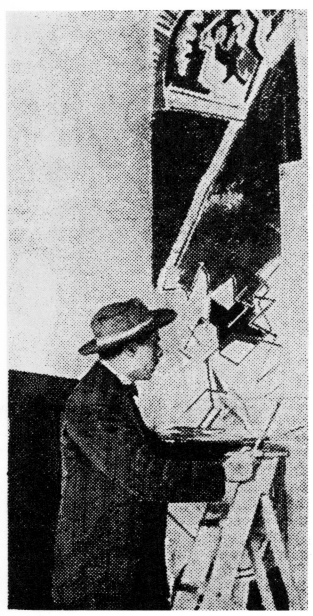

△Photograph of Lewis painting a mural at the Rebel Art Centre, 1914

△Helen Saunders *The Oast House* (?), *c.* 1912–13

Lechmere, visited the Centre and published a photograph with 'the caption in large letters "Artists a disappointment in real life." Velvet jackets and floppy ties were not encouraged by Lewis and we were to be anti-aesthetic'. The confusion did not, however, prevent the *Daily Mirror* from sending a photographer along to record the eager activity filling the Centre's headquarters at the end of March. Lewis was pictured in the act of painting a totally abstract mural on the wall, which although never completed can be seen more satisfactorily in a photograph of Kate Lechmere sewing Rebel Art Centre curtains. Its colours are unrecorded, but they were startling enough for Violet Hunt to be reminded of 'a butcher's shop full of prime cuts . . . as noisy as red paint could make them'.[16] And although the *Mirror*'s photographer could not show any other decorations to back up the Prospectus's claim that 'Ormond Street is being decorated by several artists . . . with a series of large mural paintings and friezes', he did take a shot of a whole group of the rebels hanging Wadsworth's abstract painting *Caprice* in the large room. The *Evening Standard* followed this, on the very same day, with a group portrait of Kate Lechmere and three rebels surrounded by their work; and then *The Graphic*, not to be outdone in its coverage of this new avant-garde sensation, reproduced a photograph of another, closely related Wadsworth painting hanging above a door, contrasting rather incongruously with the angular figuration of a Lewis canvas positioned over the mantelpiece.[17] But perhaps this inconsistency was ironed out soon afterwards, for Kate Lechmere remembered that the photographers were admitted to the house before it was ready to open.[18] Her memory is corroborated by a report from Frank Rutter in the *New Weekly* on 4 April, which announces the opening of the Centre and lists Lewis as manager and Etchells, Hamilton Nevinson and Wadsworth as 'associates'.[19] So spring would have been well advanced by the time everything was completed to the joint satisfaction of the leaseholder and her protégé.

At the inaugural meeting Nevinson, true to his Futurist convictions, said 'let's not have any of these damned women', and Lewis was forced to admit with embarrassment that the Centre depended for its financial survival on the female resources of Miss Lechmere. But he shared Nevinson's prejudice in other ways, and refused to hand tea round at the Saturday afternoon gatherings held between four and six o'clock in the roof-garden. 'I had to do the honours', Miss Lechmere recalled, 'because Lewis insisted that organizing tea-parties was a job for women, not artists.'[20] The anti-suffragette feeling did not, however, prevent two female painters from joining the proceedings; and since would-be members had first of all to be invited by Lewis, they must have entered with his explicit approval.

One of them was Helen Saunders, who had studied at the Slade between 1906 and 1907 but left for the Central School of Art before the rebel generation arrived there. Little is known of her formative years, beyond the fact that it needed great independence on her part to break away from a very respectable middle-class background where daughters were not expected to work, let alone become artists.[21] But a lost *Portrait* she exhibited at the 1912 AAA Salon was forward-looking enough to receive special praise from Fry, who thought that it 'shows a real feeling for planning the structure of a design, and is excellent as far as its unambitious presentment of form goes'.[22] His opinion was seconded by Clive Bell, who thought her AAA contributions 'creditable' and 'painted surely under the influence of Mr Etchells'.[23]

If a surviving early landscape can be identified as the painting of an *Oasthouse* she contributed to the 1913 Salon, Fry's commendation is immediately understandable: its muted colours and mildly Cézannesque composition is close to the landscapes Fry himself was executing at the time.[24] But one visitor to the

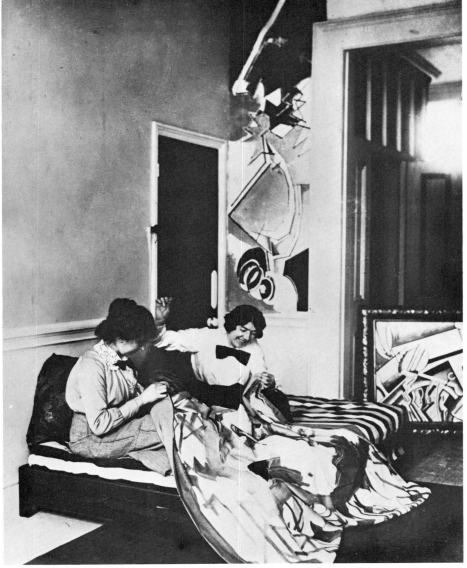

Hanging up a "work" called "Caprice."

△Photograph of (from left to right) Hamilton (?),
Wadsworth, Nevinson and Lewis hanging
Wadsworth's painting *Caprice* at the Rebel
Art Centre, 1914

◁Photograph of Kate Lechmere and a friend
sewing curtains in the Rebel Art Centre,
1914.

▽Photograph of (standing, left to right)
Wadsworth and Lewis with (sitting, left to
right) Hamilton (?) and Kate Lechmere in
the Rebel Art Centre, 1914

◁Photographs of (left to right) Lewis's painting
*Group* (?) hanging above a mantelpiece at the
Rebel Art Centre; the façade of 38 Great
Ormond Street; and an unidentified Wadsworth
painting hanging over a door at the Rebel Art
Centre, 1914

Helen Saunders
*Untitled Gouache: Female Figures Imprisoned, c. 1913*

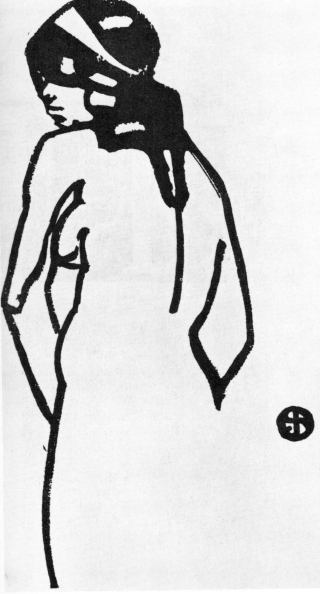

Jessica Dismorr
*Study*, 1911

show noted that Saunders' work was now 'cubist' in style;[25] and a small ink and gouache design from this period, depicting seven attenuated female figures trapped unhappily inside a cage structure presumably symbolizing the forces against which suffragettes were at that moment fighting, marks a bold step forward in the direction of semi-abstraction. Her progress is confirmed in another, related gouache showing a demonic warrior ploughing his mechanistic weapon into the ground with a vehemence which shatters the nerves of the spectator on the left and at once recalls Epstein's *Rock Drill*. From here, Saunders soon found herself drawing a frankly mechanical *Bending Figure* in a style which suggests at least a passing acquaintance with the ideas of Lewis and the other English rebels. Unlike the imprisoned females gouache, which uses curvilinear rhythms as yet unconnected with the angularity of rebel art, *Bending Figure* is close to Lewis's geometrical robots and seems to be appropriately involved in a measuring, mathematical task. It is immediately reminiscent of the celebrated 1795 colour print of *Newton* by Blake, an artist of whom Saunders was particularly fond; but the gouache certainly does not endorse Blake's condemnation of a mechanistic universe. In contrast to the noble malevolence of *Newton*, Saunders' *Bending Figure* appears both innocently and optimistically engaged in his calculating activities.

The same development can also be said to apply to Jessica Dismorr, the other woman member of the Rebel Art Centre who was likewise described as a 'cubist' when she displayed three portraits at the 1913 AAA Salon.[26] Born in 1885, the same year as Saunders, she too began her painting career at the Slade in 1902 before studying in Paris around 1910 under Segonzac, Metzinger and Fergusson at La Palette. The British Fauves absorbed her temporarily into their circle, where she made a modest reputation for herself: in *Rhythm*, the Fauves' house magazine, she published in the autumn of 1911 a drawing of Isadora Duncan which linked her unequivocally with their preoccupations. It possesses, however, an element of severity lacking in the other illustrations – some embroidering the titles of articles, others taking up a full page in their own right – which were reproduced in early editions of *Rhythm* to prove her allegiance to Fergusson's Parisian emphasis on curvilinear simplification.

Their assurance prompted Rutter to include more of Dismorr's designs in his *Art News* periodical; and when at least five of her small, richly coloured and confident paintings were exhibited at the Stafford Gallery in October 1912, all based on landscapes as various as Siena, Martiques and Avignon, she was still accompanied by Fauves like Fergusson, Peploe and Anne Estelle Rice.[27] Her style, however, must then have evolved rapidly, for a hasty doodle she executed in her copy of the June 1913 *Blue Review* is utterly devoid of figurative content, and seems to owe more to the organic abstractions of Kandinsky than Fauvism. Soon afterwards, her 'cubist' contributions to the AAA Salon probably led to a meeting with Lewis, and she was sufficiently involved in his cause at the time of the Omega row to write him a letter wondering 'how you are getting on with the Fry campaign – I am really with you in spite of my apparent want of sympathy'.[28] Such gestures of support finally earned her a place in the Rebel Art Centre ranks, even if Lewis insisted that both she and Saunders fulfil their menial roles at Great Ormond Street by serving refreshments to visitors. Kate Lechmere scornfully remembered them as 'little lap-dogs who wanted to be Lewis's slaves and do everything for him';[29] and yet their willing subservience did not mean that they were unable to contribute creatively to the pictorial experiments undertaken by the group.

Other adherents likewise gravitated towards the Centre, helping to hide the fact that the nucleus formed by Hamilton, Lewis, Nevinson, Wadsworth and Etchells was somewhat impaired by the abstention of Epstein – shut away in

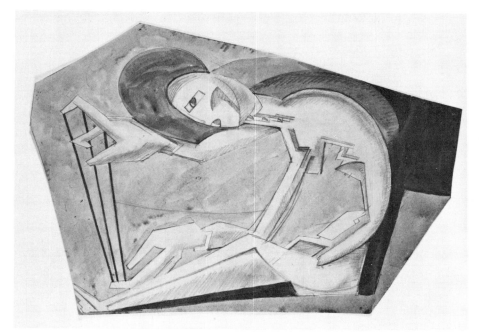

△ Helen Saunders
*Untitled Gouache: The Rock Driller, c. 1913*

◁ Helen Saunders
*Untitled Gouache: Bending Figure, c. 1913–14*

△ Jessica Dismorr
*Landscape with Cottages, c. 1911*

△ Jessica Dismorr
*Izidora, 1911*

△ Jessica Dismorr
*Monument with Figures, c. 1911–12*

◁ Jessica Dismorr
Sketch in *The Blue Review*, June 1913

the isolation of Pett Level much of the time – and Hulme, who naturally cared more for his own regular salon at Frith Street. Bomberg also remained hostile and suspicious, claiming later that 'I was not a Member or even went near the Rebel Art Centre';[30] while Kate Lechmere remembered that 'he never came to our teas, and I can still see him, a timid, thin little man who looked starving, waiting for Lewis outside the Centre. He always refused to come in'.[31] But Pound made up for their lack of enthusiasm by giving the project his whole-hearted approval, lecturing there on the connections between Imagism and the new art and introducing his poetic colleague Richard Aldington, who was by now Assistant Editor of *The Egoist*, to the rebel gatherings.

The Centre similarly attracted the sympathies of a successful portrait photographer called Malcolm Arbuthnot, who conducted a flourishing and distinguished business in his studio at 43 and 44 New Bond Street from 1914 until 1926. As early as 1908, however, he had established a quite separate reputation for radical experiment with extraordinary photographs like *The Wheel*, which summarily rejects most of the pictorial conventions of the period and opts instead for a severely schematic arrangement of essential forms. Nothing is allowed to detract from the stark silhouette of the bathing machine's spokes, save for the two bathers they frame so precisely near the horizon; and in another 1908 photograph called *The Pool* his impatience with any kind of irrelevant detail is still more marked. Its reduction to a bare silhouette is as remarkable as the way a third 1908 photograph of *The Labourer* stresses the structural geometry of the design by encircling the workman with yet another enormous wheel, the emblem of Arbuthnot's new thirst for innovation. Such audacious pictures were totally at odds with the prevalent standards of the day, and when Arbuthnot held his first one-man show of *Impressions* at the *Amateur Photographer*'s Little Gallery in March 1909, he elicited some sharp criticism. 'I would suggest that he should occasionally study human characteristics instead of disjointed and unpictorial arrangements, which may momentarily gratify a whim for something strange, but appeal to no artistic sense',[32] grumbled a typical reviewer. And *Photography*'s critic poked merciless fun at *The Wheel*, explaining that 'if you, dear reader, happened to be occupying a bathing machine, and just at the psychological moment of the interval between an aquatic and a terrestrial costume the bottom of the machine fell out and flopped you through, you would get the identical view shown. Whether you would wait to photograph it or not is a question you must decide for yourself'.

But Arbuthnot appears to have been unabashed, and stressed the proto-abstract bias of two more astonishing 1908 photographs by entitling them *A Study in Curves and Angles* and *A Study in Lines and Masses* respectively. Their calm, minimal extremism carries out the belief stated in his 1909 essay, 'A Plea for Simplification and Study in Pictorial Work', that 'there is no necessity to have what is termed a "view"; better, far better, take a portion of it . . . note how the light falls upon it, determining the tone values of each portion; scheme how to place it in such a position on the plate that the most is made of the object in conjunction with its decorative value, and, in short, get at the very soul of the little bit of nature upon which you are concentrating your attention'.[33] The result, in these two pictures supremely, was that Arbuthnot succeeded in eliminating all the narrative, picturesque and sentimental associations which photography at that period cherished. Both compositions concentrate on the most rudimentary and 'unartistic' ready-made forms for their own sake, an-nouncing an attitude towards ordinary objects and stylistic simplification quite revolutionary in either English art or photography.

Apart from the exceptional kindred spirit, such as the American pioneer photographer Alvin Langdon Coburn whom Arbuthnot portrayed around this

Malcolm Arbuthnot
*The Doorstep. A Study in Lines and Masses, c.* 1908

▽ Malcolm Arbuthnot *The Wheel, c.* 1908

△ Malcolm Arbuthnot *The Pool, c.* 1908

◁ Malcolm Arbuthnot *The Labourer, c.* 1908

▽ Malcolm Arbuthnot
*A Study in Curves and Angles, c.* 1908

Malcolm Arbuthnot
*Alvin Langdon Coburn, c.* 1907

Malcolm Arbuthnot
*Landscape,* 1910

time, his contemporaries considered such a programme ill-judged. Even a relatively sympathetic commentator like the *Photograms of the Year* editor, who wrote of these 1908 photographs that the 'quality of strong placing of simple masses is so far lacking in photography generally that Mr Arbuthnot is to be thanked for emphasising it', concluded that 'in carrying it to the extreme that he has done, he has produced some pictures which can only be taken as sketches or lessons, and which, fresh and interesting and vivid as they are, can only live as collectors' pieces, worthy of preservation as records of bold attempt and innovation. While photography suffers enormously from the want of any sort of skeleton in its pictures, the finally satisfactory photographic work will not be that in which a section of a skeleton alone is made the subject of study'.[34] Like the English art critics who rejected the successive waves of Post-Impressionism, Futurism, Cubism and now the English rebel art, photography critics simply refused to acknowledge that exciting possibilities were opened up by the deliberately reduced masses of Arbuthnot's 1908 *The Hillside*, its very mystical intensity of feeling comparable with Coburn's similar cloud studies, or his even more abstracted treatment of *The River*, where the stretch of water is rendered as a soft, whispering white curve stretching into the distance like a solitary brushstroke.[35] Looking back on Arbuthnot's career in 1916, one writer could declare that 'in many quarters he has been regarded as a stormy petrel whose outlook has ever been antagonistic to that of the conventional school';[36] and it was natural that this fierce individuality should attract him to Post-Impressionist art as well. He painted throughout his life, and Matisse actually completed Arbuthnot's portrait of the actress Teddy Gerrard while visiting his studio to be photographed. Moreover, he organized a Post-Impressionist exhibition at Liverpool in February 1913 with loans drawn from Fry's Grafton Galleries survey, ensuring a lively response from the public by parading a squad of sandwichmen through the city centre and giving lectures on the movement with Fry and Rutter while the show was on view. It was held in the Sandon Studios, and because Arbuthnot insisted that each visitor pay a shilling at a specially installed turnstile, he was able to report in his autobiography that the exhibition made 'a profit of forty pounds!'

The year before, only the three photographs of Epstein included in his Summer 1912 exhibition at the Goupil Gallery suggested that he might later ally himself with the Great Ormond Street company: the rest of his eighty *Camera Portraits* in the show ranged over a wide but reactionary spectrum of established British artists, from Alma-Tadema and Lavery to John, Brangwyn and Sickert.[37] But now, armed with his first-hand experience of Post-Impressionist crusading, he was eager to befriend the English rebels; and in the Spring of 1914 he paid a call on Lewis in his Fitzroy Street studio, where he also met Etchells and Wadsworth for good measure. The meeting was a success, and during his second visit Arbuthnot produced some examples of his current painting, which he later described as a form of 'Decorative Realism'. Lewis liked them, gave his new friend some practical advice and doubtless introduced him to the Rebel Art Centre group.[38] Arbuthnot's pictures have since been lost, but a contemporary commentary on them indicated that 'as a painter he has developed along the lines of post-impressionism, which makes a strong appeal to him for its abstract qualities of design and pattern, apart from subject. He has produced some remarkable examples of landscape work of this character, but feels it is a method of expression inapplicable to the rendering of portraits'.[39] This important reservation probably defined the limits of Arbuthnot's commitment to rebel art – he never exhibited with his artist allies, and at forty years of age was considerably older in 1914 even than Lewis – but that did not stop Pound from looking forward to posing for him. 'I haven't a decent photograph

Malcolm Arbuthnot
*The River, c.* 1908

Malcolm Arbuthnot
*The Hillside, c.* 1908

at the moment', the poet told James Joyce in July 1914, 'but Arbuthnot has asked me for a sitting and you are welcome to the result when it comes.'[40] On that level, at least, he seems to have commanded the rebels' sincere respect; while on another level he stands as a link between Vorticism and the Vortographs of his friend Coburn, who photographed Arbuthnot around 1907 and encouraged him so much during his most radical phase that by 19 April 1909 the *Liverpool Courier* could assert that 'Mr Arbuthnot follows with more or less precision in the footsteps of Mr A. L. Coburn . . . who has made for himself a peculiar place among the more advanced men by his remarkable work'.

Perhaps the most ardent of newcomers to the Centre was Lawrence Atkinson, a resolutely independent, somewhat enigmatic artist who counted singing and poetry among a multiplicity of other interests. Almost a decade older than Lewis, he had studied music in Paris and Berlin at the turn of the century, and afterwards became a concert performer while teaching singing in London and Liverpool. Then, quite suddenly, he left for Paris to begin painting under Fergusson at La Palette, and afterwards exhibited with Dismorr and the other British Fauves at the Stafford Gallery in October 1912. All his early work remains untraced, but Horace Shipp's monograph on Atkinson reveals that 'at the commencement of his career' he produced many 'landscape studies', the style of which was 'much nearer to that of Gauguin, a statement of his subject in terms of bold colour patches. Often he would emphasize the decorative value of these by definite, heavy outlines, seeing his subject as a mosaic of beautiful colour and rhythmic form'.[41] The titles of the lost pictures he sent in to the 1913 AAA Salon – *The Lady of the Hyacinths*, *The Rose Dancer* and *A Garden, a Woman and a Faun* – imply that he was still pursuing the same Fauvist style even then. And Kate Lechmere, who was taught music by Atkinson and painted with him and the British Fauves in Normandy, thought that his work only underwent a drastic metamorphosis after he had seen Lewis's pictures at the Rebel Art Centre. 'Atkinson was a regular visitor at Great Ormond Street', she recalled, 'and Lewis took a special interest in him'.[42]

For his part, Atkinson hinted at this momentous conversion in his predominantly romantic and conventional 1915 collection of poems called *Aura* where he wrote:

> The blue
> Of the moment
> Envelops me
> In her silent
> Prophecies;
> And guides my
> Rudder-less boat
> To undiscovered Countries . . .
> Dream-images,
> Inarticulate world-forms
> That steal across
> The sky-line of
> My vision, like
> Phantom derelicts
> Upon the sleeping waters
> Of my soul.[43]

But only one poem began to explain how these 'undiscovered Countries' had affected his work, and even here the elements of visual abstraction in the scene Atkinson describes are contradicted by the predominantly archaic use of language:

> . . . These vermilion-striped sunblinds
> That labour in the breeze
> And cast the pattern of each mood
> Upon the sombre classic
> Of the tanagra-fronted houses:
> From all parts high low
> These flame-bound windows
> And their lightning shadows
> Give vivid utterance of their arbitrage,
> As if to tune the stolid rhythms of the walls
> To the brilliant harmonies
> Of the greater moment – [44]

Enough can be extracted from this passage – the 'lightning shadows' and 'vermilion-striped sunblinds', for example – to parallel the abrupt, angular form of abstraction which Atkinson now began to evolve, both in coolly deliberated ink drawings and in rather more sensuous ochre and pale yellow watercolour compositions.[45] Their clearly defined contours and pronounced diagonal bias allied them to the language then being formulated out of the combined influences of

△ Lawrence Atkinson
*Vorticist Figure, c.* 1914–16

◁ Lawrence Atkinson
*Study – Café Tables, c.* 1914–18

▽ Photograph of Kate Lechmere standing in
front of curtains at the Rebel Art Centre, 1914

Cubism and Futurism by the other English rebels. Participation in the Centre's
activities must have quickly destroyed his Fauvist inclinations, for one newspaper reported on his 'designs for the curtains and awnings of the Association's
headquarters' and decided that it was 'impossible to find the slightest trace of
any regularity in the symmetry, the tonality, the colouring or any other ordinary
antediluvian practice!'[46] The *Daily News and Leader* was scarcely less startled,
describing how 'on a white curtain hung across the room points of purple and
cubes of green and yellow, intermingling with splashes of deep rose-red, formed
themselves, as one gazed at them, into fantastic human figures'.[47] And the *Daily
Mirror* even decided to reproduce a photograph of these disturbing fabric designs
with Kate Lechmere staring appreciatively up at them.

Atkinson's curtains accorded with the promises of the Centre's official prospectus, which announced the foundation of an 'Art School' offering 'instruction
in various forms of applied Art, such as painting of screens, fans, lampshades
[and] scarves'. Such aims appear disconcertingly similar to those of the Omega;
but the vital difference lay in the fact that the 'starting point and the alphabet of
the teaching' would be based on 'the principles underlying the movements in
Painting, known as Cubist, Futurist, and Expressionist ... All art with any
vitality today can be placed in one of these categories, as integrally as all vigorous
art thirty years ago entered into that of Impressionism. The only difference is

that with the movement we see today all those severe and traditional tendences [*sic*] that separated Cézanne, for instance, from the Impressionists would rather serve to ally him with the painters of the present movement'.[48] All avant-garde theories were avidly welcomed by the rebels, and *Vanity Fair*'s report emphasized this open-mindedness by asserting that 'at the Rebel Art Centre there is a Catholicism of Heresies, as it were: orthodoxy alone is anathema, and there may be seen all the possibilities and, one might say, all the powers of the new movement. There you can see curtains, carpets, tables, lampshades, fans, scarves, door panels, shawls, dresses – all in Futurism. And you see examples of Futurism, Cubism, and Expressionism, after the style of the painter Kandinsky – and an empty room for the next "ism" that comes along'.[49]

Lewis's decision to make the emptiness of one room symbolize the imminent arrival of a new movement was prophetic indeed, and showed that he would not remain satisfied for long with this eclectic policy. But he was not quite ready to launch Vorticism yet, and contented himself meanwhile with extending invitations to radical luminaries who would be willing to expound their views at the Centre. He was an organizational novice, of course, and made mistakes: 'Lewis would advertise in *The Times* a lecture to be held at the Centre, but failed to put the date', Kate Lechmere recalled, 'so a second advertisement had to be made.' But Marinetti, whose lecture at the Doré Galleries in March had been sponsored by the rebels in order to raise funds for their headquarters, was asked to talk at Great Ormond Street at the beginning of May, and Kate Lechmere remembered him 'making loud puffing noises, pretending he was a train'.[50] Atkinson may also have had a hand in enlarging the Centre's interests into the field of music, for an attempt was made to invite 'some great innovator' like 'Schoenburg or Scrabine' [*sic*] to lecture on the new music; and it was even planned to vie with the Cabaret Club by staging 'short plays or Ombres Chinoises . . . which involve considerable expense'.[51]

All these plans coincided with the policy laid down in the prospectus, which claimed that the Centre would 'by public discussion, lectures and gatherings of people . . . familiarise those who are interested with the ideas of the great modern revolution in Art'.[52] Lewis hoped that the group would give their own classes and exhibitions of their work, thereby making it possible for the Centre to act as a much-needed publicity arm and disseminator of enlightened doctrines. He even managed to persuade Ford to deliver a lecture and the novelist duly appeared, 'absent-mindedly in a tail coat'.[53] The event nearly ended in disaster, for this dignified literary figure had his efforts rewarded half-way through the talk by a sharp blow from one of Lewis's largest paintings: it had been hanging on the wall behind Ford, and suddenly pitched forward on top of him. 'Luckily, however, no harm was done', explained Kate Lechmere, 'since the frame broke loose from the picture and crashed to the floor, leaving the canvas perched harmlessly on Ford's head.'[54] As chance would have it, the painting was appropriately entitled *Plan of War*; but Ford was not the only guest at Great Ormond Street to leave in a discomfited state. Pound insisted on pinning up a poster announcing 'END OF CHRISTIAN ERA', and when Kate Lechmere's elderly aunt asked him what it meant he rounded on her fiercely and growled: 'It means, Madam, what it says.'[55]

William Roberts was, finally, introduced to the rebels as well. He had gone to work the previous year at the Omega with a letter of introduction from his friend Laurence Binyon, and helped decorate table-tops and fabrics with 'Cubist' designs; but he arrived only after Lewis and his friends had stormed out of Fitzroy Square for the last time, and later declared that 'when I joined the Omega . . . I had never heard of Lewis or his work'.[56] Although he was not then invited to exhibit at the 'Cubist Room' exhibition, he explained afterwards that

**PROSPECTUS.**

# THE REBEL ART CENTRE.

Telephone: HOLBORN 457.

38, GREAT ORMOND STREET,

QUEEN'S SQUARE, W.C.

Fee for Membership .... .... £1 : 1s.

The Rebel Art Centre is under the personal management of Mr. Wyndham Lewis. The Directors are Miss Lechmere and Mr. Wyndham Lewis.

The following privileges are attached to membership :—

Free Entrance for the space of one year, from May 1st, 1914, to all Lectures, Meetings and Picture Exhibitions, or Exhibitions of Applied Art.

On payment of half the amount of the ticket for any dances or social entertainments that may be arranged.

To the Saturday afternoon meetings of artists from 4 to 6 p.m.

It is impossible at present to give a list of the Lectures for the present year, as much depends, in getting such men to lecture as we intend, on arrangements that have to fit in with their stay in London and other engagements, and can be made only a week or two ahead.

Signor Marinetti, for instance, who will probably lecture at Ormond Street, has not yet assigned a date.

Towards the end of May, Mr. Ezra Pound will speak on " Imagisme," the most vital movement in English poetry to-day, and in which he is the principal mover.

Wyndham Lewis (?)
*Prospectus. The Rebel Art Centre*, 1914

'the fact that I was at the Omega made [Lewis] curious to meet me',[57] and he appears to have been contacted by the rebel leader soon after his departure. Never slow to befriend a potential ally, Lewis made warm overtures to this teenage malcontent, for Roberts remembered how 'I was invited one evening in the spring of 1914 to join him in an *apéritif* at the Swiss in Soho'.[58] The two artists had shared interests: *The Athenaeum* pointed out in January that 'Mr William Roberts follows Mr Lewis',[59] and their acquaintance was soon cemented by a positive act: 'it was to Cumberland Market that Lewis came one day to borrow *The Dancers* and *Religion*', Roberts recalled; 'he said he wanted to hang them in some rooms he had in Great Ormond Street, which he referred to as the Rebel Art Centre.'[60] Even if Roberts stressed that he 'visited the Rebel Art Centre only once and stayed about five minutes', he nonetheless joined the group's meetings in Lewis's flat and often accompanied them afterwards, in the evening, to a dinner at L'Etoile or Rudolph Stulik's exclusive Restaurant de la Tour Eiffel in Percy Street. And as a post-prandial finale, the rebels would end up at the now notorious Cabaret Club, where their high spirits found an ideal outlet in wild ragtime dancing. 'In my memory *la cuisine Française* and Vorticism are indissolubly linked,' remembered Roberts. 'Both Signor Rossi of the Etoile, and M. Rudolph Stulik of the Tour Eiffel should rank in the records of Vorticism as honorary members of the "Group". Lewis, who liked good food, and fine wine to go with it, kept a ringed serviette in each of these restaurants. If, as he claimed, Vorticism was the expression of a new philosophy, then it must be the newness of Rabelais, and of old Omar Khayyam's "A jug of wine, a loaf of bread and thou beside me singing . . .".'[61]

But despite all the excitement, it swiftly became apparent that these quixotic artists were not temperamentally suited to the practical business of running an organization like the Great Ormond Street atelier. Their only demonstrable group product was a Rebel Art Centre stand at the June 1914 AAA Salon, which *The Egoist*'s critic considered to be 'in unity. A desire to employ the most vigorous forms of decoration fills it with fans, scarves, boxes and a table, which are the finest of these objects I have seen'.[62] The Omega, therefore, faced formidable rivalry when the rebels actually sat down and executed some communal work; but most of them were far too embroiled in their own concerns to waste much of their time at the Centre, and even Etchells, who lived across the road, later declared that he 'didn't go to the Rebel Art Centre very frequently'.[63] Why should they have become regular callers, after all? There was no money, employment, studio space or important commissions to be obtained there. Lewis continued with his schemes for interior decoration, certainly, but there was never any suggestion that the rest of the group should join him. He alone was photographed and interviewed by the *Daily News and Leader* on 7 April and revealed that he was 'planning a design for a devotional room in a well-known society woman's house'. Blithely forgetting that he had accused Fry of using the Omega to further private interests, Lewis did not once refer to the possibility of a commission for the Centre as a whole when he outlined his ideas. 'These rooms should really become the ordinary thing', he said, 'in houses where such religion can be afforded . . . Formerly there were chapels, monasteries, and temples ready for the artist whose soul was too religious for his works to be mere entertainments and drawing-room pictures. Today there is practically nothing . . . This private chapel . . . is an obvious solution. It might be a bare room at the top of the house, where the owner could retire and get a little solitude and escape from himself. I believe the super-sensible will play a greater part both in life and art as time goes on. The spiritual world is the Polar regions of our psychic existence, and useful ghosts will meet us on its borders.'[64]

Sounding off to the Press in such a controversial style was all very fruitful for

Photograph of Lewis, 1914

Edmond X. Kapp
*Impression of Wyndham Lewis*, 1914

Lewis's career, but it contributed nothing to furthering a spirit of comradeship at Great Ormond Street. Lewis himself did offer, in a half-hearted way, to be present at the Centre 'as professor, five days a week', but only two hopeful pupils presented themselves for instruction: a man who wanted to improve the design of gas-brackets, and a lady pornographer. 'She refused to let me see her obscene drawings', recalled Kate Lechmere, 'and only allowed Lewis to view them in secret behind the door.'[65] Nobody with more serious intentions would ever have wanted Lewis as a teacher, for his volatile personality was by now a London legend. Alongside his undoubted charm, energy and intellectual brilliance, Lewis coupled a quick temper with a fatal love of intrigue. When Pound dropped in on the Centre with his wife for Saturday afternoon tea, for instance, Lewis would invite them as a mark of special favour to see his paintings in the small back room. They were, incredibly, kept firmly under lock and key 'for fear of imitators', and Dorothy Pound stated that her husband 'was at that time the only one allowed to see them'.[66] Such paranoiac suspicion of his fellow artists inevitably created a strained atmosphere which disrupted the harmonious running of the Centre: the more independent the other members of the group were, the less inclined they felt to attend an institution where Lewis held sway over all. Prospectuses firmly announced that the Centre was 'under the personal management of Mr Wyndham Lewis', and this nervous egotism effectively destroyed the fond hopes expressed at the outset that 'metal-workers, craftsmen or painters can bring their work there and go on with it, if this atmosphere is congenial to them, without interference or anything but the satisfaction of knowing that something is being done around them, and that an attempt is being made here to revive and sanify the art-instinct in this country'.[67] These promises had proved groundless: the ambience of Great Ormond Street was definitely not 'congenial', and the whole organization really began to founder when a major difference of opinion developed between Lewis and Hulme.

It all started in the spring when Lewis, Pound and Hulme each delivered a paper in Kensington Town Hall as part of a Quest Society evening of modern poetry. Kate Lechmere was in the audience with Lewis, and although she thought Pound was the only member of the trio who managed to read out his lecture without 'mumbling inaudibly into his notes', she found herself attracted to the amorous philosopher. The couple began to see each other frequently, became lovers, and then Hulme proposed to his new mistress 'in an A.B.C. teashop'. Not that he was in any hurry to get married: Epstein recalled that although Hulme 'projected a large family', he 'felt he had plenty of time for that too'.[68] He was as uninhibited with Kate Lechmere as with his other mistresses, informing her one day that the shape of a knuckleduster he always carried in his pocket was basically sexual. 'The two pieces curving out sideways at the bottom are the woman's parted legs', he explained, 'the central hole is her vagina, and the four holes in a row at the top are the woman's head tossing and turning as she achieves orgasm.'[69] To celebrate this revelation, the pair decided to call each other 'knuckleduster'.

Their relationship infuriated Lewis, who according to Kate Lechmere 'quite lost his head and when he accused me of this Hulme attachment I said he had shown little attention to me of late, and his remark was that it was not good for a woman to have too much notice taken of her!' He made his growing antagonism perfectly plain when he advised Beatrice Hastings, the sub-editor of *The New Age*, to 'get rid of this hautise of the Hulme[?]-Kibbelwhite[?] combination. They are pretty boring folk: Epstein is the only individual in that little set who does anything or has any personality. And he is not fool enough to go too far, as far as I am concerned. Let us talk of something more interesting'.[70] Frith Street was now as despised in his eyes as the Omega, rejected with a venom increased by the realization that Hulme was more committed to Epstein's art than to his. 'Epstein . . . was unquestionably Hulme's man (or perhaps I should say Hulme was Epstein's man) upon the social plane', Lewis explained later. 'They were great friends, where I never stood in that relation to Hulme at all. Hulme wrote at great length about Epstein, he had a great personal admiration for him, almost, I daresay, a big doglike devotion. Me, he did not like so well.'[71]

Before long, therefore, Lewis's victimization complex had constructed a fairy-tale plot whereby Hulme was scheming with his sculptor friend to oust him from the Rebel Art Centre and install Epstein as the new leader in his place. Such absurd suspicions were groundless, but Lewis believed in them sufficiently to take Kate Lechmere out to a teashop and warn her repeatedly that 'Hulme is Epstein and Epstein is Hulme'. The whole foolish melodrama came to a memorable climax when Lewis set out one evening in the direction of Mrs Kibblewhite's house swearing to kill the philosopher. Miss Lechmere pursued him all the way through Piccadilly shouting 'please don't kill him, please don't', but without avail: Lewis marched straight into Hulme's salon and seized him by the throat. His victim, however, was a heavily-built man. He dragged Lewis downstairs and out into Soho Square, where he hung him up ignominiously by his trouser turn-ups on the iron railings and calmly returned to his soirée.[72] Years afterwards, Lewis still insisted that he never saw the summerhouse in the middle of Soho Square without 'remembering how I saw it upside down.'[73] The dispute ultimately made co-operation between Lewis and his financial backer more or less impossible; and Miss Lechmere, who realized that the Centre was not repaying the money she devoted to it in any way, became increasingly disenchanted with the project. 'By now my very small bit of capital was running out', she remembered. 'No effort had been made by Lewis to get art students or members. After all the vitality and enthusiasm we had for the Rebel Art Centre it now seemed to go sour and to be arriving at nothing. I told Lewis he and his friends must carry on without me and that I could not pay the next quarter's rent. Some days later I went out in the afternoon and on returning found the Studio in confusion and denuded of most of its contents.' At the end of July, tired of all the childish squabbling, she finally decided to close down the entire establishment and let it out for the rest of the lease to a dancing teacher. The rebels' adventure was over.

But if the organizational side of the group had proved to be a disastrous flop, the artists themselves were still forging ahead undismayed with their own paintings and sculpture. In March, a large show had opened at the Goupil Gallery to prove they had not been at all idle since the 'Cubist Room' days: it was the first official exhibition of the London Group. Despite Lewis's political manoeuvrings at the Brighton show the previous December, all the members of the London Group, save one, believed in its value and duly sent in their best work to be displayed there. The lone absentee was the embittered Sickert, who had become so alienated by the rebels' contributions that he flatly refused to exhibit any of his paintings. His decision was predictable, for the Goupil show housed startling evidence of rampant extremism that the critics were not slow to comment on. 'The "London Group", which appears to be made up of the former "Camden Town Group", the seceders from Mr Roger Fry's "Omega Workshops" and other English Post-Impressionists, Cubists and Futurists, is holding its first exhibition', wrote Konody in the *Observer*. 'The very aggressive blue of the invitation card might have been taken as an indication of the defiant attitude of the members, although it would need a whole combination of crude hues to prepare one for the violent assaults that have been planned by these London "Indépendants". Both the Grafton and Doré Galleries are left miles

Edmond X. Kapp
*Jacob Epstein*, 1914

Wyndham Lewis
*Plan of War*, 1914

behind; and even the once disconcerting jigsaw puzzles of the Italian Futurists would appear childishly simple beside the latest geometrical obfuscations upon which Mr David Bomberg and Mr Wyndham Lewis have expended their energies. In the light of this latest development, Mr Nevinson's disjointed world in motion becomes as intelligible as photographic realism.'[74]

Once again, controversy raged around Lewis's five exhibits, all of which – save for *Enemy of the Stars* – have since disappeared. The most important seem to have been two large paintings entitled *Christopher Columbus* and *Eisteddfod*, and even Fry was moved to praise his political rival when confronted with them in the Gallery. 'Lewis', he wrote in *The Nation*, 'is by nature highly gifted, and by training, highly accomplished, so that whatever he does has a certain facility and completeness.' And if he did not actually approve of these puzzling new abstract pictures, he still admitted that 'in front of his abstract designs one has to admit their close consistency, the clear and definite organizing power that lies behind them.'[75] *The Times'* critic echoed Fry's approval by admitting that *Eisteddfod* 'has a certain logic for the eye, the kind of logic we find in some complicated piece of machinery whose working we do not understand'. But in complete contrast to this carefully objective appraisal, a sarcastic reporter from the *Daily News* chose the most commanding of Lewis's contributions as the victim for a satirical attack. 'Lewis's chef-d'œuvre is entitled "Christopher Columbus" – which is precisely what you will exclaim when you see it', he wrote gleefully. 'A crowd tried its best to find the explorer. Mr Lewis, pointing rapidly to odd corners of the canvas, said: "There's his head, there's his hand, that's his leg. Don't you get me?" It seemed as clear as London fog. "Our object is to bewilder", said he; "we want to shock the senses and get you into a condition of mind in which you'll grasp what our intentions are." '[76] The Press was clearly in no mood to cultivate Lewis's proposed 'condition of mind': the *Westminster Gazette* merely shrugged its shoulders and dismissed the painting as a 'highly coloured tesselated pavement'. No-one seemed to realize that Lewis's title was a serious reference rather than a frivolous joke, celebrating as it did Clive Bell's declaration that Cézanne was 'the Christopher Columbus of a new continent of form'.[77] Sir Claude Phillips, however, was marginally more constructive. In a vivid phrase, which makes the loss of the picture all the more to be regretted, he suggested that 'here was perhaps a symbolical representation of the Integral Calculus', adding that 'Mr Lewis's magnum opus' was 'a huge kaleidoscopic design, painted, it must be owned, with a rare decision of the brush.'[78]

If Lewis really wanted to broach total abstraction, he should have had enough confidence in his own power as a painter to rely on his pictures' emotional meaning communicating itself. But to cover his tracks by giving them relatively figurative details was to add unnecessarily to the critical confusion. He may have recognized the disparity himself, for another major abstract painting executed early in 1914 was given the far more appropriate title of *Plan of War*. This, the picture that had the doubtful honour of balancing on Ford's head, seems on the evidence of the surviving photograph to have been stylistically in advance of Lewis's Goupil Gallery exhibits. It must have been an imposing work, for its size was recorded as spanning more than 8 ft in height and well over 4 ft in width, while one description remarked on its 'strongly contrasted colours'.[79]

The monumental scale was peculiarly suited to its austere design, for Lewis has here rearranged the jostling forms of his 1913 *Composition* into a slower, grander and more balanced stasis. There is movement in the forceful diagonals disposed across the picture-surface and tension, too, in the contrast between the solid blocks of colour and the large expanses of uninhabited canvas. Lewis has

Frantisek Kupka
*Philosophical Architecture*, 1913–23

been careful to employ his sense of pictorial interval, so that the full force of each directional shape registers itself within the rigidly ordered pattern of the whole. But the various components are firmly impacted: they do not break each other up, and are delineated with a clarity that gives every diagrammatic inch of the composition its own unassailable authority. In the face of such a self-sufficient achievement, it would be idle to speculate too freely about the precise meaning of the title. Lewis himself stated that it was painted 'six months before the Great War "broke out" ',[80] and it ought to be admired for its ability to combine a prophetic awareness of world militarism with an outstandingly radical demonstration of Lewis's new-found abstract style. Vorticism would soon display a similar bias towards collision without interpenetration, aggression rather than confusion, and explosive vitality tempered with cool detachment. In this original synthesis of Cubist and Futurist impulses, *Plan of War* can be seen as the first large-scale expression of the Vorticist aesthetic.

But Rutter, who knew Lewis fairly well at this period and ought therefore to be heeded, was not content to let the matter rest there. 'This painting was no more "abstract" than the blocks of wood used in the War Game', he asserted later. 'What Lewis had done was to take for his point of departure the familiar diagram of a battle that we see in history books, with rectangles for infantry divisions, little squares for cavalry, white for the British, shaded for the enemy, and so on.' Rutter's identification of Lewis's source-material may well be correct, and he was right to point out that 'it was characteristic of the mental alertness of the artist to feel early in 1914 that there was "war in the air", and to begin a series of these strange designs all with titles taken from a military text book, and all based on the tactical dispositions of *Kriegspiel*'.

Where Rutter erred, however, was to interpret these sources too literally, declaring that *Plan of War*'s 'heavy blocks in the top right-hand corner are intended to express the extended left wing of one army which has turned, out-flanked, and is now "falling like a ton of bricks" to crush and disintegrate the right wing of the other army'.[81] Lewis would never have been interested in this kind of military cartography, which simply cannot be applied to a painting as abstract as *Plan of War*; and by describing the picture's contents with such faulty logic, Rutter succeeded only in limiting its area of reference, reducing it from an imaginative metaphor to a far less interesting essay in banal transcription. Taking diagrams of battles as a springboard for work does not automatically mean that an artist wants to reproduce tactical plans in his final painting.

In order to emphasize its temerity, *Plan of War* can be compared with one of the few similarly abstract paintings being executed elsewhere in Europe at this early stage in the history of Modernism. Only Kupka's pictures, exhibited at the Paris Salon des Indépendants in 1911, 1912, and again in 1913, bear any resemblance to Lewis's masterpiece. The Czech disposes his geometrical segments on a large scale with the same calculating precision as Lewis, even if his paintings bear less relation to an identifiable external reality. He was the creator of one of the earliest non-representational paintings in European art: *Amphora, Fugue in Two Colours*, which was exhibited at the Salon d'Automne in 1912. Lewis could possibly have seen this or some of Kupka's other publicly displayed paintings on one of his many trips to Paris, and they might have given him the extra impetus he needed to pursue his pictorial experiments. Kupka's Salon d'Automne exhibits were admired in England even in 1912, when *Rhythm* declared that their 'every line and curve suggests rhythmic motion and virility',[82] and Lewis's interest may first have been aroused by such praise. Another link may have been established through Delaunay, whose Orphic paintings of 1912 were among the first abstract works produced by a French artist. Delaunay himself had been represented at Rutter's Doré Galleries show in 1913 by his major canvas of *The Cardiff Football Team*. Was there a real connexion between the theories and achievements of the three men? It may never be known for certain, but speculation can only help to place Lewis in his rightful niche as one of the most advanced artists of his age.

Although *Plan of War* was more extreme than any other experiment with abstraction in English art up until that time, it earned a surprisingly favourable reception when exhibited at the 1914 Allied Artists' Salon. Reviewing Lewis's contributions to the show – which otherwise consisted of *Night Attack* and *Signalling* – the critic of *The New Weekly* praised their 'iron sense of construction', compared them with Bach, and concluded that 'the severe emphasis on geometrical forms seems to enhance the intensity of the colour, and their value as decoration must be admitted even by those who cannot accept them as pictures'.[83] The critics were struggling to come to terms with something completely without precedent in English art, trying to reconcile their aesthetic principles with the realization that Lewis's blasphemous abstractions were impressive. They were completely disoriented; and apart from Hulme, none of the other professional reviewers was able to adopt a firm standpoint and either reject or commit himself to the outlook embodied in Rebel Art Centre paintings. Rutter remembered seeing 'Augustus John standing in admiration before Wyndham Lewis's "Night Attack" ',[84] but nobody actually expressed any outright praise in print.

Nobody, that is, except one young artist who had been commissioned by Aldington to air his views in *The Egoist* on the subject of this very AAA Salon. And he, at least, harboured no doubts at all about the overwhelming importance of Lewis's exhibits. 'Wyndham Lewis has made enormous progress in his painting', he announced decisively. 'The two small abstractions "Night Attack" and "Signalling" are such very complete individual expressions that no praise is sufficient to adequately point out their qualities.' If *Night Attack* can be linked with – or perhaps even identified as – the surviving photograph of a painting called *Slow Attack*, it is clear that the writer admired Lewis's most uncompromising style.[85] He seems to clinch the resemblance by maintaining that 'these are designs of wilful, limited shapes contained in a whole in motion – and this acquired with the simplest means – ochres and blacks'. And he ended up with a forthright declaration of their importance as stepping-stones in the inauguration of a modern, abstract art. 'Lewis's abstractions are of a decided type', he wrote, praising their stylistic homogeneity, 'and their composition is so successful that I feel right in seeing in them the start of a new evolution in painting.'[86]

The man who had so proudly proclaimed his loyalty to Rebel Art Centre aesthetics was a 22-year-old sculptor with the unlikely name of Henri Gaudier-Brzeska: he was born plain Henri Gaudier in France but added the Polish suffix when he settled in England in January 1911 with his close friend Sophie Brzeska. They lived together ostensibly as brother and sister under their strange joint name and Gaudier claimed the relationship was platonic – but then, he often delighted in asserting he was homosexual as well. After a brief period of obscurity as clerk to a shipping broker in the City, he became associated with the British Fauves' magazine *Rhythm* and, like Dismorr before him, published in its pages several sketches that already bore witness to an exuberant artistic personality. He believed passionately in the spontaneity of drawing, its capacity for lightning speed and rapid improvisation. 'The people in the class are so stupid,' he complained to Sophie while he was attending life classes in November 1912; 'they only do two or three drawings in two or three hours, and think me mad because I work without stopping – especially while the model is resting, because that is much more interesting than the poses. I do from 150 to 200 drawings each time,

Wyndham Lewis
*Slow Attack*, 1914

and that intrigues them no end'.[87]

His aptitude for prolific sketching, however, formed only a part of his determination to prove his versatility in the more challenging medium of sculpture. Nothing pleased him more, at the beginning of his short working life, than to impress friends like Horace Brodzky and *Rhythm*'s editor Middleton Murry with his ability to switch from one style over to another without so much as a pause for breath. He would, for instance, make a piece like the 1912 *Workman Fallen from a Scaffold*, where he attempted a direct emulation of his great countryman, Rodin. Its forms are modelled with the intensely fluid, almost molten texture that was Rodin's sculptural signature, even if its fragmentary state was an accident rather than a tribute to Rodin's experiments with disjointed or truncated shapes. 'As modelled by Brzeska this figure had both arms complete, and depicted the man in the act of raising himself from the ground in agony', recalled Brodzky, who wrote that the figure was based on 'an incident that Brzeska remembered having seen in Paris'.[88] But before being cast in bronze the original clay model lost its arms, which were unwittingly used by its owner's charlady for whitening the doorstep of his house.

Henri Gaudier-Brzeska
*Workman Fallen from a Scaffold*, 1912

Nevertheless the young sculptor did begin his career by holding Rodin in perfectly understandable esteem. At the age of 19, before he made the decisive move to England, he told his friend Uhlemayer in a letter that 'we shall never see a greater sculptor than Rodin',[89] and a year later he was still enthusing to Sophie over Rodin's *Old Woman*. 'Beautiful – for beauty is life', he exclaimed. 'The forms of this Old Woman are lovely because they have character.'[90] But he was not content to allow his precocious skill to vie only with the immediate past. With fantastic dexterity, he set about mastering a whole range of styles, jumping from an exotic South American *Ornamental Mask* to a frankly classical study of a female *Torso*.[91] Only a few months separate the execution of these two wildly differing sculptures, and Gaudier revelled in the bewildered admiration of his widening circle of friends as they watched his encyclopaedic ambitions run their course. There was a streak of the showman in his temperament which demanded constant recognition, even adulation. He described the *Torso* to Major Smythies as 'a marble statue of a girl in the natural way, in order to show my accomplishment as a sculptor',[92] and this polished imitation of a Greek original – extended even to the broken arms and neck – showed to what extremes he was prepared to go in order to satisfy his Faustian appetite for universal expertise. Behind the dazzling facility lay an unshakeable self-confidence, a quality that enabled him to remain impervious to dire poverty as long as he was able to work at his sculpture. 'Gaudier had a profound belief in himself,' wrote Ede; 'he would often say: "It was an honour for So-and-so to be in my company".'[93]

Not that this assurance should be confused with empty smugness or pride. Gaudier always hated complacency of any kind, and indeed defended his deliberately eclectic programme on the grounds that it acted as a buffer against self-satisfaction. 'Life, according to Bergson and the later philosophers, is simply intuition of the passing moment, and time, which flows continually, eternally, makes itself known by change', he told Sophie in October 1912. 'The conceited man is one who stops at a certain phase of his work or of his thought, and cries out loud, like you, "When I say something, I believe it – I'm sure of myself", etc. I'm not a bit like that . . . I notice how everything differs, mingles with and knocks up against everything else, I am never sure that what I think is true, still less that what I have thought or said is true; and I can't bring myself to sacrifice new ideas, quite different from those I had yesterday, just because the old ones happened to have the honour of passing through my head and I advocated them ferociously.'[94]

But there was, at the same time, a detached quality about these hurried experiments. Gaudier stood outside the styles he had borrowed so freely; and while he indulged his talent for entering into the spirit of diverse cultures he was simultaneously appraising them all, asking himself what formal lessons they could teach him. The fundamental constituents of sculpture were kept firmly in view the whole time, for even in 1911 he had listed some basic precepts which anticipated his later adoption of abstraction. 'The great thing is: that sculpture consists in placing planes according to a rhythm', he wrote; 'that painting consists in placing colours according to a rhythm.'[95] His sentiments would have been approved by Lewis as well as the British Fauves with whom Gaudier first came into contact; and it remains true that there are striking parallels between the theories of the Fauves and the Vorticists. The Rebel Art Centre could have found nothing to contradict in some of *Rhythm*'s editorial statements: in the very first issue, for instance, Murry declared that 'aestheticism has had its day and done its work . . . We need an art that strikes deeper, that touches a profounder reality, that passes outside the bounds of a narrow aestheticism . . . Before art can be human, it must learn to be brutal'.[96]

With hindsight, the announcement can be seen as a possible native source for

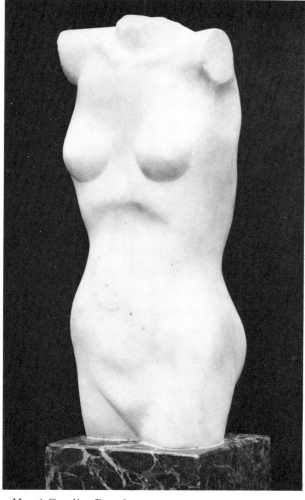

Henri Gaudier-Brzeska
*Torso*, 1913

Henri Gaudier-Brzeska
*Ornamental Mask*, 1912

Henri Gaudier-Brzeska
*Sophie Brzeska*, 1913

the Vorticists' credo, just as Michael Sadleir's article in the same issue of *Rhythm* contains sentiments that could almost have been printed in a Great Ormond Street prospectus. The British Fauves, he wrote, were opposed to 'the lifeless mechanism of pointillism . . . the moribund flickerings of the aesthetic movement . . . Fauvism is a fresh reaction from the precious. It stands for strength and decision, alike of line, colour and feeling'.[97] Gaudier warmed to such impassioned outbursts, and put *Rhythm*'s theories into practice in a work like the 1913 pastel portrait of *Sophie*, where his eccentric companion is placed in a strident arrangement of decorative outlines and hot, impulsive colour contrasts. The style of the pastel, an idiosyncratic blend of Gauguin and Matisse, appears to owe its heightened colour to the direct influence of his friend Alfred Wolmark, who was at this time setting an uninhibited example to his Fauvist colleagues by pitching his tonal divisions into a higher key than any of them. Gaudier modelled his bust in 1913, and it ended up celebrating Wolmark's individuality in a face that strongly resembled Beethoven: this time, the young sculptor seemed to be copying the Romantic abandon of Bourdelle.

A far more important mentor, however, was Epstein, who rented a flat in the upper storey of Harold Monro's Charing Cross Road Poetry Bookshop at the time when Gaudier was exhibiting some of his early works downstairs with other contributors to *Rhythm*. The American first received an official visit from Gaudier in 1911, 'while I was at work on the Oscar Wilde tomb in my Chelsea studio'. Gaudier may have been fired to experiment with different styles of the past by looking at the Assyrian inspiration of the flying angel being created for Père Lachaise, for Epstein remembered that 'a young fellow called on me one Sunday morning and asked if he could see the carving. It was Gaudier Brzeska, a picturesque, slight figure with lively eyes, and a sprouting beard'. There can be little doubt that the older man exerted a powerful influence over Gaudier, who is even supposed to have been asked by Epstein 'if he carved direct, and that, afraid to acknowledge that he hadn't, he hurried home and immediately started a carving.'[98] The incident amused Epstein, who recalled that his 'relations with Gaudier were very friendly. We were interested in each other's work. In the French fashion of the younger to the older artist he wrote to me and addressed me as Cher Maître.'[99] There is a distinct note of admiring rivalry in the letter Gaudier wrote to Sophie in October 1913, where he mentioned going 'with one Jew to see the Other Jew, Epstein; he's doing most extraordinary statues, absolute copies of Polynesian work with Brancusi-like noses'.[100] And the two sculptors spent a great deal of time together. Gaudier visited Epstein while he was at work in the Cabaret Club – where the young Frenchman may well have met Lewis for the first time – and Epstein introduced him to the delights of Hulme's salon.[101]

It may have been the philosopher's enthusiasm for strictly contemporary forms of art that first persuaded Gaudier to forget about the past and try his hand at a more advanced form of sculpture. When he embarked on a bust of his friend Brodzky in the spring or early summer of 1913, he decided to abandon the naturalistic language that still lingered on in the contemporaneous bust of Wolmark. Now it was Cubism which engaged his interest, for Brodzky recalled that his bust, 'to use [Gaudier's] own words, was "cubic" '.[102] And although hints of Rodinesque modelling can still be discerned in the construction of this dramatic head, it nevertheless shows Gaudier attempting to split up the sections of the face, hair and shoulders into the angular planes that Picasso had introduced into sculpture four years earlier in his *Head of a Woman*. Gaudier was in Paris at the time Picasso executed the *Head*, but he was at once too young and too full of admiration for nineteenth-century achievements to have been inspired by its radicalism. And even in 1913 he could not bring himself to discard as

Henri Gaudier-Brzeska
*Bust of Alfred Wolmark*, 1913

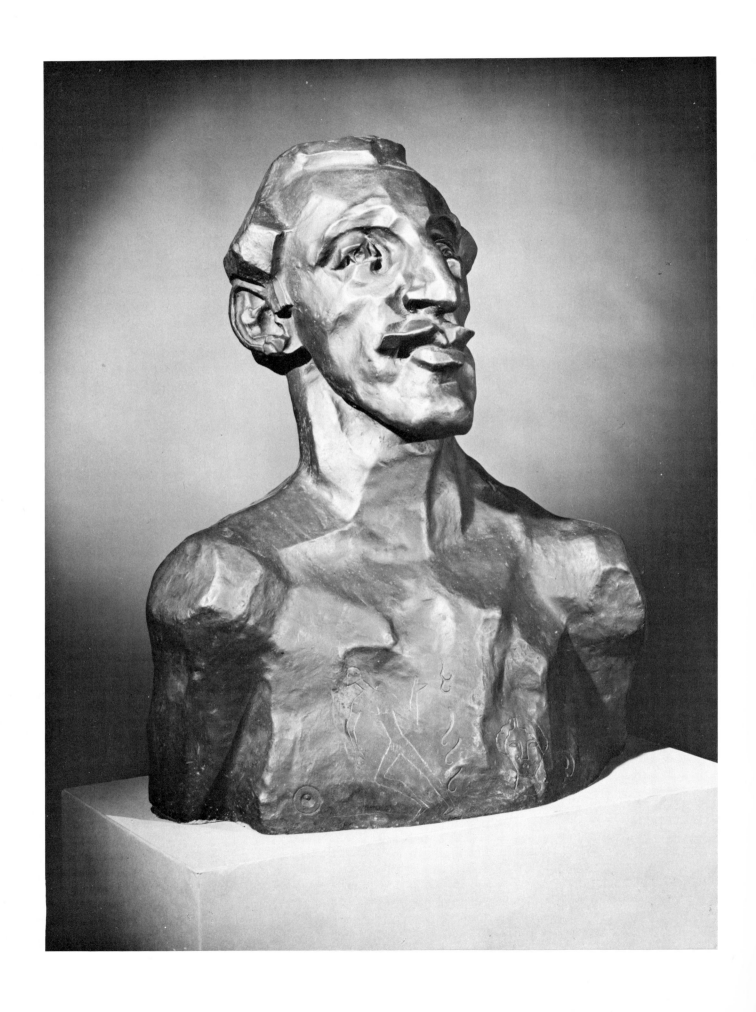

much of external appearances as Picasso. Compared with the brutal fragmentation employed in *Head of a Woman*, where representation has been rejected in favour of ruthless simplification and semi-abstract clusters of form, Gaudier's bust still clings to an academic tradition. He has imposed a superficial version of faceted Cubism onto a conventional framework, and only the notable vigour of its characterization saves the work from appearing timid.

The image almost teeters into caricature, but its exaggeration does not spring from a desire to amuse; rather does it reflect Gaudier's own frantic energy, wilfully imposing itself on the cadaverous forms of his model's features. 'He worked in a most alarming fashion', Brodzky recalled, 'jabbering all the time. He did not appear to go at it methodically, although I suppose he had a method, but he thumped the clay about, gouged out furrows, and all the time he was telling amusing stories. He seemed to get fun out of work.' Gaudier's impish wit finally got the better of him when it came to finishing off the chest: 'in a moment', he outlined the shape of a gesturing male nude and a girl's head, with a few scattered doodles thrown in for good measure. 'He did not explain the significance of these incised drawings', wrote his sitter. 'And I am quite sure there was none.'[103] Brodzky was right: Gaudier simply knew how to enjoy himself.

The Brodzky *Bust* was put on show in July 1913 at the Allied Artists' Salon, along with his bust of Wolmark and four other works.[104] It was Gaudier's debut in the world of London's public exhibitions, and any expectations he may have harboured about being hailed as a genius were doomed to disappointment. The critics accused him of mere sensationalism, and after such a depressing mauling Gaudier must have wondered how he could ever continue to scrape together a living solely from his work. The few commissions he had ever received were largely engineered for him through the good offices of friends, and lack of money had forced him to move out of the centre of town to ramshackle studio quarters at Railway Arch 25, where he and Sophie lived literally underneath a bridge. And even here, where 'electric trains rumbled all day' overhead, he 'occupied only half the arch, which had been divided lengthways by a wooden partition'.[105] Gaudier had inherited a knowledge of materials and some of his technical skill from his father, who was a village carpenter, but practical expertise could not ensure that the building was waterproof. 'He slept one day in the studio', recalled Pound, 'and woke up to find himself inundated with rain and lying in several inches of water.'[106] Gaudier was resilient enough to make the best of his abject surroundings, reheating one single mixture of stew every night for weeks on end for supper, and painting on the inside of the double doors in heavy black lines the 'Gaudier-Brzeska phallic monogram'.[107] He was cheerful, hard-working and brimming over with new ideas; but he had to live, and support Sophie as well as himself.

The solution was inevitable, and Gaudier eventually snatched at it with alacrity. Fry's proffered Omega subsidy would provide him with bare necessities, and so he enrolled at Fitzroy Square soon after the rebels had walked out in October 1913. 'He never actually worked there but we sold drawings of his and small pieces of sculpture on commission, and he looked in fairly often, probably to see if we owed him anything and to bring in fresh stuff', recalled Winifred Gill. 'He never stayed for long.'[108] But the very fact that he had been accepted by the Omega meant his talents were becoming recognised, and since he was the only sculptor attached to the Workshops his contributions rapidly registered their own individual impact. Easily the most charming were the glazed earthenware *Cats* executed soon after his entry: they exemplified another, more tender side of his personality that Fry may well have found more appealing than the robust, outspoken drama of his larger works.[109] Yet for all their ingratiating

△ Pablo Picasso
*Head of a Woman*, 1909–10

◁ Henri Gaudier-Brzeska
*Bust of Horace Brodzky*, 1913

▽ Henri Gaudier-Brzeska
*Cat*, c. 1913

Henri Gaudier-Brzeska
*Study for*
*Red Stone Dancer*, 1913

Oriental delicacy, these tiny pottery animals are constructed with great severity. Gaudier has stripped their forms of all superfluous detail, concentrated on a series of essential shapes and distorted their bodies in a surprisingly acute manner.

When the young sculptor turned his hand to the designing of trays, he evolved for the first time his own version of the style being simultaneously developed by the 'Cubist Room' group. In a successful *Inlaid Tray* he used wood with a vital and personal effect: two wrestlers struggle with each other in a welter of jagged segments that link up not only with Grant's *Elephant Tray* but also with the stylistic experiments of Lewis, Bomberg and Roberts. The men's bodies are enmeshed in a sophisticated interplay between description and abstraction that lifts the design out of simple decoration onto a more complex plane of creative activity, and it is easy to see how this combination of frenetic vitality, diagonally oriented movement and clear-cut definition prepared the way for Gaudier's adoption of Vorticist precepts.

Henri Gaudier-Brzeska
*Inlaid Tray, c.* 1913

There seems at first to have been far less tension between Gaudier and Fry than had existed when Lewis and his friends were working at Fitzroy Square. The Frenchman remained connected with the Omega for some months, and even exhibited with the Bloomsbury circle at the Grafton Group's Alpine Gallery show in January 1914. Yet he was moving forward very rapidly towards total abstraction: the *Red Stone Dancer* he displayed at the exhibition demonstrated that he had forgotten the tentative Cubism of the *Brodzky* bust and opted for a far more extreme essay in sculptural geometry. One of the preparatory studies for the sculpture, a freely executed ink wash drawing which Hulme reproduced in *The New Age*, shows with admirable élan that Gaudier now wanted to inject a more dynamic apprehension of movement into his work.[110] Three alternative figures blend into one burgeoning image, their heads, arms and legs all jostling with each other to present a paradigm of Futurist simul-

taneity. The Italian movement obviously helped Gaudier to incorporate so many successive stages of motion in a single sketch, and its vitality reflects the liberation which Futurist theories seemed to offer him. But it would be unwise to limit such a wide-ranging artist to the inspiration of Futurism alone: in one letter to Sophie he mentioned that during 'a short visit to the British Museum' his omnivorous appetite 'took particular notice of all the primitive statues, negro, yellow, red and white races, Gothic and Greek',[111] and it would hardly be fanciful to suggest that the abandon of a multi-limbed Indian dancer also lies behind Gaudier's study.

The final carving, however, rejects any Boccioni-like ideas about apeing a sequence of movement in sculpture. Now it is the unprecedented degree of abstraction which commands attention, for Gaudier has dispensed with facial features altogether and incised a large triangle on the empty oval of the dancer's head, complementing it with a circle on the right breast and a rectangle on the left in place of nipples. If these motifs sound in theory dangerously dogmatic, they are given plastic life by the rest of the figure as it unfolds in a remarkable series of intertwining arabesques. The spiral of movement initiated by the round plinth and the turning of the left foot towards its neighbour is continued and accelerated further up the body as the torso comes to rest at right-angles to the pelvis. Then the wildly elongated right arm takes up the spiral with renewed force, wrapping itself right round the impossibly tilted head in an extended serpentine curve which only comes to rest when it meets the top of the left breast. Gaudier takes the most astonishing liberties with anatomy, moulding it like rubber to fit in with the abstract rhythms of the sculpture: the left arm approaches a breast, merges with it for a moment to provide a surface for the rectangular nipple, and then somehow defies all corporeal laws by leaping over it so that the left hand can finally insert itself as a contrasting angular wedge between the rounded masses of both breasts. But all this perversity is forgotten from the side, where the overlapping limbs take on an autonomous life of their own, barely connected with their figurative role as parts of a human dancer. And so the result, viewed in its totality, is both tortuous and lyrical, labyrinthine and disarmingly simple.

This sculpture marks a decisive moment in Gaudier's career. For here he puts eclecticism on one side and embraces the new geometrical art propounded by Hulme's Quest Society lecture, which was delivered at a time when *Red Stone Dancer* was on full public view at the Alpine Gallery. The philosopher's theories may well have impressed Gaudier at the Frith Street salons, for although the *Dancer* possesses plenty of spontaneity and organic life, it looks almost as if it was constructed according to a geometrical theory of art that the sculptor wanted to advertise as brazenly as possible. Pound noticed this, and chose to expatiate upon the sculpture in one of his most closely argued passages of criticism. 'This . . . is almost a thesis of [Gaudier's] ideas upon the use of pure form', he wrote. 'We have the triangle and the circle asserted, *labled* [*sic*] almost, upon the face and right breast. Into these so-called "abstractions" life flows, the circle moves and elongates into the oval, it increases and takes volume in the sphere or hemisphere of the breast. The triangle moves toward organism, it becomes a spherical triangle (the central life-form common to both Brzeska and Lewis). These two developed motifs work as themes in a fugue. We have the whole series of spherical triangles, as in the arm over the head, all combining and culminating in the great sweep of the back of the shoulders, as fine as any surface in all sculpture. The "abstract" or mathematical bareness of the triangle and circle are fully incarnate, made flesh, full of vitality and of energy. The whole form-series ends, passes into stasis with the circular base or platform.'[112]

Although Pound's interpretation is altogether too neat and conceptual to serve as an accurate summary of Gaudier's intentions, it can stand as compelling

△ Henri Gaudier-Brzeska
*Red Stone Dancer*, 1913 (1st view)

◁ Henri Gaudier-Brzeska
*Red Stone Dancer*, 1913 (2nd view)

Henri Gaudier-Brzeska
*The Dancer*, 1913

evidence of the sculptor's new willingness to adhere to the principles of the rebel group. An enormous stylistic gulf separates *Red Stone Dancer* from *The Dancer* – his earlier version of the same theme – and he must have realized that there was no going back on the radicalism of the later piece. Where the previous version belongs squarely in the nineteenth-century tradition, and beguiles with its sensitive treatment of a naturalistic language, *Red Stone Dancer* discards all conventions and constructs something fresh and disturbing. And while the earlier *Dancer* succeeds by observing all the Rodinesque rules, conveying a moment in time through gracefully proportioned limbs and delicate gestures, the second version's squat body denies all that attenuated charm and seeks to impress through a display of solid sculptural muscle. *The Dancer* is an ember dying in the ashes of the old century, but *Red Stone Dancer* is a flame, angrily bursting into life to herald the beginning of a new order.

Gaudier had, of course, been able to lean on the advice of the Continental avant-garde before he took this final plunge into modernism. Just as Epstein was inspired by Brancusi's *Pigeons* when he carved the marble dove groups, so Gaudier was stimulated by a meeting with the Roumanian at the 1913 Allied Artists' Salon. 'Brzeska and myself were at the exhibition before the opening', recalled Brodzky, 'and we noticed a black-bearded man, obviously a foreigner, hovering near an abstract work. The bearded one seemed amiable and Brzeska approached him, and got into conversation, when he learnt that it was Brancusi, and the sculptor of the abstract work in question. Brzeska was delighted. Brancusi was a "fine fellow", and I am sure that the Roumanian sculptor had a temporary influence upon Brzeska's work.'[113] That 'influence' is immediately apparent when *Sleeping Muse II*, which Brancusi exhibited as *Muse Endormie* in the 1913 Salon, is compared with the head created by Gaudier for *Red Stone Dancer*. For despite the traces of descriptive features still lingering in Brancusi's bronze head, its viability as a purely abstract oval is emphasized above all else. It could almost have been transferred wholesale, without the facial detail, onto the neck of Gaudier's figure, executed only a few months after the young sculptor had seen *Sleeping Muse II* and talked with its creator.

The way was now clear for Gaudier to throw in his lot with the Rebel Art Centre, and he supported the activities at Great Ormond Street with enormous enthusiasm when it was opened in the spring of 1914. His effervescent personality, no less than his obvious talent as a sculptor, ensured that he rapidly became one of the most popular adherents to the rebel cause. A natural love of exhibitionism made him willing to expound the most high-flown doctrines, often as a form of personal amusement to see how his listeners would react. 'They labelled him a "barbarian" ' and 'made a fuss of him', wrote Brodzky, who disapproved of the new direction his friend had taken, 'and I am quite sure that Brzeska became a little conceited and began to act the part expected of him'.[114] But it was surely invidious to make moral judgements on the behaviour of such an instinctively theatrical individual. Whatever his oddities and blatant eccentricities, Gaudier usually managed to divorce them from the serious business of carving, modelling and drawing: and as he became personally more ebullient, his work and aesthetic theories grew increasingly committed to one totally serious line of development. He was even able to combine the lighthearted and the sober in his personality, explaining his change of heart to Brodzky in a characteristically frivolous way. 'He swore he would never shave', recalled Brodzky. 'He was a free man and would remain one. "Damn shaving!" And to be quite consistent, later on he appeared entirely clean-shaven – much to my surprise. He looked so clean. Where was his freedom? I asked him, and for what higher value had he sold it? His answer was equally surprising. Staccato, and with curled lips, he replied, "Pure form!" '[115]

Gaudier's own work was, in time, immensely strengthened by his contact with the Rebel Art Centre. The callow stylistic fireworks became far less apparent, and he settled down to pursue a consistent course of action. Meeting other artists engaged in developing similar aesthetic theories helped him to fortify his resolve, put imitation behind him and strike out on his own as one of the most forward-looking sculptors in Europe. And as new loyalties established themselves in his own mind, so he became increasingly dissatisfied with Fitzroy Square. Discussing the Omega's operations with Lewis may have convinced him that Bloomsbury should be despised, for his friend Haldane Macfall recorded that 'Gaudier spoke bitterly about Fry's gang, the Omega Workshops or some such name, as having "sucked his brains" and "swindled him" '.[116] He may have come to feel, too, that his individuality was lost in the Omega's communal anonymity; and this suspicion was reinforced by his dislike of the Workshops' approach to decorative commissions. In the same *Egoist* review where he had praised Lewis's contributions to the 1914 Allied Artists' Salon, Gaudier lashed out against the lounge which the Omega had installed at the exhibition.

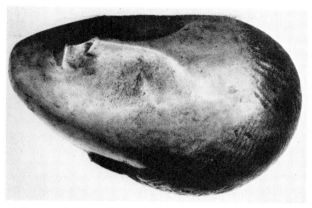

Constantin Brancusi
*Sleeping Muse*, 1910

'The chairs, the cushions and especially a screen with two natural swans and the hangings of patched work irritate me – there is too much prettiness', he declared, contrasting it unfavourably with the work displayed by the Great Ormond Street group and thereby making clear the dramatic change in his own sympathies. 'Happily the Rebel stand shows that the new painting is capable of great strength and manliness in decoration', his review continued, hitting out also against Kandinsky's exhibits – 'my temperament does not allow of formless, vague assertions' – and the Futurist contributions by Nevinson: 'it is impressionism using false weapons. The emotions are of a superficial character, merging on the vulgar.' Gaudier was the 1914 chairman of the Salon's artists' committee, but the post did not prevent him from airing his partisan views. The only sculptors he admired in the show were Brancusi, Zadkine and Epstein, 'whom I consider the foremost in the small number of good sculptors in Europe'; as for the rest, he brushed them off in a splendidly arrogant sentence as 'an agglomeration of Rodin-Maillol mixture and valueless academism [*sic*] – with here and there some one trying to be naughty: curled nubilities and discreet slits'. The man who had modelled pastiches of Rodin only two years before now had eyes only for 'the Rebel art', and he concluded by stating that 'people like Miss Dismorr [and] Miss Saunders . . . are well worth encouraging in their endeavours towards the new light. With them stops the revolutionary spirit of the exhibition'.[117]

One of the most fruitful results of Gaudier's contact with Great Ormond Street was the close friendship he struck up with Pound, whose poems the sculptor liked to compare with the *Red Stone Dancer*. They had first come across each other at the 1913 Allied Artists' exhibition, when Pound and Olivia Shakespear were wandering about 'the upper galleries hunting for new work and trying to find some good amid much bad'. Suddenly, Pound realized that they were being followed at a distance by 'a young man . . . like a well-made young wolf or some soft-moving, bright-eyed wild thing'. The poet was 'playing the fool' and Gaudier 'was willing to be amused by the performance', no doubt sharing Pound's irreverent contempt for the vast majority of work on display. But the two visitors' lightheartedness turned into surprised admiration when 'on the ground floor we stopped before a figure with bunchy muscles done in clay painted green'. It was Gaudier's *Wrestler*, and 'one of a group of interesting things', so Pound 'turned to the catalogue and began to take liberties with the appalling assemblage of consonants: "Brzxjk—" I began. I tried again, "Burrzisskzk—" I drew back, breathed deeply and took another run at the hurdle, sneezed, coughed, rumbled, got as far as "Burdidis—" when there was a dart from behind the pedestal and I heard a voice speaking with the gentlest fury in the world: "Cela s'appelle tout simplement Jaersh-ka. C'est moi qui les ai sculptés." And he disappeared like a Greek god in a vision'. Pound's curiosity was aroused, and he 'wrote at once inviting him to dinner, having found his address in the catalogue'. Gaudier did not arrive, but his would-be host received a letter 'the morning after my date' calling him 'Madame' and inviting him to the Putney studio.[118] The relationship developed from there and Pound, with characteristic generosity, did his best to help his young friend in the most practical way he could. Short of money himself, he nevertheless spent some of the £40 given to him by Yeats from a prize awarded by *Poetry* magazine on two small sculptures by Gaudier. The sculptor must have been delighted by the purchases, but no more so than Pound himself, who told William Carlos Williams in December 1913 that he had 'just bought two statuettes from *the* coming sculptor, Gaudier-Brzeska. I like him very much. He is the only person with whom I can really be "Altaforte" . . . We are getting our little gang after five years of waiting'.[119] Pound's reference to one of his own early poems was appropriate, for Gaudier was sufficiently excited by his poem on 'Piere Vidal' – who ran 'mad as a wolf' through the mountains of Cabaret – to present Pound with a pen drawing of an old wolf, inscribing it 'à mon ami Ezra Pound en admiration de "Piere Vidal Old" '.[120] And on 18 January 1914 Pound joined Yeats, Aldington, Sturge Moore and other poets in a committee to present Wilfred Scawen Blunt with a Gaudier reliquary of a reclining female nude carved in pentelican marble. It was a token of their regard for the 74-year-old poet's opposition to the British Empire and all its institutions, and in his account of the presentation in the March issue of *Poetry*, Pound took the opportunity to praise Gaudier as 'a brilliant young sculptor'.

But it was not the first time that he had celebrated his friend's work in print. By the beginning of the new year, Pound found himself so involved in the progress of the 'Cubist Room' artists that he started to write about them in magazines where formerly he had written only about poetry. He was becoming more interested in society as a whole, and was anxious to demonstrate that the arts had a rightful place in any enlightened community. These views were first elaborated in a trio of articles on 'The Serious Artist' published in *The New Freewoman* between October and November 1913, where Pound claimed that the arts could be justified because they were a science, 'just as chemistry is'. The 'touchstone of art', he maintained, was 'its precision', and this discipline showed itself in writing when an author firmly controlled his own energies and wrote only what he meant to express 'with complete clarity and simplicity', using the least possible number of words. In a prophetic phrase, he characterized poetry as the 'maximum efficiency of expression' – a description he would carry over almost intact to his Vorticist theories – even though he also insisted that in verse the 'thinking, word-arranging, clarifying faculty must move and leap with the energizing, sentient, musical faculties'.[121]

His dissatisfaction with the progress of Imagism made him turn increasingly towards the more significant achievements of radical English artists, and a few months later he decided to take up his pen in the cause of 'The New Sculpture'. The article he wrote – published in *The Egoist* on 16 February – was basically a defence of Epstein and Gaudier, but he widened it out to include his evolving theories on art and civilization. He was no longer content merely to claim a place for art in society: the work of his two sculptor friends proved to him that there was no point in the artist continuing to be a humanist and hoping to convert an 'unbearably stupid' humanity. Now it should be obvious that the arts were openly at war with the world, and that the only solution was bloodshed. 'The artist has been at peace with his oppressors long enough', Pound asserted. 'He has dabbled in democracy and he is now done with that folly. We turn back, we artists, to the powers of the air, to the djinns who were our allies aforetime, to the spirits of our ancestors.' The poet equated carvings like *Red Stone Dancer* and Epstein's flenite women with the power of witchdoctors, and considered that their magical qualities would enable the artist to rule the world as firmly as he did in primitive times. 'The aristocracy of entail and of title is decayed, the aristocracy of commerce is decaying, the aristocracy of the arts is ready again for its service', he cried rhetorically, 'and we who are the heirs of the witch-doctor and the voodoo, we artists who have been so long the despised are about to take over control'.[122]

Pound's sentiments represented a more melodramatic version of the theories outlined by Hulme in his lecture three weeks before, and Gaudier agreed with them. Avant-garde artists and writers in London were realizing more and more that they shared the same theories about the direction modern art should take, and in March Gaudier wrote a letter to *The Egoist* voicing opinions that concurred with those of his two theorist friends. 'The modern sculptor is a man who works with instinct as his inspiring force', he began, showing himself to be in sympathy with Pound's ideas about the need for a return to the primitive subconscious. 'His work is emotional. The shape of a leg, or the curve of an eyebrow, etc., etc., have to him no significance whatsoever; light voluptuous modelling is to him insipid – what he feels he does so intensely and his work is nothing more nor less than the abstraction of this intense feeling.' He made clear that this 'intense feeling' was the same as Pound's 'power of the voodoo' by insisting that 'this sculpture has no relation to classic Greek, but ... is continuing the tradition of the barbaric peoples of the earth (for whom we have sympathy and admiration)'.[123] And Gaudier was not content to state his 'admiration' only in writing. By the time he sat down to compose the *Egoist* letter he was engaged on a monumental portrait of Pound that put these theories into compelling form.

Gaudier probably began the preliminary studies in January or February 1914, after his sitter had returned from a winter at Coleman's Hatch with Yeats. 'Normally he could not afford marble, at least, not large pieces', Pound recalled. 'As we passed the cemetery which lies by the bus-route to Putney he would damn that "waste of good stone"'. Financial limitations seemed to dictate that he choose plaster, 'a most detestable medium', wrote Pound, 'to which I had naturally objected.' The poet therefore decided to help by purchasing the stone himself, 'not having any idea of the amount of hard work I was letting [Gaudier] in for'. During an arduous and dangerous period of physical work, cutting Pound's block down to a manageable size, Gaudier sketched a whole series of studies of his model, brushing in the main lines of neck, face and mane of hair with decisive strokes of indian ink. 'In many of them he had undoubtedly no further intention than that of testing a contour', Pound explained, and their swift summary of basic outlines demonstrate that from the outset Gaudier intended to create a hieratic, austerely simplified image. A photograph showing him hard at work on the marble proves that he then envisaged the eyes as diamonds rather than narrow slits, and that Pound's moustache curled up above his nostrils. And the poet was warned while he sat for him that 'it will not look like you, it *will ... not ... look* ... like you. It will be the expression of certain emotions which I get from your character'. But however much Gaudier explained, he could never have prepared his sitter – perched 'on a shilling wooden chair in a not over-heated studio with the railroad trains rushing overhead' – for the final product of these superhuman exertions.[124]

This time, he seems to have gone to the British Museum's primitive collections – like Epstein before him – and been deeply influenced by a gigantic

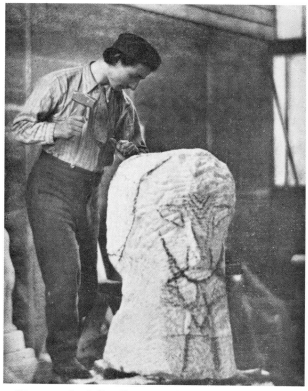

Photograph of Gaudier at work on the *Bust of Ezra Pound*, 1914

△Henri Gaudier-Brzeska
*Study for Bust of Ezra Pound*, 1914

△ Henri Gaudier-Brzeska
*Study for Bust of Ezra Pound*, 1914

▷▷Henri Gaudier-Brzeska
*Bust of Ezra Pound*, 1914 (1st view)

▷Henri Gaudier-Brzeska
*Bust of Ezra Pound*, 1914 (2nd view)

Anon
*Hoa-Haka-Nana-Ia* ('Breaking Waves') (detail)

carved figure called *Hoa-Haka-Nana-Ia*, from the Easter Island cult village of Orongo. Ever since entering the Museum in 1869 it had reigned over the Polynesian collections, a towering testimony to primitive man's ability to create potent symbols of his own magical beliefs. Gaudier could not fail to have been impressed by such irrefutable proof of the power of prehistoric art, and his marble *Bust* shows that he kept the Easter Island figure securely in the back of his mind as he disposed the various sections of his carving into their unpredictable format. If particular similarities between the two images centre on the area of eyes and mouth, it appears likely that Gaudier has been inspired above all by the whole vertical identity of the Orongo figure, thrusting its way up into the air in one compact cubic mass of stone. Just as the head of *Hoa-Haka-Nana-Ia* is wedged onto its torso without any regard for the thin shape of an intervening neck, so Pound's face rests on a wide base which exists only to ensure that the outlines of the whole sculpture travel up in one consistent form towards the wider block of hair at the top. The overall silhouette thereby succeeds in suggesting a circumcised penis, and Epstein – who visited his friend while he was at work on the *Bust* – recalled that 'Pound had asked him to make it virile and this Gaudier was endeavouring to do, explaining to me the general biological significance'.[125] This interpretation is confirmed by the disapproving Brodzky, who thought that 'there was too much sex-art talk' at the Rebel Art Centre: he coldly declared that the *Bust*'s 'purpose and beginnings were entirely pornographic. Both the sculptor and the sitter had decided upon that'.[126] And Lewis, despite his earlier protestations to Sickert about obscenity in art, described the finished carving with disarming candour as 'Ezra in the form of a marble phallus'.[127]

But there is nothing self-indulgent about this monolithic tour de force. Pound, with his almost sacred belief in the importance of artistic discipline, would have been the first to complain if his portrait had become merely immoderate, a dirty joke done for a snigger. Gaudier, likewise, would not have been prepared to expend so much of his time and energy on the creation of a mere caprice, and the *Bust* itself bears out the seriousness of his intentions. Compared with the eery blend of realism and stylization employed in the Easter Island figure, the carving appears to be tight and schematic, certainly. But the geometry is subtle, even devious. No one part of the face has been placed at the same angle as that of its companions; they are all of them tilted slightly off-balance, so that a palpable tension results. Each separate feature, carefully isolated from the others by a generous expanse of bare marble so that its shape can register with the greatest possible impact, is at odds with its neighbours. Gaudier, despising conventional regularity, has opted for a series of slight disparities in order to keep the massive block of stone alive with uneasy rhythms. And he has not overstepped himself in his desire for formal contrasts: in the final stages of the carving he deliberately cut out much of its dramatic swagger, fearing no doubt that he had gone too far in his desire for a grand theatrical statement. Pound recorded that the *Bust* 'was most striking, perhaps, two weeks before it was finished. I do not mean to say that it was better, it was perhaps a *kinesis*, whereas it is now a *stasis*; but before the back was cut out, and before the middle lock was cut down, there was in the marble a titanic energy, it was like a great stubby catapult, the two masses bent for a blow'. The sitter himself was evidently torn between his excitement over the earlier state of the carving, and the realization that it was probably too exaggerated. 'The unfinished stone caught the eye', he remembered. 'Maybe it would have wearied it.'[128]

Pound was, nevertheless, satisfied with the results of Gaudier's last-minute alterations. 'There is in the final condition of the stone a great calm', he wrote, as if in recognition of the fact that Gaudier had seen him as an implacable

Buddha in at least one of the preliminary sketches. When the carving was eventually put on display in May 1914 as part of the Whitechapel Art Gallery's survey of *Twentieth Century Art*, it must have signified Gaudier's definitive adherence to Rebel Art Centre aesthetics; but its brusque simplifications could not have looked at their best in the crowded gallery of a mixed exhibition. The *Bust* is essentially a public image, and the features chiselled so boldly onto its surface were clearly meant to be admired from a suitable distance. Just as its Easter Island prototype dominated its surroundings in the British Museum, so Gaudier – who was fundamentally a maker of small, intimate sculpture – wanted just once to construct something larger than life, to prove that his admiration for the 'barbaric peoples' could be translated into a carving that would not pale in comparison with its primitive predecessors. And he justified the phallic metaphor of the *Bust* by describing in an article how the Oceanic races, falling 'into contemplation before their sex: the site of their great energy: THEIR CONVEX MATURITY ... pulled the sphere lengthways and made the cylinder'.[129] His carving is, therefore, as much of a tribute to the powerful shape of an abstract cylinder as it is a symbol of virility, and in that sense its primitivism leads directly on to the mechanistic geometry of Gaudier's Vorticist sculpture.

Henri Gaudier-Brzeska
*Study for Bust of Ezra Pound*, 1914

Within weeks, the *Bust* found itself placed in a pastoral setting: the front garden of South Lodge, an 'unpretentious semi-detached villa in Campden Hill Road'[130] where Ford lived with Violet Hunt. South Lodge was an appropriate site for a work that so loudly proclaimed loyalties towards the modern movement, for the house had recently established itself as one of the main meeting places of the English avant-garde. It was only a short walk up the hill from Pound's lodgings at 10 Church Walk, where he lived until marriage dictated a move to larger quarters. Violet Hunt liked the poet so much that she lent him a group of Victorian watercolours by William Henry Hunt to hang in his room, where they must have appeared ill at ease with the Gaudier carvings and the woodcut of *Flushing* by Wadsworth which were also housed there.[131] But Pound returned Miss Hunt's compliment by establishing himself at South Lodge 'as a kind of social master of ceremonies'. Both Ford and his mistress were delighted to play host to such a gregarious young man, for Goldring wrote that they 'adored every form of entertaining and loved to be surrounded by crowds of friends'. Pound, therefore, 'subjugated Ford by his American exuberance', and was allowed to invite his artist friends along to enjoy the hospitality at Campden Hill Road.

'The garden was taken over', remembered Goldring, 'and every afternoon a motley collection of people, in the oddest costumes, invaded it at Ezra's instigation, and afterwards repaired to South Lodge.'[132] There, in the evenings, a salon as extraordinary as that held in Frith Street assembled inside the house. 'Wonderful young ambitious poets of [Pound's] *trempe*, confirmed artists of all kinds, mingled in our courts', Violet Hunt recalled in her florid prose, 'with the wistful Walter de la Mare and the spanking Amy Lowell, the sinister but delightful Madame Strindberg with her marmosets, painters like Jacob Epstein and Wyndham Lewis, Richard Nevinson and Gaudier Brzeska'.[133]

Her gushing description reflects the excitement with which both she and Ford greeted each fresh arrival; and it was a measure of the vitality of London's artistic life during these hectic pre-war months, when so many new and intoxicating ideas were being passed around from poet to painter, philosopher to sculptor, that such broadly-based meetings were able to take place. Practitioners of every form of creative expression mixed happily together, delighted to have the opportunity to exchange views, denounce each other's principles or thrash out a controversial question. Occasionally, of course, the outspoken rebels

Edward Wadsworth
*Harbour of Flushing*, c. 1914

clashed head-on with a figurehead of the order they were so anxious to subvert. Aldington laughingly recalled the discomfort of a 'Great Poet' who arrived at a South Lodge salon only to find that 'he had to listen to Ezra Pound, Gaudier, and myself playing verbal nine-pins with the Post-Victorians, the Royal Academy, and a variety of other pompiers' institutions. Ford Hueffer saw him down to the door, and came back chuckling. We asked what the joke was, and he said: "When we got to the front door he asked very anxiously: 'Are all the young men like that?' and I said: 'Oh, they're comparatively mild', and he said: 'Oh, my God!' and ran away." '[134]

But when Ford wrote to Lewis asking him to bring Marinetti and Nevinson along to a South Lodge evening, he could declare quite truthfully that his parties attracted 'generally some of the swell and wealthy, together with literary gents and picture buyers and people who help on MOVEMENTS'. And he also counselled Lewis, in the same letter, to have patience with the irritating Madame Strindberg, who for all her faults was attempting to mould the Cabaret into a genuine meeting place for all those engaged in creative activities. 'She is trying to build up a palace of all the Arts with three oyster shells and stale patchouli and sawdust and creme and vers libre and champagne corks', he explained, 'which, is what . . . we are all of us trying to do in one field or the other.'[135] Despite its minor insanities, the Cabaret was in its own way just as helpful to the spirit of aesthetic ferment as the gatherings at South Lodge, the Great Ormond Street tea parties, suppers at the Tour Eiffel, Café Royal absinthes or the Frith Street salon. They were all a part of that unique fabric of London's intellectual life which the First World War was so effectively to destroy; and Ford was perfectly accurate when he claimed that 'for a moment in the just-before-the-war days, the Fine, the Plastic and the Literary Arts touched hands with an unusual intimacy and what is called oneness of purpose'. Revolution was in the air, and the older generation was at last beginning to realize that there was more to modern art than Royal Academy summer shows, Edwardian verse, the New English Art Club and Augustus John.

Ford, himself a member of that generation, seemed 'seriously to have come to the conclusion that the Flaubertian Impressionism of which he and Conrad had been for so long the principal English exponents was, as Lewis said, dead and done for'.[136] And he bore this uncomfortable realization with so much good humour and verve, so keen a thirst for renewal, that he was able afterwards to admit with some pride that 'I was I suppose identified with the Vorticists', and fondly recalled how 'those young people had done their best to make a man of me. They had dragged me around to conspiracies, night-clubs, lectures where Marinetti howled and made noises like machine-guns. They had even tried to involve me in their splits . . . So they pranced and roared and blew blasts on their bugles and round them the monuments of London tottered'.[137] It was an unlikely and even miraculous alliance, but life was then unpredictable enough for anything to happen. And the flexible structure of the city's increasingly turbulent artistic circles meant that it was possible for this middle-aged man of letters to walk down Holland Street with Pound arguing 'incessantly on one side of me in his incomprehensible Philadelphian', and Lewis on the other, 'dark, a little less hirsute but more and more like a conspirator', telling him 'on and on in a vitriolic murmur' that ' "*Tu sais, tu es foûtu! Foûtu!* Finished! Exploded! Done for! . . . What people want is me, not you. They want to see me. A Vortex. To liven them up . . . I . . . I . . . I . . ." He struck his chest dramatically and repeated: "I . . . I . . . I . . . The Vortex. Blast all the rest." '[138] And even while he muttered imprecations into Ford's ear, Lewis was planning to launch both the 'Vortex' and 'Blast' upon the whole of the English establishment, so that rebellion could at last be turned into a tangible reality.

# Chapter 8: Hulme the Critic and Champion of Bomberg

The battle between traditional values and the radical theories of the young rebels was given new edge when Hulme decided to take up a journalist's pen in their defence. He assumed this new role of professional art critic almost accidentally, provoked by the howls of rage which had greeted the opening of Epstein's first one-man show at the Twenty-One Gallery in December 1913. It was a small exhibition – no more than nine drawings and five sculptures in all – but the presence of two *Carvings in Flenite* and a marble *Group of Birds* ensured that the critics' reaction was vicious to the point of outright defamation.[1] Infuriated by the mauling his hero had received, Hulme sprang to the sculptor's defence in the Christmas Day issue of *The New Age* with a lengthy article entitled 'Mr. Epstein and the Critics'. He apologized for the improvised nature of the piece, stating that 'when I see the critics attempting to corrupt the mind of the spectators and trying to hinder their appreciation of a great artist, I feel an indignation which must be my excuse for these clumsy, hurriedly written and unrevised notes'. The explanation was needed, for Hulme's column veered alarmingly between closely reasoned argument and personal abuse. But in some sections of the article he managed to escape from mere spleen and rebut what he saw as 'two separate prejudices'. The first, he claimed, was 'that an artist has no business to use formulae taken from another civilisation'; and the second 'that, even if the formula the artist uses is the natural means of expressing certain of his emotions, yet these emotions must be unnatural in him, a modern Western'.

Hulme's defence centred on the self-evident fact that these very formulae 'constitute a constant and permanent alphabet', and that an artist's individuality 'comes out in the way the formulae are used'. Human emotions, he declared, have never changed throughout history: and therefore, 'given the same emotion, the same broad formula comes naturally to the hands of any people in any century'. It was an elaboration of his favourite theory about the re-emergence of 'geometrical' art, and he defended one of the flenite sculptures by claiming that the carving, 'by an extreme abstraction, by the selection of certain lines, gives an effect of tragic greatness'. This, he thought, was 'the real root of the objection to these statues, that they express emotions which are, as a matter of fact, entirely alien and unnatural to the critic'. And he summarized his defence by asserting that 'my justification of these statues would be then: (1) that an alien formula is justifiable when it is the necessary expression of a certain attitude; and (2) that in the peculiar conditions in which we find ourselves, which are really the breaking up of an era, it has again become quite possible for people here and there to have the attitude expressed by these formulae'.[2]

Although the slander he indulged in elsewhere in the essay alienated many *New Age* readers, Lewis publicly backed Hulme up by writing a letter to the magazine claiming that the review of Epstein's show by its other art critic, Anthony Ludovici, was 'the grimmest pig-wash vouchsafed at present to a public fed on husks',[3] and the editor, Orage, was sufficiently impressed by Hulme's outstanding sense of conviction to allow him the space for a whole series of articles on 'Modern Art' during the spring and summer of 1914. They rapidly became regarded by the rebels as one of the clearest, sanest, and most sustained defences of their standpoint, for Hulme started off in forthright style on 15 January with an uninhibited attack on the Bloomsbury Grafton Group exhibition. He despised it as heartily as the other critics had hated Epstein's show, declaring that 'the departure of Mr Wyndham Lewis, Mr Etchells and Mr Nevinson and several others has left concentrated in a purer form all the worked-out and dead elements' in Fry's group.

'As you enter the room you almost know what to expect, from the effect of the general colour', he wrote. 'It consists almost uniformly of pallid chalky blues, yellows and strawberry colours with a strong family resemblance between all the pictures; in every case a kind of anaemic effect showing no personal or constructive use of colour.' He also scoffed at the subjects of the pictures: 'one may recognise the whole familiar bag of tricks – the usual Cézanne landscapes, the still-lifes, the Eves in their gardens, and the botched Byzantine.' And his own venom was particularly acute when he came round to 'Mr Fry's landscape', which demonstrated his 'inability to follow a method to its proper conclusion'. Hulme scorned the 'sentimental and pretty' colour of the painting, and dismissed it out of hand by stating that Fry 'accomplishes the extraordinary feat of adapting the austere Cézanne into something quite fitted for chocolate boxes'. Behind Hulme's abuse lay a firm conviction that Fry's group did not treat avant-garde ideas with the seriousness they deserved. He saw the Bloomsbury artists as fatally over-sophisticated, aesthetic dandies who were not capable of the emotional profundity Epstein had injected into the flenite carvings. Fitzroy Square, he believed, simply borrowed modernist conventions in a superficial way without beginning to express the fundamental change that Western thought was undergoing. 'One might separate the modern movement into three parts, to be roughly indicated as Post-Impressionism, analytical Cubism and a new constructive geometrical art', he wrote elsewhere in his article. 'The first of these, and to a certain extent the second, seem to me to be necessary but entirely transitional stages leading up to the third, which is the only one containing possibilities of development.'[4]

Such strictures must have been greeted with delight by Lewis and his allies: here, right on cue, was a writer intelligent and committed enough to take up their cause in print. But Fry, for his part, greeted the appearance of this new Savonarola with characteristic coolness. 'The Lewis group have got hold of the *New Age* critic', he told Grant on 26 January, 'and he's written an amusing thing which I send you; please send it back.'[5] As far as Fry was concerned, this dispute was going to be a cold war, in which he would retain his dignity and a suitable detachment amidst all the squabbles and pettifogging intrigues buzzing around his organization and the work of his friends.

Hulme, however, was not content to hit out only at the Bloomsbury artists. His second *New Age* column on 'Modern Art' attacked the important manifesto on 'Neo-Realism' that Ginner had contributed to the magazine on 1 January. The ideas entirely contradicted Hulme's view of modern art, and he declared that Ginner's 'statements are based on such an extraordinarily confused and complicated mass of assumptions that I cannot give any proper refutation'. But he did give one vital clue as to his feelings about abstraction when he asserted that 'both realism and abstraction, then, can only be *engendered* out of nature, but while the first's only idea of living seems to be that of hanging on to its progenitor, the second cuts its umbilical cord'.[6] The statement was published on 12 February, at a time when Lewis was painting several abstract compositions like *Plan of War* containing no overt reference to 'nature' at all. This would be the limit of Hulme's sympathy with rebel art: he could not bring himself to admit that abstraction was acceptable as an autonomous language. If a painting did not refer back to natural appearance in some way, then he considered it to have severed all connections with the vitality of great art.

His thesis was only properly developed with reference to specific works by the rebel artists when he came to review the First London Group show in *The New Age* of 26 March. Quickly sorting them out from the former Camden Town and Cumberland Market artists, he did go so far as to admit that Gore's *The Wood*, Gilman's *Eating House* and Ginner's *La Balayeuse* were 'infinitely better than the faked stuff produced by Mr Roger Fry and his friends'. But he insisted on thinking it 'possible to point out, however, in looking at this kind of painting, the dissatisfaction which inclines one towards Cubism'. For Hulme considered that the pictures painted by Gore and his compatriots were 'filled by contours which . . . one can only describe as meaningless. They are full of detail which is entirely accidental in character, only justified by the fact that these accidents did actually occur in the particular piece of nature which was being painted. One feels a repugnance to such accidents – and desires painting where nothing is accidental, where all the contours are closely knit together into definite structural shapes.' In other words, he favoured the work of the rebel artists, seeing in their paintings and sculptures 'the re-emergence of a sensibility akin to that behind the geometrical arts of the past'.

Yet he was now particularly anxious to point out that nothing could justify the prolonged and wholesale borrowing of archaic forms. It was natural for the rebel movement, 'at its first rather fumbling search for an appropriate means of expression', to go 'back to these past forms'; and works like Epstein's *Flenite Relief* and Gaudier's *Decorative Mask* had exemplified this stage of development. 'But this state has been clearly left behind', Hulme emphasized. 'The new sensibility is finding for itself a direct and modern means of expression, having very little resemblance to these past geometric forms.' Gaudier's *Bust of Pound* is a good instance of the way in which a primitive prototype has been used, not simply as an excuse for imitation, but as a springboard for the creation of a piece of 'new geometric and monumental art'. Admirable as it is, however, the *Bust* would not have satisfied Hulme's expectations completely: what he really welcomed in the London Group exhibition was the use of those 'machine forms' he had advocated in his Quest Society lecture. 'A whole picture', he wrote excitedly, 'is sometimes dominated by a composition based on hard, mechanical shapes in a way which previous art would have shrunk from. It is not the emphasis on form which is the distinguishing characteristic of the new movement, then, but the emphasis on this particular kind of form.' At last, Hulme felt he was able to see the ideas he had been expounding in his weekly salon for some months being put into practice.

But it was not to Lewis that Hulme looked for a champion of his theories. Their growing divergence of opinion was reflected in his criticism of the rebel leader's exhibits. 'In Mr Lewis's work there are always certain qualities of dash and decision', he declared, 'but it has the defects of these qualities. His sense of form seems to me to be sequent rather than integral, by which I mean that one form probably springs out of the preceding one as he works, instead of being conceived as part of a whole. His imagination being quick and never fumbling, very interesting relations are generated in this way, but the whole sometimes lacks cohesion and unity.' Just as Bell had censured Lewis in his review of the Doré show the previous October for being 'inclined to modify his forms in the interest of drama and psychology to the detriment of pure design', so Hulme now considered that Lewis's enjoyment of particular areas in his design marred the formal coherence of the whole. ' "Christopher Columbus" is hard and gay, contains many admirable inventions', he wrote, 'but is best regarded as a field where certain qualities are displayed, rather than as a complete work of art.'

Naturally enough, Hulme considered that 'the qualities of Mr Lewis's work are seen to better advantage in his quite remarkable drawing, "Enemy of the Stars" ', a work which could almost have been executed as an illustration of the philosopher's theories. But he was, in the end, far more enthusiastic about Wadsworth, whose lost painting of *Scherzo* was 'most successful' in the way it managed to ensure that 'a number of lively ascending forms are balanced by broad planes at the top'. Hamilton, similarly, was 'the painter whose work shows the greatest advance . . . His "Two Figures" shows a great sense of construction, and is one of the best paintings in this section'. And Hulme considered Etchells' drawings to be 'admirably firm and hard in character', even if their style was

William Roberts
*Study for Dancers*, 1913–14

still too indecisive for the philosopher to feel entirely happy about them. 'It would obviously be premature to form any sure judgement about this artist's work', he asserted, 'at a time when he almost seems to be holding himself back, in a search for a new method of expression.' Even Nevinson was commended, despite Hulme's avowed dislike of Futurism, and qualified approval was given to Gaudier's sculpture: 'the tendencies it displays are sound though the abstractions used do not seem to me to be always thoroughly thought out'. For all his clearly stated allegiances, Hulme was determined to be critical when his sensibility so dictated, and the sole contributor about whom he was entirely happy was Epstein, the creator of 'the only really satisfying and complete work in this section'. He thought that the sculptor had 'arrived at an interesting point in his development'; for having started from 'a very efficient realism', and 'passed through a more or less archaic period', Epstein had now 'left that behind and, so far as one can judge from the drawings for sculpture he exhibits, to have arrived at an entirely personal and modern method of expression'. He was ready to praise Epstein's sculpture unreservedly as the fulfilment of all his theories, but *Carving in Flenite* – which 'comes at the end of the second period' – and *Bird Pluming Itself* – 'quite light in character' – were not challenging enough for him to laud them unreservedly.[7]

It was a pity that Roberts was not represented at the exhibition, for he had recently executed the one painting Hulme could have seen as approximating most closely to his theories: *Dancers*.[8] It had, however, been hung by Lewis at the Rebel Art Centre; and Hulme must have admired it on one of his rare visits to Great Ormond Street, for in *The New Age* of 16 April he reproduced Roberts' *Study* for the painting as the second in a new series of reproductions of 'Contemporary Drawings'.[9] The *Study* represents an enormous and dramatic advance on *The Return of Ulysses*, painted the previous year.[10] In place of the relatively straightforward stick-like simplifications employed in that earlier work, Roberts has now developed a formal language that coincides remarkably with Hulme's mechanistic ideal. He later insisted that 'my relation to Hulme is limited to one short walk I took with him and Ashley Dukes, the dramatic critic, through Soho one night homeward from the Café Royal'.[11] But his dancers' limbs are nevertheless enclosed in Hulmean metallic sheaths, and they lever their way across the shallow, one-dimensional surface of the design with the impersonality of robots. There is no human passion in their movements; only a regularized interaction between geometrical forms that slot into each other and freeze, confined by a scaffolding of angular outlines.

Occasionally a figurative reference crops up in among the maze of component parts, and the strange, primitive violence of *Ulysses* still lingers on, for the whole group seems to be not so much dancing as engaged in some cold, dehumanized struggle. Each shape can be read either as an abstract or a representational form, and Roberts has constructed his composition with such diligence that nothing can be identified with complete confidence. The forms link up with each other in a tangled but carefully defined mass, and finally disappear into the fragmentation of the background. Ambiguity has been sustained so consistently throughout the design that Hulme – although he confidently stated that 'this drawing contains four figures' – thought Roberts was concerned only with the formal qualities of the design. 'I could point out the position of these figures in more detail,' he wrote, 'but I think such detailed indication misleading. No artist can create abstract form spontaneously; it is always generated, or at least suggested, by the consideration of some outside concrete shapes. But such shapes are only interesting if you want to explain the psychology of the process of composition in the artist's mind. The interest of the drawing itself depends on the forms it contains. The fact that such forms were suggested by human figures is of no importance'.[12]

The comment shows a curious ambivalence in Hulme's thinking. On the one hand, he remained faithful to his earlier insistence that an abstract work must originate in 'nature', and affirmed that it is 'suggested' by 'outside concrete shapes'. Yet he appears simultaneously to contradict himself by claiming that the 'forms' somehow become autonomous in their appeal, and in no way dependent on their origin in external reality. He was obviously unclear in his own mind about the viability of abstraction, and it is significant that Roberts himself later repudiated the philosopher's interpretation of the *Study*. 'The artist is always careful to retain some traces of the natural forms that have inspired him and upon which his composition is built', he declared. 'It is these suggestive fragments of natural forms scattered throughout the design that give the abstract shapes it contains their vitality and significance.'[13] His rebuttal was written many years afterwards; but so far as is known Roberts never created a consciously abstract work during these early years, and his remarks can therefore be applied to this period without fear of too much distortion.

In the final, lost painting of *Dancers* he has followed the drawing very faithfully, concentrating on the figures alone and enlarging them to a monumental scale so that they fill the entire picture-space with their clanking movement.[14] But the painting does succeed in carrying the process of abstraction one stage further. The shaded background on the far left of the *Study* has now been split up into a complex of fragments which accord more fully with the ambiguity of the rest of the picture. And the few scattered indications of human anatomy included in the drawing have been ruthlessly weeded out. Perhaps the additional dimension of colour encouraged Roberts to move further away from his overt theme towards a consistent, overall pattern of frenetic shapes: the inadequate surviving photograph indicates that some of the colours were pitched in a high key, possibly as extreme in their contrasts as Bomberg's *Vision of Ezekiel*, and that Roberts also succeeded in conveying the gestural energy of his figures through fierce, unexpected colour oppositions.

It seems almost incredible that *Dancers* should have been painted by Roberts when he was only 18 years old, 'shortly after I had left the Slade School'.[15] Kate Lechmere remembered him as 'appearing little more than a child', but he was still mature enough to digest the lessons of Picasso, Picabia and his friend Bomberg and produce a singleminded achievement of his own. The only relevant Continental comparison to be drawn is with Léger, who had executed paintings like *The Staircase* in 1913, the year in which Roberts visited France on his European travels. The English teenager may well have seen Léger's work on that occasion, for both artists equate human movement with the altogether more impersonal motion of machines and transform their figures into mindless automatons. But whereas Roberts makes great play with the duality of his semi-abstract forms, Léger insists rather on reducing his figures to their simplest, clearest number of spare parts. The Frenchman's cylindrical shapes are only incidentally mechanical, in that they arise from his desire to return to the essential alphabet of art. The staircase is plainly described, in a childlike manner, and every portion of the design is spelt out with deliberate naïvety. In *Dancers*, however, it is unclear whether the form on the right is one figure or an amalgam of two, locked together in a balletic position. Roberts, with precocious subtlety, leaves the question open.

He did precisely the same in the related watercolour of *Religion*, which he remembered as being of the same period as *Dancers* and which was also exhibited by Lewis at the Rebel Art Centre.[16] But Roberts' use of ambiguity reaches new extremes in this tortuous composition: the figures tumbling over

William Roberts
*Dancers*, 1913–14

Fernand Léger
*The Staircase*, 1913

William Roberts
*Religion*, 1913–14

each other in a slow, circular movement are couched in a plethora of conflicting styles. Roberts appears to be indulging in a form of wilful Mannerism, switching over from the naturalistic to the abstract with prodigal speed. Certain sections are easily identifiable but they make no sense when viewed together. It would be tempting to conclude that Roberts, in his desire to juggle with different brands of modernism, lost himself in an incoherent mêlée. But only a poor photograph remains on which to form a judgement, and the watercolour medium may have helped resolve all the disparities. Perhaps he deliberately wanted to express the bewildering variety of world religions in the formal conflicts of his unwieldy allegory, treating the various idioms he employs as so many arbitrary conventions and blithely juxtaposing a realistic group of fingers or a crouching ape with more autonomous segments of form.

All the same, *Religion* does seem irritatingly literary when set beside the contemporaneous work of Roberts' friend Bomberg, who was rapidly becoming Hulme's favourite painter among the rebel group. The philosopher reproduced his drawing of *Chinnereth* in the 2 April issue of *The New Age*, and its close

David Bomberg
*Chinnereth, c.* 1914

connection with Roberts's *Study for Dancers* prompted Hulme to describe it in an identical fashion.[17] Once again he stated quite categorically that 'Mr Bomberg's drawing contains four upright figures in various attitudes', but without this information it would be impossible to know for certain. For *Chinnereth* enjoys the interplay between figurative limbs and abstract shapes as wholeheartedly as Roberts' study for *Dancers*; and Bomberg's earlier *Vision of Ezekiel* was clarity itself in comparison with the jumble of arms, heads, hands and feet employed in this *New Age* drawing. 'If you ask why the legs look like cylinders and are not realistically treated', wrote Hulme in his comment on *Chinnereth*, 'the answer I should give you would be this – the pleasure you are intended to take in such a drawing is a pleasure not in representation, but in the relations between certain abstract forms.' He was exhibiting once again his schizophrenic attitude towards abstraction, and it lingered on in the detailed exposition he decided to mount in *Chinnereth*'s defence. While showing himself sensitive enough to the appeal of the drawing, Hulme still seemed to confuse an extreme simplification of representational form with abstraction. *Chinnereth* is sufficiently rooted in a description of human bodies for it to be impossible simply to enjoy

David Bomberg
*Acrobats*, 1913–14

Piet Mondrian
*Composition in Line and Colour*, 1913

'the relations between certain abstract forms'. And although Bomberg has here and there inserted an abstract passage he has remained more faithful to the normal appearance of his figures than Roberts.

*Chinnereth* was, however, the exception rather than the rule. Far more typical of his drawings at this time is the magnificent black chalk study of *Acrobats*, where the dark background has virtually been eliminated and ambiguous forms spread their weight over the entire sheet. Figurative references have certainly been retained, but for the most part Bomberg refuses to limit his shapes to a descriptive role. Striking an admirable balance between his congenital love of solidity and a feeling for graceful movement, he allows the contours of the figures to run into each other. They thereby depart from their representational function, and the constant intercutting of arcs and right angles creates its own, purely abstract network of lines.

The logical extreme of this method would be strangely reminiscent of Mondrian's contemporaneous work; and so it may be significant that the Dutchman was living in Paris and exhibiting at the Salon des Indépendants in 1913, the very year in which Bomberg visited the city with Epstein. Could there be any connection between a 1913 Mondrian like *Composition in Line and Colour*, which largely restricts itself to a criss-cross of horizontal and vertical lines, and the less radical but overt linear structure employed in the *Acrobats*? There is probably no question of a direct influence, for the two artists seem to have arrived at similar conclusions through diametrically opposed ways of working. Mondrian's vision of the totality of nature was fundamentally transcendental: he found he could express his feelings for the world in their most concentrated form by the vital intersection of two lines. And the motif had its precedent in Schoenmaker's mystical conception of the cross as 'above everything else a construction of nature's reality'.[18] But Bomberg derives his scaffolding of intercutting lines from a far more straightforward source. His version of the technique was the result of relentlessly stripping away all the inessentials from an experience received whilst actually watching acrobats performing. For all his daring, he is still working within the broad context of the Slade figure composition, whereas

David Bomberg
*Composition*, 1914

Mondrian is beginning to impose a spiritual order onto the flux and chaos of nature. There may, nevertheless, have been a link between them, for Robert Van T'Hoff – a future member of De Stijl – was, as Bomberg recorded, 'my friend when he arrived in London . . . between 1912 and 1913'.[19] The Englishman's knowledge of Mondrian's work could perhaps have been established through this very friendship.

The most remarkable aspect of Bomberg's work, however, lies in its stubborn sense of independence. Although links with other European artists can be postulated, he remains such an individualist in his approach to the problem of abstraction that the game of influence-spotting soon falls to the ground. Faced with the beautiful conté and chalk study entitled *Composition*, it must be admitted that no real precedent or parallel exists in the work of his contemporaries to which it can be usefully related. Despite his youth, Bomberg proves himself in such a drawing to be out on his own as an artist: for *Composition* takes the principles established in *Acrobats* one stage further towards an ideal statement of pictorial fundamentals. There is an attractive logic in his progression from one study to the next – one member of Bomberg's family even considered that 'if fate had not conspired to make David an artist, he would have been a mathematician'[20] – but no theoretical dryness is allowed to affect the works themselves. In *Composition*, the summary of form created in the earlier drawing is simplified even further, refined and given new meaning.

Bomberg now has no need to fill his sheet with tensile outlines in order to compensate for the lack of descriptive elaboration in his figures. Concentrating instead on an absolute minimum of linear definition and far fewer shapes, he demonstrates that bareness does not automatically entail vacuity. The upper halves of the two protagonists can still be discerned in the beguiling pattern of the design, but they are the true subject no longer. Their limbs disappear quietly into the counterpoint set up between contour and internal modelling, as Bomberg lets his shapes wander calmly in an undefined spatial area where recession and depth are allowed to coexist with the emphatic flatness of the sepia shading. Sometimes, the lines take on a life of their own and travel around at will, completely liberated from their representational function. And three triangles of plain white paper jut down at different angles from the top of the sheet, adding their brittle tension to the whole. But they do not disturb the slow, measured tempo of the drawing, or detract from the mystery of the forms as they loom out of the darkness, waver for a moment and then vanish once more into the void.

With *Composition*, Bomberg moved decisively towards a far greater reliance on form for its own sake than his friend Roberts. Many years later, he aptly described this period in his career as 'a phase of geometrical abstraction . . . working out a purist theory of colour, light and form as an integrated organic unity relating to an inherent sense of mass'.[21] And this concise summary of his early intentions is borne out by these admirable drawings, as courageous in their way as anything then being produced throughout Europe. In the relative privacy of such studies he felt free to cast off the last remaining inhibitions of a Slade training, learning to be true to the demands of his own individuality.

Even if he always clung to some shred of recognizable subject-matter when it came to a painting, he was still able to carry his daring over to the scale of a monumental canvas: one of the preliminary sketches for *In the Hold*, the largest and most uncompromising of the pictures he exhibited at the first London Group show, is as abstract as *Acrobats* or *Composition*. It is, too, one of his

David Bomberg
*Study for In the Hold*, 1913

most muscular images, transforming the theme of men working in the hold of
a ship into a series of straight lines and decisive strokes of black crayon. Bomberg
had witnessed the scene many times while sketching in the dockland area near
Whitechapel, and he decided that he would exchange ordinary cargo for a group
of human beings. Instead of crates, sacks or parcels, therefore, his workers are
busily engaged in lifting their fellow men from one section of the boat to another,
providing the artist with a tailor-made composition of figures gesturing in a
confined space – a motif standing in a direct line of development from earlier
paintings like *Ju-Jitsu* and *Ezekiel*.

The crayon drawing is handled with tremendous verve and speed, conceiving
the design entirely in terms of pure line which models the vigorous shapes
hurling their weight around inside the picture, defines their edges or shoots
off on its own to give the composition a needle-sharp precision. Its extremism
suggests that Bomberg was determined to make his painting escape from
naturalism altogether, and in another study he uses conte crayon in a manner
similar to *Composition* in order to simplify his labourers' bodies even further.
Now line is used as a container for light and shade alone, divided up into clearly
defined blocks of white or grey. And if the jumble of forms which seemed so
indecipherable at the top of the previous drawing are now more identifiable as
figures in their own right, it is noticeable how Bomberg has reduced the contents
of his design to a more minimal number of elements.

Then, if an outstanding black chalk and wash drawing usually known as
*Acrobats* can be seen instead as an advanced study for *In the Hold*, he took one

David Bomberg
*Study for In the Hold*, 1913–14

section of the proposed picture and broke it up even further into more or less abstract components. The strong tripartite form thrusting out of the lower left corner could well be one of the hands stretching up from the hold of the ship, but by this time Bomberg does not permit anything to be identified on a straightforward representational level. His 'inherent sense of mass' has now taken over almost entirely from a desire to refer to outward appearances, and a solemn configuration of volumes fill the picture with their dour movement. The powerful light source helps to throw them into relief, and this sculptural element gives them a heroic strength. They are proud, self-sufficient entities, for all their tangled activity, and Bomberg obviously felt he had invested them with enough significance to stand on their own, unaided by any specific figurative intentions.

What a shock it is, then, to turn from such an extreme of bareness and find the final drawing for *In the Hold* retreating from this freedom, relying on a conventional rendering of the human form and banishing both the ambiguity and the vitality of the previous study! Squared up for a faithful transposition to the canvas itself, it is a stiff, almost dutiful record of the definitive composition, carefully placing the profusion of struggling heads and limbs into surroundings as austere as the room employed in *Ju-Jitsu*. If Bomberg had produced a painting which exactly mirrored the arrangement of this last drawing, it would have been a very disappointing affair, experimental only in the sense that it subjected academically constructed figures to a facile process of simplification. But fortunately he had other, more startling ideas about the structure his huge, eight-foot-wide canvas should assume. The careful squaring-up of the last drawing gives a clue to his intentions: for Bomberg's painting succeeded in shattering the ponderous bulk of his figures into a myriad broken fragments. Confronted with the dionysiac abandon of *In the Hold*, the artist's reasons for reverting to a recognizable formula in the bodies of his protagonists are immediately apparent. For without this framework of identifiable references, the picture would disintegrate into a shower of abstract particles. Only the architectural outlines of the two figures who take up so much of the picture-space

◁ ◁ David Bomberg
*Study for In the Hold* (?), 1913–14

◁ David Bomberg
*Study for In the Hold*, 1913–14

prevent the canvas from degenerating into total incoherence.

The sixty-four-square grid, which imposed its own heraldic discipline on the shapes of *Ju-Jitsu*, has here become the main instrument of confusion: it provides an excuse for Bomberg to render the forms as he pleases. No single object – be it the steps of the ladder leading up from below deck, the wooden post at the lower left of the composition or the outstretched arms of the main figure – is allowed to spread itself further than half a square before it is interrupted, denied, pushed off course or in some way disrupted by a hail of geometrical minutiae. The central figure's torso, which could have provided a calm anchor in the middle of the storm raging all around, is riddled with syncopated bullets of black matter. They dance all over the man's body, reasserting the dominion of their enclosing squares over the descriptive contours of his back, shoulder and arm. Representation and abstraction are set on a suicidal course towards each other, and out of the head-on collision come sixty-four separate non-figurative paintings, further fragmented by the four triangular subdivisions which slice across each of the squares. They can either be enjoyed in their own right or taken in their entirety as the splintered parts of some awesomely rigorous whole.

*In the Hold* is such a calculated painting, so methodical in its planning and execution, that it could easily have become just a monument to Bomberg's own cerebral powers. But it avoids the dangers inherent in such an ordered structure by leaving room for improvisation as well. Within its rigid format, the artist has clearly enjoyed himself as well as exercising a fantastic diligence. For all the finality of the shapes, many of them are the result of happy accidents, inspired coincidences and spontaneous additions. The eye of the largest figure, for instance, is a continuation of the bottom line of one of the squares, and can equally well be read as a tiny triangle of abstract form. Nothing has been permitted to exist solely as a realistic passage: everything is consumed in the holocaust of glittering segments, and Bomberg must have found it difficult to decide when to stop. A close look reveals hesitancies and minor struggles in the painting, where the twin claims of grid and figuration have not finally been settled either one way or the other. They are still at pictorial loggerheads, and Bomberg's indecision vitalizes the intellectuality of his overall scheme.

He is sensitive enough to realize when a particular problem should be left unresolved, where to imply rather than state a definitive solution. But above everything else, his canvas is brought to life through the use of a spectrum of colours, serving both a functional and an emotive purpose. On one level, they act as a guide to the contents of the scene, picking out the identity of the main worker, the figure being hoisted up in the arms of another navvy or the pair of legs clambering out of the hold in the top left-hand section of the picture. And on another level, their fierce tonal oppositions express the energy of the men themselves as they labour in the ship. Bomberg welcomes hard-edge confrontations between ochre and puce, vanilla and grey, orange and ice-blue; and they manage to set up their own furious rhythms in contradiction to the rectilinear order of the grid. They tease the eye, one minute seeming to establish a great circle of movement that skirts the four corners of the canvas, and the next undulating in more wayward directions, weaving in and out of the geometry which tries so hard to contain them. Each broken portion of a square is as much a colour as it is a shape; and they flicker and dart with kinetic force all over the troubled surface of this prodigious painting.

*In the Hold* was the first picture that appears to have aroused Hulme's enthusiastic admiration for Bomberg's work. In his *New Age* review of the London Group show, the philosopher singled him out and devoted a long paragraph to this one exhibit, emphasizing its remarkable originality. 'In all

suggestion of large volumes and movements'. He could not bring himself to 'say that it touched or pleased' him, but he did think it indicated 'new plastic possibilities, and a new kind of orchestration of colour. It clearly might become something, if it is, as I suspect, more than mere ingenuity'.[23]

Such fulsome praise, coming from a powerful figurehead like Fry, confirmed the supremacy of Bomberg's five exhibits at the London Group show. The combined impact of *In the Hold* and *Ju-Jitsu* – listed in the catalogue under its alternative title of *Japanese Play* – ensured that he received more attention from the reviewers than any of the other English radicals.[24] *The Athenaeum* even went so far as to announce that *In the Hold* was 'the most entirely successful painting in the exhibition and has the attraction which belongs to complete success'.[25] Imagine how Lewis, cultivating his position as self-styled leader of the rebel artists, must have felt when he read such praise! Here was a painter, almost eight years younger than himself, earning more admiration than he had ever experienced. His reaction, if Roberts' memories are to be trusted, was characteristically ruthless: before the London Group show was even opened to the public, he put his talent for political machination to malicious purpose. 'At the hanging of the pictures, Bomberg had secured himself an excellent central position for his painting and was feeling very happy indeed about it', Roberts recalled. 'But on the day of the Private View he made a discovery that left him speechless: astounded, he saw hanging in this much-coveted spot on the wall a painting by Wyndham Lewis, and his own rehung in a less prominent position.'

Bomberg was not a man to let such an outrage go unrevenged, and he had a perfect opportunity to hit back at Lewis. Both of them had arranged with Roberts to have dinner together at a Jewish restaurant in Whitechapel that very evening; and so, 'in a fury', Bomberg 'laid plans for a showdown with Lewis at our dinner party'. The only problem was one of relative physical strength. 'Bomberg, although pugnacious and spirited, is but half the stature of Lewis', Roberts wrote, 'so instead of beautiful brunettes Bomberg brought to our rendezvous his boxer brother, "American Mowie". After the soup, Bomberg, raising his voice to a loud strident pitch, said suddenly to Lewis, "Say, Wyndham, what do you mean by taking my painting down and sticking your own up in its place?" If "American Mowie" was expecting to be able to display his pugilistic talents he was disappointed, for although at first Lewis made an attempt to protest, he stopped, rose suddenly from his seat, and throwing his theatre ticket upon the table abruptly left the restaurant in haste to escape from the hostile atmosphere of the East End back to the friendly gaiety of Soho.'[26]

Lewis must have been further stung by his young rival's additional success four months later, when the Chenil Gallery mounted Bomberg's one-man show of no less than fifty-five works in July 1914. None of the Rebel Art Centre members had ever received such an accolade, while even Epstein – as much of an outsider as Bomberg himself and a far older man, after all – had only managed to obtain a much smaller exhibition for himself the previous December. The Chenil Gallery show gave Bomberg's fellow artists their first opportunity to appreciate the full range of his radicalism, and the visitors included distinguished continental pioneers: Brancusi, Duchamp-Villon and – inevitably – Marinetti, who again attempted to 'convert' Bomberg to the Italian Futurist point of view. His overtures were, of course, 'flatly rejected', and Bomberg told him that 'this show of mine does not owe anything to Italian "Futurism". You can no more make a claim on me than on Bernard Berenson or for that matter, Michelangelo'.[27] For he had by now discovered his own, totally individual direction, and was too deeply entrenched in a personal programme ever to be seduced by the theories of others.

Indeed, the statement he printed in the front of his catalogue gave defiant, exclamatory expression to his new sense of self-confidence. Sonia Joslen, a close friend at that time, testified to Bomberg's assurance when she recalled that 'one of the most characteristic things David ever told me then was that he lacked ambition. He said he didn't *need* it: he *knew* success and acclaim were his due, like the Chenil Gallery show'.[28] The views of Marinetti did, it is true, lie behind the catalogue credo's provocative announcement that 'I hate the colours of the East, the Modern Mediaevalist, and the Fat Man of the Renaissance'. And Futurist theories obviously inspired his declaration that 'I look upon *Nature*, while I live in a *steel city*'. But apart from these understandable debts to avant-garde predecessors, Bomberg's manifesto reflected his private concerns, and celebrated them in aggressively dogmatic prose. 'I APPEAL to a *Sense of Form*', he began, declaring his central obsession from the outset. 'In some of the work I show in the first room, I completely abandon *Naturalism* and Tradition. I am *searching for an Intenser* expression. In other work in this room, where I use Naturalistic Form, I have *stripped it of all* irrelevant matter.' And then, in the final paragraph of his statement, Bomberg echoed Hulme's earlier description of him as an artist who confined himself to 'form in itself tout pur': the manifesto emphasized that 'where decoration happens, it is accidental. My object is the *construction of Pure Form*. I reject everything in painting that is not Pure Form'.[29]

But it was not only Hulme's writings that the manifesto appeared to invoke. Bomberg's doctrinaire insistence on the importance of 'form' to the exclusion of all else cannot fail to suggest a knowledge of Clive Bell's outspoken treatise on *Art*, written between 1912 and 1913 and published in February 1914, five months before the Chenil Gallery one-man show. If Bomberg never actually read the book, he would have come across the controversial theories it expounded in Bell's regular art criticism; and when he was temporarily allied with the Omega, he may conceivably have discussed its issues with the author himself. For the intellectual links between these two men – so disparate both in background and subjective tastes – become clear immediately *Art* is examined.

Bell's main thesis attempted to establish the 'common quality' shared by all great works of art, and his solution was to propose another version of Bomberg's pure form theory. 'Only one answer seems possible – significant form', Bell wrote. 'In each, lines and colours combined in a particular way, certain forms and relations of forms, stir our aesthetic emotions. These relations and combinations of lines and colours, these aesthetically moving forms, I call "Significant Form"; and "Significant Form" is the one quality common to all works of visual art.' Bell championed the supremacy of the 'geometric' tradition as wholeheartedly as Hulme, insisting that 'the whole output of the fourteenth and fifteenth centuries is immeasurably inferior to the great Byzantine and Romanesque production of the eleventh and twelfth'. And he reserved his greatest praise, like Hulme again, for primitive art: 'either from want of skill or want of will, primitives neither create illusions, nor make display of extravagant accomplishment, but concentrate their energies on the one thing needful – the creation of form. Thus have they created the finest works of art that we possess.'[30] The measure of the difference between the rebels and the Bloomsbury Post-Impressionists is that where Hulme hoped for a new geometric movement making use of mechanical forms, Bell's expectations were at once less specific and more attached to the achievements of Cézanne. 'In so far as one man can be said to inspire a whole age, Cézanne inspires the contemporary movement', he averred in a chapter frankly entitled 'The Debt to Cézanne'.[31] The book's encyclopaedic knowledge of past art, suggesting as it did a wealth of erudition, defined the gap in sensibility between the Omega and the Rebel Art Centre. Moreover, *Art* implicitly opposed Hulme when it discounted the theory that Post-Impressionism 'is an expression of the ideas and feelings of that spiritual renaissance which is now growing into a lusty revolution'. Bell insisted that 'with this I cannot, of course, agree. If art expresses anything, it expresses some profound and general emotion common, or at least possible, to all ages, and peculiar to none'.

*Art* was on the side of the work produced by Bell's own closest friends: in a list of contemporary painters he admired, Grant and Fry were the only Englishmen apart from Lewis to be included among Matisse, Picasso, Derain, Brancusi, and other European radicals. And Lewis's presence is probably to be explained by the fact that Bell finished writing the book before the Omega rumpus took place. The preface is dated November 1913, and by the time it was published he may well have regretted Lewis's inclusion in the list. Compared with the pronouncements of Hulme, Lewis, and Bomberg, *Art*'s standpoint is diffuse and prefers generalizations to particular commitment. Bell certainly makes clear his approval of 'this passion for works that are admirable as wholes, this fierce insistence on design, this willingness to leave bare the construction if by so doing the spectators of the Impressionist age are vexed by the naked bones and muscles of Post-Impressionist pictures'. But he never gets around to defining this new art, placing himself squarely in its favour, or describing particular paintings – English or otherwise – to back up his vague support. It is typical of Bell's relative detachment that he should conclude a chapter on 'Simplification and Design' by stating that 'for my own part, even though these young artists insisted on a bareness and baldness exceeding anything we have yet seen, I should be far from blaming a band of ascetics who in an age of unorganised prettiness insisted on the paramount importance of design'.[32] Such cautious pronouncements came from a man too disengaged ever to plunge wholeheartedly into combat like rebels of Bomberg's mettle.

Occasionally, the book reads like an outspoken Bloomsbury version of a Marinetti manifesto: 'What will not cause a riot is probably not worth saying', Bell declared in one of the most unbuttoned passages. But although he rails against the Royal Academy, insists that 'art schools must go', damns 'culture' for adoring 'the man who is clever enough to imitate, not any particular work of art, but art itself', and asks 'society' to 'do something for itself and for art by blowing out of the museums and galleries the dust of erudition and the stale incense of hero-worship' – despite all these lively fireworks, the author's loyalties are nowhere definitively set down. His book could never, therefore, have had a profound effect on Bomberg's thinking, even if some of its pronouncements seem to be echoed by the Chenil Gallery foreword. And so there is probably a tenuous link at best between Bomberg's cry for pure form and Bell's statement that 'if a representative form has value, it is as form, not as representation. The representative element in a work of art may or may not be harmful; always it is irrelevant'.[33] All the same, the similarity between the two men's theories does serve to demonstrate how closely allied all the advanced factions of English art were at this time, how shared ideas of the most inflammatory kind ricocheted from one camp over to the other.

By the time his one-man show opened, Bomberg had become an original force, secure in theories derived from no-one but himself. The 'sense of mass' which he later considered one of the fundamental concerns of his early work had become, 'as my work developed . . . identified as a basic structure inherent in the gravitational forces that subject us to nature's laws'.[34] The explanation is compressed and obscurely phrased, but it does throw some light on the purist obsession with weight, volume and movement that finally produced the masterpiece of his pre-war period: *The Mud Bath*. Bomberg must have realized the paramount importance of the picture, for the catalogue not only listed it proudly as the first exhibit, but announced that 'this painting, "The Mud Bath", has been hung *outside* the Gallery premises that it may have every advantage of lighting and space'. It was the centrepiece of the whole show and displayed, as the *Daily Chronicle* related, with a positively festive flair. 'What, I wonder, would the Fat Man of the Renaissance think of Mr Bomberg's "The Mud Bath",' the critic asked in amazement, 'which hangs outside the Chenil Galleries, on the outer wall of the house, rained upon, baked by the sun and garlanded with flags?' Bomberg was afterwards amused to recall how 'the horses drawing the 29 bus used to shy at it as they came round the corner of King's Road';[35] but the painting's unconventional presentation did not prompt the public to step inside the exhibition. 'The passers-by make no comment', noted the *Chronicle*, 'because they do not recognise it as a picture.'[36]

Nor would they have been able to identify the precise locale it depicted, even if they had bothered to look at the painting. For Schevzik's Steam Baths in Brick Lane – the probable inspiration of the room previously portrayed in *Ju-Jitsu* – does not seem to have contained a mud bath at all. 'There was no *mud bath*', wrote the Borough Librarian of Tower Hamlets in 1969. 'Two residents in this area, aged 65 and 84, remember the Baths very well, and have confirmed this.'[37] And Bomberg's brother-in-law, James Newmark, could not recall a mud bath either. 'I remember being taken around 1910 to Schevzik's Baths by my father', he wrote in 1968. 'The baths were constructed with a row of separate bathrooms and a small pool at the end. This had steps leading down into the tepid water. The pool was used communally. Men and women used it on different days of the week. It is my recollection that the pool was very small (perhaps 10 ft square).'[38] According to Bomberg's first wife, 'he was intrigued by the attitudes of the various figures as they clambered out of the bath and ran their hands along their bodies';[39] and Lilian Bomberg revealed that when she first visited the site of the former Steam Baths in 1969, 'I thought, my God, no wonder David was so excited by this place. He must have stood on the balcony above the bath and observed the figures in movement down below, surrounded by those bare, tiled walls – it was a perfect subject for him'.[40] So the Baths and the bathers it housed, not a specific mud bath, would seem to have aroused Bomberg's interest.

Could the title chosen by Bomberg for his painting therefore be a product of his own imagination? An affirmative answer is reinforced by the nature of the earliest picture which has been related to *The Mud Bath*, a small oil sketch of a *Bathing Scene*. Its comparative naturalism and pale, delicate colours place the study in the Slade period, and suggest that Bomberg considered using a water motif instead of his usual platform as early as 1912. *Island of Joy*'s inclusion of a foreground pool confirms this supposition, too; but Bomberg seems to have discarded the idea temporarily, for both *Ezekiel* and *Ju-Jitsu* used surroundings as dry as they are arid. The probability is, then, that Bomberg came across *Bathing Scene* and used it when he was planning a major canvas in 1914: if so, the overt mythological content of *Bathing Scene*, with its brandished club and attendant animals, suggests that *The Mud Bath*'s title was selected for its ritualistic associations rather than as a documentary reference to Schevzik's steamfilled interior.

There has, likewise, been a widespread tendency to place the final canvas too early in Bomberg's career. William Lipke's monograph on the artist even seems willing to place it in the Slade period, merely because of the link with *Bathing Scene*: he states that *The Mud Bath* was executed 'prior to 1914'.[41] But this interpretation makes nonsense of Bomberg's immensely logical progress towards his stated ideal of 'pure form', and contradicts the available evidence as well. For a preparatory drawing has survived, dated 1914, to prove that the artist –

David Bomberg
*Bathing Scene*, 1912–13

David Bomberg
*Study for The Mud Bath*, 1914

David Bomberg
*Crayon Study for The Mud Bath* (verso), 1914

David Bomberg
*Gouache Study for The Mud Bath II* (recto),
1914

of the forms even more.

The artist's indecision serves to stress how important a role colour played in his new vocabulary. For it was, in the true sense of the word, constructive: not only modelling the figures and defining their contours, but also giving them that essential vitality and significance which informs the final canvas. In a picture concerned above all with violent motion, wild and abandoned enough to come out of a primeval orgy, the colour had to match up to the extreme physical tension contained in the disposition of the figures. All these problems are thrashed out, with painful deliberation, in this gouache *Study*. Even the size of the individual limbs has been enlarged slightly, so that each will register its full plastic impact. Nothing has been left to chance: each square inch of the design has been worried over, and the final canvas gains enormously from this intensive preparatory work.

In *The Mud Bath* itself, it is difficult to identify anything with complete confidence. The figures are no longer recognizable forms confused by a superimposed grid that forces the spectator to forget their naturalistic attributes. The shapes in this brash, seven-foot wide painting are far more self-sufficient than they were in the kaleidoscope of *In the Hold*. They are what they appear to be: tensely coiled, springing mechanisms that demand to be read as embodiments of energy and stress *in themselves*, and not because they refer to a frenetic subject like the loading of a ship. No ostensible theme detracts attention from the vitality of these strange, hybrid amalgams of body and machine, human anatomy and geometric abstraction. The true significance of their furious movements comes through straightaway, unhindered by any wilful fragmentation. And the mud bath motif of the title has been interpreted so freely as to be meaningless: these configurations could just as easily be hurling themselves in a crazy chain around some primitive totem pole.

Bomberg has dispensed with all the usual descriptive and associative props, leaving his audience free to interpret the contents of the picture at will. He has managed, at last, to create a personal pictorial world, with its own laws and its own highly original logic. And he is arrogant enough to expect his spectators to study the rules of this game in order to understand the workings of the painting. He is asking them whether they possess the necessary humility and lack of prejudice to forget traditional visual language, and learn the syntax of a new one: simpler and more immediate in impact than the old, but harder to accept and trust. In other words, his painting demands either total adherence or total rejection. There are no half-measures. These leaping shapes crowd out of the picture-frame, overpowering both in their physical vigour and their stylistic extremism. They make a frontal assault on the senses, determined to bully conservatism so mercilessly that it will either recoil in horror or capitulate altogether to the new way of seeing. Battle has been joined, and Bomberg wanted nothing less than a struggle to the death.

A steeply inclined aerial viewpoint has been selected, so that everything can be laid down and explained on the surface of the design in the most clear-cut, open fashion. The confused colours of the gouache *Study* have been dispensed with entirely, exchanged for the clangour of red, white and blue. Bright highlights on the limbs ensure that they stand out sharply from their surroundings, and the unrelieved scarlet of the bath area helps the shapes between the figures to take on as much abstract significance as the figures themselves. The patterns formed independently by all three colours jostle with each other on one flat pictorial plane, each fighting for its own supremacy. Their abstract war is being waged alongside the more immediate war of solid limbs, so that there is a fierce tension between the two levels of activity, tugging the eye from one over to the other and back again with remorseless cunning. On the figurative plane, each story finally makes absolute sense: however committed Bomberg may have been to the need for extreme renewal when he executed *The Mud Bath*, his hatred of 'the Fat Man of the Renaissance' did not extend to Michelangelo. He was still enough of a Slade school product to overcome his prejudices when it came to *The Entombment*, and realize that the muscular disposition of thrusting, diagonally oriented forms in this remarkable panel could be acknowledged as an inspiration for his own, strictly twentieth-century efforts to achieve the same qualities in a major statement like *The Mud Bath*. In this sense, Bomberg's masterpiece can still be linked with the Slade figure composition tradition summed up by John's *Moses and the Brazen Serpent*, even if *The Mud Bath* ends up expressing the taut pressures of modern man's urban experience with tremendous innovatory power as well.

Needless to say, the critics failed to recognize this achievement in their abusive reviews of the show, and the exhibition remained largely unsold. John managed to persuade the American collector John Quinn to purchase two of the earlier works on view – *Head of a Poet* and *Meditation* – but they were both naturalistic in treatment and not at all typical of Bomberg's mature style. The artist himself later remembered that the director of the Chenil Gallery 'offered me a contract to buy for his stock, everything that I did in the style of the drawing exhibited in the spring exhibition of the NEAC of 1913'. But Bomberg's reaction to the proposal was inevitable. 'This was impossible for me to accept, in the sense that having already learned how to make a scrap of metal, I was more concerned how to learn to make the hammer to beat it with.'[43] His one-man show was a financial disaster, and *The Mud Bath* – along with *In the Hold*, *Ezekiel* and many other items – was returned unsold to its creator, and left to languish for decades in the obscurity of a garage. Now it can be seen as the most outstanding English painting of its period, a work that looks as if it could have been painted yesterday instead of over sixty years ago. For Bomberg to mount a whole exhibition of such pictures in the London of 1914 must have required considerable courage, and he certainly did not expect to earn any thanks from the Press. Rather did he have to content himself with feeling grateful for being reviewed at all, however unfavourably. 'The imputations daily in the press that the reason the English cubists painted cubisticly was incompetence, though damaging to ourselves we regarded as the natural public prejudice against any change in the art forms of the day', he explained later. 'It seemed to me preferable to the calculated indifference of the polite gentlemanly critics.'[44] He was forced to be philosophical about the vilification, even though adverse publicity itself led to accusations of self-advertisement.

The one solitary gleam of consolation came from Hulme, whose admiration was so thoroughly aroused by the exhibition that he devoted the whole of his fourth essay on 'Modern Art' in *The New Age* to a lengthy discussion of its implications. He even took it upon himself to be Bomberg's champion against the scorn of other critics, just as he had defended Epstein's one-man show some months before. After quoting the complaints of the *Pall Mall Gazette*, he declared such judgements 'to be entirely unjust', claiming that all Bomberg's work 'shows emphasis on, and understanding of, that quality which, while it may only be one element in the excellence of a naturalistic drawing, is yet the whole of a more abstract one – a sense of form. That seems to have been always excellent. He has all the time, and apparently quite spontaneously, and without imitation, been more interested in form than anything else'. To Hulme, such singlemindedness was wholly commendable, and sufficiently rare in the art he saw around him to merit vigorous praise. 'That his work shows the impatience the critic regrets is only to be expected', he wrote, his loathing of writers who lacked definite loyalties by now fully aroused. 'People with any guts in them do

Michelangelo
*The Entombment* (unfinished), *c*. 1505–6

not have catholic tastes. If they realise in a personal and vivid way the importance of *one* element, if they feel that they have anything fresh to say about that, they are naturally impatient with the other elements. Why, if you are only interested in form, should you be asked – once you have got down the elements of that form adequately – to add to it the alien elements which would make it into a solid realistic representation?'

On a calmer and more analytical note, he took the exhibition as a pretext to sort out in his own mind his feelings about abstraction. 'Is pure form alone', he asked, 'a sufficient basis for interest in art?' His answer was equivocal. Among his unpublished notes is a long précis of Volkelt's argument against the existence of a separate 'aesthetic emotion', and he put it to good use in his article when he asserted that 'there is no such thing as a specific *aesthetic* emotion, a peculiar kind of emotion produced by *form* alone, only of interest to aesthetes. I think it could be shown that the emotions produced by abstract form, are the ordinary everyday human emotions – they are produced in a different way, that is all'. His statement set itself up in complete opposition to the theory Bell had just outlined in *Art*, and Hulme may have used the opportunity this review gave him to reject the Bloomsbury standpoint. For Bell, in his vital opening chapter on 'The Aesthetic Hypothesis', claimed that 'to appreciate a work of art we need bring with us nothing from life, no knowledge of its ideas and affairs, no familiarity with its emotions. Art transports us from the world of man's activity to a world of aesthetic exaltation. For a moment we are shut off from human interests; our anticipations and memories are arrested; we are lifted above the stream of life'. Bell postulated a radical version of the time-honoured Romantic concept of aesthetic delight, one that stretches right back to Wordsworth's mystical emotions in front of Tintern Abbey. 'The rapt philosopher, and he who contemplates a work of art, inhabit a world with an intense and peculiar significance of its own', he continued; 'that significance is unrelated to the significance of life. In this world the emotions of life find no place. It is a world with emotions of its own.' Hulme may have been a philosopher, but he never became 'rapt' enough to agree with the ideas put forward in *Art*. He was at once less élitist and more down-to-earth than Bell, and insisted in his article that 'if form has no dramatic or human interest, then it is obviously stupid for a human to be interested in it'.

What Hulme believed, once again applying the theories of a German thinker to his own experience of contemporary art, was that art's raison d'être lay in its capacity to arouse 'the ordinary everyday emotions'. He even censured Bomberg's 'use of form' for satisfying 'a too purely sensuous or intellectual interest'. Hulme, wanting something wider in its appeal, was disappointed that this form 'is not often used to intensify a more general emotion'. And in one of his most categorical statements on the nature of art, he stressed that the 'possibility of living our own emotions *into* outside shapes and colours is the basic fact on which the whole of plastic art rests'. This cherished belief was the stumbling block that made him seem to contradict himself. For the 'more general emotion' he missed in Bomberg's work seemed to depend for its existence on retaining some kind of link with the outside world. So Hulme swung from one side of the fence to the other, declaring that abstraction must be rooted in normal human reality, and at the same time stating that 'pure form' should be self-sufficient. 'There is nothing mysterious in this process by which *form* becomes the *porter* or *carrier* of internal emotions', he wrote, in support of his theory that abstraction should have 'dramatic or human interest'. But then, a couple of paragraphs later, he went back on himself by asserting that 'the fact that the abstract element did occur as a matter of fact in external nature mixed up with other things is of no importance. The forms are either interesting in themselves, or not. They derive no justification from their natural occurrence'. He was still willing abstraction to be two things at once, for the very next sentence declared that 'the only importance of nature in this connection is that it does suggest forms, which the artist can develop; the mind here, as elsewhere, having very little natural spontaneity'.

Hulme's confusion was eminently forgivable: he was, after all, feeling his way with something completely new in English art. The only way he was able to explain why he thought Bomberg was employing a 'merely intellectual use of abstraction', was to compare him with Epstein. 'I do not feel, then, the same absolute certainty about his work that I do about Epstein's', he wrote. 'In Mr Epstein's work the abstractions have been got at gradually, and always intensify, as abstractions, the general feeling of the whole work. But then Mr Epstein is in a class by himself.' Could it be that he preferred Epstein because the sculptor's work was more allied to representation than Bomberg's? If he did, then Hulme was not even now in wholehearted sympathy with 'pure form', despite his protestations to the contrary. Although he praised *The Mud Bath* as 'one of the best things Mr Bomberg has done', noting that 'the colour is used in an entirely constructive way, and in no sense derivative from nature', he considered 'the best' painting to be *Reading from Torah*, because 'the abstract shapes here do reinforce a quite human and even dramatic effect'. This is what Hulme was really after: some figurative theme which could at least be connected with the abstraction of the forms. *Reading from Torah* is now lost, but Hulme's statement that it 'developed' out of the same drawing which also inspired *The Mud Bath* suggests that a surviving gouache called *Composition* may be a study for it.[45] The pictorial language *Composition* employs is identical to that used in the gouache *Study for The Mud Bath*, and it looks very much like a preliminary sketch for a projected painting: the supposition may, therefore, be correct. And *Composition* does contain precisely those 'human' and 'dramatic' connotations that *The Mud Bath* seeks to reject, with its two identifiable figures clasping each other in the centre of a circle of gesticulating forms. Hulme obviously preferred such recognizable references, and praised *Reading from Torah* accordingly.

Many years later, Bomberg paid tribute to Hulme's perceptive support when he stated that the philosopher 'helped innovators by trying to explain the deeper significance of visual form', even if Hulme's explanations 'were in terms of speech and therefore had no influence on the artists'. What really counted was the boost Hulme gave to the morale of the young painter, and Bomberg gratefully recorded that he 'did me much honour'.[46] It was no more than the philosopher deserved, since he alone had lent Bomberg his wholehearted support at a time when most other critics decried the formidable body of work on view at the Chenil Gallery. And there was an additional mark of approval in Hulme's review of the exhibition, too. For while he emphasized the young painter's originality by declaring that 'his work has always been personal and independent – much more independent than that of most Cubists – and never reminiscent', he also pointed out that 'Mr Bomberg stands somewhat apart from the other English Cubists', and lauded him at the expense of the other rebels when he asserted that Bomberg's paintings were 'certainly much more individual and less derivative than the work of the members of that group. The tendency to abstraction does seem in his case to have been a logical development of tendencies which were always present even in his earlier drawings, and not merely the result of a feverish hurry to copy the latest thing from Paris'.[47] Hulme was falling out of sympathy with the increasingly abstract bias of rebel art and thereby, at the very moment when Vorticism was poised to establish itself as a vital force in England, managed to dissociate himself from the movement he had done so much to anticipate.

David Bomberg
*Composition: Study for Reading from Torah* (?) (recto), *c.* 1914

# Chapter 9: Marinetti and Nevinson's Role in Provoking the Arrival of Vorticism

Hulme's disenchantment with the progress of the Rebel Art Centre group was by no means a sudden, impulsive affair. As early as March 1914, when he praised their contributions to the London Group exhibition, he had been simultaneously at pains to announce his lack of sympathy with a disturbing new departure in their work. For the philosopher was annoyed that his cherished 'new geometrical and monumental art making use of mechanical forms' was not as much in evidence as he would have liked, and so he described how his own ideal movement 'has now generated a second movement based simply on the idea that abstract form, i.e: form without any representative content, can be an adequate means of expression. In this, instead of hard, structural work like Picasso's you get the much more scattered use of abstractions of artists like Kandinsky. It seems, judging by its development up to now, to be only a more or less amusing by-product of the first. Lacking the controlled sensibility, the feeling for mechanical structure, which makes use of abstractions a necessity, it seems rather dilletante . . . I do not think this minor movement is destined to survive. I look upon it rather as a kind of romantic heresy'.[1]

Edward Wadsworth
*Radiation*, 1913–14

Pitifully few of the rebels' London Group exhibits have survived, and therefore it is difficult to know precisely what kind of stylistic traits Hulme was complaining about. But an old photograph of *Radiation*, one of Wadsworth's contributions, does seem to exemplify the paintings which upset his critical sense so greatly.[2] It represents a dramatic advance on the Futurist inspiration so evident in *L'Omnibus* the year before, even if the title of another of Wadsworth's London Group exhibits, *Funicular*, recalls the theme of that earlier painting. Now representation has been eliminated almost entirely in favour of a whole jumble of heterogeneous shapes. Konody noticed Wadsworth's espousal of abstraction in his review of the show in the *Observer*, remarking that 'when Mr E. A. Wadsworth gaily splashes about his primaries and fills his canvas with angles and curves, he labels his pictures "Radiation" or "Scherzo", thus indicating that he deals with form in the abstract, expressing his emotions, or rather sensations, in terms of colour and rhythmic lines without any representative character'.[3] *The Athenaeum* was more alarmed, and thought that *Scherzo*, 'with its screaming violence of pitch, appeals to an instinct which may be decadent'; while *The Times* was utterly horrified by Wadsworth's new direction, declaring that ' "Radiation" expresses a confusion of the senses . . . so complete that we cannot tell from his picture what has caused it'.

Pound, doubtless acting on information provided by Wadsworth himself, insisted in his review of the exhibition on *Radiation*'s connection with industrial reality, explaining that it represented 'the "pictorial equivalent" of a foundry as perceived . . . by the retina of the intelligence'.[4] Judging by the cogs, shafts and spokes in the painting, he may be right; but this theme does not fit *March*, where Wadsworth makes a strange collection of embryonic forms wriggle their way across the surface of the canvas, mixed in with other, still less figurative elements.[5] Neither of his paintings recalls the influence of Kandinsky directly – *March* even borrows Futurist lines of force – but Hulme was nevertheless right to invoke the name of the German painter in his review. For Wadsworth's sudden adherence to abstraction seems to have been in part the outcome of his intensive study of Kandinsky's theoretical writings.

The German pioneer's treatise, *On The Spiritual in Art*, had by this time been widely read and discussed in English avant-garde circles: it had originally been translated in 1914 and Pound, for one, recorded that 'when I came to read Kandinsky's chapter on the language of form and colour, I found little that was new to me. I only felt that some one else understood what I understood, and had written it out very clearly'.[6] Wadsworth may have felt the same, but he made his special interest in the book clear by publishing a translation and

Edward Wadsworth
*March*, 1913–14

commentary on selected passages of *Ueber das Geistige in der Kurst* [*sic*] in July 1914.[7] His knowledge of German dated from his pre-Slade days of 1906 when he studied engineering in Munich and painted at the Knirr School in his spare time; and he used his command of the language, aided by an English translation which Constable's had just published as *The Art of Spiritual Harmony*, to produce a detailed exposition of Kandinsky's principle of *Inner Necessity*. 'This book is a most important contribution to the psychology of modern art', he wrote enthusiastically in his article. 'Herr Kandinsky . . . is a psychologist and a metaphysician of rare intuition and inspired enthusiasm. He writes of art – not in its relation to the drawing-room or the modern exhibition, but in its relation to the universe and the soul of man. He writes, not as an art historian, but essentially as an artist to whom form and colour are as much the vital and integral parts of the cosmic organisation as they are his means of expression.'[8] Considerable praise indeed, coming as it did from an artist whose own pictures bore scarcely any imprint of Kandinsky's work. Wadsworth's admiration doubtless reflected his own delight in reading the theories of a man who was not afraid to broach total abstraction, and Kandinsky's articulate defence of complete expressive freedom must have helped the Englishman to leave *L'Omnibus* behind and embrace the less representational extremism of *March* and *Radiation*.

Wadsworth's article suggested as much when it came round to discussing the climax of Kandinsky's thesis: the introduction of the concept of a 'form' which 'represents no real object'. For he translated this important section of the text thus: 'Such pure abstract entities, which as such have their life, their influence and their effect, are a square, a circle, a triangle, a rhombus, a trapezium, and the other innumerable forms which become ever more complicated and possess no mathematical significance. All these forms are citizens of the abstract empire with equal rights.' After reproducing the passage, Wadsworth proceeded to comment on its implications, stating that 'once having accepted the emotional significance of form and colour as such, it follows that the necessity for expressing oneself exclusively with forms that are based on nature is only a temporary limitation similar to, though less foolish than, the eighteenth century brown-tree convention'. Does Wadsworth's explanation celebrate the feeling of liberation he himself experienced when he first came across Kandinsky's doctrines? They might well have helped him enormously, for the Englishman went on to declare that 'logically this axiom must be accepted: that the artist can employ any forms (natural, abstracted or abstract) to express himself, if his feelings demand it'.[9] This last sentence is vital for an understanding of English rebel art. Wadsworth, like Lewis, does not feel committed to an exclusively abstract vocabulary: he interprets Kandinsky's teachings more as a confirmation of the artist's right to use any combination of forms he desires, at will, in the same composition. In *Radiation*, for instance, the wheel cogs and the floodlights are both basically naturalistic elements included in an otherwise non-figurative design. And Lewis's lost *Eisteddfod*, similarly, made 'long tranquil planes of colour, sweeping up from the left, encounter a realistically painted piece of ironwork'.[10] The English radicals did not want to restrict their range of expression in any way, even if they usually felt that an abstract idiom was the most efficient means of reflecting the true quality of modern experience. Abstraction, for them, was inextricably connected with the form-language of machinery and industrialised civilisation as a whole; and none of the rebels produced, even at the height of the Vorticist period, work which can be described as totally non-objective. It always remained rooted in their specific yet metaphorical response to the changing fabric of twentieth century life.

Kandinsky was, without a doubt, one of the artists who spurred them on in their attempts to free their art from the limitations of the representational tradition. His book was published in English for all to see and imbibe, but more important still were the pictures he sent over to London for display at successive Allied Artists' Salons. The consignments began as far back as 1909, when Kandinsky exhibited two paintings and twelve engravings at the AAA. The following year he contributed three more paintings, two of which are identifiable and significant works: *Improvisation Number Six* and *Composition Number One*. At that stage, no-one in England would have been willing to learn from Kandinsky's extreme simplification of form. Lewis was far too involved in the lessons of Parisian Cubism, and he was not prepared, anyway, to reduce his pictures to such an abstracted orchestration of line and colour as Kandinsky had done in *Improvisation Number Six*. The British Fauves would have been most deeply stirred by the heightened colour and loose brushwork of the German's exhibits, but they did not get another chance to see his paintings until 1913. Possibly disillusioned by the marked lack of critical attention in London, Kandinsky only sent six woodcuts with an album and text to the 1911 Salon, and the following year decided to submit nothing at all. But he more than compensated for his absence in the 1913 Salon, where he not only displayed *Improvisation Number Twenty-Nine* and *Landscape with River Poppeln* but also one of the masterpieces of his early period: *Improvisation No. 30 (Cannons)*.[11]

Now, finally, his presence was appreciated by the most perceptive critics, and Fry was moved to write one of the first appreciations in English of Kandinsky's most abstract works. 'One finds that after a time the improvisations become more definite, more logical, and closely knit in structure, more surprisingly beautiful in their colour oppositions, more exact in their equilibrium', he wrote excitedly in the 2 August edition of *The Nation*, obviously surprised to find that abstractions could affect him so profoundly. 'They are pure visual music, but I cannot any longer doubt the possibility of emotional expression by such abstract visual signs.'[12] The revelation may have prompted him to admit the viability of abstract art in his own work at the newly-founded Omega, while Bell was sufficiently impressed to include Kandinsky in his list of the best 'Post-Impressionists' in *Art*.[13] And the German's fame spread further when Arthur Jerome Eddy, a Chicago collector, acquired the *Cannons* painting and wrote to Kandinsky asking him about the precise meaning of the sub-title; for the artist replied in words that were absorbed by many when Eddy published them in his 1914 book on *Cubists and Post-Impressionism*, a pioneering examination of recent avant-garde painting. 'The designation *Cannons*', wrote Kandinsky, 'selected by me *for my own use*, is not to be conceived as indicating the "contents" of the picture. These contents are indeed what the spectator *lives*, or *feels* while under the effect of the *form and colour combinations* of the picture.' But he did admit that 'the presence of the cannons in the picture could probably be explained by the constant war talk that had been going on throughout the year', even if he insisted that 'I did not intend to give a representation of war; to do so would have required different pictorial means'. He concluded by declaring that 'this entire description is chiefly an analysis of the picture which I have painted rather subconsciously in a state of strong inner tension. So intensively did I feel the necessity of some of the forms that I remember having given loud-voiced directions to myself, as for instance, "But the corners must be heavy!"'[14] Kandinsky had explicitly stated one of the most important tenets in English abstraction: that artistic creation requires the willing co-operation of the subconscious, and that the spectator, too, must relax his cognitive faculties if he wants to be able to understand and enjoy the abstractions presented by the artist.

Lewis's work, with its emphatic linear definition, could not be more dramatically opposed to Kandinsky's. When the German sent in his final trio of paintings – *Picture with Yellow Colouring, Study for Improvisation Number*

Wassily Kandinsky
*Improvisation No. 30 (Cannons)*, 1913

*Seven* and *Painting 1914* – to the AAA Salon of 1914, the critic of *The New Weekly* clearly distinguished between the two artists. 'Kandinsky's aim, as he has explained in a recent book, is to create a colour music independent of representational elements, and his three paintings are purely sensuous and emotional', he wrote. 'We do not find in them anything of that iron sense of construction which is present in the works of Mr Wyndham Lewis, whether large or small, and, therefore, following the musical analogy, we are justified in saying that Mr Wyndham Lewis plays Bach to Herr Kandinsky's Chopin.'[15] Nevertheless, they were both numbered among the handful of radicals in Europe producing completely abstract pictures; and there had even been super- ficial similarities between their work two years before, in the freewheeling forms of Lewis's prophetic *Abstract Design*, the first surviving non-representational drawing in English art.

When, moreover, Lewis later wrote down his most comprehensive explanation of the working process behind his early abstractions, he proved himself to have been as interested in the creative subconscious as Kandinsky. Instancing his 1913 drawing of *Planners (A Happy Day)*,[16] he emphasized that ' "*Planners*" is *a title* merely found for this drawing for the purposes of exhibition', just as Kandinsky had insisted that he chose the title of *Cannons* for his own use, and

Wyndham Lewis
*Planners (A Happy Day)*, *c.* 1913

not as a guide to the 'contents' of his painting. 'The way those things were done', Lewis wrote of all his drawings like *Planners*, 'is that a mental-emotive impulse – and by this is meant subjective intellection, like magic or religion – is let loose upon a lot of blocks and lines of various dimensions, and encouraged to push them around and to arrange them as it will. It is of course not an accidental, isolated, mood: but it is recurrent groups of emotions and coagulations of thinking, as it were, that is involved'.[17] Both artists, then, employed a method of controlled improvisation, and Lewis's comparison with magic recalls that he, too, felt as much sympathy with the intuitive art of primitive races as did Gaudier, Epstein or Pound. He relied on the inspiration of his subconscious as heavily as Kandinsky, even if the end results did not bear the slightest resem- blance to each other. Lewis, in fact, upbraided Kandinsky in 1915 for failing to define figurative hints like the cannons. 'He would have done better to

ACKNOWLEDGE that he had (by accident) reproduced a form in Nature', Lewis declared, 'and have taken more trouble with it FOR ITS OWN SAKE AS A FRANKLY REPRESENTATIVE ITEM.'[18] For this is exactly what Lewis himself had done in *Planners*, where the brooding outline of a giant head is formed out of the same jagged shapes as the other, more abstract parts of the drawing. The ambiguity, Lewis seems to be arguing, is still retained; but at least it is not shirked and tentative, like the cannons.

Nevertheless, the presence of great canvases by Kandinsky in London at the time when they were needed most by the English rebels must have been a great source of comfort to them. Nevinson even went so far as to announce at a public lecture in 1914 that 'the three paintings by Kandinsky at the Allied Artists are to my mind three of the finest modern pictures I have seen'.[19] And this was particularly high praise, coming as it did from the one English artist who had embraced Marinetti's cause without any reservations, misgivings or loss of personal pride. By the time he exhibited in the first London Group show in March 1914 Nevinson's Futurist affiliations were self-evident, and Konody could state that 'Mr Nevinson more than ever proclaims himself an English disciple of Severini and the other Italians of the memorable Sackville Gallery show'. Remembering especially Nevinson's lost painting of *The Non-Stop*, Konody wrote that 'he is obsessed with the idea of speed, devotes himself to conveying by pictorial means the sensation of speed in railway trains and other means of locomotion, and gives the idea of movement by displacing objects, making them penetrate each other, in fact, making several successive moments simultaneous. The result would be intolerable confusion if it were not for the artist's fine sense of rhythm, which saves his utterance from absolute incoherence'.[20]

Konody was by now becoming quite thankful for Nevinson's pictures, if only as a relief from what he considered to be the unintelligible confusion of Lewis, Bomberg, Wadsworth and the other rebels. And his gratitude was echoed by the critic of the *Westminster Gazette*, who maintained that 'in "The Non-Stop" Mr C. R. W. Nevinson differs from many of his colleagues in the group by letting us see something of what is in his mind. That mixture of streaks of light, and fragments of advertisements, and curves, and colour, with lines that suggest straphangers here and there, is quite obviously an impression of a compartment on the Underground'. By executing a painting that sought to interpret the urban excitement of a London tube journey, Nevinson was literally fulfilling Marinetti's exhortation to young English artists in his interview with the *Evening News* two years before. No visual record of *The Non-Stop* has survived, but the critics' descriptions suggest a picture prescribed by the Futurist leader, who had told the *Evening News* that on the Underground 'I had got what I wanted – not enjoyment, but a totally new idea of motion, of speed'. *The Non-Stop* must have been an especially successful transcription of Marinettian doctrines, for Rutter later declared that 'I well remember one of [Nevinson's] paintings of this period, a circular picture of the interior of a compartment in a "Tube" in which the vibration of seated figures and strap-hangers was kaleidoscopically expressed in vivid bright colours'.[21] And Fry clinched Nevinson's Futurist connections by describing *The Non-Stop* in his review of the London Group show as 'almost a copy of a work by Severini'. If Nevinson's lively study *At the Dance-hall* had been included in the exhibition, Fry's remarks would be fully justified; for this gouache, squared up in preparation for a lost painting, employs inflammatory colour combinations and a whole repertoire of forms borrowed from Severini's *The "Pan-Pan" Dance at the Monico* to establish his identity as the only committed English Futurist.

As Nevinson himself would have wished, his paintings were now managing

△ Christopher Nevinson
*The Strand, c.* 1914

◁ Christopher Nevinson
*At the Dance-hall,* 1913–14

to communicate to a wider cross-section of the public than those of his compatriots. Visitors to the London Group exhibition must have felt mystified by *In the Hold* or *Radiation*, and pleased when they turned to his lost painting of *The Strand* and realized that they could discern the faces of a crowd of people at the bottom of the canvas. He had retained enough figurative references in this picture to reassure an audience bemused by the extremism of Lewis's *Christopher Columbus*. Nevinson was satisfying popular emotions, and used watered-down Futurist techniques to transmit them in the most sensational way. *The Strand* comes dangerously near to looking like a plain man's guide to modernist conventions, but the press responded by giving his work extensive coverage. The *Manchester Guardian*, for instance, reproduced the only extant photograph of *The Strand* under a banner headline announcing 'A FUTURIST'S CONCEPTION OF A LONDON STREET', knowing full well that its readers, even if cynical about the merits of Futurism, would be able to identify with this celebration of the capital's turbulent pre-war night life.

But *The Strand* was not a thoroughbred Futurist work – it contained as much of Cubism as of the Italian movement – and Nevinson was determined to demonstrate his loyalty to the cause on the largest conceivable scale. He wanted to paint a tour de force of English Futurism, bold and ambitious enough to stand beside Severini's *"Pan-Pan" at the Monico* or Boccioni's *The City Rises* without fear of odious comparisons. And so he set to work, helped by Ethelbert White, on an enormous canvas for the 1914 Allied Artists' Salon, and made his

Christopher Nevinson
*Tum-Tiddly-Um-Tum-Pom-Pom*, 1914

defiant intentions abundantly plain by calling it *Tum-Tiddly-Um-Tum-Pom-Pom*.[22] Once again the original has failed to survive, but by great good fortune the *Western Mail* carried a photograph of the painting with the artist himself standing gravely beside it, palette and brush in hand, under the heavily ironic headline of 'A FUTURIST MASTERPIECE'. And the *Mail*'s reporter claimed, with his tongue lodged firmly in his cheek, that 'it represents Hampstead Heath on a Bank Holiday. Real confetti has been showered into the paint. The picture shows – at least the artist claims that it shows – the chaotic movement, noise, and enthusiasm of the Bank Holiday crowd'.

Nevinson had hit on yet another immediately popular theme, and he squeezed as much drama and dynamism out of it as he possibly could. There is a blatant stylistic division between the upper and lower halves of the design, between representation and abstraction, and no attempt has been made to reconcile this alarming disparity. Nevinson positively revels in his own fantastic extravagance, heaping forms on top of each other without seeming to care whether they cohere or cancel each other out. The sheer exuberance of the whole exercise, its sense of mad adventure, counteracts the obvious vulgarity of its formal arrangement. Nevinson's folly is so high-spirited that it does not wholly matter if his composition appears hopelessly disorganized and ineloquent. It hits out at the sensibilities of aesthetes with all the boorish conviction of a fist, and the force of the blow was all that the artist really cared about.

For once, the critics were able to label the picture with complete accuracy. *The New Weekly* declared that it was 'pure Futurism', and guardedly considered that 'to a sympathetic eye it is certainly expressive of the glare and movement of a Bank Holiday on Hampstead Heath'.[23] But Gaudier, in his *Egoist* review of the Salon, loathed the picture and went so far as to declare that 'the emotions are of a superficial character, merging on the vulgar', impatiently dismissing its 'union jacks, lace stockings and other tommy rot'.[24] Part of his hostility sprang from Nevinson's loudly proclaimed loyalty to Futurism, which Gaudier and the other English rebels could neither sympathise with nor stomach. For the stylistic ancestors of *Tum-Tiddly-Um-Tum-Pom-Pom* are all too easy to discover. The gigantic smiling face in the upper centre of the painting, its mouth open wide enough to show two unpleasant rows of teeth, is lifted wholesale from the face of the recumbent woman in Boccioni's *The Laugh*, which Nevinson would have remembered from the 1912 Sackville Gallery exhibition. The Futurist painting, as much of a hotch-potch of diverse stylistic conventions as the Englishman's picture, conveys the same sensation of hysterical confusion. And both works take as their text the passage in the 'Technical Manifesto of Futurist Painting' which announced that 'the time has passed for our sensations in painting to be whispered. We wish them in future to sing and re-echo upon our canvases in deafening and triumphant flourishes'.[25]

Gino Severini
*Dynamic Hieroglyph of the Bal Tabarin*, 1912

Nothing could more aptly sum up the feelings contained in Nevinson's picture, but it does specifically recall another Futurist painting as well: Severini's *Dynamic Hieroglyph of the Bal Tabarin*. As a friend of the artist, Nevinson would have seen the painting in Severini's Paris studio, for he visited the French capital in 1912, the year in which it was executed.[26] And just as he summarized his impressions of a Bank Holiday crowd, so Severini's disjointed rhythms enclose vivid memories of the night-club he habitually frequented. The Englishman, incorporating the word COCOA and the numeral 3 in his picture, follows the Futurist example: *Dynamic Hieroglyph* employs the irregular POLKA and the smooth VALSE to bring musical associations into the mind. Moreover, Severini's use of glistening applied sequins – a device originally recommended to him by Apollinaire – has its counterpart in the confetti showered so liberally into Nevinson's paint. *Tum-Tiddly-Um-Tum-Pom-Pom* is, therefore, a form of homage to the impact of the Italian movement on English art. It is a dictionary of Futurist quotations.

'He has the true Futurist sensibility', wrote Konody in his London Group review, and to prove his point instanced Nevinson's lost *Portrait of a Motorist* in which 'bits of glass are embedded in the paint to indicate goggles, and an actual button is stuck onto the coat.' Konody could not bring himself to agree with such techniques, and complained that 'I have never been able to fathom how such childishly crude realism can be compatible with the abstract rhythm at which this group of artists professes to aim'.[27] It is no longer possible to ascertain whether his criticism was justified, but Hulme was sufficiently impressed to pronounce it Nevinson's 'best picture' in the show, describing it as a 'very solid' work that 'develops an interesting contrast between round and angular shapes'.[28] The philosopher even reproduced Nevinson's drawing of a *Chauffeur* – calling it 'the study for the picture he has exhibited in the London Group' – in *The New Age* of 30 April as part of his series of 'Contemporary Drawings'.[29] It gives a clear indication of the appearance of the lost painting: the goggles are there, as is the button with the words 'MOTOR UNIT' inscribed on its circular surface; but most striking of all are the headlights which play over the form of the driver, splitting up his cap, face and coat lapels alike into a pattern of jagged segments.

The man's expression is mindless, almost brutal: he looks like a mechanized product of the new age of speed. And although Hulme would have warmed to the mechanical aspect of the drawing, he was less likely to appreciate the motives behind 'the elongation of the right side of the face', which he described as 'an attempt to show the distortion produced by light'. For this was a classic Futurist obsession, one that received its most exaggerated expression in Boccioni's multi-media sculpture entitled *Fusion of a Head and a Window*. Nevinson experienced this work at first-hand, as one of the main exhibits in the third and final Futurist exhibition in London, held at the Doré Galleries in April 1914. The novelty of the show was certainly the four sculptures displayed by Boccioni: he called them *Ensembles Plastiques* and reprinted his 1912 'Technical Manifesto of Futurist Sculpture' to introduce this departure into a new medium. It announced the Futurists' decision to 'cast all aside and proclaim the ABSOLUTE AND COMPLETE ABOLITION OF DEFINITE LINES AND

Christopher Nevinson
*The Chauffeur*, c. 1914

△Umberto Boccioni
*Fusion of a Head and a Window*, 1912

▷Christopher Nevinson
*Automobilist* or *Machine Slave, c.* 1914–15

CLOSED SCULPTURE. WE BREAK OPEN THE FIGURE AND ENCLOSE IT IN ENVIRONMENT. We proclaim that the environment must be part of the plastic block which is a world in itself with its own laws; that the sidewalk can jump up on your table and your head be transported across the street, while your lamp spins a web of plaster rays between one house and another'.[30]

Those very 'rays' explode outwards down the side of the face in Boccioni's macabre *Fusion* sculpture, and Nevinson must have been impressed by their dynamic force: soon afterwards, he tried his hand at a lost sculptural version of his *Chauffeur* and called it *Automobilist*.[31] It splits up the left side of the motorist's face with the same violence as Boccioni's *Fusion*, but the experiment is even less satisfactory than it is in the Futurist work. Deprived of the' environment' with which Boccioni surrounded his face, the slabs of light in *Automobilist* fail to convey their proper meaning: they merely look like slabs of metal inserted for some mysterious reason into the structure of cheek and jawbone. If Nevinson had been able to build up the motorist's surroundings as he did in the *Chauffeur* drawing, with the headlights cutting through the whole figure, then the device might have appeared convincing. But he has opted instead for a hybrid style, half Cubist and half Futurist, so that the power of the cadaverous features and sunken eyes is negated by his divided sculptural loyalties. Boccioni compels respect through sheer extremism, but Nevinson cannot avoid modelling the *Automobilist*'s left ear with naturalistic contours entirely out of keeping with the faceted planes used elsewhere in the bust.

To judge from the few works that have survived from his Futurist period, Nevinson did not really manage to curb the urge to illustrate, and he never moved on to a more advanced, non-representational language. He later insisted that he had been 'busily experimenting on, but not exhibiting, many pictures of a purely abstract nature', which attempted to 'convey movement: the dynamic rather than the static'.[32] None of these paintings has come to light, and it is surely significant that he decided not to display them in the galleries. For Nevinson wanted above all to communicate with his public, rather than shutting himself away in a misunderstood clique with the other rebels. His decision to become a Futurist may have been in part the outcome of his unwillingness to alienate, for the Italian movement was becoming far more widely understood and respected

backstage at the end of the farcical performance, only to find Marinetti 'in the best of spirits, dismissing the unanimous condemnation of the audience and calmly announcing to the Press, "C'était un cabal" '. The Futurist leader was as irrepressible as he was determined to continue at the Coliseum for the whole week, and so a compromise was arrived at. 'For the next performance', remembered Nevinson, 'Stoll introduced a gramophone record by Elgar to bring a little melody into the act. It helped, and the effort was received in stony silence. Marinetti described it as a "succés fou".'[38]

By this time, London had taken Futurism to its heart as the latest trend, and Marinetti himself was caricatured by cartoonists like Adrian Allinson as a darling of society. To the Press, this outrageous new movement was a godsend, and for the idle rich it provided an amusing pastime with the added advantage of cultural connotations. It was, in a word, *artistic*. Almost overnight, anything new and shocking was saddled with the arbitrary nickname of 'Futurist': men's pyjamas, lampshades, cravats, silk purses, quilts and bathing suits, not to mention interior decorating schemes and backdrops at the theatre. The *Daily Mirror* even carried a photograph of three wildly divergent types of painted scenery which all masqueraded under the name of Futurism, although the stark chess-board motif employed in the centre picture had more in common with the

Adrian Allinson
*Marinetti Reciting one of his Restful Futurist Poems, c.* 1913–14

abstractionist principles of a rebel painting like *In the Hold*.[39] Clearly, the advertising machine had taken over; and if Futurist paintings were still looked upon with bewilderment by the general public, Futurist underpants sold like wildfire. The movement had become so much a part of the nation's consciousness that its name was bandied about indiscriminately to describe any new development in the arts. Inevitably, the English rebels found it extremely difficult to establish themselves with an individual identity, and much of their posing and publicity-hunting was a simple matter of self-defence, a necessary counter-attack that would divorce them from the Futurist stereotype. They were understandably touchy about their own independence, and even the enamoured Nevinson had the tact to dissuade Marinetti from attempting to promote the artists who had sponsored the Florence Restaurant dinner in his honour the previous November.[40] The Italian was already too dominant a figure in the English art world, as Edward Storer affirmed in *The New Witness* when he wrote that 'the history of that [Rebel Art Centre] group in England will make an interesting chapter one day. It was a case of speedy conversion for the most part. St. Augustine could not have had such success with the rude Saxons as Marinetti achieved with Messrs Lewis, Bomberg, Nevinson, Wadsworth, etc.'[41]

△A Trio of Futurist Flower Robes, 1914

▷London Music Hall Experiments with Futurist Scenery, 1914

The public was only too ready to accept such a distorted interpretation of the facts at its face value, and the rebels realized that they were in danger of being written off as little more than satellites, meekly revolving around the glaring sun of Marinetti's charismatic personality. How could they possibly escape from his orbit, when journalists as widely respected as Nevinson's war correspondent father extolled his virtues and made him into a high priest of revolution? 'Into our ancient life of precedents and perpetual repetition he burst like a shell', wrote Henry Nevinson in the Newark *Evening News*, mirroring his son's enthusiasm. 'Antiquity exploded. Tradition ceased to breathe... I have heard many recitations, and have tried to describe many battles. But listen to Marinetti's recitation of one of his battle scenes ... the noise, the confusion, the surprise of death, the terror and courage, the shouting, curses, blood and agony – all were recalled by that amazing succession of words, performed or enacted by the poet with such passion of abandonment that no-one could escape the spell of listening.'[42]

Such rhetoric is only ever lavished on men who have become cult figures, and Marinetti was without doubt a fad among the smart intelligentsia of London. There was no other avant-garde leader to match him on the lecture platform, where he persuaded people to commit themselves – however superficially – to his cause. Even Lewis, as Miss Lechmere recalled, was 'inaudible' at public readings, keeping 'his head buried firmly in his notes'.[43] And yet the English rebels disagreed so profoundly with so many aspects of Futurist aesthetics that they needed a leader of their own, someone who could present their alternative case with the requisite clarity and panache. Lewis himself was the first to realize this. He knew, now, that he had made a fatal mistake by pinning his hopes on Marinetti after the Omega debacle: by doing so, he had merely substituted one father-figure for another, and the anti-Futurist remarks inserted into the 'Cubist Room' foreword prove that by the end of 1913 he was already beginning to diverge from the path of Marinettian truth.

Small wonder, then, that by the early summer of 1914 he had fallen completely out of love with his Futurist rival, just as he had previously become disenchanted with John, Sickert and Fry. If Lewis was an exhilarating man to have as a friend, he was a truly lethal enemy, and Marinetti was the new target. He seems to have started his offensive fairly quietly, with the occasional malicious remark: Goldring remembered that 'Lewis, who from the first regarded Marinetti with deep suspicion, used to say that the lavish funds which he had at his disposal were derived from a chain of de luxe brothels in Egypt, controlled by Marinetti père'.[44] But before long, private slander had turned into open disagreement on important matters of aesthetic principle. One evening, Lewis later recalled, the two of them were 'passing into a lavabo together' for Marinetti to wash 'after a lecture where he had drenched himself in sweat'. A heated argument broke out between them, and Lewis's reconstruction of the scene is a vital document that clarifies his own restlessness with Futurist dogma. Marinetti, he remembered, saw the occasion as an ideal opportunity to convert the Englishman and enlist him in the Futurist ranks.

' "Why don't you announce that you are a futurist!" he asked me squarely.

"Because I am not one", I answered, just as point-blank and to the point.

"Yes. But what's it matter!" said he with great impatience.

"It's most important", I replied rather coldly.

"Not at all!" said he. "Futurism is good. It is all right."

"Not too bad", said I. "It has its points. But you Wops insist too much on the Machine. You're always on about these driving-belts, you are always exploding about internal combustion. We've had machines here in England for a donkey's years. They're no novelty to *us*."

"You have never understood your machines! You have never known the *ivresse* of travelling at a kilometre a minute. Have you ever travelled at a kilometre a minute?"

"Never." I shook my head energetically. "Never. I loathe anything that goes too quickly. If it goes too quickly, it is not there."

"It is not there!" he thundered for this had touched him on the raw. "It is *only* when it goes quickly that it *is* there!"

"That is nonsense", I said. "I cannot see a thing that is going too quickly."

"See it – see it! Why should you want to *see*?" he exclaimed. "But you *do* see it. You see it multiplied a thousand times. You see a thousand things instead of one thing."

I shrugged my shoulders – this was not the first time I had had this argument.

"That's just what I don't want to see. I am not a futurist", I said. "I prefer *one* thing."

"There is no such thing as *one* thing."

"There is if I wish to have it so. And I wish to have it so."

"You are a monist!" he said at this, with a contemptuous glance, curling his lip.

"All right. I am not a futurist anyway. *Je hais le mouvement qui déplace les lignes.*"

At this quotation he broke into a hundred angry pieces.

"And you 'never weep' – I know, I know. *Ah zut alors*! What a thing to be an Englishman!" '[45]

Beneath the rather theatrical badinage lay a basic divergence of artistic belief, which Lewis summarized very succinctly with his reference to a line from Baudelaire's *La Beauté*. And his decision to use that particular quotation was in itself a direct challenge to Futurist theoretical writings, for Boccioni had only recently attacked it in his 1914 book on *Pittura Scultura Futuriste*: 'Only a slack and sleepy mind could claim that the static concept behind all art up to the present day proves that immobility is the essential element of the masterpiece', Boccioni wrote. 'And here the stupidity of this marvellous sentence can be seen: "Je hais le mouvement qui déplace la ligne" [*sic*] . . . It is not immobility that fascinates us in a masterpiece, but the serenity that flows from certainty in the laws that guide it!'[46]

Lewis obviously disagreed with Boccioni's cunning argument, and in his turn chose to employ the Baudelaire line as a dramatization of the divide separating him from Futurism. Where Marinetti was a diehard Romantic, who revelled in the flux of modern life, its speed, uproar and confusion, the sympathies of his English opponent resided in Classical control, preferring to stand back and appraise twentieth-century phenomena with a cold, aggressive passion. And while Futurism expressed itself in terms of multiform images, Lewis clung instead to the viability of separate, precisely defined objects. Neither was this a mere whim on his part. It was the consensus of opinion among the English rebels: even Bomberg, who would never have dreamed of aligning himself with Lewis, demonstrated in paintings like *The Mud Bath* that he would have had a similar argument with Marinetti had the occasion arisen. And the same applied to the works executed by other artists in Lewis's immediate circle, even if they were likewise loath to assemble under the banner of his leadership: Roberts' *Dancers*, for example, or Epstein's *Marble Doves*.

The Futurist leader must have recognized this opposition after a while, but he was far too resilient to be ousted without a public battle. Nevinson was a confirmed disciple, after all, and so Marinetti collaborated with him on a written article couched in language so extreme that it would serve either to confirm or destroy Futurism's hold over the English rebels. This final 'Putsch', as Lewis afterwards described it, took the form of a declaration of faith entitled 'VITAL ENGLISH ART. FUTURIST MANIFESTO', signed jointly by Marinetti himself and the faithful Nevinson. It was their version of the 'Round Robin'; and just as Lewis had sent copies of his earlier broadside to the Press, so the Futurists' Manifesto was published in the *Observer* on 7 June

# VITAL ENGLISH ART

## FUTURIST MANIFESTO.

I am an Italian Futurist poet, and a passionate admirer of England. I wish, however, to cure English Art of that most grave of all maladies—passéism. I have the right to speak plainly and without compromise, and together with my friend Nevinson, an English Futurist painter, to give the signal for battle

## AGAINST:

**1** — The worship of tradition, and the conservatism of Academies, the commercial acquiescence of English artists, the effeminacy of their art and their complete absorption towards a purely decorative sense.

**2.** — The pessimistic, sceptical and narrow views of the English public, who stupidly adore the pretty-pretty, the commonplace, the soft, sweet, and mediocre, the sickly revivals of mediævalism, the Garden Cities with their curfews and artificial battlements, the Maypole Morris dances, Aestheticism, Oscar Wilde, the Pre-Raphaelites, Neo-primitives and Paris.

**3.** — The perverted snob who ignores or despises all English daring, originality and invention, but welcomes eagerly all foreign

1914, and subsequently in *The Times* and the *Daily Mail*. 'But we were not content with that', recalled Nevinson, 'and I used to go to the galleries of theatres and shower the manifestos on the heads of the unsuspecting people in the stalls and the dress circle. When I was located I was escorted from the building by the largest commissionaire'.[47]

The style of the Manifesto clearly proclaimed its origins in earlier Futurist prototypes; and, as if in confirmation of these allegiances, it was reprinted in the 15 July issue of *Lacerba*, the principle Futurist organ. Marinetti's voice was predominant from the outset, too: 'I am an Italian Futurist poet, and a passionate admirer of England', the text began. 'I wish, however, to cure English Art of that most grave of all maladies – passéism. I have the right to speak plainly and without compromise, and together with my friend Nevinson, an English Futurist painter, to give the signal for battle.' The ensuing text was divided up neatly into two sections: 'AGAINST' and 'WE WANT', although the first, merely destructive section was by far the longest and most specific. The authors decided that eleven distinct elements in English art ought to be purged, and they began in an abrasive vein by attacking 'the worship of tradition, and the conservatism of Academies, the commercial acquiescence of English artists, the effeminacy of their art and their complete absorption towards a purely decorative sense'. The refusal to mention any names meant that their insults could be interpreted in the widest possible sense, stretching from Sir Edward Poynter at one end of the scale to the Omega at the other. And the second onslaught was equally generalized, so much so that Marinetti insisted on vaguely portraying England as a cloud-cuckoo land of prejudice and downright idiocy. It hit out at 'the pessimistic, sceptical and narrow views of the English public, who stupidly adore the pretty-pretty, the commonplace, the soft, sweet, and mediocre, the sickly revivals of mediævalism, the Garden Cities with their curfews and artificial battlements, the Maypole Morris dances, Aestheticism, Oscar Wilde, the Pre-Raphaelites, Neo-primitives and Paris'. The convoluted list of evils said more about Marinetti's melodramatic imagination than the real state of the nation. His obvious relish for the satirical game threatened to castrate the cogency of his assault. There was an abundance of ills to be denounced in England, certainly, but long-winded lists of adjectives were not the most efficient weapons to use against them.

Ensuing grievances were, fortunately, expressed in both a shorter and more coherent vein. The Manifesto successively castigated the 'perverted snob who ignores or despises all English daring, originality and invention, but welcomes eagerly all foreign originality and daring'; the 'sham revolutionaries of the New English Art Club, who, having destroyed the prestige of the Royal Academy, now show themselves grossly hostile to the later movements of the advance guard'; and 'the indifference of the King, the State and the politicians towards all arts'. It even railed against those 'pioneers suffering from arrested development' who merely emulated primitive art, and it declared that 'if it has been necessary in painting and sculpture to have *naïveté*, deformation and archaism, it was only because it was essential to break away violently from the academic and the graceful before going further towards the plastic dynamism of painting'. Hulme might have agreed with the idea that primitive imitation ought only to be the stepping-stone towards a specifically modern movement, but he would have joined the other English rebels in dissociating themselves from the ideal of 'plastic dynamism'. Nor would any of them have felt very strongly about the last and most exclamatory of the Manifesto's complaints, the 'mania for immortality'. Marinetti, surrounded as he was in his home country by the intimidating achievements of the Renaissance, categorically announced that 'a masterpiece must disappear with its author. Immortality in Art is a disgrace.' And then, as a final flourish to anticipate the victory of Futurism in London, he roared: 'Forward! HURRAH for motors! HURRAH for speed! HURRAH for draughts! HURRAH for lightning!' But the fervour of the war-cries was of little use without positive, constructive proposals about the kind of art that the Manifesto wished to see thriving in England. And this was precisely where it failed, providing no indication of the character of this art apart from woolly clichés. Marinetti and Nevinson called for an 'Art that is strong, virile and anti-sentimental'; demanded that 'English artists strengthen their Art by a recuperative optimism, a fearless desire of adventure, a heroic instinct of discovery, a worship of strength and a physical and moral courage, all sturdy virtues of the English race'; and degenerated into whimsicality by demanding that 'Sport' be 'considered an essential element in Art'.

They were, perhaps, anxious to avoid repeating the theories already advanced in previous Futurist manifestos; for the all-important last paragraph attempted to drag all the English rebels into the net of the movement. In a rash conclusion which implied that Lewis and his colleagues were in agreement with the principles of the manifesto, the two Futurists called upon 'the English public to support, defend, and glorify the genius of the great Futurist painters or pioneers and advance-forces of vital English Art – ATKINSON, BOMBERG, EPSTEIN, ETCHELLS, HAMILTON, NEVINSON, ROBERTS, WADSWORTH, WYNDHAM LEWIS'.[48] The list included all those artists connected with the Rebel Art Centre whom the co-authors considered to be potential Futurists: the only people to be omitted were Gaudier, whose French nationality probably ruled him out, and Dismorr and Saunders, whose sex contradicted the fundamental Futurist belief in masculinity. And it was Marinetti's greatest tactical blunder. He had no right to take it upon himself even to suggest that the rebels had defected to his own cause, and yet this was precisely what his last paragraph alleged. The rebels' fury knew no bounds: how could Marinetti have been so presumptuous to use their names in a piece of straightforward Futurist propaganda without seeking their permission before-hand? The outrage made them realize, once and for all, how urgently they needed to repel the Italian's advances; and Lewis, with his shrewd eye for political timing, knew at last that Marinetti's mistake provided him with a perfect opportunity. Now, surely, he could persuade his associates that they needed a fully-fledged movement of their own, and galvanize them into a concerted show of strength.

Before the appearance of the Vital English Art manifesto, it would have been difficult for him to do so. The rebels were a tough group of individualists, as determined to maintain their own artistic personalities as they were suspicious of Lewis's obvious desire to group them all together under his leadership. Roberts described the situation very well when he wrote, many years later, that the English avant-garde was 'composed not with the figure of a single "Leader" in the person of Wyndham Lewis surrounded by a herd of Adherents, Disciples and Professed Followers, influence-drenched and impact-dazed, but on the contrary a criss-cross of opposed interests between rivals eager to establish themselves and their own particular brand of abstract art . . . "No Disciples! No Adherents!" was the battle-cry in those days'.[49] Lewis had his close personal allies, of course – notably Wadsworth, Etchells, Pound, Gaudier and Saunders – but their friendship did not automatically mean that they were willing to become subservient to Lewis's sole hegemony. Most of them were young men in their early twenties, not yet settled enough in their own minds to agree about the kind of aesthetic principles that would constitute a new English movement in the true meaning of the term. They had exhibited together as a group in the 'Cubist Room', certainly, but only as part of a larger show; and Lewis's foreword undoubtedly exaggerated the community feeling of the exhibits. Even the much-vaunted Rebel Art Centre, which started off with so many hopes and pretensions, rapidly petered out through internal dissension and lack of the mutual enthusiasms that made a movement like Futurism stay alive. The English rebels were a heterogeneous collection of personalities, ambitious and combative enough to make a stand against the existing art establishment, but neither ready nor willing to commit their separate identities to the kind of group that Lewis tried so energetically to foster.

The only real collective endeavour they had agreed to take part in before the Futurist Manifesto entirely transformed the nature of the situation, was a magazine which Lewis proposed to edit. Backed with funds to the tune of £100 from the faithful Kate Lechmere, the periodical was to make its revolutionary bias abundantly plain in its aggressive title: *Blast*. Plans were first mooted towards the end of 1913, for Wadsworth wrote to Lewis on 17 December – the day after the 'Cubist Room' opened – that 'I have not been able to think of another name for *Blast* and I am not convinced yet really that *Blast* is bad . . . In any case I don't think we ought to change the name unless for something *better*'.[50] The letter not only proves that the project and the title were being actively discussed before the new year: it also demonstrates the communal nature of the enterprise. Lewis had asked Wadsworth – and, no doubt, other of his rebel friends as well – about the suitability of the name *Blast*, and he must have been commissioning articles and drawings for the periodical at the same time. The allies probably thought it an appropriate title, not only because of its onomatopoeic attack but also its implicit reference to the blast-furnaces of industrial England which Vorticism would highlight.

Less than a month later, on 8 January 1914, the first published announcement of this magazine appeared in *The New Age*'s editorial column, written under the pseudonym of 'R.H.C.' 'I hear', he wrote, 'that a magazine, to be named *Blast*, will shortly appear under the editorship of Mr Wyndham Lewis to provide a platform for the discussion of Cubism and other aesthetic phenomena.'[51] The rebels had, therefore, only agreed to contribute to *Blast* on the understanding that no independent movement of Lewis's own making would be launched within its pages. Just as the Rebel Art Centre's prospectus supported a whole range of Continental avant-garde movements, so this proposed periodical did not at first attempt to be anything more than a mouthpiece for 'Cubist Room' artists, united by their desire to experiment with abstraction but otherwise uncommitted to any form of political association. So much is made clear in a letter Pound wrote to Joyce early in 1914, where he mentions that 'Lewis is starting a new Futurist, Cubist, Imagiste Quarterly. I think he might take some of your essays, I cant tell, it is mostly a painter's magazine with me to do the poems'.[52] Even Pound, already a formidable propagandist of literary causes, had not at this stage helped to formulate an independent movement for the artists he knew and supported. Only one thing was agreed upon: the magazine wanted to set itself up in direct opposition to Fitzroy Square aesthetics, for Wadsworth told Lewis in a letter on 4 February that 'Constables asked whether "Blast" had any connection with the Omega so I disillusioned them on that point and said the Omega was *dead*'.[53] From there, it was a natural step to associate the periodical with the Rebel Art Centre, and a prospectus – probably issued from Great Ormond Street at the beginning of April – duly promised that 'there will be in the course of the next six weeks, a "Blast" evening, or meeting to celebrate the foundation and appearance of the review of that name. A manifesto of rebel art will be read and addresses read, to the sound of carefully-chosen trumpets'.[54]

Perhaps it was Lewis's original willingness to include Futurist theories in the 'quarterly' that encouraged Marinetti and Nevinson to make such a high-handed allegation about the rebels' loyalties in their Futurist Manifesto. But such an action was inexcusable in the eyes of the artists named in its final paragraph; and Lewis himself must have interpreted Nevinson's action as a challenge to his own hopes for leadership. Nevinson had very stupidly given the Rebel Art Centre as the address beneath his signature in the Manifesto, and this tactlessness constituted the final insult. Lewis would not have forgotten how much the upstart Futurist disciple owed to his own early encouragement and ideas: they had, after all, been sufficiently close at the end of 1913 to talk over plans for *Blast* together. 'Lewis was at that time anxious to produce a paper somewhat on the lines of the Futurist manifestos', Nevinson recalled later. 'He asked me to help him and I went so far as to suggest the title, which was *Blast*. We used to meet at Verrey's to discuss the first issues.'[55] And late in January 1914, they went off together in search of a publisher for the magazine, armed with a useful letter of introduction from Nevinson's father. 'Let me introduce to you my son Richard and his friend Wyndham Lewis', Henry Nevinson had obligingly written to one of his publishing contacts, describing them both as 'revolutionary artists of Futurist fame, who want to consult you about bringing out an artistic magazine they have in mind'.[56] Lewis was then content to see himself referred to openly as 'Futurist'; but during the months that followed, his relationship with Nevinson deteriorated. Kate Lechmere, who gave her rash promise to pay for the rebel organ when the manuscript was brought to the Rebel Art Centre so that Lewis and Dismorr could spend their mornings 'trying to translate *Blast* to a puzzled and bewildered typist', remembered Lewis telling her that 'everything Nevinson does has a touch of vulgarity about it';[57] and the complaint may well have referred to Nevinson's increasingly partisan friendship with Marinetti. Hostility came to a head with the appearance of the Futurist Manifesto: banging drums at lectures was harmless enough, but this list of names smacked too strongly of clumsy political manoeuvring.

Lewis's reaction was as explosive as it was in his earlier dénouement with Fry. On 12 June, five days after the Manifesto appeared in the *Observer*, he gathered together the artists whose reputations had been abused and plotted with them to disrupt a Futurist demonstration scheduled that very evening for the Doré Galleries. Since Marinetti and Nevinson were going to promote their cause, and Nevinson planned to read out the entire text of 'Vital English Art', it was a perfect opportunity for the rebels to display their wrath in a concerted 'counter-putsch'. 'I assembled in Greek Street a determined band of miscellaneous anti-futurists', Lewis remembered. 'Mr Epstein was there: Gaudier Brzeska, T. E. Hulme, Edward Wadsworth . . . There were about ten of us. After a hearty meal we shuffled bellicosely round to the Doré Gallery. Marinetti had entrenched himself upon a high lecture platform, and he put down a tremendous barrage in French as we entered. Gaudier went into action at once. He was very good at the *parlez-vous* . . . He was sniping him without intermission, standing up in his place in the audience all the while. The remainder of our party maintained a confused uproar. The Italian intruder was worsted.'[58] And when it came to Nevinson's turn to read out the contentious manifesto, complete bedlam broke loose. Gaudier made a point of correcting his mispronunciation of 'Vortickists', a reporter from the *Evening News* wrote that 'when Mr. Nevinson made a passionate outcry for motors, speed and lightning, a Vorticist set off some fireworks in the centre doorway', and the beleaguered Futurist disciple eventually sat down 'amid laughter and the shouting of names'.[59] One of the most significant aspects of the demonstration was the sudden appearance of a new name: 'Vorticists'. *The New Age*, which described the evening's events in colourful detail, considered them to be the product of 'Futile-ism'; but a report in the *Manchester Guardian*, which appeared the next morning, was far more accurate when it mentioned 'the new Seceders from the Marinetti group, Messrs Wyndham Lewis, and Co., who now call themselves the Vorticists'.[60]

Out of the blue, the title of an independent English movement had been created, but it had not yet received the official approval of Lewis's companions. No mention of its name was included in a letter the rebels printed in the 14 June issue of the *Observer* – a week after the appearance of the Futurist Manifesto – but their feelings about Marinetti and Nevinson were all the same made abundantly obvious. Signed jointly by Aldington, Atkinson, Bomberg, Etchells, Gaudier, Hamilton, Pound, Roberts, Wadsworth and Lewis, the letter's tone was cold and antagonistic. 'To read or hear the praises of oneself or one's friends is always pleasant', it began curtly. 'There are forms of praise, however, which are so compounded with innuendo as to be most embarrassing. One may find oneself, for instance, so praised as to make it appear that one's opinions coincide with those of the person who praises, in which case one finds oneself in the difficult position of disclaiming the laudation or of even slightly resenting it.' After this preliminary rebuttal, the letter became more specific. 'There are certain artists in England who do not belong to the Royal Academy nor to any of the passéist groups, and who do not on that account agree with the futurism of Signor Marinetti. An assumption of such agreement either by Signor Marinetti or by his followers is an impertinence.' By refusing to mention Nevinson's name, and merely referring to him as an anonymous 'follower' of Marinetti, the rebels insulted him in the most effective way. And their final sentence made clear that they wanted nothing whatsoever to do with the Italian movement. 'We, the undersigned, whose ideals were mentioned or implied, or who might by the opinions of others be implicated, beg to dissociate ourselves from the "Futurist" manifesto which appeared in the pages of THE OBSERVER of Sunday, June 7.'[61] The letter was addressed from the Rebel Art Centre, which might help to explain Epstein's absence from the list of signatories; but Bomberg also insisted on making his total independence absolutely manifest in a postscript, where the editor of the *Observer* wrote that 'Mr Bomberg asks us to say that he signed the letter not as a member of the Art Rebel Centre (being unconnected with that group), but independently'.

The fact that stubborn individualists like Bomberg had agreed to sign such a political letter, however, showed how deeply their pride had been affronted by the Futurist Manifesto. In vain did Nevinson send a letter to Lewis on 13 June, pleading that 'I regret having been the cause of so much trouble and expense to the R.A.C. on account of my "irresponsibility" regarding the manifesto . . . I had no idea you felt so strongly against Futurism, because in some prospectus I remember seeing you even mention it as a "vital form of art"'.[62] Nevinson may not have realized the resistance that had developed to the Italian movement among his former colleagues; but any hopes he entertained about an absolution must have been shattered by the publication of their *Observer* letter. A week later, he had come to realize that the Manifesto had precipitated an irrevocable split between the rebels and Marinetti, for on 20 June he wrote a letter to *The New Weekly* – this time addressed from his Hampstead home – explaining his motives in a far less apologetic tone. 'As a Futurist, the fight before me is too great to feel very interested in the petty and personal polemics or the ridiculous technical differences that the directors of the Rebel Art Centre seem so much to enjoy', he began, assuming a position of lofty disdain. 'But, much as I should like utterly to ignore their letter, it is necessary for me to contradict a few misstatements. I would point out: (1) That there was no need for the artists referred to in the manifesto to dissociate themselves from Futurism, as they were quite distinctly and invariably named as "pioneers or advanced forces of vital English art", which they undoubtedly are. Nor was there the smallest hint that they endorsed the ideals of Signor Marinetti or myself.'

His excuse was patently unconvincing: the Manifesto's last sentence had been composed so ambiguously as to suggest that the rebels agreed with the sentiments expressed in the rest of the text. But Nevinson was determined to mount a defence, however unconvincing it may have appeared to even the most impartial observer. His second point was that 'we are at perfect liberty to praise (or criticise) an artist without his consent', which succeeded in proving nothing either one way or the other. And the third point was equally irrelevant – 'Signor Marinetti never used the address of the Rebel Art Centre as stated, but his address of the Futurist movement, Milan' – because he proceeded to negate it in the very next sentence by 'willingly' admitting that 'I made an error of judgement in using the address of the Rebel Art Centre, considering its autocratic constitution'. It was useless for him to protest that he 'used it simply as a member uses the address of his club, and without the slightest evil intent'.[63] The damage was done, and no amount of letters to the Press would ever restore his once amicable relations with the other rebels.

Indeed, the rift was made definitive in the very same issue of *The New*

*Weekly*, where Lewis wrote a brief essay pouring scorn on the Futurists' worship of speed and 'automobilism', claiming that England 'practically invented this civilisation that Signor Marinetti has come to preach to us about', and declaring that the Italian propagandist and his 'innocent disciple' had used a 'stupid polemic' to brand as Futurists a group of artists who were not 'automobilists'. 'Now', he announced prophetically, 'it is time for definition.'[64] There was a note of exultation in the article, for Lewis knew that the time was now propitious for the launching of the English avant-garde movement he had cherished for so long. Pound had already been quick to capitalize on the new situation, declaring in *The Egoist* on 15 June that 'we have in Mr Lewis our most articulate voice, and we shall sweep out the past century as surely as Attila swept across Europe'.[65] His tone was confident, since he knew that Nevinson's blunder had made his colleagues realize the need for consolidation within the ranks; and that Lewis now found himself able to seize on this unprecedented new mood as a signal for the birth of Vorticism.

The Press, after all, was playing right into his hands by announcing its arrival before the rebels had a chance to realize it themselves. 'Futurism in this country has hardly been born before it has budded off into Vorticism', asserted the *Yorkshire Observer* on 15 June, only one day after the publication of the rebels' letter in the *Observer*. 'The split occurred last week, and it now seems as if Signor Marinetti and Mr Nevinson, the best-believed and most devoted of his disciples, are the only orthodox Futurists left in England. When Signor Marinetti leaves us, Mr Nevinson will have the distinction of Abdiel – "Faithful among the faithless only he." ' The *Yorkshire Observer* was amazingly well informed on the latest developments in the quarrel, even if it had some disparaging remarks to make about the new splinter group. 'The seceding Vorticists', it continued, 'have already published a sort of preliminary manifesto, though the full manifesto has yet to come . . . They are all very ardent and articulate young men, amazingly strong on matters of principle. In achievement they seem neither articulate, nor ardent, nor copious; but, if these movements and sub-movements are at present all talk, it is very good talk.'[66]

The criticisms were, in a sense, justified. This strange name, Vorticism, was the product not of a homogeneous group of painters and sculptors proclaiming theories as original as Cubism or Futurism. Rather was it the brainchild of Lewis's political ambitions, a collective term which he was able to bestow on the rebels' work after the Futurist Manifesto had offended their sense of national pride. Would this designation ever have come into official existence without the catalyst provided by Nevinson's misjudged manoeuvre? The question needs to be asked, for a *Blast* advertisement published in *The Egoist* as late as 1 April contained no mention of Vorticism at all. And six days later, a lengthy interview with Lewis centering on the subject of *Blast* in the *Daily News and Leader* did not mention the movement's name, either. Lewis merely explained that ' "Blast" signifies something destructive and constructive. It means the blowing away of dead ideas and worn-out notions. It means (according to the Anglo-Saxon interpretation) a fire or flame. In "Blast" we will deal only with those aspects of art which are worth consideration'.[67] This note of studied generalization was continued in a 15 April announcement in *The Egoist* as well, for although it promised that the magazine would be ready in April, it still maintained that *Blast* would present an unspecific 'Discussion of Cubism, Futurism, Imagisme and all Vital Forms of Modern Art'.[68] At this stage Lewis would surely have liked his journal to propagate an independent movement: a note in his handwriting still exists with the words 'Blast – the bimonthly organ of Blasticism' scribbled on it.[69] But his allies' hostility to the idea had always deterred him

*Blast* advertisement in *The Egoist*, 1914

from suggesting it to them before Nevinson blundered in to save the day.

As for the name itself, Pound seems to have used it first in a letter written on 19 December 1913, where he told his friend William Carlos Williams that 'you may get something slogging away by yourself that you would miss in The Vortex – and that we miss'.[70] Even at this early date, Pound appears to be referring to the word as a concept shared and understood by his own circle of fellow-artists. Admittedly, he is not yet sure whether it expresses a desirable state of affairs or not: Carlos Williams, he thinks, might actually profit by absenting himself from it. But that Pound should have coined the name before anyone else was wholly appropriate, for he it was who applied it to the rebel movement, probably with reference to Lewis's pictures. A couple of years later, he wrote to John Quinn praising Lewis's work and explaining that 'it is not merely knowledge of technique, or skill, it is intelligence and knowledge of life, of the whole of it, beauty, heaven, hell, sarcasm, every kind of whirlwind of force and emotion. Vortex. That is the right word, if I did find it myself'.[71] Roberts later stated that 'Pound invented the word in that fateful month of June 1914',[72] but his memory simply reflects the limitations of his intimacy with the poet at the time. The truth is that Pound must have discussed the possibility of employing the name with Lewis during the early days at the Rebel Art Centre – if not before – and the two men obviously decided that it was as yet impossible to persuade the other rebels to accept it. Their hands, momentarily at least, were tied.

But the advent of the Futurist Manifesto gave their hopes for a movement a sudden new lease of life. Only six days after Marinetti and Nevinson's joint text was published, Lewis placed an advertisement in the 13 June issue of *The Spectator* announcing for the very first time that *Blast* would include a 'Manifesto of the Vorticists'. He clearly thought that the other rebels, stung by Nevinson's bid for Futurist supremacy, would now allow him to group them under the collective umbrella of the Vortex. And the plan worked: none of them, not even the independent Epstein who had committed himself to contributing two drawings to the magazine, seems to have objected to the change of emphasis. It could be claimed that they were not properly equipped to voice their dissent, for Roberts afterwards cynically asserted that, 'from the point of view of a Leader, the rotating forces of this Vortex were in perfect equilibrium; none of these artists were [*sic*] writers, but just painters who put their trust in brush and palette; such implements could never challenge leadership, for that a pen would be necessary'.[73] Perhaps Roberts protests too much, however: the fact remains that not one of the rebels who found himself christened a Vorticist in *Blast* ever felt that he had to repudiate the name by writing to the Press in the accepted way.

The only problem now confronting Lewis lay in the deadline for the journal's publication. 20 June is the date printed on its title-page, and that must surely have been decided upon well before the appearance of the Futurist Manifesto. Even if the specifically Vorticist material was prepared as early as May, Lewis had little time to edit it before *Blast* finally appeared on 2 July. But he did manage to place 'Review of the Great English Vortex' underneath the word *Blast* on the title-page, add a short credo called 'Long Live the Vortex!' before the preliminary manifesto, tag on a final section entitled 'Our Vortex' to the major collection of essays he had written for the magazine, and procure from Gaudier and Pound – the two other main enthusiasts for the movement – personal articles of faith simply entitled 'Vortex'. Brodzky, in fact, celebrated the particular militancy of this triumvirate of Vorticist propagandists in a lively little cartoon reproduced in *The Egoist* on 15 July, calling it *The L-B-P Troupe*. And Pound later confirmed the central importance of the parts which he, Gaudier and Lewis played by

THE LEWIS-BRZESKA-POUND TROUPE.
Blasting their own trumpets before the walls of Jericho.

Horace Brodzky
*The Lewis-Brzeska-Pound Troupe,* 1914

telling the artist Gladys Hynes that 'W.L. certainly *made* vorticism. To him alone we owe the existence of *Blast*. It is true that he started by wanting a forum for the several ACTIVE varieties of CONTEMPORARY art/cub/expressionist/ post-imp etc. BUT in conversation with E.P. there emerged the idea of defining what WE wanted & having a name for it. Ultimately Gaudier for sculpture, E.P. for poetry, and W.L., the main mover, set down their personal requirements'.[74]

No proof has survived either from the publishers, The Bodley Head, or the printing firm of Leveridge and Co., to substantiate these last-minute insertions. But the evidence contained in *Blast No.1* itself is enough to support the hypothesis. To judge by the binding of the periodical, for instance, all the writings which mention the word Vortex could easily have been added after the main body of text was set up for printing: apart from Lewis's 'Our Vortex' article and the title of his essays, 'Vortices and Notes', every other reference to Vorticism is contained either in the first or the last signature of *Blast*. And in between, the great mass of intervening writing in the periodical – taking up over 150 pages – scarcely contains an acknowledgement of Vorticism's existence.

Still more conclusive, however, are the opinions expressed by Lewis in 'The Melodrama of Modernity', one of the essays he wrote for *Blast No.1* before Vorticism's existence was mooted. Here he shows himself to be perfectly happy to accept the label of Futurism applied so often by the critics to him and his friends. 'Of all the tags going, "Futurist", for general application, serves as well as any for the active painters of to-day', he declared. 'It is picturesque and easily inclusive. It is especially justifiable here in England where no particular care or knowledge of the exact (or any other in matters of art) signification of this word exist.' It would be hard to imagine a more convincing demonstration of Lewis's earlier willingness to concur with the non-partisan feelings of his allies. When he wrote 'The Melodrama of Modernity', he no more thought that they would agree to be known as Vorticists than he himself expected to become the next President of the Royal Academy. Aspirations to leadership had merely to be implied through his editorship of *Blast*, and his lengthy theoretical contributions printed in its pages. 'As "Futurist", in England, does not mean anything more than a painter, either a little, or very much, occupying himself with questions of a renovation of art, and showing a tendency to rebellion against the domination of the Past', his 'Melodrama of Modernity' article continued, 'it is not necessary to correct it.' Any hopes for a new movement were confined to one brief sentence, tactful and vague enough to hurt the pride of no-one. 'We may hope before long', he added wistfully, 'to find a new word.'[75]

The presence of such sentiments in a magazine later transformed into a public announcement of the Vorticist movement now looks nonsensical. If Lewis had felt able to delay *Blast No.1*'s publication a month longer, he could have deleted these outdated passages and restored consistency to his arguments. But he was sufficiently shrewd to realize that it should be issued while the memory of the Futurist Manifesto still rankled in the minds of his fellow rebels. They must, for instance, have been delighted to read the headline of a report in an Italian newspaper claiming that 'THE VORTICISTS SURPASS THE FUTURISTS IN DARING'. The article, which appeared in Trieste's *Il Piccolo della Sera* and was sent to Pound as a joke by James Joyce, asserted that 'the futurists have been overtaken, artistically and intellectually, by a new trend, which has revealed itself among some fine English literary and artistic contemporaries who have founded a new school . . . that of the "Vorticists". Is not life itself a vortex? Apparently it is, and having admitted that, it is natural that even art and literature should become vortices, absorbing in their spirals all the products of the human intellect. No rule, no measure, no special mark is necessary in order to be a vorticist painter or sculptor. The greatest, most absolute freedom is accorded the followers of the new theory. Let them do what they want, and how they want, provided that they produce something which has never been seen before now'.[76] The rebels would have warmed to such a declaration of Vorticism's victory over Futurist dogma, and the 'freedom' described in the report might have gone some way towards appeasing their desire for individual liberty.

Lewis, moreover, was a master tactician, and he attempted to foster a real 'group' atmosphere by arranging a grand *Blast* dinner at the Dieudonné Restaurant in Ryder Street on 15 July to mark its publication. 'The appearance of *Blast* was celebrated in due state at "Dieudonné", on July 7th', recalled Pound. 'Or rather the tickets were issued for July 7th, and the ceremony performed on July 15th, such being the usual proceeding of "il capo riconosciuto".'[77] The meal was, by all accounts, both memorable and hilarious. Gaudier, who could not afford a 10-shilling ticket, arrived with a *Fawn* carving which he placed on Pound's plate as an alternative form of payment. 'I was summoned to attend by telegram', wrote Goldring, 'but, to my lasting regret, my *guru* refused to allow me to go ... Those who attended the function still speak of it with emotion: it must have been a remarkable evening.'[78] And Pound helped to account for Goldring's sorrow when he remembered that 'the feast was a great success, every one talked a great deal ... Gaudier himself spent a good part of the meal in speculating upon the relation of planes nude of one of our guests, though this was kept to his own particular corner'.[79] Kate Lechmere, who as the financial backer of the periodical came as a guest of honour, recalled one very angry and perplexed guest 'getting up from the table in the middle of the meal and announcing that he had given up trying to read *Blast* in despair, and passed it over to his children in the hope that they would make more sense of it. So Lewis promptly tapped on the table and told the guest that "you have insulted Miss Lechmere, who paid for the magazine and is present here tonight with fifty copies piled up underneath her chair!" '[80]

The dinner must, above all, have been Lewis's finest hour: against all the odds, he found himself drinking the health of a movement he had only just allowed himself to think about, formulate and unleash on a hostile world. A month before, Pound pointed out in an *Egoist* article that 'Mr Lewis has been for a decade one of the most silent men in London';[81] and apart from relatively minor outbursts like the Omega rumpus and the Rebel Art Centre, it was true. But now Lewis was to break that silence in the most spectacular and irrevocable way, pitting the rebel forces not only against contemporary English art but also against the philistine and reactionary character of an entire nation. He heralded the broad nature of this attack, as well as the declamatory style of the *Blast* manifestos, in a tirade written for *The Outlook* in July, where he chanted:

'Well then! This is what it is time to do.
We must kill John Bull.
We must kill John Bull with art!
Russia, France, Germany, all have their national beast to slay. And each of these animals has its special vulnerability: there is something that is deadly to each. Art is what our fellow butts madly against, for he has a premonition he will end by that.
Russia's brute is only a Bear.
But ours is the *real Bull* – the *John Bull*!
I think we should kill him because he has triumphed too often, and it is up to us to do so. And no Bull can live for ever. It is time we had a new one.'[82]

The resolve was clear enough, and mirrored Lewis's determination to put into dramatic practice the advice he had recently given in a letter to his old sparring partner Augustus John. The only course of action to take against 'the Town of

London', Lewis had insisted, was to 'smite it hip and thigh! I should not be sorry if you made an end of it once and for all, artistically. Let it be an authentic earthquake!!! – a really prodigious and elemental disturbance'.[83] John, needless to say, had not acted on Lewis's heated exhortation, but he hardly needed to. For Vorticism was imminent, and *Blast* would do its best to ensure that the whole of London was shaken by its seismic impact.

## Chapter 10: Blast No. 1 and the Vorticist Aesthetic

> $\boxed{1}$
>
> **BLAST First** (from politeness) **ENGLAND**
>
> **CURSE ITS CLIMATE FOR ITS SINS AND INFECTIONS**
>
> **DISMAL SYMBOL, SET round our bodies,**
>
> **of effeminate lout within.**

So screamed the thick black capitals of *Blast No. 1*'s opening manifesto.[1] The *Review of the Great English Vortex* – or what Lewis himself more vividly dubbed 'this puce monster'[2] – had arrived, and it intended to make itself heard. Everything, from the brazen pink covers with the title in giant letters stamped diagonally across them like lightning, through to the freewheeling and exclamatory typography, was designed to launch a frontal assault on the sensibilities and prejudices of its readers. 'To make the rich of the community shed their education skin, to destroy politeness, standardization and academic, that is civilized, vision, is the task we have set ourselves', cried Lewis in his preliminary declaration called 'Long Live the Vortex!' And in order to make his insurrection punch its way home, he made sure that the magazine's prose was as uninhibited as it was insulting. Only by turning himself into the literary equivalent of an unscrupulous prize-fighter, pulling no punches, taking on all opponents, hitting below the belt where need be and pausing on occasions to tickle his adversary's ribs, could the editor of *Blast* produce the verbal acrobatics which served in themselves as a model of the energy Vorticism wanted to unleash.

'WE ONLY WANT THE WORLD TO LIVE, and to feel its crude energy flowing through us', Lewis shouted, exhilarated at the prospect of making his unholy dissatisfaction with every aspect of English culture sing out from the huge pages of the journal he had nursed for so many months. 'Blast sets out to be an avenue for all those vivid and violent ideas that could reach the Public in no other way', he averred, and made clear from the outset that his rumbustious brainchild aimed to be democratic in the widest sense of the word. 'It will not appeal to any particular class, but to the fundamental and popular instincts in every class and description of people, TO THE INDIVIDUAL', his editorial insisted. 'The moment a man feels or realizes himself as an artist, he ceases to belong to any milieu or time. Blast is created for this timeless, fundamental Artist that exists in everybody.' And Lewis, never for one moment forgetting that wit can be just as potent in propaganda as invective, refused to place a sane limit on his hopes for potential disciples. 'We will convert the King if possible', he declared. 'A VORTICIST KING! WHY NOT? DO YOU THINK LLOYD GEORGE HAS THE VORTEX IN HIM?'[3]

This intoxicating mixture of gravity and sheer high spirits set the tone for the whole of the rebels' astonishing periodical. Lewis summarized his ambivalent aims very neatly when he told Lord Carlow, in a letter enclosing a copy of *Blast No. 1*, that 'such things as *Blast* have to be undertaken for the artist to exist at all. When you have removed all that is *necessarily* strident, much sound

Cover of *Blast No. 1*, 1914

art-doctrine is to be found'.⁴ But so far as the first eighteen pages of the introductory manifesto were concerned, naughtiness prevailed over serious aesthetic debate. 'A 1000 MILE LONG, 2 KILOMETER Deep BODY OF WATER even, is pushed against us from the Floridas, TO MAKE US MILD', it announced, using a magnificently spurious form of geography to account for the lamentable lack of muscle in English life. 'CURSE the flabby sky that can manufacture no snow, but can only drop the sea on us in a drizzle like a poem by Mr Robert Bridges.' Enraged by what it saw as the 'VICTORIAN VAMPIRE, the LONDON cloud' that 'sucks the TOWN'S heart', the giant lettering called for the destruction of obsolete traditions bequeathed by nineteenth-century culture. 'BLAST years 1837 to 1900' it cried, spiralling off immediately into a satirical attack on nineties aestheticism – 'raptures and roses of the erotic bookshelves culminating in PURGATORY OF PUTNEY' – and rather less specifically at the 'RHETORIC of EUNUCH and STYLIST', the 'good-for-nothing Guineveres' and 'FRATERNIZING WITH MONKEYS'. Lewis was out to enjoy himself and indulge his flair for outrageous verbal salvos. He even went out of his way to jeer at the country that had produced Cubism, blasting France for its 'pig plagiarism, BELLY, SLIPPERS, POODLE TEMPER, BAD MUSIC' and SENTIMENTAL GALLIC GUSH'.⁵ The English had genuflected before the altar of French cultural domination for too long, and damning 'PARISIAN PAROCHIALISM' was one way of redressing the balance.

But the central target was England, and its indigenous follies were railed at again and again. 'BLAST HUMOUR', exclaimed the heading to one page, 'Quack ENGLISH drug for stupidity and sleepiness. Arch enemy of REAL, conventionalizing like gunshot, freezing supple REAL in ferocious chemistry of laughter.' Infuriated by a public which refused to treat rebel art with the attention it deserved, Lewis lashed out at those who jeered at abstraction rather than attempting to understand it. Not that he was under any illusion that these very pages would somehow elicit a more favourable response: 'CURSE those who will hang over this Manifesto with SILLY CANINES exposed' he stormed, throwing the ridicule of philistines back in their own faces. And then, after lamenting the 'impossibility for Englishman to be grave and keep his end up, psychologically', he suddenly trained his batteries on another great perennial English foible. 'BLAST SPORT', exploded the capitals, 'HUMOUR'S FIRST COUSIN AND ACCOMPLICE.' Perhaps the greatest venom of all, however, was reserved for the species of emasculated good taste that educated upper classes affected to possess. 'CURSE WITH EXPLETIVE OF WHIRLWIND THE BRITANNIC AESTHETE', Lewis roared, inveighing against a personalized amalgam of Bloomsbury, the Slade, the Academy, rich picture financiers and art connoisseurs. 'CREAM OF THE SNOBBISH EARTH' was how he denounced them in one of his most Baroque flights, 'ROSE OF SHARON OF GOD-PRIG OF SIMIAN VANITY SNEAK AND SWOT OF THE SCHOOL-ROOM.' And as a final parting shot, he sniped away successively at the 'AMATEUR', the 'SCIOLAST' [sic], the 'ART-PIMP', the 'JOURNALIST', the 'SELF MAN' (a rather ironical quality for Lewis to be blasting), and the 'NO-ORGAN MAN'.⁶

All the bitterness and frustration accumulated by years of antagonism from the public and hostility from the Press found its cathartic outlet in these outspoken preliminaries; and in an orgiastic climax, Lewis printed a whole page of names he considered worthy of blasting. In this extraordinary list of over fifty personalities, products and institutions, hatred mingled with mockery in the most irresistible manner. Codliver Oil was damned alongside the Lyceum

Club, Brangwyn insulted in the same breath as the 'Bishop of London and all his posterity', and Elgar dismissed along with the hair-raising conglomerate of 'Beecham (Pills, Opera, Thomas)'. Sidney Webb, the Post Office, Tagore, Galsworthy, Captain Cook, Bergson, Croce and Marie Corelli were all consigned to the ignominious rubbish-heap of *Blast No. 1*'s over-heated imagination, and there left to moulder with George Grossmith, the British Academy and the Countess of Warwick. This fatuous mêlée had, presumably, helped to propagate the malaise already outlined in the preceding manifesto, and they were as culpable as 'the lazy air that cannot stiffen the back of the SERPENTINE, or put Aquatic steel half way down the MANCHESTER CANAL'. They represented the 'CHAOS OF ENOCH ARDENS', who loved to 'crack their whips and tumble in Piccadilly Circus, as though London were a provincial town'. To Lewis, who wanted to make England's capital city a truly cosmopolitan centre which would mould the finest aspects of avant-garde world art into a national synthesis, the insularity of the British was a cardinal sin. 'WE WHISPER IN YOUR EAR A GREAT SECRET', he wrote in conspicuously loud type. 'LONDON IS NOT A PROVINCIAL TOWN. We will allow Wonder Zoos. But we do not want the GLOOMY VICTORIAN CIRCUS in Piccadilly Circus. IT IS PICCADILLY'S CIRCUS!' In other words, it ought to become the hub of the radical art movement which Lewis wanted to see sweeping through a country that 'is just as unkind and inimical to Art as the Arctic zone is to Life', a veritable 'Siberia of the mind'.[7]

At this point, having reached the height of destructive wit and fury, seven pages of benediction ensued – 'an example', as Lewis later cheekily explained, 'of English "fairness!" '[8] The nation which had just been battered with sarcasm and ridicule was now applauded, but still in the same quizzical vein. 'BLESS ENGLAND!' commanded the capitals, concentrating this time on the maritime virtues of the race. 'BIG BETS' were to be placed on 'ITS SHIPS, which switchback on Blue, Green and Red SEAS all around the PINK EARTH-BALL'. And a specifically artistic cause was celebrated when it came to blessing 'ALL SEAFARERS', for 'THEY exchange not one LAND for another, but one ELEMENT for ANOTHER. The MORE against the LESS ABSTRACT'. The sea positively encouraged artists to evolve a non-figurative style, and so 'the vast planetary abstraction of the OCEAN' was blessed unequivocally. Besides, the sea was capable of a fury and an energy singularly lacking in the land it surrounded. 'BLESS THE ARABS OF THE ATLANTIC', the manifesto insisted. 'THIS ISLAND MUST BE CONTRASTED WITH THE BLEAK WAVES.' The only places worthy of praise on the land itself were 'the great PORTS' – enumerated in a reverent roll-call stretching from Hull through Liverpool, London and Newcastle to Bristol and Glasgow – and they were likened to the 'RESTLESS MACHINES' which the rebels were beginning to incorporate in the vocabulary of their pictures. Indeed, the first full-page illustration in *Blast No. 1* reproduced Wadsworth's woodcut of *Newcastle*, an extremely abstract saw-toothed design which provided an appropriate pictorial equivalent for Lewis's theories. Apart from this celebration of nautical life, however, the other blessings were bestowed more or less frivolously. The 'HAIRDRESSER' was approved of, for instance, since 'he makes systematic mercenary war on this WILDNESS' and, like every true Vorticist, 'trims aimless and retrograde growths into CLEAN ARCHED SHAPES and ANGULAR PLOTS'. And, with unabashed inconsistency, 'ENGLISH HUMOUR' was blessed for being 'the great barbarous weapon of the genius among races', the 'wild MOUNTAIN RAILWAY from IDEA to IDEA, in the ancient Fair of LIFE'.[9]

Edward Wadsworth
*Newcastle*, 1913

It was absurd, of course, to laud the very things that had been castigated a moment before, but the whole style of this opening tract revelled in paradox and bloody-minded impudence. To 'BLESS the separating, ungregarious BRITISH GRIN' made nonsense of the previous assault on English humour; just as the blessing of France 'for its BUSHELS of VITALITY to the square inch' and its 'MASTERLY PORNOGRAPHY (great enemy of progress)'[10] flatly contradicted the earlier satire on Gallic shortcomings. Lewis wanted to madden his readers, teasing and bullying them by turn. He was determined to start the periodical off spectacularly, lace it with controversial firewater; and he did genuinely love the country he lambasted with such un-inhibited verve. England had potential: he was sure of that, and the amount of vitriol he poured into his attacks only reflected the measure of his hopes for a national Vorticist movement. When, therefore, he asked his readers to 'BLESS cold, magnanimous, delicate, gauche, fanciful, stupid ENGLISH-MEN', it was not simply a matter of displaying an undergraduate sense of fun. The contrasting group of adjectives also went some way towards expressing his own double-edged feelings about the country he had elected to transform. In this sense, the blasting/blessing format was an organised and constructive dialectic, purging the nation of its besetting maladies in order to isolate its positive qualities the more clearly.

The blessing section of the magazine terminated the frivolities and led on to the undoubtedly serious, even impassioned part of the crusade. But Lewis ensured, all the same, that it ended up on a note of hilarity with a list of well over seventy 'blessed' names which were, if possible, even more delirious than their 'blasted' counterparts. Now it was the Pope who found himself favoured with a mention, followed closely by Madame Strindberg, the Salvation Army, Charlotte Corday and the Commercial Process Company. The juxtapositions were delightfully insane: Castor Oil set beside James Joyce; Frank Harris rubbing shoulders with Lady Aberconway; and Kate Lechmere pushed up against Henry Newbolt.[11] All the names, from Cromwell to George Robey, had obviously been chosen with the utmost glee, and the spirit of fun is as alive now when the list is examined as it undoubtedly was in the summer of 1914.

It comes as no surprise, then, to learn that the composition of these contrasting lists – which may have been partially inspired by Blake's fifty-seventh proverb of Hell, 'Damn braces. Bless relaxes' – was conducted in a mood of holiday levity. 'The inaugural tea-party that preceded publication, at which editorial policy was laid down and a list of the people to be blasted and blessed drawn up, was held in Lewis's studio in Fitzroy Street, and presided over by Lewis and Ezra', recalled Douglas Goldring. 'The "blasted" names, apparently, consisted very largely of "eminent" figures whose publicity was considered boringly excessive, and the "blessed" were often the particular favourites of Ford and Violet Hunt.' Kate Lechmere was a rare exception: Lewis had 'wanted me to do a drawing for Blast but at the time the atmosphere was so difficult that I was not able to do so; but as a compensation I was put in the "bless" column!' On the whole, Goldring thought, the tea-party 'was a solemn occasion, except, I suspected, for the two prophets – who, when unobserved by the disciples, occasionally exchanged knowing grins – and for myself, who had frequently to suppress irreverent giggles'.[12] The active presence of Pound and Ford guaran-teed that Blast No. 1 would be – for all its purely pictorial ambitions – heavily biased towards literature as well. Ford himself contributed the first part of a little tale called 'The Saddest Story', the opening chapters of his best novel *The Good Soldier*, which the author accurately described as a 'bird . . . no louder than a thrush in the pages of Blast'[13]; the precocious Rebecca West, who was invited to participate 'because Lewis had met me at South Lodge and liked some things of mine in *The New Freewoman*',[14] wrote a melodramatic short story entitled 'Indissoluble Matrimony'; and Pound himself displayed a heterogeneous selection of twelve poems, one of which almost prevented the publication of the whole magazine. The American had never been afraid of incorporating frankly erotic imagery in his work: in the March 1914 issue of *Poetry and Drama* he had published a poem called 'Coitus' that started:

The gilded phaloi of the crocuses are thrusting at the spring air.

But that was mild compared to his final offering in *Blast*, 'Fratres Minores', which satirized the woolly approach to love favoured by latter-day Romantic poets:

With minds still hovering above their testicles
Certain poets here and in France
Still sigh over established and natural fact
Long since fully discussed by Ovid.
They howl. They complain in delicate and exhausted metres
That the twitching of three abdominal nerves
Is incapable of producing a lasting Nirvana.[15]

Lewis was probably delighted to be able to include such a scurrilous morsel in his periodical: Pound later wrote to the 'Old Vort' asking him whether 'you remember yr/first cheery invitation, to provide you with "something nasty for Blast"'; and the poem did accord well with the subversive intentions of the entire venture. But when Lewis discovered that his friend's admirably clear-eyed poem might cause *Blast No. 1* to be banned by the censor, he had to make sure that the first and final two lines of 'Fratres Minores' were blocked out of each separate copy. 'Happily the black bars laid across them . . . were transparent', Lewis recalled. 'This helped the sales.'[16] And yet it can hardly have helped the 'young maidens' who were employed to carry out this painstaking, not to say delicate task. Whether Pound's cancelled lines were actually approved of by the maidens themselves is unrecorded; but if Jessie Dismorr and Helen Saunders were among them, it seems unlikely. Kate Lechmere, who by this time was thoroughly enjoying herself as Hulme's mistress, remembered the two female Vorticists as 'terribly proper women who both came up to me at the *Blast* tea-party when my name was added to the "Bless" list and said, very huffily, that "some people *need* blessing"'.[17]

The rest of the issue, apart from the 'Vortex' articles of faith by Pound and Gaudier and Wadsworth's Kandinsky translations, was written entirely by the indefatigable Lewis. He must have regarded it as the ideal opportunity to display his literary as well as his artistic talents. Not only did he compose the lengthy introductory manifestos and a substantial collection of theoretical essays; he also published an ambitious thirty-six page piece of fiction called 'The Enemy of the Stars', a hybrid cross between a play and a story which was as stylistically experimental as the paintings and drawings he chose to reproduce in the magazine. 'You are I am sure right in thinking that Lewis *was* to all intents and purposes *Blast*', Helen Saunders admitted later, 'and carried the rest of the team with him, some from conviction and some no doubt for their own purposes of advertisement.'[18] The self-styled Vorticist leader was determined to make an impact, and knew full well that it was up to him to establish his cherished movement straightaway as a force to be reckoned with. Marinetti and Nevinson, who doubtless realized that the publication of *Blast No. 1* was imminent when they brought out their Futurist Manifesto, had quite deliberately tried to take the wind out of Lewis's propagandist sails; and it was doubly vital that their attempt to effect a rival coup should be quashed once and for all. Indeed, Goldring recounted that Nevinson actually 'turned up' to the *Blast* tea-party 'to observe, and had a fierce argument with Lewis before he finally swept out in disgust'.[19] The incident rings true, for Nevinson's hostility was probably tinged with chagrin. Even if he would never admit it himself, he must have instinctively recognized that the ill-judged Futurist broadside had already petered out into a disregarded whimper, and that the immense superiority of *Blast No. 1*'s contents would soon ensure that his tactless publicity stunt was entirely forgotten.

The most cursory glance at the Vorticists' second 'Manifesto' would have told him that Lewis had succeeded in expounding the rebel cause with a far more compelling amount of panache and conviction than he had managed to produce even with the aid of a seasoned campaigner like Marinetti. Divided up into seven curt sections, this half of *Blast No. 1*'s introductory credo eschewed mere derision in order to concentrate on positive beliefs, set out this time in a series of hard-hitting single sentences. The tone was ruthlessly aggressive, establishing the new-born Vorticists as a breed of warriors who would stop at nothing to achieve their aims. 'We are Primitive Mercenaries in the Modern World', declared the first section, which went on to announce its willingness to 'fight first on one side, then on the other' if such a strategy would 'stir up Civil War among peaceful apes'. For Lewis saw himself as the leader of a band of shock troops, and insisted that he had no time for anything that diverted art from the path of true militancy. 'We only want Humour if it has fought like Tragedy', he cried, clarifying the paradoxical theme of the 'blasts' and 'blesses' into a bloodthirsty religion. And, conversely, he stressed that 'we only want Tragedy if it can clench its side-muscles like hands on its belly, and bring to the surface a laugh like a bomb'.[20] This was his ideal pictorial language: one that relieved English art of its tiresome anachronisms by shattering them with the force of a semi-abstract explosion. For the past two years at least he had been drawing or painting the kind of figures and shapes best equipped to effect such a revolution, and now he was bolstering the bleakness of those pictures with a prose no less iconoclastic in its implications.

But this destructive impulse was also fortified with optimism, as succeeding pages of the manifesto proved. 'We hear from America and the Continent all sorts of disagreeable things about England: "the unmusical, anti-artistic, un-philosophic country"', lamented the second section, adding sternly that 'we quite agree'. The entire nation was horrifyingly decadent and ingrown, rotting away through an excess of 'luxury, sport, the famous English "Humour", the thrilling ascendancy and idée fixe of Class, producing the most intense snobbery in the World; heavy stagnant pools of Saxon blood, incapable of anything but the song of a frog, in home-counties'. Yet precisely because the cancer was so malignant, Lewis was filled with the hope that his reforms would be correspondingly fruitful: a 'movement towards art and imagination could burst up here, from this lump of compressed life, with more force than anywhere else'. And there would be nothing feeble about the revolt, either. Lewis refused to castrate his programme with even a hint of an Omega-like desire to enhance the beauty of everyday surroundings. 'To believe that it is necessary for or conducive to art, to "improve" life, for instance – make architecture, dress, ornament, in "better taste", is absurd', he stormed, scotching the idea of the artist as a cultural missionary who bestows the products of his superior sensibility upon a visually uneducated public. 'The Art-instinct is permanently primitive', he repeated, celebrating an impulse as utterly divorced from Bloomsbury aesthetics as it was from the ' "advanced", perfected, democratic, Futurist individual of

Mr Marinetti's limited imagination'. The truly inspired 'artist of the modern movement' had to be 'a savage', and Lewis emphasized that 'this enormous, jangling, journalistic, fairy desert of modern life serves him as Nature did more technically primitive man'.[21]

There was little difference between this theory of the artist's relationship with the world and Pound's idea about the 'heirs of the witch-doctor and the voodoo', Gaudier's 'sympathy and admiration' for the 'barbaric peoples of the earth', or Hulme's exaltation of the man willing to exorcize art of the 'sloppy dregs of the Renaissance'. And Lewis justified this concept by thinking of English art as essentially Gothic in character: 'we assert that the art for these climates, then, must be a northern flower', as true to its origins as was Shakespeare when he 'reflected in his imagination a mysticism, madness and delicacy peculiar to the North'. This, he felt, was the real meaning of national pride, even though he dissociated himself from Nevinson's manifesto by hastily avowing 'that there is nothing Chauvinistic or picturesquely patriotic about our contentions'.[22] Lewis's hopes for England centred on his belief that 'any great Northern Art will partake of this insidious and volcanic chaos' – a far cry indeed from the qualities admired by the jingoistic flag-wavers of the Royal Academy.

*Blast No. 1* wanted to escape once and for all from the image of England perpetrated by Burlington House and the New English Art Club. The art fostered by such reactionary institutions avoided the challenge of coming to terms with the mechanized environment which England had done so much to create. 'Our industries, and the Will that determined, face to face with its needs, the direction of the modern world', wrote Lewis, 'has reared up steel trees where the green ones were lacking; has exploded in useful growths, and found wilder intricacies than those of Nature.'[23] Confronted with the excitement of this great phenomenon, it was obviously the artist's duty to incorporate it in his work, draw inspiration from its visual splendour and bring British art face to face with the realities of twentieth-century life. Instead of hiding their heads in the sands of the Victorian tradition, English painters and sculptors had to become aesthetic guerillas, and harness the wild strength of a mechanical civilization to express the genuine spirit of their own country. How could anyone concentrate on studying the flesh tones of a nude on a bed in Mornington Crescent's decaying gentility when such an invigorating task lay waiting to be tackled?

Marinetti had, of course, been the first to preach the importance of the machine-world, and many readers of *Blast No. 1* scornfully dismissed its doctrines as a secondhand attempt to serve up Futurist recipes in a spicier dressing. But by doing so, they were only demonstrating that they had not read the manifestos closely enough; for Lewis was supremely adamant in his determination to produce an independent alternative to the European avant-garde. 'Just as we believe that an Art must be organic with its Time', he explained, 'so we insist that what is actual and vital for the South, is ineffectual and unactual in the North.' Convinced that all his fellow rebels shared a 'violent boredom with that feeble Europeanism, abasement of the miserable "intellectual" before anything coming from Paris, Cosmopolitan sentimentality, which prevails in so many quarters', he pointed out that 'the Modern World is due almost entirely to Anglo-Saxon genius, – its appearance and its spirit'. Why, therefore, if 'machinery, trains, steam-ships, all that distinguishes externally our time, came far more from here than anywhere else', could not the English produce an art that interpreted contemporary life with as much pioneering originality as it put into constructing the external fabric of that life? 'In dress, manners, mechanical inventions, LIFE, that is, ENGLAND, has influenced Europe in the same way that France has in Art', cried Lewis, and he saw no reason why England

Abstract design from *Blast No. 1*, 1914

should not now take over the Gallic role as well. Simply because the British had been so 'busy with this L I F E-E F F O R T' that they were 'the last to become conscious of the Art that is an organism of this new Order and Will of Man', it did not automatically follow that they would never be capable of creating an artistic movement to match the prowess of their scientists and practical visionaries.[24] 'Once this consciousness towards the new possibilities of expression in present life has come, however', the manifesto continued, 'it will be more the legitimate property of Englishmen than of any other people in Europe.'

The form taken by this vital new national art would directly oppose the absurdly hysterical enthusiasm for the industrial world displayed by Marinetti and his cohorts. 'The Latins are at present, for instance, in their "discovery" of sport, their Futuristic gush over machines, aeroplanes, etc., the most romantic and sentimental "moderns" to be found', announced Lewis, ridiculing the Italians' childlike worship of twentieth-century inventions. The English, he insisted, would be far cooler and more objective about the dynamics of modern civilization; 'for, in the forms of machinery, Factories, new and vaster buildings, bridges and works, we have all that, naturally, around us.' This world was the English people's birthright, and, 'as it is by origin theirs', so it should 'inspire them more forcibly and directly', replacing emotional Futurist flabbiness with cerebral Vorticist sinew. 'They are the inventors of this bareness and hardness', explained Lewis, 'and should be the great enemies of Romance.'[25]

This, then, was the slice of pictorial territory Lewis saw the rebels exploring: an area of synthesis, essentially, that would temper Futurist melodramatics with Cubist sobriety, Italian movement with French monumentality. Despising Futurism for its unconditional love of machinery, and Cubism for avoiding the theme altogether in favour of the old studio repertoire of portraits and still life, he aimed for a half-way house situated neatly between the two, tapping the strengths of both and leaving their weaknesses severely alone. How far he was justified in speaking of his allies' art as well as his own in this categorical fashion will always remain a matter for dispute. But the inescapable fact remains that a good number of the illustrations in *Blast No. 1* – including Wadsworth's *March* and *Radiation*, Roberts' *Religion* and *Dancers*, a Flenite *Drawing* by Epstein and Hamilton's *Group* – back up his theoretical assertions in a most striking way. Looking at their contributions, it is hard to imagine any of these artists reasonably objecting to Lewis's militant statement of intent, or to the resolutely abstract designs which he reproduced in the magazine to reinforce the exclamatory impact of the typography.

There was a full-page list of 'Signatures for Manifesto' at the end of his tracts, too, naming in alphabetical order Aldington, Arbuthnot, Atkinson, Brzeska, Dismorr, Hamilton, Pound, Roberts, Saunders, Wadsworth and Wyndham Lewis himself.[26] But this roll-call of eleven should not be treated as a definitive proof of loyalty to the cause. Few of the signatories, for one thing, donated their names with any great seriousness or profound contemplation of Lewis's written testament. Of those who did actually sign in person, and had some inkling of *Blast No. 1*'s contents, only Wadsworth, Pound, Gaudier and the two women can have approached the task with complete responsibility. Aldington probably summed up the attitude of the others by recording, in the same year, that 'Mr Lewis has carefully and wittily compiled a series of manifestos, to which we have all gleefully applied our names'.[27] To him, *Blast No. 1* was nothing more nor less than a lively firework which he heartily approved of, in a non-partisan way, as a bracing tonic for English culture. He would no more have thought of himself as a committed Vorticist than Arbuthnot, Atkinson or Hamilton, all of whom probably agreed to add their signatures at a light-hearted meeting like

Abstract design from *Blast No. 1*, 1914

the tea-party in Lewis's studio where the 'blasts' and 'blesses' were first compiled. And as for Roberts, he later recalled in an understandably acid memoir that 'if anyone were to imagine we signed this Manifesto, pen in hand, in solemn assembly, they would be making a big mistake. I, in fact, personally signed nothing. The first knowledge I had of a Vorticist Manifesto's existence was when Lewis, one fine Sunday morning in the summer of 1914, knocked at my door and placed in my hands this chubby, rosy, problem-child Blast'.[28]

Even if Roberts had previously given some vague verbal assent to the idea of signing a magazine devoted only to a general discussion of radical English art, Lewis had still treated him in a very cavalier manner. Presumably he must at some stage have agreed to the reproduction of his pictures, *Religion* and *Dancers*; but he obviously did not imagine that Lewis had made him into a fully-fledged Vorticist without his consent. Etchells, by contrast, who is the strangest and most conspicuous absentee from the list, did realize the full significance of a signature in *Blast No. 1*. Although he displayed no less than four drawings in the periodical, he afterwards explained that 'I got out of signing the manifesto because I was very cagey about the whole idea. I remember the terrific discussions we used to have: Lewis would talk and talk, and Wadsworth's wife used to say she could see me shrinking away from it all. I was never a willing captive for Lewis, despite our strong friendship, because I always thought Vorticism was a manufactured, faked movement'.[29]

Etchells, like Roberts, wanted to retain his independence and stay resolutely outside the politics of the avant-garde. Neither of them actively disagreed with Lewis – it is possible, indeed, to see Lewis's influence in both men's work – but they remained suspicious of his desire to rally them under his own egotistical banner. Lewis was in many ways a dynamic and inspiring example to his friends in their search for new art forms, but he was also maddeningly insensitive when it came to asserting his sole dominance. Something of the irritation he must have caused is vividly conveyed in a passage from his autobiography, where he recalled how 'I assumed too that artists always formed militant groups. I supposed they had to do this, seeing how "bourgeois" all Publics were – or all Publics of which I had any experience. And I concluded that as a matter of course some romantic figure must always emerge, to captain the "group". Like myself! How otherwise could a "group" get about, and above all *talk*. For it had to have a mouthpiece didn't it? I was so little of a communist that it never occurred to me that left to itself a group might express itself *in chorus*. The "leadership" principle, you will observe, was in my bones'.[30]

If such arrogance was distasteful to Roberts and Etchells, it was positively unbearable to a rampant individualist like Bomberg. He refused to countenance any suggestion of being included in the periodical, even in the spring of 1914 when Vorticism had not yet been properly formulated. Bomberg's widow remembered 'David once telling me that Lewis wanted to take some photographs of his pictures at the first London Group show, and reproduce them in *Blast*; but David was adamant. He not only told Lewis that he did not want any of his work published in *Blast* – he also threatened to sue Lewis if anything did appear in the magazine'.[31] Lewis was obviously regarded as totally untrustworthy by Bomberg, who always resisted any attempt to pin a stylistic label onto his art. He was his own man and belonged to nobody else, despite the fact that none of his 1914 work would have looked at all out of place in *Blast No. 1*. Many of the arguments outlined in Lewis's manifesto could be applied without any sense of incongruity to an aggressive painting like *The Mud Bath*; but Bomberg was determined to stand alone, as free from Vorticism as he was from the Omega, Sickert or Marinetti.

His standpoint was wholeheartedly endorsed by Hulme, whose personal rift

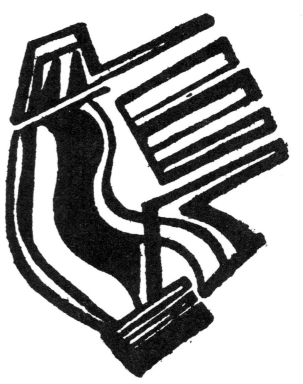

Abstract design from *Blast No. 1*, 1914

with Lewis made the presence of his signature an impossibility from the beginning. Ideally, the philosopher ought to have commemorated his earlier involvement in the movement by publishing in *Blast* the essay on Epstein which he had once intended to write for the magazine. At one stage, he expected to do so;[32] but now he even went so far as to publicly approve of the abstaining postscript Bomberg had appended to the rebels' letter repudiating Nevinson's Manifesto. 'I noticed that in signing a collective protest, published a few weeks ago, [Bomberg] added in a footnote that he had nothing whatever to do with the Rebel Art Centre', Hulme wrote in his July review of the Chenil one-man show, pointing out that he thought Bomberg had acted 'very wisely, in my opinion, for his work is certainly much more individual and less derivative than the work of the other members of that group.'[33] The remark was above all a calculated snub to Lewis's pride; and Hulme was by this time no better disposed towards Pound, either. 'Someone once asked him how long he would tolerate Ezra Pound', recalled Epstein, 'and Hulme thought for a moment and then said that he knew exactly when he would have to kick him downstairs.'[34] In view of the philosopher's feelings, it is hardly surprising that Epstein himself, always Hulme's great hero, likewise left his name out of the *Blast No. 1* list. He had allowed two drawings to be reproduced, and that – to the pugnacious sculptor who spent so much of his time in self-imposed isolation at Pett Level, anyway – was as far as he was willing to involve himself in Lewis's devious machinations.

It is against this turbulent background of internal dissent and petty rivalries that *Blast No. 1*'s claim to be seen as the representative document of a new group's ideas must be viewed. Vorticism was never, even at its inception, a closely-knit movement like Futurism. When the Italians put their names at the bottom of their own manifestos, they did so as the active contributors to an aesthetic they had all helped to formulate; but no such collective endeavour lay behind the launching of the 'Great English Vortex'. Just as Picasso and Braque left it to Gleizes and Metzinger to lay down their interpretation of Cubist principles and always abstained from dogmatic pronouncements about the movement themselves, so most of the English rebels shied away from Lewis's attempts to tie them down to a fixed, theoretical point of view. But it must not, on the other hand, be therefore assumed that a group ambience did not really exist among the English rebels. They had fought against common enemies, exhibited together several times, met each other frequently, discussed their ideas together, and contributed examples of their work to a magazine. If some of them resisted the idea of becoming Vorticists, their work nevertheless makes excellent sense when it is viewed as the product of the first English abstract art movement. And a surprisingly large number of the paintings, drawings and sculptures they were to execute during the course of 1914 and 1915 can usefully be examined from the albeit distorted vantage-point of Lewis's writings. For all his political trickery, he did succeed in defining a number of tenets which can be applied to the work of the rebels without fear of misinterpreting the true situation. At heart, they were all striving for an art sufficiently divorced from the aims of Futurism and Cubism to be considered as a national style in its own right. And the fact remains that many of Lewis's pronouncements in *Blast No. 1* were an accurate reflection of the way they thought, argued and worked in London at this vital moment in the history of English art.

None of them could reasonably complain, anyway, that the magazine abused his intentions by presenting him as the practitioner of one rigidly defined style. There was scarcely any specific theorizing about Vorticism: for Lewis, having laid down the broad direction that rebel art should take in his admirably succinct prefatory manifestos, was at this formative stage more concerned to attack

Futurism than elaborate on exactly how he thought a Vorticist should paint or sculpt. In his twenty-one page dissertation on contemporary aesthetics, 'Vorteces and Notes', the recurrent theme focuses on a sustained hostility to Marinetti and all his doctrines. Perhaps Lewis was conscious of the debt he owed to Futurist principles, and wanted to lay the ghost for ever by making his disagreement plain. He must have known that the Italians would realize, as soon as they picked up a copy of *Blast No. 1*, that its very format was inspired not only by the *parole in libertà* exemplified in Marinetti's book *Zang Tumb Tuuum*, but also by Apollinaire's manifesto, *Futurist Anti-Tradition*, which had been published by *Lacerba* on 15 September 1913. The similarities were too striking to ignore: Apollinaire likewise used giant capital letters to announce 'DISTRUZIONE' and then counterbalanced it in the same type with 'COSTRUZIONE'; he devised a dynamic layout that set the sentences down on the page with a startling lack of regard for conventional rules of presentation; and most of all he grouped the list of names he hated and loved under the headings 'MERDA' and 'ROSE' respectively. Set a copy of *L'Antitradizione Futurista* down alongside two comparable pages from *Blast No. 1*'s manifesto, and the connections are immediately apparent. Lewis would have come across this document at precisely the time when he first began to toy with the idea of a magazine, and Apollinaire's impatience with traditional forms of printed presentation clearly came as an inspiration to him.

*Blast No. 1* takes Apollinaire's example much further, of course – Lissitsky, one of the creators of modern typography, freely acknowledged a debt to the

Filippo Marinetti
Cover for *Zang Tumb Tuuum*, 1914

Guillaume Apollinaire
*Futurist Anti-Tradition Manifesto*, 1913

Vorticist journal – but Lewis would have felt happier if he had created it all by himself without the initial aid of *Lacerba*. 'As Blast was designed to be totally unlike any previous publication in its typography and lay-out', wrote Goldring, who was clearly unaware of Apollinaire's precedent, '[Lewis] required a printer humble enough blindly to carry out his instructions.' Lewis the editor was no different from Lewis the would-be group leader: he had to exert the strictest possible control over every facet of the magazine's production, and made his leading role in the creation of its typographical style absolutely clear by printing his *Blast*-like preface to the catalogue of *Exhibition, Leeds* in May 1914 in a format which directly anticipates the greater excess of the Vorticists' journal.[35] This forerunner of *Blast No. 1* proves how much of a product of Lewis's own imperious initiative the July manifestos really were, and Goldring acted with great understanding when he decided that the firm of Leveridge and Co. should print *Blast* itself. 'After making enquiries', he recalled, 'I found him a small jobbing printer in the outlying suburb of Harlesden who seems to have done what he was told to do.'[36] Leveridge obeyed Lewis's exacting instructions faithfully enough, and succeeded in printing a magazine which shouts out the rebel manifesto like a loud-hailer, isolating each expletive so that its typographical format curses at the reader, and dividing up the pages into the abstract blocks, lines and dissonant fragments of a Vorticist picture. It is no accident that as many as eleven professional fighters and music-hall entertainers were blessed in *Blast No. 1*: the manifestos combine the aggression of the boxing-ring with the raucous aplomb of a music-hall song, and the result is identifiably English in its sturdy, almost Hogarthian vigour. The very size of the periodical, its weight and its peculiarly thick, coarse paper all possess a four-square pugnacity, which links

△ Wyndham Lewis: Preface to the catalogue of *Exhibition, Leeds*, 1914

up with the bulldog attack of the typography to create something significantly different from either Apollinaire's manifesto or Marinetti's more feverish precedents.

But Lewis still wanted to make his divorce from Futurism absolutely final by reminding his readers of it time and again through a hundred insulting references. 'The Futurist statue will move: then it will live a little', he jeered in his 'Vorteces and Notes'; 'but any idiot can do better than that with his good wife, round the corner.' He was intent on satirizing what he saw as Futurism's foolish attempt to ape the banal aspects of reality, and repeatedly hit out at the state of mind behind such a philosophy. 'Everywhere', he complained, 'LIFE is said instead of ART', and went on to stress the paramount importance of the artist's own creative imagination. 'There is only one thing better than "Life" – than using your eyes, nose, ears and muscles – and that is something very abstruse and splendid, in no way directly dependent on "Life"', he wrote. 'It is no EQUIV-ALENT for Life, but ANOTHER Life, as NECESSARY to existence as the former. This NECESSITY is what the indolent and vulgar journalist mind chiefly denies it. All the accusations of "mere intelligence" or "cold intellectuality" centre round misconception of this fact.'[37]

Possessed by the idea of art as something which refined experience, Lewis shrank away from the Futurists' romantic abandon in front of modern life. 'With their careful choice of motor omnibuses, cars, lifes, aeroplanes, etc., the Automobilist pictures were too "picturesque", melodramatic and spectacular', he explained, 'besides being undigested and naturalistic to a fault.' For Lewis, such an attitude denied the whole raison d'être of art: to impose an ordered structure onto the messiness and confusion of reality, and to rely more on the

Wyndham Lewis (ed.)
Manifesto from *Blast No. 1*, 1914, pages 18 and 19; 22 and 23

**BLESS ENGLAND!**

**BLESS ENGLAND**

FOR ITS SHIPS

which switchback on Blue, Green and Red SEAS all around the PINK EARTH-BALL,

BIG BETS ON EACH.

**BLESS ALL SEAFARERS.**

THEY exchange not one LAND for another, but one ELEMENT for ANOTHER. The MORE against the LESS ABSTRACT.

———

**BLESS** the vast planetary abstraction of the **OCEAN.**

———

**BLESS** THE ARABS OF THE **ATLANTIC.**

THIS ISLAND MUST BE CONTRASTED WITH THE BLEAK WAVES.

22

**BLESS ALL PORTS.**

PORTS, RESTLESS MACHINES of | scooped out basins
heavy insect dredgers
monotonous cranes
stations
lighthouses, blazing through the frosty starlight, cutting the storm like a cake
beaks of infant boats, side by side,
heavy chaos of wharves,
steep walls of factories
womanly town

BLESS these MACHINES that work the little boats across clean liquid space, in beelines.

**BLESS** the great **PORTS** | HULL
LIVERPOOL
LONDON
NEWCASTLE-ON-TYNE
BRISTOL
GLASGOW

**BLESS ENGLAND,**

industrial island machine, pyramidal

23

shaping power of your own creativity than on an impulse provided by life itself. Instead of interpreting reality, and reorganizing it into a formal language with its own self-sufficient terms of reference, the Futurists plunged into an unthinking, vulgar celebration of the visible world around them. 'AUTOMOBILISM (Marinetteism) bores us', Lewis declared impatiently. 'We don't want to go about making a hullo-bulloo about motor cars, anymore than about knives and forks, elephants or gas-pipes.' The Futurists succeeded merely in stating the obvious facts about life rather than finding a proper equivalent for it, and their paintings had the childishness of a kindergarten primer: 'Elephants are VERY BIG. Motor cars go quickly.' Only by escaping from this fatuous desire to cling to external reality – a desire that moved Lewis to label the Italian movement as 'largely Impressionism up-to-date' – could the Futurists ever hope to produce worthwhile work. 'If, divested of this element of illustration, H. G. Wells romance, and pedantic naturalism, Marinetti's movement could produce profounder visions with this faith of novelty', he declared, 'something fine might be done.' But as it was, only Severini's 'feeling for pattern, and certain clearness and restraint' and Balla's 'purely abstract' paintings were worthy of the slightest attention. They at least tried to escape from representational clichés; whereas their companions sank lower and lower into the slough of unadulterated life. 'Cannot Marinetti, sensible and energetic man that he is, be induced to throw over this sentimental rubbish about Automobiles and Aeroplanes, and follow his friend Balla into a purer region of art?' asked Lewis. 'Unless he wants to become a rapidly fossilizing monument of puerility, cheap reaction and sensationalism, he had better do so.'[38]

Nothing could have been more bitingly expressed than *Blast No. 1*'s disdain for Futurism. And, conversely, nothing could have been so subtly proclaimed as Lewis's attitude towards total abstraction. His complaints about the Futurists' appetite for life suggested that he himself wanted to retreat completely into a non-figurative world of the artist's own making. But this was not the case, as Lewis's illustrations in *Blast No. 1* – varying from the abstraction of *Slow Attack* to the figurative connotations of *Enemy of the Stars* – proved in themselves. He was content to remain flexible on this most delicate of issues, and thereby feel free to swing from representational content over to non-figuration at will. 'It is all a matter of the most delicate adjustment between voracity of Art and digestive quality of Life', he declared in his 'Vorteces and Notes'. For in one mood he was ready to assert that 'at any period an artist should have been able to remain in his studio, imagining form, and provided he could transmit the substance and logic of his inventions to another man, could have, without putting brush to canvas, be the best artist of his day'. And in another, less dogmatic frame of mind he warned of the dangers of total abstraction, emphasizing that 'to dream is the same thing as to lie: anybody but an invalid or a canaille feels the discomfort and repugnance of something not clean in it'. But ultimately, it was a question of striking the right balance, and recognizing that 'reality is in the artist, the image only in life, and he should only approach so near as is necessary for a good view'. This was the basis of his working philosophy, and he summed it up concisely when he wrote that 'the finest Art is not pure Abstraction, nor is it unorganised life'.[39]

Lewis was consciously leaving both himself and his fellow rebels room to manoeuvre: they could include representation if they so wished, but only if the underlying discipline of abstract form was retained as well. And he articulated his personal feelings about the nature of creative inspiration best of all when, in an essay on 'Fêng Shui and Contemporary Form', he discussed the value of geomancy. 'I do not suppose that good Geomancers are more frequent than good artists', he admitted. 'But their functions and intellectual equipment should by very alike.' In order to demonstrate precisely how he meant the parallel to be taken, he described the way in which he fed his visual imagination. 'Sensitiveness to volume, to the life and passion of lines, meaning of water, hurried conversation of the sky, or silence, impossible propinquity of endless clay nothing will right, a mountain that is a genius (good or evil) or a bore, makes the artist', he wrote in an eloquent passage; and then listed the kind of phenomena – half of them abstract, the other half drawn directly from reality – which fired him in his art. 'A certain position of the eyes, their fires crossing; black (as a sort of red) as sinister; white the mourning colour of China; white flowers, in the West, signifying death – white, the radium among colours, and the colour that comes from farthest off: 13, a terrible number: such are much more important discoveries than gravitation.'[40] This mysterious sentence chants the sources of Lewis's excitement with the same compound of emotional intensity and intellectual energy that he injected into his pictorial work. It is the ideal verbal counterpart to the near-abstract drawings and paintings he executed during 1914 and the following year.

'Vorteces and Notes' makes plain Lewis's conviction that only English rebel art was capable of evolving a lasting synthesis out of all the pictorial experiments conducted on the continent. And this searchingly critical attitude towards the European avant-garde signified the death of England's artistic provincialism. Critics like Bell and Fry had, of course, already promoted an awareness of international radicalism; but until Lewis let fly in *Blast*, the English had never been supplied with a national alternative which sought to improve on the latest developments from abroad. Lewis presumed to tell his readers exactly where he thought the European movements had erred, and thereby hauled his country out of its crippling insularity. He did not manage to compile a comprehensive critique of European radicalism until 1915, when he published his ambitious 'Review of Contemporary Art' in *Blast No. 2*. But *Blast No. 1* did take a few side-swipes at movements other than Futurism. Expressionism, for instance, was censured by implication: in an appreciative 'Note' written originally for an exhibition catalogue of *Modern German Art* at the Twenty-One Gallery in the spring of 1914, Lewis succeeded in belittling the movement by limiting its achievement to one minor medium. 'At this miniature sculpture, the Woodcut', he wrote, 'Germans have always excelled.' And when he mentioned Kandinsky in an essay on 'Orchestra of Media', it was only as a useful comparison with the 'pleasantly Chinese' Matisse. 'Kandinsky at his best is much more original and bitter', he declared; but swiftly added that 'there are fields of discord untouched', and announced the Vorticists' intention to explore this particular area: 'the possibilities of colour, exploitation of discords, odious combinations, etc., have been little exploited'.[41]

Cubism, on the other hand, was dealt with at length, but only with reference to the 'small structures in cardboard, wood, zinc, glass, string, etc.', which Picasso had 'last shown as his'. Despite their undoubted use of semi-abstraction, these Synthetic Cubist sculptures were castigated for attempting to emulate the appearance of life. Just as the Futurists had erred in that direction, so 'these little models of Picasso's reproduce the surface and texture of objects. So directly so, that, should a portion of human form occur, he would hardly be content until he could include in his work a plot of human flesh'. And Picasso, unlike the Futurists, did not even tackle the best subject-matter, concentrating exclusively on the stuffy 'NATURES-MORTES' of the Old Masters. 'He no longer so much interprets, as definitely MAKES, nature', Lewis cavilled, '(and "DEAD" nature at that).'[42]

The implication was that Vorticism stood alone in its ambition to extract the formal essence from the panorama of the modern world and put it down on paper, canvas, stone or bronze with the maximum amount of aggressive punch. The task was urgent and profoundly invigorating: there was no time to be wasted destroying history, as the Futurists so obsessively demanded. 'Our vortex is not afraid of the Past', cried Lewis in his final 'Vorteces and Notes' essay; 'it has forgotten its existence.' And, similarly, he insisted that 'the Future is distant, like the Past, and therefore sentimental'. For in order to 'produce a New Living Abstraction', Lewis declared that 'we wish the Past and Future with us, the Past to mop up our melancholy, the Future to absorb our troublesome optimism'. The crux of the matter lay in the simple fact that 'with our Vortex the Present is the only active thing. Life is the Past and the Future. The Present is Art'. It was vital that Life and Art be considered apart, as entirely separate entities. 'Our Vortex insists on water-tight compartments', wrote Lewis, explaining that 'we must have the Past and the Future, Life simple, that is, to discharge ourselves in, and keep us pure for non-life, that is Art.'[43]

This idea of reducing chaotic life to the death-like stillness of artistic, or real, life recalls the theories of Hulme's mentor, Worringer, who believed that the true significance of abstraction lay in its absence of life. Primitive art, being a product of the will as opposed to the senses, was therefore a precedent for the classical objectivity of Vorticism. And yet Lewis was anxious to make sure, in the impassioned closing sentences of 'Vorteces and Notes', that this quality of cold detachment was not interpreted by his enemies as in any way pacific. 'As to the lean belated Impressionism at present attempting to eke out a little life in these islands', he shouted:

> Our Vortex is fed up with your dispersals, reasonable chicken-men.
> Our Vortex is proud of its polished sides.
> Our Vortex will not hear of anything but its disastrous polished dance.
> Our Vortex desires the immobile rhythm of its swiftness.
> Our Vortex rushes out like an angry dog at your Impressionistic fuss.
> Our Vortex is white and abstract with its red-hot swiftness.[44]

The war-cry was magnificently defiant, but what exactly *was* this 'vortex' which Lewis kept referring to with such pride? As the principal midwife of the movement, he should have made it his duty to lay down an authoritative explanation of the term in his own magazine. But he failed to do so, either because he was loath to restrict the word to one simple literal meaning – preferring instead to let its powerful associations work their own way into the imaginations of his readers – or because he took a characteristically cussed delight in creating a mystery. The only contemporary record that now exists to explain Lewis's own interpretation of the image is provided by Goldring, who remembered Lewis telling him to 'think at once of a whirlpool . . . At the heart of the whirlpool is a great silent place where all the energy is concentrated. And there, at the point of concentration, is the Vorticist'.[45]

The combative overtones of the word were ready-made: Lewis saw the Vorticist as a man inhabiting the calm centre of a rotating holocaust where all the other rival movements were spinning helplessly around and destroying themselves. He himself confirmed this interpretation later, when he explained that 'the origin of the term "Vorticism" was the idea of a mass of excited thinking, engrossed in a whirling centre. We all know, without applying to the dictionary, what is meant by a vortex. It is a violent central activity attracting everything to itself, absorbing all that is around it into a violent whirling – a violent central engulfing. An ingenious critic noticed that my position was offensively central, that I was at once calm and whirling, that I was at once magnetic and incandescent'.[46] The appeal of such a concept is immediately understandable. It symbolized not only a weapon of destruction – Lewis used it in this way when he declared in *Blast No. 1* that 'the Turner Vortex rushed at Europe with a wave of light' – but also incorporated at the same time his cherished idea of art as 'non-life'.[47] The 'great silent place' he had described to Goldring was the ideal location for such an exalted activity, and it goes a long way towards elucidating the proud assertion in 'Our Vortex' that:

> The Vorticist is at his maximum point of energy when stillest.
> The Vorticist is not the Slave of Commotion, but its Master.
> The Vorticist does not suck up to Life.
> He lets Life know its place in a Vorticist Universe![48]

This emphasis on the cold, hard, static nature of art stands in direct refutation of the dictionary definition of a 'vorticist' as the 'metaphysical' notion of a 'person regarding the universe, with Descartes, as a plenum in which motion propagates itself in circles'. Lewis would have been the first to reject any suggestion that he was concerned with 'motion', let alone the cursive rhythms entailed in the dictionary's reference to circles. He and his colleagues always preferred staccato, angular forms and sharp diagonals which broke masses up into fragments rather than rendering them in a rounded, flowing sequence. Curvilinear multiplication characterized the Futurist style, after all, and the Vorticists would have nothing to do with the Italians' obsessive interest in speed.

Marinetti's idea of dynamism was irrevocably caught up in the outer chaos of the vortex whirlpool, a piece of hopelessly romanticized flotsam drowning itself in its own undisciplined frenzy. It stood at the other end of the scale to Lewis's interpretation of the word, despite the strong possibility that either he or Pound may have originally borrowed the vortex symbol from the Futurists' theories. There is no way of proving this connection beyond all doubt; but Frank Rutter, who knew the English rebels well at that time, categorically stated years later that Vorticism's 'name is derived from a term used in the preface to Boccioni's book on Futurism, where the emotional state of the Futurist artist is described as being a "vortex"'.[49] And although Rutter's memory played him false over the reference being situated in the preface, he was indeed correct in remembering that Boccioni's 1914 book, *Pittura Scultura Futuriste*, contained such a passage elsewhere in its pages. During his exposition of Simultaneity, the Italian theorist declared that 'I cannot forget the scepticism and the derision with which our extremely violent affirmations of faith in modernity were received, above all in Italy, by artists young and old, public and press. These affirmations concerned the indisputable need to trample on the *artistic* and the mania for culture; the need to become brutal, rapid and precise; the need to Americanise ourselves, to enter into the overwhelming vortex of modernity by way of its crowds, its automobiles, its telegraph systems, its naked popular quarters, its noises, its shrieks, its violence, its cruelty, its cynicism, its implacable ambition; the exaltation, in other words, of all the savage anti-artistic aspects of our epoch'.[50]

The passage makes clear that Futurism used the word vortex only in a generalized sense, to signify the bracing dynamism of contemporary life as a whole. And so although Lewis or Pound may well have first found it employed in this incidental way by Futurist manifestos, they made sure that the English movement took the vortex over, refined its meaning and turned it into a central clarion-call for the rebel doctrines.[51]

On a purely pictorial level, the Italians had of course already exploited the idea of a primal energy that drew inwards to a dynamic vortex; and Balla went so far as to execute no less than eight pictures between 1913 and 1914 entitled *Vortex*.[52] They were never actually exhibited in London – Balla was not represented in the Sackville Gallery show and they were not included in his 1914 Doré Galleries contributions either – but Lewis admired his work more than the other Futurists. 'Balla is a good painter, you know',[53] he admitted to Etchells

Giacomo Balla
*Vortex, c.* 1913

in a letter written at the time of the Futurists' second London exhibition in April 1914; and in *Blast No. 1* he pointed out that 'if "dynamic" considerations intoxicate Balla and make him produce significant patterns (as they do), all is well. But . . . Balla is not a "Futurist" in the Automobilist sense. He is a rather violent and geometric sort of Expressionist'.[54] Such praise implies that Lewis looked closely at Balla's work, and he may perhaps have studied reproductions of the *Vortex* pictures. Not out of any desire to borrow their stylistic mannerisms, but simply because their abstract structure fired him with the notion of using a vortex for his own, totally different ends.

Possibly, too, his attention was drawn to the Balla paintings by Pound, since it was he who had thought of using the vortex idea in the first place. During the course of 1913, the American poet had become increasingly dissatisfied with the progress of Imagism, the literary movement he had launched with such crusading fervour the year before. The more he came into contact with young rebel artists like Gaudier, the more he realized that Imagism was not succeeding in creating the poetic revolution he so eagerly desired. Consolidating his old relationship with the fiery and restless Lewis may well have brought the shortcomings of his movement home to him with more vividness. The paintings and sculpture he saw at Rutter's Doré Galleries exhibition that autumn probably convinced him that the Imagists were not pushing their literary experiments half as far as this courageous group of artists. ' "England" is dead as mutton', he wrote sourly to Harriet Monroe in November 1913, around the time when the alternative attractions of Vorticism began to present themselves to him. 'Until "we" accept what I've been insisting on for a decade, i.e., a universal standard which pays no attention to time or country – a Weltlitteratur standard – there is no hope. England hasn't yet accepted such a standard, so we've plenty of chance to do it first.'[55] Behind the tone of aggressive optimism, a certain measure of desperation can be glimpsed in Pound's plea: was it advisable, anyway, to carry on trying to resuscitate the Imagist movement? Would it not be better to forget about the whole venture and concentrate instead on formulating with his artist friends an alternative movement based on the motif of a vortex? The position of centrality which this new word signified would have chimed at once with Pound's own determination to pit himself the highest international achievements in art – he was only half in jest when he told Kate Buss in March 1916 that his 'first connection with vorticist movement [was] during the blizzard of '87 when I came East, having decided that the position of Hailey was not sufficiently central for my activities'.[56] For a young American writer who had exiled himself to measure up to the most exacting creative standards the world could offer, this aspect of the term vortex was appealing indeed.

It was entirely fitting, then, that Pound's loyalties were by the end of 1913 transferred from Imagism to Vorticism. His first recorded reference to 'The Vortex' in his December letter to Carlos Williams shows that he had by that time made up his mind to join forces with Lewis in a new co-operative which would unite the combined resources of literature and art.[57] The advantage of this merger resided in the far greater potential strength of its attack: how would the reactionaries be able to withstand the onslaught of London's most adventurous painter, charging alongside the city's most hotly debated young poet and polemicist? Pound was no more doubtful than Lewis about the answer to that question, and he proved the sincerity of his intentions by throwing himself into the activities of the Rebel Art Centre with irrepressible élan. He enjoyed the invigorating company of his artist friends – years later he remembered 38 Great Ormond Street with affection as a 'serious VORT centre, supported by the pure in heart'[58] – and made his own most important contribution to the formulation of Vorticism in a lecture he delivered there in the spring of 1914. Although ostensibly concerned with Imagism, Pound afterwards recorded that the substance of the talk was identical with the essay on 'Vorticism' he published later on in the year. 'In September, 1914, I had an article in the *Fortnightly Review*, which was for the most part a closer form of a rather informal lecture given at the Rebel Art Centre in Ormond Street the preceding spring',[59] he explained, thereby proving that the most positive single essay ever written to expound the meaning of the Vorticist aesthetic was originally read out to a motley collection of malcontents assembled in the large first-floor studio of Kate Lechmere's rented atelier.

By the time he composed this vital dissertation, Pound had obviously decided to assume the mantle of official poetic spokesman for Vorticism, just as Apollinaire and Marinetti had done for their respective movements. He even sought to remind his readers of the parallel by pointing out at the beginning of the essay that 'we are all futurists to the extent of believing with Guillaume Appollonaire [*sic*] that "On ne peut pas porter *partout* avec soi le cadavre de son père" '. But after this preliminary declaration of solidarity with Vorticism's European counterparts, Pound soon made it clear that he was at pains to define the independent character of the English movement. And this entailed as specific a denunciation of Futurist precepts as Lewis published in *Blast No. 1*. 'The vorticist has not this curious tic for destroying past glories', Pound insisted. 'I have no doubt that Italy needed Mr Marinetti, but he did not set on the egg that hatched me, and as I am wholly opposed to his aesthetic principles I see no reason why I, and various men who agree with me, should be expected to call ourselves futurists. We do not desire to evade comparison with the past. We prefer that the comparison be made by some intelligent person whose idea of "the tradition" is not limited by the conventional taste of four or five centuries and one continent.'[60] Elsewhere, in his *Egoist* article of 15 June, Pound had elaborated on Vorticism's admiration for more primitive cultures by declaring that 'the futurists are evidently ignorant of tradition. They have learned from their grandfathers that such and such things were done in 1850 and they conclude that 1850 was all "the past". We do not desire to cut ourselves off from the past. We do not desire to cut ourselves off from great art of any period, we only demand a recognition of contemporary great art, which cannot possibly be just like the great art of any other period'.[61]

Having clarified the different attitudes of the two movements towards their artistic predecessors, Pound went on to rephrase the arguments Worringer had outlined in *Abstraction and Empathy* – the book which had provided Hulme with so much fundamental inspiration – by stating that 'there are two opposed ways of thinking of a man: firstly, you may think of him as that toward which perception moves, as the toy of circumstance, as the plastic substance *receiving* impressions; secondly, you may think of him as directing a certain fluid force against circumstance, as *conceiving* instead of merely reflecting and observing'. This, for Pound, was the basic distinction to be drawn between Futurism and Vorticism. Despite their use of ostensibly abstract stylistic conventions, the Italians were still passively content to reproduce nature in a way that derived from Impressionism. But, Pound stressed, 'the organization of forms is a much more energetic and creative action than the copying or imitating of light on a haystack', and the Vorticists were as directly opposed to the Futurist method of working as the Symbolists had been to Impressionism at the end of the last century. 'In the 'eighties there were symbolists opposed to impressionists', he wrote; 'now you have vorticism, which is, roughly speaking, expressionism, neo-cubism, and imagism gathered together in one camp and futurism in the other.'

Pound had an endless capacity for broad generalizations, and his encyclopaedic mind delighted in making sweeping statements that slotted the various artistic groups of the previous hundred years into arbitrary pigeon-holes of his own making. It made no logical sense to type Vorticism as an amalgam of three widely differing movements, yet he enjoyed formulating definitions that would startle people into thinking about these various terminologies in a new way. And he did, in fact, possess an eccentric intelligence which guaranteed that his theories always cohered in the last analysis. Vorticism did have an urgency and harshness akin to the excoriating art of the Expressionists; it did, too, emphasize static and monumental forms like the Cubists; and there was a link, finally, between its attempt to return to pictorial fundamentals and Imagism's determination to jettison the obsolete clichés of Victorian verse. All of this, and more, was circulating in Pound's agile mind when he coined that strange, seemingly inaccurate description of the Vorticist style.

But the most important single aspect of the new movement still lay in its resemblance to the poetic revolution he had instigated two years before, and a large part of the article was taken up with an attempt to justify his shift of loyalties from Imagism over to Vorticism. The process had begun as early as March 1914, when he admitted in his *Egoist* review of the London Group show that he found it difficult to write about the exhibits because they were 'perhaps so close to one's poetic habit of creation'. He even went so far as to admit that his own 'surest critic' was 'a contemporary painter who knows my good work from my bad – NOT by a critical process, at least not by a technical process'. This was the reason for his new collaboration with Lewis: the exhilarating realization that there was 'a "life" or sameness somewhere that we are both trying with our imperfect means to get at'.[62] So miraculous was this coincidence that Pound still remained surprised about it in 1956, when he asked Lewis 'whether you note convergence (from two quite distinct angles) on agreement of 1913 or whatever. At any rate there was a convergence not merely a connexion'.

Lewis, for his part, was probably not quite as enthusiastic about Pound's verse as the American poet was about Lewis's pictures. '[Pound's] poetry to the mind of the more fanatical of the group was a series of pastiches', he wrote some years afterwards. 'Its novelty consisted largely in the distance it went *back*, not *forward*; in archaism, not in new creation . . . But this discrepancy between what Pound said – what he supported and held up as an example – and what he did, was striking enough to impress itself on anybody.'[63] Lewis's relations with Pound had soured somewhat by the time he committed these reservations to print; but it certainly remained true that Pound was always more involved with the past than his impatient friend. His poems in *Blast No. 1* included translations from the seventh century poet Fu I, and they go some way towards explaining Lewis's later complaint that 'I thought of the inclusion of poems by Pound etc. in "Blast" as compromising. I wanted a battering ram that was all of one metal. A good deal of what got in seemed to me soft and highly impure . . . My literary contemporaries I looked upon as too bookish and not keeping pace with the visual revolution'.[64] But the fact remains that many of Pound's *Blast No. 1* poems were perfectly attuned to the defiant mood of Lewis's magazine, stylistically as well as emotionally:

Let us deride the smugness of 'The Times':
GUFFAW!
So much the gagged reviewers,
It will pay them when the worms are wriggling in their vitals;
These were they who objected to newness,
HERE are their TOMB-STONES.

cried 'Salutation the Third', the first of Pound's poems in the periodical.

> They supported the gag and the ring:
> A little black BOX contains them.
>      so shall you be also,
> You slut-bellied obstructionist,
>      You sworn foe to free speech and good letters,
> You fungus, you continuous gangrene.

There is nothing 'soft' about these swaggering sentiments, and nothing 'impure' about the way in which Pound uses *vers libre* with such conspicuous emancipation, isolating lines at will to reinforce the militant meaning of the poem. It is hard to imagine how Lewis could possibly have objected to the contributions of a man who concluded 'Salutation the Third' with this swingeing attack:

> HERE is the taste of my BOOT,
>      CARESS it, lick off the BLACKING.[65]

Were, then, Lewis's reservations simply the product of his congenital jealousy? Did he resent Pound's talent for expounding the principles of Vorticism in public? There may be some truth in such speculations, for the American possessed just as much of a talent for art politics as the progenitor of *Blast* himself. Soon after Pound had anonymously edited the first official anthology of Imagist poetry, *Des Imagistes*, published in March 1914, he felt that his leadership was being usurped by the formidable Amy Lowell, a rich and determined Lady Poetess from across the Atlantic whose previous efforts to join the Imagist movement had failed because, as Aldington explained, 'at that time she had published only one book, which H.D. and I agreed was the fluid, fruity, facile stuff we most wanted to avoid. We wanted clear outlines, directness, concision, unhackneyed rhythms'.[66] His suspicions were ultimately confirmed when Miss Lowell arrived in London in July 1914, accompanied by a conspicuously outsize chauffeur-driven motorcar, and ensconced herself at the Berkeley Hotel. After attending the *Blast No. 1* dinner at the Dieudonné on 15 July, she threw a grand 'Imagist Dinner' at the same restaurant two days later, attended by Pound and his wife, Aldington, Flint, John Cournos, H.D., Ford and possibly Gaudier. Their hostess had one objective in view, and she was determined to achieve it: a second Imagist anthology, more comprehensive than its predecessor, and selected by the contributors rather than an editor like Pound. She even offered to contact an important, established American publisher – thereby promoting the movement on a far more respectable scale than Pound, whose anthology had been issued through the relatively humble auspices of the Poetry Bookshop.

Her suggestion was greeted with approval by most of the Imagists, who were growing increasingly dissatisfied with Pound's affiliation with Vorticism. Even Aldington was restless, in spite of his earlier willingness to sign the *Blast No. 1* manifesto, and he later recalled how Amy Lowell had become 'fed up with Ezra. So were others . . . Ezra had now attached himself to the *Blast* group, and was busy patenting a new movement, Vorticism . . . The first number of *Blast* was indeed a brilliant production, but most of the brilliance was due to the editor and chief contributor . . . *Blast* didn't seem quite the right medium for the rest of us'.[67] The other Imagists could not possibly feel at home with this new, predominantly pictorial movement; and although *Blast No. 1* betrayed a strong literary bias, the only Imagist poems to appear in its pages were by Pound, apart from one short poem by H.D. which Pound quoted in his 'Vortex' essay as a putative example of verbal Vorticism:

> Whirl up sea –
> Whirl your pointed pines,
> Splash your great pines
> On our rocks,

> Hurl your green over us,
> Cover us with your pools of fir.[68]

It did not really link up with the main body of the Vorticist movement, and Lewis later admitted his lukewarm attitude towards the Imagists when he revealed that 'my only trouble was that nothing was being written just then that seemed within a million leagues of the stark radicalism of the *visuals*'.[69]

For his part, Pound was just as dissatisfied with the shape that Imagism threatened to assume under the control of Amy Lowell. 'I should like the name "Imagisme" to retain some sort of a meaning', he wrote to her aggrievedly in August 1914. 'It stands, or I should like it to stand for hard light, clear edges. I can not trust any democratized committee to maintain that standard. Some will be splay-footed and some sentimental.'[70] In other words, he feared that the original impulse behind Imagism would be watered down into a compromised affair: wider in scope, perhaps, but with ideals lowered to a fatal degree. He asked his rival to call her new anthology *Vers Libre*; but she was adamant, returned to America in September with the loyalty of five contributors – Flint, D. H. Lawrence, Aldington, H.D., and John Gould Fletcher – and went on to publish three anthologies in succeeding years under the collective title of *Some Imagist Poets*. 'H.D. and I pleaded with Ezra to stay in, but he refused to play ball,' recorded Aldington, who described the whole bloodless coup as Amy Lowell's 'Boston Tea Party'.[71] For Pound, it constituted the final blow to his already waning interest in Imagism, and he wrote the movement's unofficial obituary by rechristening it with the derisive nickname of 'Amygism'. Vorticism was now his only hope.

This is the context in which his *Fortnightly Review* essay should be placed. It was, above all, Pound's attempt to square up Imagism with Vorticism, and it is impossible entirely to refute the suspicion that Lewis may have been slightly annoyed when he read the article. His hypersensitive pride might well have been offended by Pound's personal interpretation of the Vortex as 'the primary pigment' of all the arts. And Lewis could easily have balked at his friend's declaration that 'the image is the poet's pigment. The painter should use his colour because he sees it or feels it. I don't much care whether he is representative or non-representative. He should *depend*, of course, on the creative, not upon the mimetic or representational part in his work. It is the same in writing poems, the author must use his *image* because he sees it or feels it, *not* because he thinks he can use it to back up some creed or some system of ethics or economics'.[72] If Lewis did indeed despise Imagist poetry, this categorical statement may have been unpalatable to his imperious intellect. He was a writer himself, and afterwards stated that his 'kind of play, "The Enemy of the Stars" . . . was my attempt to show [the Imagists] the way'.[73] Lewis's undoubted literary ambitions were not entirely compatible with Pound's, and when the poet explained in his 'Vorticism' article that 'the image is itself the speech. The image is the word beyond formulated language', Lewis's creative ego possibly objected to this correlation of the poet's image with the artist's abstract language.

How, moreover, did Lewis react to Pound's dogmatic linking of the Image with the Vortex, Imagism with Vorticism? In the most vital passage of the article, Pound finally announced that 'the image is not an idea. It is a radiant node or cluster; it is what I can, and must perforce, call a VORTEX, from which, and through which, and into which, ideas are constantly rushing. In decency one can only call it a VORTEX. And from this necessity came the name "vorticism". *Nomina sunt consequentia rerum*, and never was that statement of Aquinas more true than in the case of the vorticist movement'.[74] Maybe Lewis's overweening vanity was wounded by the knowledge that Pound had first thought of the Vortex idea: if it was, then he was bound to smart at this openly political identification of another man's poetic movement with his beloved Vorticism.

The resentment must not, however, be exaggerated: it was only many years afterwards that Lewis actually protested 'that *vorticism* was purely a painters affair (as *imagism* was a purely literary movement, having no relation whatever to *vorticism*, nor anything in common with it)'.[75] And it should be realized that Pound's description of the vortex as a focal point which gathered all the purest and most energetic artistic impulses into a brilliant refinement accorded well with the definition Lewis had himself provided in *Blast No. 1*. There is no reason to suppose that the editor of *Blast No. 1* harboured any profound objections to Pound's 'Vortex' article – virtually a précis of the 'Vorticism' essay in the *Fortnightly Review* – which appeared between the pink covers of his magazine. Did not the poet's introductory definition of the vortex as 'the point of maximum energy' echo Lewis's own explanation in the periodical? He must have warmed to Pound's assertion that the vortex 'represents, in mechanics, the greatest efficiency', and concurred no less readily with the idea that 'the vorticist relies on this alone; on the primary pigment of his art, nothing else'. Pound insisted on the importance of returning to the vitality contained in the basic constituents of all art, pointing out that 'every conception, every emotion presents itself to the vivid consciousness in some primary form. It is the picture that means a hundred poems, the music that means a hundred pictures, the most highly energized statement, the statement that has not yet SPENT itself in expression, but which is the most capable of expressing'. He was obsessed with the idea of the vortex whirlpool as a kind of powerful spring, coiled up into a multitude of tight circles so that the germ of a creative intuition was both encapsulated in the middle and poised to leap out on the sensibilities of the spectator. It was a metaphor after Lewis's own heart, and he would have been delighted to read Pound's exuberant announcement that 'all experience rushes into this vortex. All the energized past, all the past that is living and worthy to live. All MOMENTUM, which is the past bearing upon us, RACE, RACE-MEMORY, instinct charging the PLACID, NON-ENERGIZED FUTURE. The DESIGN of the future in the grip of the human vortex. All the past that is vital, all the past that is capable of living into the future, is pregnant in the vortex, NOW'.[76]

It was the potential bursting out of the heart of the whirlpool that excited Pound, who saw it as a uniquely powerful confluence, a synthesis in the present moment of the most valuable elements ever produced in the past or adumbrated in the future. And this emphasis on the decisive importance of 'now' automatically guaranteed that the Futurists were redundant, a sentimental relic broken up in the slipstream of the vortex turbine. 'Futurism is the disgorging spray of a vortex with no drive behind it, DISPERSAL', wrote Pound scornfully, dismissing the movement as 'an accelerated sort of impressionism' made up merely of 'the CORPSES of VORTICES'. How could it be otherwise? Any movement which lost sight of the 'primary pigment' consigned itself to mediocrity and dealt only with irrelevant considerations. 'Elaboration, expression of second intensities, of dispersedness belong to the secondary sort of artist', said Pound. 'Dispersed arts HAD a vortex.' Instead of being just another offshoot from theories originally evolved on the continent, Vorticism stood for all the most potent qualities of any artistic language. 'EVERY CONCEPT, EVERY EMOTION PRESENTS ITSELF TO THE VIVID CONSCIOUSNESS IN SOME PRIMARY FORM', Pound repeated in loud capitals. 'IT BELONGS TO THE ART OF THIS FORM. IF SOUND, TO MUSIC; IF FORMED WORDS, TO LITERA-

TURE; THE IMAGE, TO POETRY; FORM, TO DESIGN; COLOUR IN POSITION, TO PAINTING; FORM OR DESIGN IN THREE PLANES, to SCULPTURE; MOVEMENT TO THE DANCE OR TO THE RHYTHM OF MUSIC OR OF VERSES.' Only the Vorticists were capable of holding fast to these life-giving essentials, and they thereby ensured that 'VORTICISM is art before it has spread itself into a state of flaccidity, of elaboration, of secondary applications'.[77]

Nothing, in fact, could have been more immediately comprehensible than this one great central tenet of the Vorticist aesthetic. Pound's 'Vortex' article affirmed that art operates at its fullest capacity when the artist exploits his medium's intrinsic strength; and he allied that with abstraction by misquoting from Pater – 'all arts approach the conditions of music' – and Whistler, who had once explained that 'you are interested in a certain painting because it is an arrangement of lines and colours'.[78] The vortex was able, therefore, to contain within itself the varying theoretical interpretations placed upon it by both Lewis and Pound. Where Lewis favoured its iconoclastic potential as well as the calmness of its 'still centre', Pound tended towards a more pacific and comprehensive meaning, based on his unfulfilled yearning for a movement that would encompass all the arts. He virtually acknowledged the advantages of the vortex image's ability to embrace these alternative viewpoints when he explained in his 'Vorticism' article that whereas 'the symbolist's *symbols* have a fixed value, like numbers in arithmetic, like 1, 2 and 7 . . . the imagiste's images have a variable significance, like the signs *a*, *b*, and *x* in algebra.' Hence Pound's choice of a vortex, which could combine combative rebellion with geometrical detachment. He even declared in his *Blast No. 1* essay that among Vorticism's ancestors were 'Picasso, Kandinski, father and mother, classicism and romanticism of the movement'. It was a justifiable claim, for Vorticism did strive to attain a centralising amalgam of the romantic and the classical, the explosive urge and the passion for ordered control. This dichotomy provided the rebels' best works with much of their essential tension: the typically diagonal forms of a Vorticist design are thrusting outwards, as if straining to burst the bounds of the picture-frame; but they are constrained, even so, by an insistence on precise contours and a solidity of construction often almost sculptural in its weight. Time and again the Vorticist appears to fragment his composition to the point of total dispersal, and then recant by locking all his forms together into an inevitable and thoroughly immoveable structure.

But despite the formidable amount of literary and artistic talent that had been poured into the crucible of *Blast No. 1*, it failed to communicate its meaning to anyone outside the small clique of partisans who had backed it in the first place. Both critics and public alike were instantly alienated by the anarchic presentation of its material. This unprecedented typographical excess constituted a barrier which separated the words jumping off the page from the meaning they were intended to convey. The majority of readers did not sympathize with the abstraction of the illustrations *Blast No. 1* carried, and so why should they bother to study and understand the full meaning of the theories behind the mysterious pictures? The puzzled reaction of the crowd was amusingly summed up by the experience of Dorothy Pound, who aired the periodical during a journey from Kensington to Tottenham Court Road. As she alighted from her bus, a couple of youths stared in astonishment at the cover of *Blast No. 1* so prominently exhibited under her arm, turned to each other and exclaimed 'Blawst?' '*Blawst?*'

The vocabulary employed by Lewis and Pound to expatiate their beliefs now seems like an inspired outward equivalent of the rumbustious defiance of their inward beliefs, but to the public of 1914 it appeared to be merely one more source of annoyance. There was no point at all in Lewis giving the vortex visual form in *Blast No. 1* as an appropriately solid and stable cone spinning round a rigid perpendicular line: the diagram only perplexed his audience even further, and reminded them of the movement's dauntingly conceptual bias. And as for the very last words printed in the magazine – 'Will and consciousness are our VORTEX'[79] – what was the general public to make of such a broad statement? If they were neither willing nor able to enter into the spirit of the movement, then there was certainly no hope of them ever admiring the tenacity and conviction that this final sentence undoubtedly signified.

As it turned out, the response elicited from the critics degenerated into the brand of merciless sarcasm they had already heaped upon the rebel exhibitions. 'The long-promised review "Blast", the organ of the English Vorticists – or Avorticists – has at last made its appearance in a paper cover of a peculiarly aggressive pucey pink', wrote Konody in the *Observer*; 'a bulky quarto volume printed in type of a size that would make it ideally suitable reading for a railway journey, were it not that the bulk of the reading matter is couched in language so obscure and unintelligible that it is not advisable to dip into the vortex of "Blast" without a handy pail of ice for application to one's head.' Konody viewed the magazine as a foolish prank, extreme enough to merit a few journalistic quips, perhaps, but certainly not worthy of proper critical attention. 'Blast is a strange mixture of seriousness and facetiousness, common sense and obscurity', he continued, but soon made it clear that he did not intend to bother about examining the 'serious' aspect of its contents. 'Much of it reads like the production of naughty boys who are impelled by love of mischief. The desire to shock accounts for many of the epigrams, and perhaps the desire to mystify for many of the pages of wildly extravagant and often ungrammatical nonsense.' There was no real acknowledgement of the startling originality of *Blast No. 1*'s ideas, its illustrations or its layout; and neither was there any suggestion that a leaven of inspiration might conceivably lie below the dough that Konody chose to find in the periodical.

The final accusation inserted into his tirade was, moreover, the most serious and damaging of all. 'Throughout "Blast" there runs a note of hostility to Marinetti and Marinettism', Konody concluded. 'And yet, without Marinetti "Blast" would have been inconceivable.'[80] The implications of this complaint were grave. Despite all that Lewis and his friends had done to establish a standpoint in direct contradistinction to the principles of Futurism, a commentator as intelligent and relatively informed as Konody refused to accept the independence of the Vorticist aesthetic. He was not even prepared to realize, on the most superficial level, that *Blast No. 1*'s warning to suffragettes to 'LEAVE ART ALONE, BRAVE COMRADES!' for fear that 'YOU MIGHT SOME DAY DESTROY A GOOD PICTURE BY ACCIDENT'[81] was utterly divorced from the Futurists' cry for the destruction of museums. He wanted to see only the damaging resemblances, and humiliate Vorticism by describing it as a second-hand pastiche of Italian theories. Nevinson, needless to say, was quick to capitalize on Konody's strictures. He hurriedly penned a cheeky letter to the *Observer* on 12 July to explain that there was indeed a difference between the two movements. 'Surely Mr Konody, in his amusing criticism of "Blast", either failed to follow his own advice and apply enough ice to his head in order to grasp the distinction between Vorticism and Futurism', wrote Marinetti's disciple, '. . . or (though it is not made clear what Divinity is going to carry out their orders) he is quite pardonably intending to get himself among the damned and blasted in the next number which will appear in October'.

Delighted as Nevinson so obviously was by the reception *Blast No. 1* had been accorded by the *Observer*, he was determined to distinguish his own

Wyndham Lewis (ed.)
Vortex cone from *Blast No. 1*, 1914

beliefs from those of his rivals. 'Mr Konody nearly nips the "Northern Flower" in the bud and (to use the Vorticist metaphors) strangles "the angry dog" at birth when he says that the Vorticists "praise machinery of every kind". Only the Futurists do this. The Vorticists have a peculiar prejudice, which they claim to be insular, against the "internal combustion" engine, and they only bless more obsolete machinery. This statement may come as a great shock to many of the Vorticists, who obviously imagine that the motive power of motors, aeroplanes etc., is not a mechanical one.' The satire was as clumsy as it was inaccurate. Lewis never for a moment claimed that he was 'prejudiced' against any kind of machinery: all he insisted on was a degree of detachment, as a necessary antidote to Futurist romanticism and sentimentality. But Nevinson did not concern himself with a faithful representation of the views promulgated in *Blast No. 1*. He wanted at all costs to demolish the enemy stronghold, and pressed on regardless into mere whimsicality. 'In fact, their mechanics seem as primitive and inaccurate as their arithmetic', he jeered. 'On the title-page I notice the subscription is 2s. 6d. quarterly and 10s. 6d. annually!' And he ended up with his own version of Lewisian satire by insisting that 'it would be a pity to have the two movements confused, especially as it is so entertaining to watch these ex-Futurist professors performing intellectual contortions "within the stationary centre of a whirlpool!" that the strong and swift-flowing stream of Futurism was bound to cause and has left behind'.[82]

Nevinson's parting burst was a pointed inversion of Pound's vortex, but to anyone unacquainted with the finer points of avant-garde debate such squabbling and continuous back-biting seemed tedious to the point of downright childishness. Small wonder that the *Observer* also carried, in the same month, a spoof letter written by one 'Marionetti Bombelewis' and sent hotfoot from 'The Only Art Centre'. Proclaiming the emergence of a new group of artists called 'THE INFINITISTS', the anonymous correspondent declared that 'we paint pictures with morning dew and moonshine mixed with a little Thames mud to ensure consistency'. He went out of his way to explain that 'where other ists grovel in the mundane, rejoicing in motors, whirlpools, vortices, and such like inanities, *we* lift our eyes to the vaulted heavens, and piercing the empyrean with our eagle eyes roam through space, ignoring time'. The letter consciously guyed the Futurist manifesto as much as *Blast No. 1*, exhorting its readers to shout 'Hurrah! then for the void; Hurrah! for the Comet; Hurrah! for the Stardust. Gee-whiz-bang! Hurrah! for Infinitism'. And it consolidated its official position in the hierarchy of the radical art world by announcing the forthcoming publication of 'a biennial journal to be entitled "The Dam"'.[83] Lewis may have blasted humour for its ability to reduce the most urgent topics to a roar of hearty English mirth, but it made no difference to his audience, who persisted in mocking a movement they could not be bothered to comprehend. *Blast No. 1* made their task easier, admittedly, by casting so much of its argument in satirical terms itself, and its editor recognized this loophole later when he recalled that 'Vorticism was replete with humour, of course; it was acclaimed the best joke ever . . . "Kill John Bull with Art!" I shouted. And John and Mrs Bull leapt for joy, in a cynical convulsion. For they felt as safe as houses. So did I'.[84] And so did the people who were specifically cursed in the manifestos: Arbuthnot remembered in his autobiography that when *Blast No. 1* appeared 'I was rather perturbed to find that I had "blasted" several friends, including Martin Harvey. I thought perhaps he would be annoyed, but he thought it was "great fun"'.

How could Lewis expect the reaction to *Blast* to be anything other than frivolous? The Press simply treated it as the latest in a long series of cranky Bohemian publicity stunts, inseparably connected with the colourful propaganda of that arch-showman Marinetti. The *Morning Post* even described it as 'the first futurist quarterly . . . full of irrepressible imbecility which is not easily distinguished from the words and works of Marinetti's disciples'.[85] Clearly, the *Post* had not even begun to 'distinguish', and would never have the slightest intention of doing so. It was useless for Aldington to claim in his first *Egoist* review that *Blast No. 1* was 'the most amazing, energised, stimulating production I have ever seen'.[86] London did not agree, and refused to regard it as anything other than the work of verbose madmen. 'Sang old Rabelais in a ribald song to do with the adventures of Amorous Toss Pot, "A very small rain lays a very high wind" ', wrote a reviewer for *Truth*. 'Flatulence is a dull and boring complaint, both in sheep and artists. Please God send the rain.'[87] And when the Vorticists did not find themselves ridiculed for their pretentiousness, they were black-balled on almost moral grounds for their connexions with such a questionable periodical. Pound, for instance, received an extraordinary rebuttal in October from G. W. Prothero, editor of the *Quarterly Review*, thanking him for his 'letter of the other day', and then declaring that 'I am afraid that I must say frankly that I do not think I can open the columns of the Q.R. – at any rate, at present – to anyone associated publicly with such a publication as *Blast*. It stamps a man too disadvantageously'.[88]

But perhaps the saddest opinion of all was expressed by the poet Gordon Bottomley, who remained utterly unmoved by the magazine and perused its contents with patronizing disdain. 'It looks amusingly stale and old-fashioned already, now', he told Paul Nash on 2 October. 'The text would be trite if it were not so very black, and the pictures look like theories that have gone cold too soon.' Imagine how deflated Lewis would have been if he had read this letter, and realized that *Blast No. 1* sometimes did not even succeed in arousing strong feelings, either one way or the other! 'The only pictures by the living men that appeal to me, and that seem to have an original feeling for beauty are the two [*Dancers* and *Religion*] by W. Roberts', Bottomley continued; 'as for the pictures by Lewis, Wadsworth et Cie, they would look far more convincing, reasonable, and valuable, if carried out by the yard and made into opera cloaks.'[89]

The one consolation to be gleaned from this harvest of antagonism and cynical levity was that Vorticism was taken up, momentarily at least, as a fashionable craze. It was 'all the rage in 1914' according to the ubiquitous Violet Hunt, who gathered some fellow sympathizers around her and 'dressed Vorticist' in garish clothes that celebrated the fluorescent colour of *Blast No. 1*'s cover.[90] Instead of enjoying the emergence of a movement with a European reputation, Lewis had to content himself with witnessing the growth of yet another ephemeral gimmick. It must have been an ironic experience for the man who had insisted in his own magazine that 'we do not want to make people wear Futurist Patches, or fuss men to take to pink and sky-blue trousers. We are not their wives or tailors'.[91] But at least he could squeeze some wry satisfaction out of the grisly spectacle afforded by a city falling over itself to catch up with the latest trend. 'Everyone by way of being fashionably interested in art, and many who had never opened a book or bought so much as a sporting-print, much less "an oil", wanted to look at this new oddity, thrown up by that amusing spook, the Zeitgeist', he remembered, drily dissecting the idiocies of his own generation. 'So the luncheon and dinner-tables of Mayfair were turned into show-booths. For a few months I was on constant exhibition. I cannot here enumerate all the sightseers, of noble houses or of questionable Finance, who passed me under review. They were legion. Coronetted envelopes showered into my letter-box. The editor of *Blast* must at all costs be viewed; and its immense puce cover was the standing joke in the fashionable drawing-room, from Waterloo Place to the border-line in Belgravia.'[92]

Such an effusive response, if a little flattering and entertaining for a while, was irrelevant. Lewis saw his much-vaunted new spirit in art dissipated by the interminable buzz of cocktail chatter. Instead of being hailed as a courageous pioneer of English abstraction, he found himself treated as a celebrity, famous for nothing more specific than a capacity for 'boldness' and unconventional ideas. 'I might have been at the head of a social revolution, instead of merely being the prophet of a new fashion in art',[93] he wrote with bemused disbelief. 'I passed my time in the usual way when a "Lion" is born. I saw a great deal of what is called "society".'[94] However gratifying this reception must have been to Lewis's inexhaustible ego, it must ultimately have become enormously frustrating. The British establishment's notorious talent for squashing dissent by inviting malcontents into its own home, making a fuss of them and flattering them so much that they warm to the existing hierarchy here reached its apogee. The Vorticist who had pledged himself in *Blast No. 1* to fight like 'a mercenary' in order to achieve his subversive aims, now watched his insurrection being disarmed by the bubbling gaiety of dinner parties and smart soirées. And the irony of the whole situation reached the heights of wild absurdity when Lewis was introduced to Prime Minister Asquith at one of Lady Ottoline Morrell's gatherings in her house at Bedford Square. Immediately the two men met, Lewis found himself 'cross-questioned at length about my principles. I remember especially that he asked me "whether I was in touch with people of similar views in other countries". Yes, I admitted, I had corresponded with continental painters, critics, and men of letters. He nodded his head thoughtfully at this . . . Here was a movement masking itself beneath the harmless trappings of the fine arts, and camouflaged as a fashionable stunt of the studios, but with wide ramifications in all countries, and with unavowed political objectives'.[95]

Fêted by hostesses and suspected by politicians, Lewis's hopes for the rise of Vorticism as a serious and respected art movement gradually waned. It seemed as if the fears for *Blast No. 1* expressed by the editor of *The New Age* as far back as January 1914 were going to be entirely borne out by events. 'It will, of course, be amusing for an issue or two, and connoisseurs will purchase early numbers as an investment for their old age', he had written; 'but will it encourage discussion, the one thing needed?'[96] All it did appear to encourage was social banter, and an attitude which regarded *Blast No. 1* as an entertaining curiosity rather than an impassioned treatise that sought to cure English art of its provincial malaise. Fifteen years later its fame as a source of mere amusement still lingered on in Evelyn Waugh's *Vile Bodies*, where Johnnie Hoop takes pride in modelling his up to date invitation cards on '*Blast* and Marinetti's *Futurist Manifesto*. These had two columns of close print; in one was a list of all the things Johnnie hated, and in the other all the things he thought he liked'.[97] What a fate for an epoch-making publication, the first to launch the idea of a home-grown abstraction on a stagnant and philistine English art world! Pound was wasting his time when he protested in *The New Age* that 'if *Blast* itself were no more than an eccentrically printed volume issued by a half a dozen aimless young men, then you could afford to neglect it. *Blast* has not been neglected. *Blast* has been greatly reviled'.[98] It was an irrefutable fact that the brave venture had misfired badly, and the so-called 'quarterly' never produced its promised second issue before 1914 came to an end.

Seeking to account for the hostile reception of the magazine, Pound suggested that 'the sterile, having with pain acquired one ready made set of ideas from deceased creators of ideas, are above all else enraged at being told that the creation of ideas did not stop at the date of their birth; that they were, by their advent into this life, unable to produce a state of static awe and stolidity'. His words have the ring of a requiem about them: even before the movement had been given a chance to live, expand and mature, it looked as if it would be forced to crawl away and expire in an untimely grave. 'The common or homo canis snarls violently at the thought of there being ideas which he doesn't know', continued Pound, wincing at the size of the task still confronting the Vorticists. 'He dies a death of lingering horror at the thought that even after he has learned even the newest set of made ideas, there will still be more ideas, that the horrid things will grow, will go on growing in spite of him.'[99]

But would they carry on growing as easily as Pound persisted in hoping? Received notions, prejudices, fashionable praise and even indifference can be overcome if a movement and its members are given the requisite time and opportunities to develop their ideas. Vorticism was denied that vital chance. A month had hardly elapsed after *Blast No. 1* was let loose before the inconceivable happened, and a full-scale war finally burst upon an unsuspecting world.

# Chapter 11: Vorticism's Progress under the Shadow of War

Looking back on that fateful summer of 1914, Pound afterwards recounted with understandable bitterness how 'in less than three weeks after the [*Blast*] dinner the gigantic stupidity of this war was upon us, the accumulated asininity of that race which "N'a jamais pu qu'organiser sa barbarie", and the vanity of an epileptic had tumbled us into the whirlpool'.[1] This time, however, it was a whirlpool of real blood as opposed to a vortex of creative destruction, and it spelt death for avant-garde ideas as well as human beings. 'On the night of August 4', Bomberg remembered, 'I was in the Café Royal sitting at a table with Augustus John when the news . . . of the declaration of war was carried by one of our friends among the waiters to where we were. John, very perturbed said: "David, this news . . . is going to be bad for art".'[2] It was fatal for Vorticism. The whole cultural ambience of London was rapidly overturned, and the city's attention diverted from an obsession with creative experiment towards an even more fanatical interest in battle. At the Café Royal itself, an habitual rendezvous for the English rebels, the exuberance of aesthetic debate was replaced by grim thoughts of enlistment and patriotic sacrifice. 'The dots of khaki on the red plush benches toned down the vivid colour scheme', wrote the historians of the Café. 'A tired little batch of artists would totter in each lunch-time and at night, Augustus John and Edward Wadsworth among them, and demand beer. They were being drilled for Home Defence in – of all places – the yard of Burlington House. Every day a few more uniforms appeared. The barbers did bumper business lopping off . . . long hair.'[3] And those who resisted the demands of the scissors found themselves rejected by the nation: Bomberg attempted to join the service at the end of the summer, but was turned away because of his suspicious accent and the dimensions of his beard.

The most serious consequence of war for the rebel cause was that it drowned the noisiness of *Blast No. 1* in far louder and more urgent cries to defend the homeland. There had, admittedly, been a mood of strident hysteria in London from the beginning of the year: Douglas Goldring recalled that 'the Season of 1914 was a positive frenzy of gaiety', and described with some puzzlement how, 'long before there was any shadow of war, I remember feeling that it couldn't go on, that something *had* to happen'.[4] But although the advent of the Vorticists was one of the most dramatic manifestations of this suicidal mood, the war's arrival wrecked whatever chance they had of converting the amusement of society into constructive commissions, new adherents and a palpable victory over the forces of reaction. And the most unbearable irony of all lay in the prophetic way the Vorticists had specifically reflected the spirit of universal conflict before world war was mooted. Even though only a handful of enlightened admirers understood the stylistic extremism of their paintings and sculpture, it still remained true that their combative character – *Slow Attack, March, Enemy of the Stars* – foreshadowed the course of political events with uncanny accuracy. Writing much later, on the eve of the Second World War, Lewis confessed that 'it is somewhat depressing to consider how as an artist one is always holding the mirror up to politics without knowing it. My picture called "The Plan of War" painted six months before the Great War "broke out", as we say, depresses me . . . With me war and art have been mixed up from the start. It is still. I wish I could get away from war'.[5]

But did he feel the same about it in 1914, when he positioned himself at the head of a band of artistic warriors? Would not the war provide the revolution for which they had been yearning, and signify the extinction of the old order in the most efficient manner imaginable? It is difficult to tell. In one sense, the Vorticists must have welcomed war, and seen it almost as a confirmation of everything they had been struggling to achieve. Now, with any luck, the 'GLOOMY VICTORIAN CIRCUS' which *Blast No. 1* had lampooned so

fiercely would be destroyed by enemy bombs, and the 'VICTORIAN VAM-
PIRE' well and truly ousted. Yet Lewis categorically stated in 1915 that 'as to
Desirability, nobody but Marinetti, the Kaiser, and professional soldiers WANT
War'. And he must soon have reluctantly recognized that military iconoclasm
spelt death for creative iconoclasm, discovering with dismay that Vorticism's
potential audience found it hard to distinguish rebellious manifestos from the
propagandist tirades of the war-effort. 'All the artists and men of letters had gone
into action before the bank-clerks were clapped into khaki and despatched to
the land of Flanders Poppies to do their bit', Lewis remembered, highlighting
the unpleasant fact that there was no longer any distinction between painter and
soldier. 'Life was one big bloodless brawl, prior to the Great Bloodletting'[6] he
concluded, and thereby helped to account for Vorticism's failure to register its
desired impact on a country confused by a universal upheaval. Rebel demonstrations became as much of an everyday occurrence as rabble-rousing speeches
for volunteers, and the public could not in fairness be blamed for confusing art
with politics. Roberts, who recalled how 'the first three months of the war were
particularly difficult for us', forcing him to work 'some weeks making bomb parts
in a Tufnell Park munitions factory', claimed that 'despite Lord Kitchener's
image with its commanding finger pointing down from the hoardings, during
most of 1915 I paid more attention to matters of art and picture-making (as did
most of the artists with whom I associated) than to the war taking place in
France'.[7] But everyone else forgot about the challenge of controversial aesthetics
and concentrated instead on the far more formidable German menace advancing
through Europe.

Just how greatly the Vorticist cause suffered through the arrival of war may
be gauged by the critical response to the work they displayed some months
later in the second London Group exhibition of March 1915. Several of the
rebels were represented there in force – Lewis and Wadsworth both showed
two major canvases, Epstein had four important sculptures on view, Gaudier
was much in evidence and so was Roberts – but the inexorable escalation of
battle fever took a severe toll on the Press's capacity to respond to pictorial
experiment. Instead of attempting to come to terms with abstraction, reviewers
simply saw the exhibits as a pale imitation of the true military impulse.

'In having degenerated so suddenly into such a bore, the Vorticists, or whatever they used to call themselves, have been a little unlucky', Collins Baker
wrote in the *Saturday Review* on 20 March. 'I am inclined to think that their
reputation as amusing creatures and puzzle painters might, in normal conditions,
have carried them through another season (provided that a rival group had not
been yet more amusing). But Life decreed that something serious should come
to the rescue of a costive world, whose ennui was barely mitigated by all sorts
of ingenuity and elaborate bright notions. So in August, to our horror, we were
tipped into things that really mattered. And now, when we have the opportunity
to look again at those old ingenious notions, our nerves still tingling with the
impact of reality, we simply wonder what on earth was up with us that we should
ever have been entertained by them.' Even if the war had never occurred,
writers like Collins Baker would have continued to abuse Vorticism by discussing it exclusively in terms of novelty and sensationalism. But now, with the
drama of an international holocaust reverberating through his mind, he concluded his article by declaring that 'the trouble with the Vortex school is that
its members are either dull or dishonest. Some of them are both'. And the
critic of *The Times* shovelled the last spade of abuse onto the Vorticists' coffin
by describing their second London Group contributions as 'Prussian in spirit'.
Under the disparaging headline 'JUNKERISM IN ART', he announced
that 'these painters seem to execute a kind of goose-step, where other artists are

content to walk more or less naturally. Perhaps if the Junkers could be induced to take to art, instead of disturbing the peace of Europe, they would paint so and enjoy it. But we do not feel that these gentlemen enjoy it. They are not Prussian enough for their theories of art'.[8]

As might be expected, Lewis resiliently defended his movement against the implications of these remarks. He retorted that 'the Junker, obviously, if he painted, would do florid and disreputable canvasses of nymphs and dryads, or very sentimental "portraits of the Junker's mother" '; and he took *The Times* review as the pretext for a spirited defence of the so-called 'Prussian' character of Vorticist art. 'Because these paintings are rather strange at first sight, they are regarded as ferocious and unfriendly', he wrote. 'They are neither, although they have no pretence to an excessive gentleness or especial love for the general public. We are not cannibals. Our rigid head-dresses and disciplined movements, which cause misgivings in the unobservant as to our intentions, are aesthetic phenomena: our goddess is Beauty, like any Royal Academician's though we have different ideas as to how she should be depicted or carved.' But explanations were useless. When Lewis asked whether, 'as an antidote to the slop of Cambridge Post Aestheticism (Post-Impressionism is an insult to Manet and Cézanne) or the Gypsy Botticellis of Mill Street, may not such "rigidity" be welcomed?' he was hurling a futile question into a wilderness of Anglo-Saxon philistinism.[9] The damage was done, and the ambitious programme outlined in *Blast No. 1* dwindled into an unregarded cul-de-sac where the rebels' work remained unsold and patrons never appeared.

Sporadically, the odd commission was bestowed upon Lewis and his allies. In June 1914, Mrs Mary Turner asked him to design furniture and decorate the drawing-room of her house in Park Lane, but nothing has survived to indicate how Lewis may have approached the project. She also negotiated the purchase of a number of his paintings, including *Slow Attack*; yet in the end their relationship deteriorated and Mrs Turner told him that she would have the pictures collected by her solicitor and put into storage.

Then, towards the end of the year, a more positive move was made by Violet Hunt, who proposed that Lewis should transform Ford's first-floor study at South Lodge, with its conventional aura of 'innumerable pipes on a table, its special machine for cutting tobacco, its books, its air of comfort', into a Vorticist showpiece.[10] Again, no trace of the work executed there remains, and a frustratingly brief description by Goldring is the only record of the scheme which now exists. 'To surmount the chimney-piece in the study', he wrote, 'Ford commissioned Wyndham Lewis to paint the large abstract decoration, with the accompanying red paint on the doors and skirting boards which gave the room its special character.'[11] Goldring's recollection outlines enough to suggest that the South Lodge study was conceived as a contrasting sequel to Lady Drogheda's dining-room: where her walls were shrouded in black, Ford found himself assaulted by strident red, and Violet Hunt supplied 'three brick red coloured tapestry window curtains' to complete the virulent scheme. The mantelpiece picture, likewise predominantly crimson in tone, appears to have gone much further than Lady Drogheda's decorations, however. Their figurative content was still more or less comprehensible, whereas Rebecca West later described the South Lodge painting as 'a huge, abstract work over the fireplace, very violent and explosive, and I remember Ford saying in his quizzical way that he "found it extremely restful" '.[12] It seems probable that this picture, which must have been executed on canvas or board rather than straight onto the wall like a mural,[13] was virtually non-representational. A letter of Pound's establishes that Lewis was hard at work on the room in November 1914, at a time when he was concerned with excluding figurative references from his pictures altogether.[14] And the likely size of the painting – a little under six feet wide and five feet high[15] – means that it would have constituted one of his most sustained attempts to employ a relatively abstract vocabulary.

The history of Vorticism is littered with missing pictures or the pointless destruction of vital works, all adding up to a sorry reminder of how little they were valued by their owners at the time. A fate similar to the vanished South Lodge project also befell perhaps the most important and stimulating venture Lewis was asked to undertake after the publication of *Blast No. 1*: the transformation of the 'small dining-room' at the Restaurant de la Tour Eiffel for its proprietor, Rudolph Stulik. According to Roberts, Lewis enjoyed total creative licence there, for 'Stulik liked artists, especially was he fond of Lewis; repeating to me often, in his Viennese accent, "I vould to anyting for Mr Lewis" '. The result of this friendship was that Stulik, 'to use his own words, "Gave Mr Lewis carte blanche" ', and Roberts added that 'Lewis made full use of this'.[16] Precisely how is not known – Roberts merely recorded that the chosen dining area 'became known as the Vorticist Room' because of the 'three abstract panels' which Lewis painted for its walls.[17] Once more, they sound as if they were an exciting contribution to the development of non-representational English art, as well as an ambitious bid to put the principles of Vorticism into practice on an environmental scale. But the panels, which Roberts recalled were painted with Saunders' probable help 'in the summer of 1915' and opened to view through Lewis's specially designed invitation card the following January, have all been lost; and with them goes one more landmark in the evolution of the rebel movement.

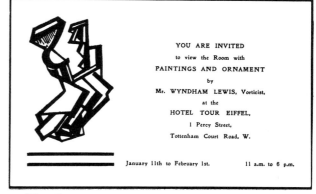

Wyndham Lewis
Invitation card for the 'Vorticist Room' at the Tour Eiffel, 1916

The invitation card specified 'Paintings and Ornament', and a review in the April 1916 issue of *Colour* reported that 'gay vorticist designs cover the walls, and call from the tablecloth', which suggests that this private upstairs room contained applied art as well as painted panels. *Colour* decided that the scheme was 'a welcome surprise', because 'we have suffered so severely from the decoration of cafés in England and abroad'; and the reviewer concluded that the paintings were 'good in colour, and very decorative, although their meaning is not self-evident'. One month later, the same magazine carried an article on 'Futurism in Furnishing' by Guy Cadogan Rothery, who reported that a 'provocative and arresting power is also to be felt when confronting the storied walls' of the Vorticist Room. 'In this case we may demur to the symbolism alleged to lurk in what the man of average perceptive faculties will consider weird creations, formless forms set down by the artist', he continued, clearly baffled by Lewis's extreme degree of abstraction; 'but the appeal of the colour is undeniable.' Rothery was in two minds about the Room, prophesying that 'those outside the vortex may, on recovering from their giddiness, retain much of what is worth incorporating in our system of applied arts. All the more so as the extreme violence of the rebels is not essential outside the battle area, within which we may occasionally desire to stray though not caring to live there'.

No photographs of the decorations appear to have survived, and the present owners of the now renamed White Tower Restaurant confirmed that 'unfortunately, when we came here in 1938, we found no trace of them. Between Stulik going and our coming, the place had become a hotel of sorts and the first floor, the "Wyndham Lewis" room, was cut up into three bedrooms'. But as luck would have it, the painter Harry Jonas was recently still able, as an habitué of the Tour Eiffel during the 1920s, to remember the paintings there, 'a big one between the windows . . . and others on the remaining walls'. The predominant colours were, he told the author, 'bright red and green' and 'very raw'; but they nevertheless 'had the effect in the room of being on the low-toned side and somewhat gave the room the deep coloured atmosphere one senses, rather than sees, in Or San Michele at Florence'. As for their general content, Jonas wrote that 'the subject matter of the pictures I should describe as semi-abstract. Buildings, etc., very "Gothick", strong lines and flat patches of colour: a geometrical treatment'. He also thought that Lewis's scheme was 'directly done on the walls . . . at any rate they were not just lodged up: for, again, I seem to recall quite a to-do to get them removed . . . I take it that the work was scrubbed off the walls'. Jonas only got to know the Vorticist Room in 1921, and 'the excitement must have cooled owing to the war. There was still some talk about the work, but no-one seemed any longer to allude to it with much enthusiasm'. By then, of course, Vorticism was dead and the degree of abstraction propounded at the Tour Eiffel had been rejected by virtually every considerable artist working in England.

The Vorticists, however, spent a lot of time in Lewis's room before the war; and Roberts, who emphasized that the rebel movement was not 'developed in the gloom of a studio, but at the Tour Eiffel over a *tourne-dos* and a bottle of Burgundy', pointed out very perceptively how 'the Blasting, Cursing, Damning and Blessing of the opening pages of our puce-coloured Manifesto have the gusto of a tavern song'. He even remembered, with understandable gastronomic relish, that 'a *Specialité de la Maison* at the Tour Eiffel was a confection Stulik called Gâteau St. Honoré. This was a large circular custard tart ornamented round its edge with big balls of pastry. Lewis was very partial to this *gâteau* and always took a second helping; he excused himself one day for this, by repeating the remark Schopenhauer is reputed to have made: "If you thought as much as I do, you would eat as much as I do"'.[18]

These three projects were the sum total of the commissions inspired by the advent of the Great English Vortex: 'with the exception', wrote Roberts, 'of a few small objects such as painted match-box holders, by Miss Dismorr and Miss Saunders, probably from Lewis's own designs'.[19] The movement failed to attract the munificence of a Shchukin or a Gertrude Stein, and none of the London dealers showed the faith in their work that Kahnweiler gave to Picasso over in Paris. It is intensely galling to wonder how the rebels would have responded to the challenge of an imaginative public commission, or what the combined talents of this eager clutch of painters and sculptors could have produced as a monument to their hopes for a truly radical national art. Something of their frustration can be guessed at by reading between the lines of Lewis's embittered admission that 'we cannot hope that after the War England will change her skin so much that she will become a wise and kind protector of the Arts. Almost alone among the countries of Europe she has proved herself incapable of producing that small band of wealthy people, who are open to ideas, ahead of the musical-comedy and academics of their age, and prepared to spend a few hundred pounds a year less on petrol or social pyrotechnics, and buy pictures or organize the success of new music or new plays'.[20]

The position was hopeless, and England's cultural vitality slumped as the war entered its second year. 'The mental temperature of London fell imperceptibly but rapidly', recalled Aldington. 'Business as usual, so popular a slogan among merchants, did not apply to intellectual activities. Literary papers quietly disappeared, literary articles were not wanted, poems had to be patriotic. The old camaraderie disappeared, and along with it the old simplicity.'[21] The rebels' dreams about a genuine renewal of art disappeared, too, and they eked out a meagre living in their studios, doggedly executing work that nobody wanted to buy. Morale sank lower still when Lewis contracted an illness in the autumn of 1914 which continued to beleaguer him for many months. Plans for the publication of a second issue of *Blast*, already prorogued by the outbreak of war, thus received an additional setback. He managed to combat ill health sufficiently to paint a series of sizeable, virtually abstract pictures which elaborated on the ideas put forward in the Vorticist Manifestos, and sometimes had his spirits restored when caprices were arranged by his friends. 'Arbuthnot has a malicious photograph of me in an article in *Leaders of Modern Movement*', he wrote laughingly to Pound around January 1915. 'There I figure with Poynter, Sargent, Jacob and John. Poynter, they say, is the leader of a "movement that is almost extinct." It is full of wit. But for Arbuthnot's behaviour I know no parallel in the history of art.'[22]

These occasional outbursts of devilment were, however, only the brief intervals in a long period of disappointment and hardship, when Lewis often had to take to his bed and vent all his pent-up spleen on the completion of his first novel, *Tarr*. Finished, according to the author himself, 'with extreme haste, during the first year of the War, during a period of illness and restless convalescence', the book represents Lewis's most ambitious attempt to carry over the radicalism of his art into the medium of the novel.[23] His 'Enemy of the Stars' in *Blast No. 1* actually approximated far more closely to his pictorial language than *Tarr* was to do, but he nevertheless set out to create the book with that ideal in mind. 'In writing *Tarr* I wanted at the same time, for it to be a novel, and to do a piece of writing worthy of the hand of the abstractist innovator (which was an impossible combination)' he explained later. 'Anyhow it was my object to eliminate anything less essential than a noun or a verb. Prepositions, pronouns, articles – the small fry – as far as might be, I would abolish. Of course I was unable to do this, but for the purposes of the novel, I produced a somewhat jagged prose.'[24] He did indeed; and quite apart from stylistic considerations, the book contains some valuable insights into the workings of Lewis's mind at this crucial stage in the progress of Vorticism.

It is a comedy of ideas, essentially, and possesses a special fascination for the reader who wants to find Lewis's ideas expressed in a more human and approachable way than they are in *Blast No. 1*. The character of Tarr himself, an egotistical painter who hovers between mistresses in bohemian Paris, endlessly discussing the problems of art and life, tallies in many respects with the personality of his creator, and feeds upon Lewis's own libertine sojourn in the French capital as well. Indeed, in replying to a literary friend who had criticized *Tarr* by complaining that 'the characters appear to me mechanical automatons, wound up in order to spout forth opinions, instead of breathing with life', Lewis admitted that 'I make Tarr too much my mouthpiece'.[25]

Only one side of Lewis's temperament was personified by Tarr – he was consciously opposed in the novel to the romantic, incompetent figure of Otto Kreisler – but it was a significant side all the same. Lewis made him the spokesman for thoughts and opinions that had already been aired in the staccato prose of *Blast No. 1*, though an element of wish-fulfilment can be detected as Lewis, powerless in his desire to free England from all the attitudes of mind he so heartily detested, lashed out through the medium of fiction as a substitute for concrete action. When Tarr complained that Kreisler's life could be viewed as 'an attempt to get out of Art back into Life again', he was enabling Lewis to condemn all the reactionary painters he despised. From the Vorticist point of view, the book's most dramatic confrontation occurs when, within a few pages of each other, Kreisler and Tarr both execute a picture. Kreisler's motif, 'the doing of a Salon artist of facile and commercial invention', was a semi-naked half-length of Bertha, whom he then goes on to rape in accordance with the best traditions of French nineteenth century studio life. The two of them 'disappeared in the whirlpool towards which they had, with a strange deliberateness and yet aimlessness, been steering', Lewis explained, presenting the episode in terms of an image that would link their undisciplined appetites with his idea of a spinning vortex which destroyed anyone not firmly established at its calm centre. The inevitable outcome of Kreisler's absurdity was suicide; whereas Tarr calmly proceeds elsewhere in Paris to execute a cruel satire on the kind of futile Salon art Kreisler had espoused. 'By the end of the afternoon he had got a witty pastiche on the way', Lewis wrote, laughing at the 'three naked youths sniffing the air, with rather worried Greek faces, and heavy nether limbs.' It was an evocation of the work he himself had produced around 1912 as an attack on the obsolete Victorian worship of the classical canon, and it afforded an ideal contrast to the mindless abandon of Kreisler. Both in its anti-sentimental colours, 'a smoky, bilious saffron, and a pale transparent lead', and its refusal to work from a model, Tarr's studio procedure was intended as a model for the working attitudes of a Vorticist artist.

But nobody cared about this revolution; or if they did, they merely treated it as the amusing outpourings of a born controversialist. Lewis made Tarr express his reluctant acknowledgement that nothing the Vorticists attempted during 1914 had awoken the English from their 'phlegmatic and hysterical dream-world, full of the delicious swirls of the switch-back, the drunkenness of the merry-go-round – screaming leaps from idea to idea'. The 'puce monster' had failed to call a halt to such a meaningless flux, the outer edges of the vortex whirlpool; and Tarr sadly confessed that 'my little weapon for bringing my man to earth – shot gun or what not – gave me good sport, too, and was of the best workmanship. I carried it slung jauntily for some time at my side – you may have noticed it. But I am in the tedious position of the man who hits the bull's eye every time'.[26] The pathos of Tarr's admission of impotence was real enough: both he and Lewis had repeatedly struck the desired target, but without either demolishing it or replacing it with a fresh structure of their own ordering. Lewis's solution, in the book as in his actual life, was to cultivate indifference towards an alien world. The decision made him move further towards a detached, ruthless abstraction, as his surviving paintings and drawings of the period prove; and they received a fictional explanation in Tarr's decision to adopt a heartless view of external reality.

His views are set out most succinctly at the end of the book, where Tarr elaborates on his fervent belief that art is an extraction from life, a purification of reality that reorganizes the messiness and inconsequence into something crisp, tough and abstracted. 'Anything living, quick and changing, is bad art, always', Tarr explains; 'naked men and women are the worst art of all, because there are fewer semi-dead things about them. . . . Soft, quivering and quick flesh is as far from art as an object can be.' Just as Pound had distinguished between Symbolism and Impressionism, Vorticism and Futurism in his *Fortnightly Review* essay, so Tarr spoke for his creator when he stressed the importance of distinguishing between 'a hippopotamus' armoured hide, a turtle's shell, feathers or machinery on the one hand; *that* opposed to naked pulsing and moving of the soft inside of life, along with infinite elasticity and consciousness of movement, on the other. – Deadness, then . . . in the limited sense in which we use that word, is the first condition of art. The second is absence of *soul*, in the sentimental human sense. The lines and masses of the statue are its soul. No restless, quick flame-like ego is imagined for the *inside* of it. It has no inside. This is another condition of art; *to have no inside*, nothing you cannot *see*. Instead, then, of being something impelled like an independent machine by a little egoistic fire inside, it lives soullessly and deadly by its frontal lines and masses'.[27] If Lewis could not persuade England of the truth contained in the vortex, he was still able to comfort himself with the expatiation of his ideals in fictional form. The writing of *Tarr* must have provided an invaluable catharsis for the repressed energy seething inside his temporarily ailing body.

Eventually, however, he rallied his strength sufficiently to organize the first – and only – Vorticist Exhibition that London was privileged to witness. The project had obviously been fermenting in his mind ever since he first decided to turn *Blast No. 1* into a vehicle for the new movement; but the war, his own physical incapacity and a probable unwillingness on the part of gallery owners to harbour such a hated and unsaleable show meant that the plan was not actually put into operation until the summer of 1915, almost a year after the publication of the Vorticist organ. And even then, it was a strangely compromised selection of work that finally opened at the Doré Galleries on 10 June. Lewis may have claimed in the catalogue that 'this is the first exhibition of a group of painters, to whom the name Vorticist has been given', and explained that although 'their work has been seen in various Exhibitions, the London Group, the Allied Artists and elsewhere . . . this is the first time in England that a Gallery has been used for the special exhibition of nothing but the work of this tendency by English artists'. But his fanfare conveniently ignored signs of further dissension within the rebel ranks. The list of 'members' printed in the catalogue now contained only seven names, as opposed to the eleven that had appeared at the end of the *Blast No. 1* Manifesto. And if Etchells had at last consented to be counted among them, his conversion did not really compensate for the departure of Hamilton and Atkinson – whom Roberts remembered having 'aspirations to leadership of his own, and promoted a kind of rival abstract painting and music centre' – or the continued abstention of both Bomberg and Epstein.[28] The loss of Epstein was only to be expected: Pound reported in March 1915 that the sculptor 'and Lewis have some feud or other which I haven't inquired into',[29] and the following month Epstein even went so far as to tell John Quinn that the Vorticists were 'plagiarists from Marinetti'.[30] But without the signatures of those who did not paint or carve (Aldington, Arbuthnot and Pound) the kernel of Vorticist aficionados looked diminished: the alphabetical roll-call cited Dismorr, Etchells, Gaudier, Roberts, Saunders, Wadsworth and Wyndham Lewis. That was all.

The brave words Lewis placed on the large poster he prepared for the exhibition were not, then, entirely borne out by the facts of the case. And the strangest aspect of the whole venture was the presence of six painters in a special section of their own, tacked onto the movement's corpus like a worried afterthought. 'In addition to the Vorticist Group several other artists similar in aim have been invited to exhibit', Lewis explained in his catalogue 'Note', 'and the show includes specimens of the work of every notable painter working at all in one or other of the new directions.' What was the point of this mysterious second group, lumped together unceremoniously in the catalogue under the generic heading of 'Those Invited to Show'? It was useful, admittedly, to have Bomberg there with three paintings and the same number of drawings: he was, after all, one of the most outstanding rebel talents, and his presence could only enhance the survey of English abstraction which the exhibition aimed at providing. Atkinson, likewise, was to be welcomed with his trio of paintings, albeit as a sheep half-way out of his former fold. But the introduction of artists as divorced from the concerns of Vorticism as Bernard Adeney, Grant, Jacob Kramer and – most ironic of all – Nevinson made nonsense of the exhibition's primary aim. One critic even thought it 'interesting to note that in this strange company Mr Nevinson's Futurist paintings look absolutely normal and almost academic!'[31] and Nevinson himself naturally insisted on the appellation 'Futurist' in brackets after his name, to make his independence absolutely clear. As for Adeney and Kramer, their presence did nothing but dilute whatever concerted impact Lewis had presumably hoped to achieve in the show. And the fact that Roger Fry had at one stage been invited to participate in this section makes the exhibition's

FIRST
VORTICIST
EXHIBITION.
PAINTINGS, DRAWINGS,
AND SCULPTURE
BY
ETCHELLS, BRZESKA,
ROBERTS, WADSWORTH,
WYNDHAM LEWIS,
DISMORR, SAUNDERS.
DORÉ GALLERY DAILY 10–6.
35, NEW BOND STREET, W.

Poster for the Vorticist Exhibition, 1915

△ Vanessa Bell
*Abstract Painting, c.* 1914

▷ Duncan Grant
*Abstract Kinetic Collage Painting with Sound*
(detail), 1914

▽ Duncan Grant
*The White Jug,* 1915–22

focus look still more blurred.

Only the inclusion of Grant might have made sense. He had already demonstrated a taste for catholic experiment at the Omega; and although never inspired by the same kind of didactic conviction that motivated the Vorticists, both he and Vanessa Bell were actually executing remarkably abstract pictures around 1915. One particularly interesting example of Bell's non-figurative work – a warmly coloured painting restricted to a bare equation of flat geometrical forms – survives to prove that she would not have appeared anomalous at the Doré Galleries exhibition. And David Garnett remembered, on a visit to Grant's studio around this time, that 'Duncan brought out a long band of green cotton on two rollers. I stood and held one roller vertically and unwound while, standing a couple of yards away, Duncan wound up the other, and a series of supposedly related, abstract shapes was displayed before our disgusted visitors'.[32] This long scroll of completely abstract *papier découpé* forms was originally intended to unroll like a kinetic picture on motorized wheels, accompanied by Bach's music; and so the three paintings Grant sent to the Vorticist show may easily have been non-representational as well. A couple of them were simply called *One* and *Two*, which lends strength to the hypothesis; and one reviewer of the show declared that 'the admission of Mr Duncan Grant's "paintings", consisting of bits of firewood glued on to a dirty canvas, with here and there a few vertical stripes of colour, carries with it the danger that the whole exhibition may be suspected of *fumisterie*'.[33] What is more, at least one of Grant's contemporaneous paintings, based entirely on a series of vertical coloured stripes, still exists – even if he later added an anomalous jug and some fruit to counteract its non-representational severity.[34]

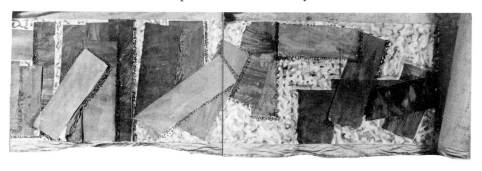

But the contributions of the Vorticists themselves must have ensured that, for all the inconsistencies inherent in the arrangement of the show, the Doré Galleries housed a spectacular survey of avant-garde English art. The stark design reproduced on the front cover of the exhibition's catalogue made clear that its contents defended the viability of abstraction, and major experiments in semi-abstraction by artists as gifted as Gaudier, Roberts, Wadsworth and Lewis would have constituted an impressive argument in favour of the new movement. If all the work they showed there could be recovered now, it would add up to a powerful condemnation of the critics who dismissed Vorticism as hocus-pocus at the time. Even Konody, that arch-enemy of Vorticism, was forced to admit in his *Observer* review of the exhibition that 'when six artists like Dismorr, Etchells, Roberts, Saunders, Wadsworth and Wyndham Lewis show such absolute oneness of purpose and similarity of method, it is reasonable to assume that they have definite aims and mutual understanding'.[35] The collective aims of the group were beginning to cohere, only a year after its formation had been announced; and a uniform Vorticist style, an independent alternative to Cubism, Futurism and Expressionism, had emerged from the tumult of a world war. It was a remarkable achievement, especially in view of Lewis's personal ability to offend so many of his potential supporters, and it signified a definitive watershed

in the development of British painting. For after this exhibition had closed, no-one could accurately say that the English still lagged behind the Continent in terms of artistic renewal. The spirit of uncompromising abstraction which Vorticism fostered even spread to isolated provincial centres such as Leeds, where B. S. Turner translated the violence of a *Boxing Match* into a formalized design that conveyed all the dynamic vitality of its theme.[36] Minor talents like Turner were, therefore, inspired by the nucleus of courageous men and women in London who were able to stand up and declare their independence of all rival European movements. Could any other comparable group in the entire history of modernism claim more than this, with a mere twelve months of battle-torn existence behind it? Vorticism was not, ultimately, as considerable in terms of creative achievement as its opponents in France, Germany and Italy; but who is to say how the comparison would have stood if the rebels had been granted a few years of peace in which to develop and consolidate their ideas?

The encroachment of war ensured that the Doré show was the only one of its kind by calling most of its participants up to the front line soon afterwards. And the critics dealt the final blow to the Vorticists' hopes with a panning that spared no-one in its derision. 'One cannot believe in collective insanity with the identical symptoms in six different men', wrote Konody, scarcely able to prevent himself from insisting that the rebels be packed off into an asylum. 'At the same time, it is permissible to hesitate to accept these pictures and drawings as legitimate works of art.' He still could not bring himself to admit any real possibility that the Vorticists were artists at all. 'If it is the function of the work of art to transmit an emotion, the transmission must be effected by some kind of intelligible language', he continued. 'The Vorticists' experiments in angular jagged rhythm . . . do not transmit any kind of emotion and, therefore, have no *raison d'être* as works of art. Abstraction carried too far becomes meaningless. What the Vorticists appear to have in common is a perfect dread lest their colour stripe jumbles should by any chance resemble some recognisable form or approach the symmetry of deliberate pattern.'[37] On the evidence of the few surviving exhibits, most of the pictures shown at the Doré Galleries did, in fact, retain identifiable references to outward reality. A number of them included configurations based clearly on the human form, but Konody seems to have found it impossible to spend time deciphering elements he considered uncongenial. A barrier had been built up by his inborn prejudices against the idea of total abstraction, and if he thought the process had been 'carried too far', then his responses ceased to function and the barrier clamped down like a guillotine on his unfortunate victims.

His disapproval was seconded by his critical colleagues, even if some of them appeared to grasp more of Vorticism's objectives than he had done. The *Glasgow Herald* was surprisingly acute when it decided that, 'casting behind them Post-Impressionism, Futurism, Cubism, and one knows not what besides, this gallant band, in theory at any rate, seems to stake all on the unrepresentational rendering of energy'.[38] It was a conclusion after Lewis's own heart, but the reviewer devoted the rest of his column to an unfavourable debate as to whether the Vorticists had succeeded in translating this 'theory' into effective practice.

Without one voice raised in defence of the Vorticist cause, the outlook was bleak indeed. This time there was no Hulme to hurry forward to the rescue, damn all the critics and champion the exhibition. The philosopher was far too much in agreement with Epstein, and too involved in the composition of articles on the Great War in *The New Age* to bestir himself once again.[39] In this no-man's-land of rejection and rampant philistinism, it was a relief to find *The Athenaeum*'s reviewer making the sensible, simple remark that 'the Vorticists, loosely included by journalists among the Futurists of yesterday, were also the Cubists of the day before, and the name clearly fits better the present work of Messrs Wyndham Lewis and Wadsworth than any previously coined'. The critic was not, of course, favourably disposed towards the exhibition, but at least he was prepared to give it the benefit of the doubt; and that, in the overall context of hostility and mistrust, assumed the proportions of a minor miracle. 'They certainly fill their canvases with systems of interacting movement, the co-ordinations and antagonisms of which are admirably stressed by a use of colour very similar to that of any other capable designer', he wrote, his studied objectivity teetering on the very edge of condescension. 'Their designs are now virtually rectilinear, the small sharp curve occasionally introduced as a kind of knot being used not for purposes of transition, but rather to envenom the clash of opposing forces. To speak of such a design as a Vortex reveals, it is true, little but what any artistically trained mind would already appreciate in it, but at least it is not a mystification.'

*The Athenaeum*'s critic had obviously looked more closely at the exhibits, and responded to them more positively, than any other reviewer. But even he eventually came down on the side of all his professional colleagues by complaining that 'we see on one canvas a vortex, on another a second vortex. They differ slightly, but are all generalised to vagueness in spite of extreme incisiveness in the means of expression'. The unprecedented degree of abstraction employed in the pictures disoriented him so thoroughly that he saw no essential variation between one composition and the next. The patterns seemed arbitrary and monotonous, for all their aggressive power, and he decided that 'while it is difficult to define the significance of these schemes of movement, there is, to our mind, much in human experience which they do not express in the least'. He even referred to the comments made by a contemporary cartoonist in his efforts to elucidate his misgivings, citing a *Punch* drawing which had appeared one day before the Doré Galleries exhibition opened.[40] Picking out the use of the word 'plan' in the cartoon, *The Athenaeum*'s reviewer wrote that 'the word is a just one: these designs are *plans*, with no distinction between upright and horizontal – that is to say, no sense of weight, of the pull of the earth. Doubtless, these distinctions are not in the ultimate sense fundamental, but even the idea of spring is almost too concrete for expression in a stark world of ideas wherein is no aspiration'. The writer failed to realize that this selfsame 'stark world of ideas' symbolized 'aspiration' of a fresh, demanding and extremely positive kind; but then, he could hardly be expected to appreciate this fact if he was deluded enough to complain about the absence of something as irrelevant as 'the pull of the earth'. Both he and his fellow critics were floundering in a

"So vast is Art, so narrow human wit."

*Cubist Artist (who is being arrested for espionage by local constable).* "MY DEAR MAN, HAVE YOU NO ÆSTHETIC SENSE? CAN'T YOU SEE THAT THIS PICTURE IS AN EMOTIONAL IMPRESSION OF THE INHERENT GLADNESS OF SPRING?"

*Constable.* "STOW IT, CLARENCE! D'YER THINK I DON'T KNOW A BLOOMIN' PLAN WHEN I SEES ONE?"

E. E. Briscoe
*So Vast is Art, So Narrow Human Wit*, 1915

slough of ignorance, and there seemed to be no way in which their superstitions could be allayed.

It was, for instance, becoming increasingly apparent that Lewis would never be able to serve them up with the kind of explanation they would be able – or prepared – to comprehend. *The Athenaeum*'s critic resented this lack of a clear rationale, a framework from which he could formulate a more balanced judgement of the Vorticists' precepts; and he stated in his review that 'these objections are provisional, Mr Lewis being as, alas! is usual – too busy pointing out the inadequacy of other methods of painting to have space adequately to explain his own'.[41] The complaint was understandable and, in a sense, just; but it must be remembered that the English movement had only just been born. In common with most of the other avant-garde groups that sprang to life in the first two decades of the twentieth century, it started off by clearing the ground, attacking both the immediate past and potential rivals. The Futurists' aesthetic position was only formulated cumulatively, in a number of manifestos stretching over several years of hectic activity; when the 'Manifesto of Futurist Painters' was defiantly proclaimed from the stage of Turin's Politeama Chiarella in March 1910 there was as yet nothing that could be fairly analysed as Futurist art. And Cubism never had a proper manifesto to expound the philosophy of its practitioners. Only the exalted prose of Apollinaire, and the one-sided, dangerously academic explanations of Gleizes and Metzinger served to unfold the mysteries of the Cubist revolution. The truth of the matter was that Lewis, despite his literary ambitions and undoubted journalistic flair, was as loath to talk about the workings of his own creative intuition as any other artist engaged on a voyage of discovery. All he did feel moved to write down were violent, poetic broadsides intended to arouse the English from their smugness and backward-looking mental habits. 'As this paper is run chiefly by Painters and for Painting', he said of *Blast* in 1915, 'and they are only incidentally Propagandists, they do their work first, and, since they must, write about it afterwards.'[42]

Besides, there still appeared to be plenty of time ahead to elaborate on the principles they had established with such panache. Although the spectre of imminent enlistment loomed up in front of all the male Vorticists, they had no reason to suppose that the Doré Galleries exhibition would provide the last opportunity to convert London to their way of thinking. They were all young; their ideas would mature with their art; and successive instalments of *Blast* would no doubt contain deeper, fuller definitions of their own singular viewpoint. For the moment, Lewis was content to enjoy himself in his 'Note' to the Doré Galleries catalogue, letting his penchant for exuberant language develop into a full-blooded verbal skirmish. 'Artists today have an immense commercialized mass of painting and every form of art to sanify or destroy', he announced, preparing himself for the fray. 'There has never been such a load of sugary, cheap, anecdotal and in every way pitiable muck poured out by the ton – or, rather, such a spectacle socially has never been witnessed before. There is not a little grocer in Balham, bromidic Baroness in Bayswater, or dejected Princess who has not a gross of artists closely attending to his or her needs, aesthetically.' The ideal antidote for this lamentable malaise – as prevalent today as it was when Lewis cursed it so vigorously in 1915 – was to take the Vorticist rebellion out into the streets where everyone could be affected by its stern message. Lewis was prepared to face the fact that 'definite POPULAR acceptance' of 'such abstract works as are found here ... should never be aimed at'. But he was still prepared to 'give a direct example of how this revolution will work in popular ways. In poster advertisement by far the most important point is a telling design. Were the walls of London carpeted with abstractions rather than the present mass of work that falls between two stools, the design usually weakened to explain some point, the effect architecturally would be much better, and the Public taste could thus be educated in a popular way to appreciate the essentials of design better than picture-galleries have ever done'.

Little did Lewis know, when he wrote those prophetic words, that the principal way in which the lessons of Vorticism were to be disseminated in England after the war was through the outstanding posters designed by McKnight-Kauffer for newspapers, department stores and the Underground. The Vorticist leader was still determined to lay down the priorities of his movement in new ways, and made a brave attempt in the catalogue 'Note' to summarize its objectives in a concise, abrasive form. 'By Vorticism', he wrote, 'we mean (a) ACTIVITY as opposed to the tasteful PASSIVITY of Picasso; (b) SIGNIFICANCE as opposed to the dull or anecdotal character to which the Naturalist is condemned; (c) ESSENTIAL MOVEMENT and ACTIVITY (such as the energy of a mind) as opposed to the imitative cinematography, the fuss and hysterics of the Futurists.' Activity, significance, essential movement: all three were qualities that Lewis wanted Vorticism to signify. And behind them, controlling, marshalling and galvanizing into dynamic action, must be a fierce intelligence – 'the energy of a mind' which he included by way of elucidation in this sharply expressed round-up of Vorticist beliefs.

Looking at the works that have survived from this one most important year of Vorticism's existence, it is easy to see how Lewis's programme provided an eloquent verbal commentary on the style of the pictures themselves. But to the critics, Lewis's latest definition merely confirmed them in their suspicion that the whole movement was rooted in mumbo-jumbo, cooked up by a gaggle of publicity-seeking phonies who disguised their lack of ideas in a cloud of obscurantist prose. The vocabulary in which Vorticist theories were transmitted was not incomprehensible: it was just that the terms of reference employed had not yet been grasped by the men for whom they were intended. The result was an insoluble stalemate.

Lewis, realizing the dimensions of the chasm separating him and his allies from the outside world, tried hard to expound on his tripartite definition in the exhibition catalogue. He knew he was dissipating his energies on a futile project, but what other options were open to him? '(a) Picasso in his latest work is rather in the same category as a dressmaker, he matches little bits of stuff he finds lying about', he wrote, elaborating on the theme of ACTIVITY. 'He puts no life into the pieces of cloth or paper he sticks side by side, but rather CON-TEMPLATES THEIR BEAUTY, placing other things near them that please. His works are monuments of taste, but too much natures-mortes the whole time.' With hindsight, it is possible to see this passage as an eminently understandable critique of all that Lewis shrank away from in Synthetic Cubism: its decorative bent, pacific charm and obsession with domestic themes. Seeking to throw light on his second point, about SIGNIFICANCE, he wrote: '(b) The impression received on a hot afternoon on the quays of some port, made up of the smell of tar and fish, the heat of the sun, the history of the place, cannot be conveyed by any imitation of a corner of it. The influences weld themselves into an hallucination or dream (which all the highest art has always been) with a mathematic of its own.' In one lucid sentence, Lewis had produced a stirring evocation of that ideal blend of fantasy and geometry towards which Vorticist pictures were striving. But the critics refused to grasp his meaning, and they resisted Lewis's explanation of ESSENTIAL MOVEMENT as well: '(c) Moods, ideas and visions have movements, associating themselves with objects or an object', Lewis continued doggedly. 'An object also has an ESSEN-TIAL movement, and essential environment, however intimate and peculiar an object it may be – even a telephone receiver or an Alpine flower.' He was affirming the importance of 'one thing' as against 'a thousand' which he had already defended in his argument with Marinetti in the lavabo. But by this time he had had enough: there was little point in these abortive justifications, and he wearily referred the reader to his long essay in the forthcoming sequel to *Blast No. 1*. 'It is difficult to condense in a short foreword these ideas in such a way as to dispel the suspicion and puzzlement of the Public in looking at these pictures', he wrote. 'In the second number of "BLAST", which is appearing in a week's time, there is a full and detailed exposition of them.'[43] The forty-one Vorticist paintings, drawings and woodcuts, along with the eight sculptures by Gaudier, would have to stand on their own merits, strung along the walls of 'part of the principal room of the Doré Gallery', as the *Glasgow Herald* reported. They were, after all, the finest artefacts the movement had yet produced, and written dogma was best left in the care of *Blast No. 2*.

As it happened, Lewis's promised essay in *Blast*'s second number, 'A Review of Contemporary Art', turned out to be at once his most elaborate and most frustrating piece of theorizing on the subject of Vorticism. Written, according to the preliminary 'Note', in the spring of 1915, it represented his biggest effort to organize his thoughts on the movement and separate out its destiny from the continental groups that persisted in obscuring the Vorticists' identity. He began his ambitious task from the widest of all possible angles, claiming that 'the painters have cut away and cut away warily, till they have trapped some essential. European painting today is like the laboratory of an anatomist: things stand up stark and denuded everywhere as the result of endless visionary examination'. All radical artists were, therefore, basically united in their aims; but what Lewis set out to do, with as much articulate passion as he could muster, was explain once and for all how Vorticism differed from Cubism, Futurism and Expressionism. He succeeded, but did not manage fully to outline the Vorticist alternative. An artist embroiled in the middle of a nascent movement could never entirely step outside his own activities and analyse them with the objectivity of an historian. Quite simply, he had not been granted enough time in which to paint, experiment and synthesize his work – let alone write down his conclusions. Indeed, Lewis gave what was tantamount to a confession of the essay's inadequacy by inserting, at the end, the promise that 'some further sections will be added to this Essay in the next number of the Magazine'.[44] But there never was a third copy of *Blast*. War intercepted, with irrevocable consequences, and 'A Review of Contemporary Art' – incomplete though it was – stands alongside Pound's 'Vorticism' essay as the best testament to Vorticist ideals that now remains. It contains only hints, but they are pregnant enough to merit careful examination.

The first few pages are once again given over to a detailed discussion of the failings perpetrated by those movements out of which the Great English Vortex had grown, and from which it now desired so urgently to divorce itself. Many of the sentiments had been expressed already in *Blast No. 1*, but not in such a coherent form. For here, Lewis first of all proceeded with magisterial disdain to refute Impressionism, and its commandment that 'your washing-stand or sideboard must be painted, with due attention to complementaries, and in form it must be Nature's empiric proportions and exactly Nature's usually insignificant arrangements'. It was directly opposed to Vorticism's philosophy of the primary pigment: the Impressionists considered that 'the pigment for its own sake and on its own merits as colour, was of no importance. It was only important in so far as it could reproduce the blendings of the prism'. Only 'Degas by violent perspectives (the theatre seen from its poulailler) or Cézanne by distortion and "bad drawing", escaped from this aesthetic legislation', and Lewis pronounced its influence to be insidious. 'So this pedantry', he wrote, 'with its scornful and snobbish verbotens, may be seen establishing its academies'; but he would not have thought it worthwhile to mention the movement at all were it not that 'one of the most important features of the painting of the C U B I S T S, and Picasso's practice, is a tenet they have taken over wholesale and unmodified from the I M P R E S S I O N I S T S'. The source of Lewis's restlessness with Cubism was rooted in the limited range of its subject-matter: 'Picasso through the whole of his "Cubist" period has always had for starting-point in his creations, however abstract, his studio-table with two apples and a mandoline, the portrait of a poet of his acquaintance, or what not'.[45] Such an approach was inconceivable to Lewis, with his yearning to reflect the whole fabric of modern civilization in his art.

But he had voiced these strictures before; and his essay was now far more anxious to point out that the Cubists' gravest error lay in their tendency to invest a slice of life with a grandeur out of all proportion to its true importance. 'Any portion of Nature we can observe is an unorganized and microscopic jumble, too profuse and too distributed to be significant', he wrote. 'If we could see with larger eyes we should no doubt be satisfied. But to make any of these minute individual areas, or individuals, too proudly compact or monumental, is probably an equal stupidity.' And then, in a passage of eloquent conviction, he explained how the Vorticists tackled the vast spectrum of reality. 'Finite and god-like lines are not for us', he insisted, 'but, rather, a powerful but remote suggestion of finality, or a momentary organization of a dark insect swarming, like the passing of a cloud's shadow or the path of a wind.' Therein lay the most exciting substance of human experience, and 'the moment the Plastic is impoverished for the Idea, we get out of direct contact with these intuitive waves of power, that only play on the rich surfaces where life is crowded and abundant'.

His tone became passionate as he impressed upon his readers the need to retain a flexible and subtle relationship with nature: one which kept itself open to the influence of evanescent sensations even as it sought to reorganize them into a rigid Vorticist structure. 'We must constantly strive to ENRICH abstraction till it is almost plain life', he cried, 'or rather to get deeply enough immersed in material life to experience the shaping power amongst its vibrations, and to accentuate and perpetuate these.'[46] This was the heart of the English rebels' programme, and Lewis stressed that 'we must not abate in our interrogation' of the problems it entailed.

There was no help to be gained from the Futurists, who upset the profound balance at which Vorticism aimed by substituting for 'the POSED MODEL, imitative and static side of CUBISM' the 'hurly-burly and exuberance of actual life'. Lewis had already exhausted his impatience with 'their doctrine . . . of maximum fluidity and interpenetration', and hurried on to criticize the Expressionists – a task he had not attempted before.

The basis of his case against Kandinsky (for it was his art alone that Lewis chose to dissect) rested on its tendency to become nothing more than a non-representational equivalent of Futurist fluidity. 'Kandinsky is the only PURELY abstract painter in Europe', he stated. 'But he is so careful to be passive and medium-like, and is committed, by his theory, to avoid almost all powerful and definite forms, that he is, at the best, wandering and slack.' It was Kandinsky, in fact, who led Lewis to the most vital contention of his essay, for he considered the German's brand of abstraction to be as bankrupt as the Academician who let mindless imitation predominate in his art. 'In what is one painting representative and another non-representative?' he asked, before posing a whole battery of other questions which strove to demonstrate the impossibility of escaping from some kind of figurative content. 'If a man is not representing people, is he not representing clouds? If he is not representing clouds, is he not representing masses of bottles? If he is not representing masses of bottles is he not representing houses and masonry? Or is he not representing in his most seemingly abstract paintings, mixtures of these, or of something else? Always REPRESENTING, at all events.'[47] This line of thought, ruling out the possibility that a work of art could ever represent nothing apart from its own arrangement of forms and colours, was the main reason for Vorticism's determination to hover on the border-line between the two alternative conventions.

The artist who had 'passed the test of seriousness in weeding sentiment out of his work' and 'left it hard, clean and plastic' need never worry about retaining representational elements in his pictures. All Kandinsky succeeded in doing, by convincing himself that he dealt with pure abstraction, was to execute paintings in which the unavoidable figurative references were enfeebled and irrelevant. 'Kandinsky, docile to the intuitive fluctuations of his soul, and anxious to render his hand and mind elastic and receptive, follows this unreal entity into its cloud-world, out of the material and solid universe', wrote Lewis, ridiculing what he saw as the formless meanderings of an artist who ought to stop deluding himself and admit the presence of representation in art. 'He allows the Bach-like will that resides in each good artist to be made war on by the slovenly and wandering Spirit', Lewis insisted. 'He allows the rigid chambers of his Brain to become a mystic house haunted by an automatic and puerile Spook, that leaves a delicate trail like a snail. It is just as useless to employ this sort of Dead, as it is to have too many dealings with the Illustrious Professional Dead, known as Old Masters.'[48]

Having settled this fundamental question in accordance with the balance between observation and rigidity recommended earlier on in the essay, Lewis now asked whether, 'under these circumstances', it was 'a fault or a weakness if your shapes and objects correspond with a poetry or a sentiment, that in itself is not plastic, but sentimental?' And he solved it for himself by arguing that it was not, so long as the sentimental did genuinely coincide with formal pre-occupations. Lewis was salving his own conscience about the literary streak in his art when he protested that 'it is natural for us to represent a man as we would wish him to be; artists have always represented men as more beautiful, more symmetrically muscular, with more commanding countenances than they usually, in nature, possess'. In all the 'grandest and most majestic art in the world', he continued, citing 'Egyptian, Central African, American', this creative wish-fulfilment 'divested man of his vital plastic qualities and changed him into a more durable, imposing and in every way harder machine'. Hence the poetic squared up very neatly with the formal, for 'this dehumanizing has corresponded happily with the unhuman character, the plastic, architectural quality, of art itself'.

Lewis had provided himself with a clever rationale for his inclination to express literary ideas in his pictures. Just how blatantly literary he could some-times be is proved by the passage in his essay where he claims that 'in our time it is natural that an artist should wish to endow his "bonhomme" when he makes one in the grip of an heroic emotion, with something of the fatality, grandeur and efficiency of a machine'. For he then makes the astonishingly revealing assertion that 'when you watch an electric crane, swinging up with extraordinary grace and ease a huge weight, your instinct to admire this power is, subcon-sciously, a selfish one. It is a pity that there are not men so strong that they can lift a house up, and fling it across a river'.[49] The implications of this remark are fascinating. Lewis was confessing that his obsession with mechanical imagery did not originate solely from a desire to make English art relevant to twentieth-century life. It also mirrored the private wish of a human being to become as potent as a machine, as capable of large-scale destruction as a bulldozer or a tank. 'In any heroic, that is, energetic representations of men today, this reflec-tion of the immense power of machines will be reflected', he concluded; and it was now transparently clear that mechanical forms excited him partly because he could imagine them effecting the kind of wholesale revolution that he had wanted for so long. The equation was cunningly watertight: Lewis had evolved his Vorticist imagery to satisfy his desire for destruction, and this very destruc-tion would be carried out to establish the hegemony of the Vorticist imagery he had first evolved. The symmetry of this full circle was worthy of Lewis's calculating intelligence.

After presenting his case with such a display of logic, he could now afford to declare that 'the human and sentimental side of things, then, is so important that it is only a question of how much, if at all, this cripples or perverts the inhuman plastic nature of painting'. This was the crux of the problem con-fronting Lewis and his allies: how best to include in their art 'as much of the material poetry of Nature as the plastic vessel will stand'. And the one con-sideration to be held steadily in view was that modern life had tilted the scales of this ideal balance perceptibly in favour of abstraction. 'Nowadays, when Nature finds itself expressed so universally in specialized mechanical counter-parts, and cities have modified our emotions, the plastic vessel, paradoxically, is more fragile. The less human it becomes, the more delicate, from this point of view.' The perfect Vorticist work of art would arrange itself so as to vie with the wonderful sense of 'rightness' that Nature often produces. 'You must be able to organize the cups, saucers and people, or their abstract plastic equivalent, as naturally as Nature', Lewis stressed, 'only with the added personal logic of Art, that gives the grouping significance.' Once this ability had been mastered, the Vorticist would be able to produce great paintings and sculpture, for 'the finest artists – and this is what Art means – are those men who are so trained and sensitized that they have a perpetually renewed power of DOING WHAT NATURE DOES, only doing it with all the beauty of accident, without the certain futility that accident implies.'[50]

It was an almost intangible synthesis of abstraction and representation that Lewis prescribed; and in case his readers lost themselves in the honeycomb of his argument, imagining that he was proposing a weak-kneed compromise to bypass the problems of extremism, he finished his essay by hitting out at the practitioners of 'Decorative Art'. These 'between-men', personified in Lewis's mind by 'the Jugend, Rhythm, [and] Mr Roger Fry's little belated Morris movement', managed only to substitute 'a banal and obvious human logic for the co-ordination and architectures that the infinite forces of Nature bring about'. Then, in order to show everyone exactly where his first loyalties would always lie, and round off his theoretical tour de force with a curse in keeping with the combative side of his movement, Lewis announced that 'there should be a Bill passed in Parliament at once FORBIDDING ANY IMAGE OR RECOGNIZABLE SHAPE TO BE STUCK UP IN ANY PUB-LIC PLACE; or as advertisement or what-not, to be used in any way publicly. Only after passing a most severe and esoteric Board and getting a CERTIFI-CATE, should a man be allowed to represent in his work Human Beings, Animals, or Trees. Mr Brangwyn, Mr Nicholson and Sir Edward Poynter would not pass this Board: driven into the Vortex, there would be nothing left of them but a few Brangwynesque bubbles on the surface of the Abstract'.[51]

This rousing finale was worthy of the first Vorticist Manifesto, and proved that *Blast No. 2* had sustained the essential combination of wit, cheekiness and aggression throughout the twelve bitter months since its predecessor had first been launched on an unwilling populace. It appeared a more mature offspring of the movement, in that few of the works reproduced in *Blast No. 1* had been executed specifically as Vorticist creations. In *Blast No. 2* they were; and yet it was, perhaps inevitably, a bleaker and less invigorating issue than *Blast No. 1*. As if in acknowledgment of the change, it was called a 'WAR NUMBER', and Lewis reinforced the message by executing a stark black-and-white drawing of advancing soldiers enmeshed in a cruel complex of military shapes for the front cover. The design was entitled, topically enough, *Before Antwerp*; and if its degree of representation comes as a surprise when compared to the other work Lewis was producing around the same time, it was still as 'hard, clean and plastic' as he could have wished and probably reflected a conscious desire to produce a relatively unambiguous image. For the war raging across the Channel was a harsh affair, and the Vorticists knew it to their cost. Not only had it diverted attention from their own efforts during the past year; it had also, by the time *Blast No. 2* appeared in July, senselessly sacrificed one of the most promising members of the group. Gaudier, who was represented in the magazine by a photograph of his *Bust of Pound* and a forceful 'VORTEX GAUDIER-BRZESKA' article 'written from the trenches', had been killed in a charge at Neuville St. Vaast on 5 June. His obituary notice, printed in a black border under the heading 'MORT POUR LA PATRIE', cast a shadow over the entire periodical; and such a terrible tragedy made the occasional outbursts of high spirits emitted by other contributors seem misplaced.

Lewis's editorial nonetheless struck a note of grim yet implacable persistence. 'BLAST finds itself surrounded by a multitude of other Blasts of all sizes and descriptions', he began, coming straight to the point. 'This puce-coloured cockleshell will, however, try and brave the waves of blood, for the serious mission it has on the other side of World-War.' Despite the alarming realization that the holocaust looked as if it would drag on for many years, he was con-

Wyndham Lewis
*Before Antwerp*: Cover of *Blast No. 2*, 1915

Four abstract designs from *Blast No. 2*, 1915

vinced that Vorticism would survive. 'The art of Pictures, the Theatre, Music, etc., has to spring up again with new questions and beauties when Europe has disposed of its difficulties', he urged. 'And just as there will be a reaction in the Public then to a more ardent gaiety, art should be fresher for the period of restraint. Blast will be there with an apposite insistence.'[52]

He struggled hard to inject some of the old venom into the second issue, even though the absence of the typographical excitement of *Blast No. 1*'s introductory manifesto was all too apparent, and some shorter, more subdued lists of 'blasts' and 'blesses' were relegated to the end of the magazine. This time, despised artists dominated the 'blast' page, headed by Brangwyn, Mestrovic, Orpen and 'Bevan, and his dry rot'. They were sprinkled, with the familiar random insouciance, among The Roman Empire, The Architect of the Regent Palace Hotel, Birth-Control and 'Lyons' shops (without exception)'.[53] For reasons best known to the compilers, the 'bless' page proceeded to heap benediction on 'All A.B.C. Tea-shops (without exception)' – presumably because Lewis took a quirky delight in patronizing these establishments. He did not explain why they were intrinsically superior to Lyons', but he had previously accounted for his enjoyment of the A.B.C. ambience in *Blast No. 1*, where he wrote that although 'every one admits that the interior of an A.B.C. shop is not as fine as the interior of some building conceived by a great artist', it would still 'probably inspire an artist today better than the more perfect building. With its trivial ornamentation, mirrors, cheap marble tables, silly spacing, etc.: it nevertheless suggests a thousand great possibilities for the painter.'[54]

Dissonance and asymmetry were of the essence in Vorticism, and this bias was further reinforced when 'the scaffolding around the Albert Memorial' was blessed in *Blast No. 2* at the expense of the hated architecture and sculpture it enclosed. Following the same train of thought, the great Japanese master Korin was blessed as well, presumably out of admiration for his striking patterns, daring stylistic distortion and startling combinations of textures and objects. Yet the rest of the 'Bless' page, with its callow listing of War Babies, Selfridge, Bombardier Wells and The War Loan, somehow failed to recapture the exuberance of its model in *Blast No. 1*. It had all been done before, with conspicuously greater verve, and only the illustrations in this war number fully upheld the high standards set by the first issue. There were, for one thing, a series of designs integrated with the text, as stern and incisive as their counterparts in *Blast No. 1*; and the majority of the pictures were equally tough, with titles like *Combat*, *War-Engine* and *On the Way to the Trenches*. They were more unified in style than the *Blast No. 1* reproductions, despite the fact that Nevinson was now granted one woodcut in the periodical he had done his best to sabotage a year ago. His temporary admission to the ranks is a great surprise, but no more so than the inclusion of a Kramer drawing called *Types of the Russian Army*, the naïvely figurative style of which completely contradicted the spirit upheld by the whole publication. It is a mystery why Lewis introduced it into his journal, especially since he had written a review of the second London Group show which described Kramer's exhibit as containing 'all sorts of objects and schools . . . in its melting-pot'.[55] Maybe it was a last-minute insertion, to compensate for the lack of drawings by Hamilton and Epstein, both of whom had contributed to *Blast No. 1*.

The one newcomer whose illustrations made absolute sense was Dorothy Pound, who sent in a sensitive *Snow Scene* under her maiden name of Shakespear. It was delicate rather than aggressive, but her husband's influence ensured that she pared her design down to a few sparse, finely poised formal ingredients. And although its pacific mood contains nothing to link her directly with Lewis's work, she afterwards testified to the beneficial effect exerted by Vorticism when recalling how she and Ezra 'went often to the "Rebel Art Centre" to Wyndham Lewis's Saturday(?) tea meetings and I watched it all with deep interest. I certainly never had any "lessons" from him but the movement came just as I needed a shove out of the Victorian.' Mrs Pound even specified one moment of particularly helpful contact, whereby 'Wyndham Lewis caught me painting one day – said it was too tight – "do something more free" '.[56]

Dorothy Shakespear
*Snow Scene, c.* 1915

Those brief words of advice, combined with the practical example set by Lewis and her husband's great friend Gaudier, were enough to liberate Dorothy Shakespear from the nineteenth-century English watercolour tradition she had upheld in earlier years. Many of her apprentice landscapes belonged unquestioningly within that tradition, and she always identified with it even at her most abstract, but the first clear sign that she was ready for renewal appeared in 1912. Then, executing her only two extant oil paintings, she announced a determination to learn both from Cézanne and the simplification of Japan in a panoramic view of *Devil's Cheese Ring*.[57] The most finished version, opting for the thin washes of an instinctive watercolourist who mistrusts the juicier pleasures of pigment, does not quite succeed in amalgamating these two influences: its distant mountain range, plainly indebted to the careful copies of Japanese prints she had carried out in her youth, fails to unite with the more proto-Cubist style of the foreground trees.

She needed the impetus provided by her Rebel Art Centre visits to fulfil her growing desire for a more innovatory synthesis, and in a fierce red, blue and grey watercolour called *War Scare, July 1914* she attained it for the very first time. On the back of the picture, a note in her hand records that it was painted 'when the Stock Exchange shut, before war was declared', and it is possible to surmise that the irregular cubic mass in the top left corner may represent this architectural symbol of the established capitalist order being invaded by the missile-like forms of an encroaching conflict. But the degree of abstraction which *War Scare* employs makes such an interpretation unnecessarily literal. The image of looming aggression, of thrusting, piercing and invading, stands by itself; and the watercolour's high-pitched tonality reflects the excitement of this 28-year-old artist as she dispenses with descriptive references altogether. Indeed, so alarmed was she by the radicalism espoused here that the note on the back insists the picture ought 'not to be shown to any body'.

△Dorothy Shakespear
*Landscape: Devil's Cheese Ring,* 1912

◁Dorothy Shakespear
*War Scare, July 1914,* 1914

△ Dorothy Shakespear
*Composition, c.* 1914

Dorothy Shakespear never exhibited her work with the other rebels, and she remains an essentially private individual who maintained links with the pastoral artistic legacy handed down by her amateur ancestors. 'Drawing is a traditional family hobby', she wrote later, remembering how her father and grandfather, a civil servant in India, always painted landscapes of 'mountains and fir-trees, very Victorian!' And their heritage is obvious even in a daring, forthright *Composition* executed in collage and watercolour around this time, where the abrupt angular transitions and icy shades of ultramarine and green are still uneasily allied to persistent echoes of picturesque hillsides or mountains. She did, however, prove her quiet allegiance to the movement in her contributions to *Blast No. 2*, including apart from the Japanese *Snow Scene* a sharp, incisive cameo of militant Vorticist figures and her outstanding cover for Pound's 1915 edition of *Ripostes*, reproduced horizontally above an advertisement for several of his books, among them his Chinese translations from notes by Ernest Fenollosa.[58] The cover's superbly organized structure succeeds in recalling the teaching of Fenollosa himself, who wrote in an essay discovered by Pound that 'the type of sentence in nature is a flash of lightning. It passes between two terms, a cloud and the earth'. Dorothy Shakespear's design seems to put this idea into pictorial action, making the elegant triangular wedges which had already appeared in her 1914 *Composition* lance from the lower to the upper black masses; and it also connects with her husband's poetry, for Pound was impressed by Fenollosa's notion that natural energy could be transferred best of all into the energy of syntax. And so, when Mrs Pound drew her impressively severe cover for Ezra's 1915 *Catholic Anthology*, she was providing a visual equivalent of his obsession with the power encapsulated in the isolated poetic image. The finely gauged contrasts between black and white shapes, floating in a calm equilibrium in keeping with the anti-romantic bias of Vorticism as a whole, faithfully obeys Pound's injunction to retain the vividness of the 'primary' forms.

△ Dorothy Shakespear
*Vorticist Figures, c.* 1915

▷ Dorothy Shakespear
Cover Design for *Ripostes, c.* 1915

▷▷ Dorothy Shakespear
Cover Design for *Catholic Anthology, c.* 1915

There is nothing in the least 'dispersed' about Dorothy Shakespear's best Vorticist work, and her quite personal sense of understated discipline makes it a matter for regret that she did not pursue her art more strenuously at that time. Lewis clearly thought so, for he wrote to Pound around January 1915 sending

as a verbal embodiment of Vorticist energy and concentration. Pound was doing his best to prove the truth of *Poetry* magazine's description of Vorticism as 'the latest official title of the latest literary and artistic revolution in England'.[64]

If anyone had bothered to examine the evidence carefully, however, it should have been obvious by this time that Vorticism was first and foremost an artists' affair, with literature involved only in a marginal way through Lewis's continuing fictional ambitions and Pound's search for an alternative to Imagism. The literary content of *Blast No. 2* was far less consequential than its predecessor's, and much of the non-theoretical writing in *Blast No. 1* had dangerously weakened the magazine's cohesion. Ford's short story was a respectable example of its author's ability, and yet it was included more as a tribute to his paternal interest in Vorticism than as a declaration that his prose represented a verbal extension of the movement. Rebecca West's contribution, 'Indissoluble Matrimony', had been permeated with images of violence, certainly, and its climax possessed a militancy which for all its florid overstatement had connections with the *Blast No. 1* manifestos: 'They were broken into a new conception of life. They perceived that God is war and his creatures are meant to fight. When dogs walk through the world cats must climb trees . . . And those who were gentle by nature and shrank from the ordained brutality were betrayers of their kind, surrendering the earth to the seed of their enemies.' But although the water George and Evadne eventually fall into is described as 'a brawling blackness in which whirled a vortex', 'Indissoluble Matrimony' was in no real sense a Vorticist short story. It is true that George's disgusted view of 'his wife as the curtain of flesh between him and celibacy, and solitude and all those delicate abstentions from life which his soul desired'[65] bore a superficial resemblance to Lewis's distinction between Art and Life or Hulme's Classicism and Romanticism dialectic. Every milieu shares some preoccupations, however, and they do not automatically turn Rebecca West into a Vorticist writer. Explosive in its emotional outpourings, her story nevertheless remained surprisingly conventional in style.

Neither she nor Ford were signatories in *Blast No. 1*, and the rebel artists probably did not want them to be. Aldington had added his name just as a friendly outsider, after all, and even Pound had signed primarily as an Apollinaire-like theoretical champion of a movement concerned at heart with painting and sculpture. He may have persuaded himself otherwise, but his own poems do not on the whole encourage any illusions about Vorticism's capacity to encompass literature as well as art. Even Lewis's 'Enemy of the Stars', a remarkably experimental attempt to inject fiction with some of the abstract economy, iconoclasm and taut vitality of visual Vorticism, properly belongs to his development as a writer rather than an artist. It is pertinent only to point out parallels between this 'play' and Lewis's contemporaneous pictures: when the characters positioned at the opening of a mine-shaft find that 'A GUST, SUCH AS IS MET IN THE CORRIDORS OF THE TUBE, MAKE THEIR CLOTHES SHIVER OR FLAP, AND BLARES UP THEIR VOICES', Lewis was clearly choosing the kind of imagery with which the Vorticists had decided to feed their art. Nor was this an isolated example. 'Enemy of the Stars' lived up to its title by evoking an entire solar system of heightened, deliberately strident elemental forces, as Arghol discovers after nightfall: 'His eyes woke first, shaken by rough moonbeams. A white, crude volume of brutal light blazed over him. Immense bleak electric advertisement of God, it crushed with wild emptiness of street. The ice field of the sky swept and crashed silently . . . The stars shone madly in the archaic blank wilderness of the universe, machines of prey . . . He rose before this cliff of cadaverous beaming force, imprisoned in a messed socket of existence. Will Energy some day reach Earth like violent civilisation, smashing or hardening all?'

Technology and primitivism are here welded together into a thunderous, baleful unity which signifies more than anything else the turbulence of Lewis's imagination, as he waits for the Armaggedon Vorticism was determined to engender. But 'Enemy of the Stars' is prevented from toppling into chaotic melodrama by a terse stylistic system which divides most of the prose into isolated sentences, pares away at orthodox syntax within those sentences and dispenses with the linear narrative which both Ford and Rebecca West had employed. By doing so, Lewis hoped to purge his writing of convention's impurities, an ambition which paralleled the evolution of his art and constituted the central debate in 'Enemy of the Stars'. For after declaring that 'our soul is wild, with primitiveness of its own', Arghol goes on to explain how 'the process and condition of life, without any exception, is a grotesque degradation, and "souillure" of the original solitude of the soul. There is no help for it, since each gesture and word partakes of it, and the child has already covered himself with mire'.[66] In other words, Lewis's desired separation of Art and Life is dramatised in fictional form by 'Enemy of the Stars', which manages to exchange the 'Life' of accepted, time-oriented literary form for the 'Art' of a disconnected prose full of bizarre imagery, sudden scene-changes and fragmented, spatially organised episodes. It is an extraordinary achievement, far more radical than *Tarr* and oddly prophetic of Samuel Beckett as well. But the fact remains that 'Enemy of the Stars' stands as a lone phenomenon in Lewis's work at this period, without any genuine forerunners or successors. In essence, it should be seen as an offshoot produced by a man whose major energies were then absorbed in visual art, its theory and polemical exposition; and in the context of Vorticism it is more like a fascinating verbal accompaniment than an integral part of the movement as a whole.

Pound, however, continued with undimmed faith to assert that there was no essential difference between his way of working and that of his artistic allies. 'An organisation of forms expresses a confluence of forces', he maintained in an 'Affirmations' article printed by *The New Age* in January 1915. 'It is only by applying a particular and suitable force that you can bring order and vitality.' As a poet, he considered himself able to deploy the ingredients of his medium in exactly the same way as the Vorticist painter worked with the pictorial elements at his command. 'The understanding that you can use form as a musician uses sound, that you can select motives of form from the forms before you, that you can recombine and recolour them and organize them into new form, this conception, this state of mental activity brings with it a great joy and refreshment.' If his explanation of the Vorticist method was more passive, even tasteful, than Lewis's – who was driven forward by the need to create militant forms as well as newly ordered ones, and would never have felt fulfilled by the emotions of 'joy and refreshment' – the underlying outlook was compatible. And in order to make his poetry move even closer to the art he admired so greatly, Pound wrote an equivalent of a Vorticist painting called 'Dogmatic Statement on the Game and Play of Chess', subtitled it 'theme for a series of pictures', and placed it proudly at the front of his collection of verse in *Blast No. 2*:

> Red knights, brown bishops, bright queens
> Striking the board, falling in strong "L's" of colour,
> Reaching and striking in angles,
>                    Holding lines of one colour:
> This board is alive with light
> These pieces are living in form,
>                    Their moves break and reform the pattern:
> Luminous greens from the rooks,
>                    Clashing with "x's" of queens,

# Notes and Index to Volume One

# Notes

The full reference to a book or publication is only given the first time it is mentioned. Page numbers are given for books and *Blast*, not for magazines, catalogues and newspapers.

**Chapter One**

1. Lewis, *Rude Assignment. A Narrative of my Career Up-to-Date* (London, 1950), pp.110–11. Lewis claims here (p.110) that Rugby's discovery of his artist's studio was a 'landmark in my career . . . which had a decisive influence upon the subsequent course of it'. He also asserts (p.111) that he was 14 years old when the episode occurred; but Geoffrey Wagner, in his *Wyndham Lewis. A Portrait of the Artist as the Enemy* (London, 1957), conclusively proves: (a) That Lewis was born in November 1882. (b) That he went to Rugby in January 1897 and left in December 1898. (Wagner, pp.5–6.) Lewis would therefore have been 16 when he left Rugby.
2. Robert Wellington, interview with the author, May 1971.
3. *Nude Boy Bending Over* is thought to be one of the works submitted by Lewis to the Slade scholarship competition, of which he was one of the winners in the 1899–1900 session.
4. Lewis, *Rude Assignment*, p.119.
5. Ibid., pp.118–19.
6. Rothenstein, *Men and Memories. Recollections of Sir William Rothenstein: 1900–22* (London, 1932), p.27. The author is grateful to Michael Holroyd for clarifying the period at which Rothenstein introduced Lewis to John. (Holroyd to the author, 14 July 1972.)
7. Lewis, *Rude Assignment*, p.115.
8. John, *Finishing Touches* (London, 1964), p.117.
9. Gore to Hubert Wellington, unpublished, owned by Robert Wellington. Not dated, but later on in the same letter Gore mentions that 'I could get no details of McEvoy's marriage except that it was very quiet'. McEvoy married Mary Spencer in 1902.
10. Lewis, *Rude Assignment*, p.119.
11. Fry, review of the 1902 NEAC exhibition in *The Athenaeum*, Virginia Woolf, *Roger Fry. A Biography* (London, 1940), p.109.
12. Lewis to Hubert Wellington, undated, but postmarked on the envelope 2 May 1902. Unpublished, owned by Robert Wellington.
13. Lewis to his mother, c.1904, *The Letters of Wyndham Lewis*, ed. W. K. Rose (London, 1963), p.11.
14. Lewis to his mother, postmarked 7 October 1904, ibid., p.13.
15. Some editions of the catalogue for the 1904 NEAC exhibition, held at the Dudley Gallery between April and May, do not list Lewis's exhibits. But all these editions are marked 'under revision', and a later edition does include *Study of a Girl's Head* in the *Exhibitors – Non-Members* section (No. 123).
16. Rutter, *Since I Was Twenty-Five* (London, 1927), pp.153, 134.
17. Lewis, *Blast No. 2* (London, 1915), p.80.
18. Lewis to his mother, c.1903, *Letters*, p.10.
19. Lewis to his mother, c.1904, ibid., p.13.
20. Lewis to his mother, c.1905, ibid., p.18.
21. Lewis to his mother, February 1905, ibid., p.17.
22. Lewis to his mother, c.April 1905, ibid., p.20.
23. Lewis to his mother, c.1907, ibid., p.35.
24. Grant, interview with the author, August 1971.
25. Lewis to his mother, c.1908, *Letters*, p.39.
26. *Blast No. 1* (London, 1914), p.21, made a point of including Bergson in its list of people to be blasted.
27. Lewis, *Rude Assignment*, p.113.
28. John, *Chiaroscuro. Fragments of Autobiography. First Series* (London, 1952), p.73.
29. Two etchings of Lewis were executed by John in January 1903, along with a drawing reproduced in Lewis's *Letters*. All these portraits, showing a clean-shaven Lewis, were probably executed two or three years before the painting reproduced here.
30. Mrs Lewis to the author, September 1972. Lewis himself paid tribute to Kropotkin many years later in *Rude Assignment*, p.23.
31. Kropotkin's *The Russian Revolution and Anarchism* was published in London in 1907.
32. Mrs Lewis to the author, September 1972.
33. Lewis, *Rude Assignment*, p.148.
34. Mrs Lewis to the author, September 1972.
35. Lewis, *Rude Assignment*, p.120.
36. Lewis, 'Enemy of the Stars', *Blast No. 1*, pp.76–7.
37. Stirner, *The Ego and His Own*, trans. Steven T. Byington (London, 1907). Arghol even has a fight with Stirner when the latter appears in 'The Enemy of the Stars'. But there are so many correspondences between *The Ego and His Own* and Lewis's philosophy of the self that Lewis must once have admired Stirner's writings. Lewis may first have come across Stirner through a study of *The Egoists*, published in America in 1909 and written by James Huneker. John Quinn knew Huneker well, and so Lewis could have heard about *The Egoists* from Augustus John or Pound, both of whom had met Quinn.
38. Grant to Lytton Strachey, 18 February 1907, unpublished, owned by King's College Library, Cambridge.
39. Lewis to his mother, postmarked 30 September 1905, *Letters*, p.21.
40. Lewis, *Rude Assignment*, p.117.
41. Ibid., p.118.
42. John, *Finishing Touches*, pp.119–20.
43. Lewis, 'The Pole', *The English Review* (May 1909).
44. Lewis to Sturge Moore (unfinished; probably not sent), c.1908, *Letters*, pp.39–40. The date of Lewis's return to London differs from published accounts, and is indebted to new research conducted by Victor M. Cassidy.
45. Ford, *Return to Yesterday. Reminiscences, 1894–1914* (London, 1931), p.407.
46. Goldring, *South Lodge. Reminiscences of Violet Hunt, Ford Madox Ford and the English Review Circle* (London, 1943), pp.39–40.
47. Mrs Lewis to the author, September 1972. Mrs Lewis also maintained (letter to the author, 14 October 1972) that Lewis lived near Picasso, but none of Lewis's recorded Paris addresses bears out her statement.
48. Lewis to Violet Schiff, 2 May 1922, unpublished, owned by British Museum Manuscripts Room.
49. Lewis to Sturge Moore, c.September 1909, unpublished, preserved in the Sturge Moore Papers, University of London Library. Lewis actually wrote the name 'Mattisse', and this mistake may indicate his limited knowledge of the artist. Several references in this undated letter, including a description of John Quinn's visit to London, assign it convincingly to September 1909.
50. The last three quotations all come from John's *Chiaroscuro*, p.69. John himself came nearest to Picasso's Blue period in a 1907 painting of a *French Fisher-Boy*, now owned by Mr and Mrs Stephen Tumim.
51. Although *The Celibate*'s abstract elements suggest a date of 1911 or 1912, it is significantly cruder in execution than either the 1911 *Girl Asleep* drawing in Manchester or the 1912 *Timon* series. From the little surviving evidence, Lewis's style during the 1909–12 period seems to have been very erratic: he tended to start off boldly in one direction and then quickly become sidetracked. So it appears more sensible cautiously to accept *The Celibate*'s inscribed date at face value, remembering that it could easily have been re-worked later, and also that whenever it can be proved that Lewis dated a picture inaccurately, he post-dated rather than pre-dated. He could be scrupulously accurate as well: a drawing called *Circus Scene* was dated 1913, and then redated 1914 when Lewis presumably worked on it again.
52. Yeats, Journal, 11 April 1909, *Memoirs. Autobiography – First Draft. Journal*, transcribed and ed. by Denis Donoghue (London, 1972), p.214.
53. The member of the hanging committee was Theodore Roussel, and the story is recounted by Frank Rutter in *Since I*

*Was Twenty-Five*, p.187.

54. Sickert, 'The Allied Artists' Association', *Art News*, 14 July 1910.

55. Ginner, 'The Camden Town Group', *Studio*, November 1945.

56. Lewis to John (fragment), 1910, *Letters*, p.45.

57. Bomberg, unpublished writings, 1957, owned by Mrs Lilian Bomberg. Latterly known as *The Green Tie*, this drawing is listed as *Architect with Green Tie* (No. 285A) in *Paintings and Sculpture. The Renowned Collection of Modern and Ultra-Modern Art Formed by the late John Quinn* (New York, 1927). Another pen drawing called *The Architect* is listed in the same catalogue.

58. Lewis to James Thrall Soby, 9 April 1947, *Letters*, p.407.

59. Emmons, *The Life and Opinions of Walter Richard Sickert* (London, 1941), p.147.

60. Lewis to Sturge Moore, c. July 1911, unpublished, owned by the Sturge Moore Papers, University of London Library. This undated letter was obviously written soon after the June 1911 exhibition, and is addressed: 11 Route d'Eu, Le Pollet, Dieppe.

61. Lewis, *Rude Assignment*, p.121. Lewis claims here that the 'fishermen' canvas was shown at 'the Ryder Street Gallery, St. James's, run by Robert Ross'. But Ross's gallery was in reality the Carfax Gallery, where the Camden Town Group held its exhibitions. Hence the connection with *Port de Mer*, listed in the December 1911 exhibition catalogue (No. 35).

62. John to Lewis, undated. Department of Rare Books, Cornell University.

63. Rutter, *Some Contemporary Artists* (London, 1922), p.180.

64. An earlier and representative exhibition of modern French painting organized by Robert Dell had been held the previous June in Brighton, but it caused less excitement than occurred a few months later in London.

65. MacCarthy, 'The Art-Quake of 1910', *The Listener*, 1 February 1945.

66. Virginia Woolf, *Roger Fry*, p.155.

67. Wilenski, *The Modern Movement in Art* (London, 1926), p.121.

68. Gill to Rothenstein, 5 December 1910, *Letters of Eric Gill*, ed. Walter Shewring (London, 1947), p.35.

69. Lewis to Sturge Moore, c. January 1911, unpublished, owned by the Sturge Moore Papers, University of London Library. This undated letter refers to Eric Gill's Chenil Gallery one-man show, held in January 1911, as the current London novelty.

70. MacCarthy, 'The Art-Quake of 1910'.

71. MacCarthy, 'The Post-Impressionists', introduction to the exhibition catalogue of *Manet and the Post-Impressionists*, Grafton Galleries (London, 1910).

72. Lewis to John (fragment), 1910, *Letters*, p.45.

73. MacCarthy, 'The Post-Impressionists'.

74. Lewis, 'Les Saltimbanques'.

75. Lewis, interview with 'M.M.B.', *The Daily News and Leader*, 7 April 1914. Lewis is photographed here standing in front of *Smiling Woman*; and in the text below it is explained that the drawing 'was a sketch for "The Laughing Woman"', which The Contemporary Arts Society purchased from Mr Wyndham Lewis last year'. *Smiling Woman* might, in fact, have been executed in 1912: Kate Lechmere, who met Lewis in 1912, remembers posing for just such a drawing (interview with the author).

76. Sickert, 'The Old Ladies of Etching-Needle Street', *The English Review*, January 1912.

77. Goldring, 'Futurism', *The Tramp*, August 1910, pp.487–8.

78. Lewis, in *Blasting and Bombardiering* (London, 1937), p.278, writes: 'I should say that was in 1910, though I have no calendar, engagement book, old letters – nothing to tell me what the year in fact was.' But Victor Cassidy has found a letter from Pound to Ford, undated but obviously written in 1909, where Pound already refers to Lewis as a personal acquaintance (Ford's papers, Cornell University). And Pound, for his part, insists in *Canto 8*: 'So it is to Mr. Binyon that I owe, initially, Mr. Lewis, Mr. P. Wyndham Lewis.'

79. Lewis, *Blasting and Bombardiering*, pp.279–81.

80. This unnamed Society rejected the Poet's Club and met for the first time, under the initiative of T. E. Hulme and F. S. Flint, on 25 March 1909.

81. Goldring, *Odd Man Out. The Autobiography of a 'Propaganda Novelist'* (London, 1935), p.100.

82. Lewis, *Blasting and Bombardiering*, p.277.

83. Ibid., p.278.

84. Floyd Dell, 'Friday Literary Review', *Chicago Evening Post*, 6 January 1911.

85. Pound used the movement's new name for the first time in a note he placed at the back of *Ripostes* to accompany the publication in book form of T. E. Hulme's *Complete Poetical Works*. 'As for the future', he wrote, '*Les Imagistes*, the descendants of the forgotten school of 1909, have that in their keeping.'

86. Pound, 'Prologomena', *Poetry Review*, February 1912.

87. Pound, 'Vorticism', *Fortnightly Review*, 1 September 1914.

88. Pound to the Editor of *Poetry*, 30 March 1913, *The Letters of Ezra Pound*, ed. D. D. Paige (London, 1951), p.53.

89. Pound, 'Prefatory Note to the Complete Poetical Works of T. E. Hulme', *Ripostes* (London, 1912).

90. Pound to Harriet Monroe, 18 August 1912, *Letters*, p.44.

91. Aldington, *Life for Life's Sake. A Book of Reminiscences* (London, 1968), p.96.

**Chapter Two**

1. All quotations are taken from the Sackville Gallery catalogue, London, March 1912, which reprinted three of the major Futurist manifestos:
   (i) 'Initial Manifesto of Futurism' (20 February 1909).
   (ii) 'Futurist Painting: Technical Manifesto' (11 April 1910).
   (iii) 'The Exhibitors to the Public' (5 February 1912).
   The painters shown at the Sackville were Boccioni, Carrà, Russolo and Severini. Balla was omitted.

2. Marinetti, 'Initial Manifesto of Futurism', from the translation in the Sackville Gallery catalogue.

3. 'Futurist Painting: Technical Manifesto', ibid.

4. Konody's review in the *Pall Mall Gazette* appeared on 1 March 1912, and his *Observer* notice was published on 3 March.

5. *Evening News*, 2 March 1912.

6. Sir Philip Burne-Jones, letter to the *Pall Mall Gazette*, 5 March 1912.

7. Ibid., 4 March 1912.

8. Sickert, 'The Futurist "Devil Among the Tailors"', *The English Review*, April 1912.

9. Marinetti to F. B. Pratella, 12 April 1912, Gambillo and Fiori, *Archivi del Futurismo* (Rome, 1958–62), Vol 1, p.237.

10. Goldring, *South Lodge*, p.64.

11. *Daily Chronicle*, 20 March 1912.

12. *The Times*, 21 March 1912.

13. *Evening News*, 4 March 1912.

14. Bomberg, unpublished memoirs, 1957, owned by Mrs Lilian Bomberg.

15. John, *Finishing Touches*, p.118.

16. Lewis, 'A Breton Innkeeper', *The Tramp*, August 1910.

17. In the 1927 sale catalogue of the Quinn Collection *Two Women* is reproduced on p.27 and called *The Starry Sky* (No. 49).

18. Ibid.

19. *Two Mechanics* can perhaps be identified as the *Two Workmen* which Lewis exhibited in Frank Rutter's Doré Galleries exhibition of October 1913 (No. 188). The drawing may at this stage have been enlarged from its original 1912 format.

20. The title of *The Vorticist* was obviously added later, after Vorticism itself had come into being.

21. Picasso's *Head of a Man* was reproduced in the Grafton Galleries exhibition catalogue, and listed as No. 68 (lent by M. Kahnweiler).

22. Nevinson, *Paint and Prejudice* (London, 1937), p.41.

23. *Preliminary Prospectus*, dated April 12, private collection.

24. John, *Chiaroscuro*, p.117.

25. Epstein, *Let There Be Sculpture* (London, 1940), p.134.

26. Sitwell, *Great Morning. Being the third volume of Left Hand, Right Hand! An Autobiography* (London, 1948), p.208.

27. Ibid., p.208.

28. Noel Stock, *The Life of Ezra Pound* (London, 1969), p.145.

29. *Cabaret Theatre Club. The Cave of the Golden Calf*, brochure dated May 1912, private collection.

30. Ibid.

31. Sitwell, *Great Morning*, p.208.

32. Hunt, *I Have This To Say* (New York, 1926), p.267. Published simultaneously in London as *The Flurried Years*.

33. The drawing, now lost, was reproduced in the May 1912 Cabaret prospectus.

34. There is no definite evidence to connect this abstract drawing with the Cabaret commission, but its style, spirit and date seem to place it in this context.

35. Madame Strindberg, unsigned note to Lewis, Department of Rare Books, Cornell University.

36. Etchells, interview with the author, 2 June 1970.

37. The May 1912 Cabaret prospectus states that 'decorations have been carried out under the guidance and supervision of Mr Spencer Gore. They include large panels by Mr Charles Ginner, Mr Spencer Gore, and Mr Percy Wyndham Lewis'.

38. Lewis, *Blast No. 1*, p.150.

39. Gore and Ginner's finished paintings were probably taken to America by Madame Strindberg during the Great War and sold there. Ginner's oil sketch is now in the collection of Mrs Charles Baty. (Cf. *The Tate Gallery: The Modern British Paintings, Drawings and Sculpture, Vol. I* (London, 1964), entry under Gore.)

40. Epstein, *Let There Be Sculpture*, p.134.

41. Lewis, *Rude Assignment*, p.125.

42. Ibid.

43. See Lewis to Hamilton, *Letters*, p.46.

44. The attribution of this drawing to Hamilton was made by Agnes Bedford.

45. Lewis, draft of a letter to Hamilton, 1913, *Letters*, p.46.

46. Rutter, *Art in My Time* (London, 1933), p.143.

47. Fry, *The Nation*, 20 July 1912. Fry must be referring to *Creation*, since this is the only exhibit by Lewis listed in the AAA's catalogue. *Creation* is included in the 'large paintings and decorative works' section, which also suggests that it is the painting which met with such a controversial critical response. But nobody who reviewed or remembered Lewis's contribution to the show ever referred to it as *Creation*. And when Clive Bell reviewed the October 1913 exhibition organised by Rutter at the Doré Galleries, he stated: 'I do not grumble at the reappearance of Wyndham Lewis's *Kermesse*, which has been altered and greatly improved since its last appearance at the London Salon.' (Bell, *The Nation*, 25 October 1913). Bell must be referring here to the 1912 AAA Salon, since the 1913 Salon certainly did not contain Lewis's *Kermesse*. And the reference to alterations and improve-ments implies that Lewis had extensively reworked the painting, perhaps altering the title from *Creation* to *Kermesse* at the same time. This hypothesis is confirmed by the memories of other writers who would have seen the picture when it was first exhibited: Rutter (see previous footnote) and Horace Brodzky, whose review of the 1917 New York Vorticist exhibition singled out 'Lewis's large "Kermess" [sic] which was shown some years ago at the Allied Artists' Association'. (Brodzky, 'Gossip from New York', *Colour*, March 1917.) It must therefore be presumed that *Creation* was *Kermesse*, and that the painting was known under several titles. After all, Lady Drogheda called it 'Norwegian Dance' when she wrote to Lewis in November 1913 and told him how much she admired it. (See Chapter Six, footnote 5.) Finally, the *Creation* listed in the 1912 AAA catalogue should not be confused with the lost *Creation* illustrated in the catalogue of Fry's 1912 Post-Impressionist exhibition. As the surviving photograph shows (reproduced in this book on page 43), this was a wash drawing rather than a 'large painting'.

48. The contract for lending *Kermesse* to Madame Strindberg is in the Wyndham Lewis Collection, Cornell University. It provides for a three-month rental of £10, and an option to purchase upon payment of another £20 which was obviously never taken up.

49. These Press comments on *Kermesse* are culled from a variety of contemporary reviews, including *The Times*, *The New Age* and the *Daily Telegraph*. Sickert's comment comes from his catalogue preface to an exhibition of Therese Lessore's paintings at the Eldar Gallery, London, November 1918.

50. *Design for a Programme Cover – Kermesse* was reproduced in *Blast No. 2*, p.75.

51. 1927 Quinn Sale Catalogue lists *Kermesse* as No. 382. The catalogue also states that *Kermesse* was 'signed lower left Wyndham Lewis and dated 1912', and that its measurements were 'height 8 feet 9 inches x length 8 feet 11 inches'.

52. Lewis to Pound, 12 April 1916, *Letters*, p. 79. Lewis was discussing Quinn's proposal to purchase *Kermesse*.

53. Rutter, *Art in My Time*, p.145.

54. This drawing was included in the 1917 New York Vorticist exhibition as either No. 6 or No. 28. Lewis himself titled it *Design for Kermesse* (No. 27) in the catalogue of his May 1949 Redfern Gallery exhibition.

55. *The Times*, 30 July 1912.

56. John to Lewis, undated, but probably 1912, Lewis Collection, Cornell University.

57. Bell, *The Athenaeum*, 27 July 1912.

58. Fry, *The Nation*, 20 July 1912.

59. Fry to Lewis, 31 July 1912, *Letters of Roger Fry*, ed. Denys Sutton (two vols.), (London, 1972), pp. 359–60.

60. Fry, 'Introduction', catalogue of the *Second Post-Impressionist Exhibition*, Grafton Galleries, October 1912.

61. *Creation* no longer exists, but it may well be connected with a large painting called *Creation* which Lewis included in the 1913–14 'Cubist Room' exhibition (No. 168).

62. Goldring, *South Lodge*, pp.63–4. For the history of Max Goschen, see Goldring's *Odd Man Out*, p.110.

63. Goldring, *South Lodge*, ibid. The Timon drawings shown at the Grafton Galleries exhibition were listed in the catalogue as follows: *Drawing for Timon of Athens; The Thebaid; A Mask of Timon; A Feast of Overmen; Timon; Timon.* These entries are taken from the first edition of the Grafton catalogue, which stated that each of the Timon drawings was 'exhibited by courtesy of the Cube Publishing Co.' All the Cube Press drawings – the reference to which proves that they were indeed included in the published portfolio, where the same name appears – were marked as not for sale in the catalogue.

64. Lewis to Pound, August 1917, *Letters*, p.90.

65. Pound, 'Vorticism', *Fortnightly Review*, 1 September 1914.

66. *The Athenaeum*, 12 October 1912. The reviewer is anonymous; but judging from his comments elsewhere in the notice about 'significant form' he was probably Clive Bell, who had already contributed to *The Athenaeum*. Earlier in the review, he declared: 'Mr Wyndham Lewis is claimed as a disciple of Picasso, and his work being far more intelligible than many of the later ones of the Frenchman, he may be charged by some with being a mere popularizer. We should rather regard him as, relatively to others of the school, a consolidatory influence laying stress in his pursuit of abstract significance of form on its geometric elements, but with a clear conviction, denied to Picasso, that it is almost impossible to have significant form quite divested of function.'

67. Lewis, *Blast No. 2*, p.26.

68. Pound, 'Wyndham Lewis', *The Egoist*, 15 June 1914.

69. Fry, 'Introduction' to *Second Post-Impressionist Exhibition* catalogue.

70. John to Lewis, 8 November 1912, Department of Rare Books, Cornell University.

71. Bell, 'The English Group', catalogue introduction to the *Second Post-Impressionist Exhibition*.

72. Strachey to Lady Ottoline Morrell, October 1912, Michael Holroyd, *Lytton Strachey. A Critical Biography. Vol. II. The Years of Achievement (1910–1932)* (London, 1968), p.74.

73. Etchells, interview with the author.

74. These Etchells watercolours are all preserved in the Victoria and Albert

Museum. They are mostly copied from the windows of Cirencester Parish Church and Kilburn Priory.

75. Etchells, interview with the author.

76. Ibid.

77. The surviving fragments of all these decorations, by Fry, Etchells, Grant, Macdonald (Max) Gill, Rutherston and Adeney, are now preserved in the Tate Gallery.

78. Grant, interview with the author, August 1971 (cf. also *The Tate Gallery: The Modern British Paintings, Drawings and Sculpture*, Vol. I, entry under Adeney).

79. *Observer*, 11 February 1912.

80. Fry to Charles Vildrac, 1 April 1912, *Letters*, p.356. The exhibition to which Fry refers was held in May 1912 at the Galerie Barbazanges, Paris.

81. Garnett, *The Golden Echo. The First Part of an Autobiography* (London, 1954), p.251.

82. Fry to Grant, autumn 1912, *Letters*, p.360.

83. Now in the Tate Gallery, London.

84. Etchells to the author, 19 July 1970.

85. *A Group of Figures* is in the Towner Art Gallery, Eastbourne. *The Entry into Jerusalem* was exhibited as *L'Entrée en Jerusalem* at Fry's Paris exhibition in May 1912 (cf. footnote 80).

86. The painting bears the date '1913' on the back, but it may just as well have been painted in 1912.

87. The Ashmolean Museum, which now owns *On the Grass*, calls the painting *Two Women Sitting on the Grass*. Etchells' other exhibits in the show, all as yet untraced, were two *Landscapes*, *The Blue Thistle* and *Courtyard* (Nos. 72, 75, 76 and 105).

88. Etchells, interview with the author.

89. See *The Tate Gallery: The Modern British Paintings, Drawings and Sculpture*, Vol. I, pp.172–3.

90. Woolf, *Beginning Again. An Autobiography of the Years 1911–18* (London, 1964), p.94.

91. Bennett, *The Journals*, selected and edited by Frank Swinnerton, new complete edition (London, 1971), p.354.

92. Bell, *Art* (London, 1914), pp.85–6.

93. Paul Nash, *Outline. An Autobiography and Other Writings* (London, 1949), p.93.

94. Sickert, *The English Review*, March 1912.

95. Bell, 'The English Group'.

96. Fry, 'Introduction' to the Second Post-Impressionist catalogue.

97. Bell, *Art*, p.21.

98. Woolf, *Beginning Again*, pp.95–6.

**Chapter Three**

1. Wadsworth studied at the Slade from 1908–12; Nevinson from 1909–12; Roberts from 1910–13; and Bomberg from 1911–13. Paul Nash, Ben Nichol-son, Mark Gertler, Isaac Rosenberg and Stanley Spencer were there at the same time.

2. Nevinson, *Paint and Prejudice*, p.26.

3. Ibid., p.29.

4. The fact that Edward Wadsworth is not included in this photograph does not affect its probable date; he simply did not attend the picnic.

5. Recollection by George Charlton, Lipke, *David Bomberg. A Critical Study of his Life and Work* (London, 1967), p.34.

6. Nevinson, *Paint and Prejudice*, p.40.

7. Roberts, *Abstract & Cubist Paintings & Drawings* (London, n.d.), 1957, p.6.

8. Nash, *Outline*, pp.92–3.

9. Roberts, *A Press View at the Tate Gallery* (London, 1956), pp. unnumbered. Roberts specified one source of his inspiration from Cubism when he wrote about the effect 'the "Angularities" of Picasso's *Guitarists* had on his student work (Roberts, 'Portrait of the Artist', *Art News and Review*, 5 November 1949).

10. From an official brochure, Fry Papers, King's College Library, Cambridge.

11. Adrian Allinson, *Painter's Pilgrimage*, unpublished autobiographical manuscript now in the possession of Miss M. Mitchell-Smith, p.37.

12. *Observer*, 11 February 1912.

13. Rutter, review of the February 1911 Friday Club exhibition, *Sunday Times*.

14. Nevinson, *Paint and Prejudice*, p.30.

15. Ibid., p.43.

16. Rutter, *Art in My Time*, p.143.

17. The most reliable visual record now existing of *A View of Bradford* is in the 1927 Quinn Sale catalogue where the painting is reproduced on p.36 and dated – without any supporting evidence – 1912. Another Nevinson painting, entitled *The Gasometers at the Last Hour*, is also dated 1912 in the 1927 Quinn catalogue. No illustration survives for this painting, but the catalogue describes it as an 'atmospheric view of gasworks by the banks of a canal, the huge inflated gasometers and the towering chimney stacks catching the fleeting reflections of a golden sun; in the foreground bargees are hauling their barge by way of the towpath. Before a cerulean blue sky flecked with the illumed smoke from the chimneys'. (No. 83). This painting may be identified with *Gasometers*, shown as No. 119 in the 1911 Friday Club exhibition at the Alpine Gallery.

18. This painting was included in the February 1912 exhibition (No. 27), which suggests that it was executed in 1911.

19. Rutter, review of the Friday Club exhibition at the Alpine Gallery, February 1912, *Sunday Times*.

20. Ibid.

21. Margaret Wynne Nevinson's article, 'Futurism and Woman', appeared in *The Vote* on 3 December 1910.

22. Allinson, *Painter's Pilgrimage*, p.39.

23. Nevinson, *Paint and Prejudice*, p.33.

24. The *Yorkshire Post*'s review is dated 10 October 1910, which contradicts the 1911 date inscribed on the *Self-Portrait* itself. Perhaps the critic was referring to an earlier, more Whistlerian version, or perhaps Wadsworth only completed the picture finally in 1911, when he signed it.

25. The only photograph which exists of this landscape is a blurred image preserved in Wadsworth's own album. The details of its date, prize and exhibition, mentioned here in the text, are inscribed on the back.

26. Allinson, *Painter's Pilgrimage*, p.40.

27. *Plague au Havre* takes its title from an entry in the 1927 Quinn Sale catalogue where it is described as a 'colourful composition'. The other Le Havre beach painting now exists only as an untitled photograph signed and dated 'Havre 1911' and inscribed 'to Helen'. Wadsworth himself wrote in the book where the print is now preserved that the original picture was 'destroyed in 1939–45'.

28. The Marquet painting is reproduced on p.39 of *French Paintings since 1900*, the catalogue of an exhibition held at the Royal Academy in 1969.

29. Rutter, *Sunday Times*, February 1912. *Long Acre* was listed as No. 99 in the Friday Club catalogue.

30. *Nature-Morte* is dated 26 June 1912 on the reverse, which means it was executed after Wadsworth left the Slade.

31. Forge, *The Slade, 1871–1960* (London, n.d.), p.23.

32. *Sleeping Men* was set as an illustration from Ecclesiastes XII, 5 for the Slade Sketch Club.

33. Bomberg, unpublished writings, 1957, owned by Lilian Bomberg.

34. Ibid.

35. Cliff Holden, 'David Bomberg: an artist as teacher', *The Studio*, March 1967.

36. For a long time this painting was known as *Primeval Decoration* (see the entry for Cat. No. 3 in *David Bomberg 1890–1957*, London, Arts Council, 1967, p.22). But Bomberg's first wife, Alice Mayes, confirmed in a letter written on 15 January 1972 that this picture is in fact the *Island of Joy* painted by Bomberg for the Slade Sketch Club's summer competition in 1912, when the theme of Joy was set as the subject. (See *The Tate Gallery 1970–72* (London, 1972), pp.87–8.)

37. Nevinson, *Paint and Prejudice*, pp.23–4.

38. Fothergill, 'Drawing', *Encyclopaedia Britannica* (London, 1910–11), Vol. 8, p.554.

39. Although Lipke, *David Bomberg*, places the *Vision of Ezekiel* in 1913, it is in fact dated 1912. And Bomberg's sister, Kathy Newmark, remembers him painting it at the family home in St Mark's Street, Aldgate, where he lived until

January 1913 (see *The Tate Gallery 1970–72*, pp.86–8). Alice Mayes remembered, too, that in 1915 'the painting he [Bomberg] wanted most to get out of store was the first lay-out for the "Vision of Ezekiel", which for the sake of the show – on another canvas – he had destroyed all its naturalism by the Cubist touch. Lilian has this first lay-out in her collection [*now in the Tate*] and it shows signs where he has – in 1915 – touched up the foreground figures. But he was unable to do what he wanted, and after he sent it back to store' (letter to the author, 17 July 1973). When Bomberg was once asked which genre *Ezekiel* belonged to, he replied 'Pure Decoration' and wrote the word 'Decoration' on the back of the picture. Indeed, he once lightheartedly described it as 'Dream of Hezekiah' (Denis Richardson, relaying information from Alice Mayes, letter to the author, 23 September 1973).

40. Roberts, *Abstract & Cubist Paintings & Drawings*, p.4.

41. This final drawing is dated 1913, which does not square with the 1912 date inscribed on the painting. However, the signature and date are less worn than the rest of the drawing, and it may be that Bomberg signed and dated it inaccurately when he sold it in 1914.

42. Phillips, *Daily Telegraph*, May 1914: review of the Whitechapel Art Gallery's *Twentieth Century Art* exhibition.

43. Lewis, *Blast No. 2*, p.41. Lewis clinched the connections with Bomberg by going on to explain that 'the grandiose and sentimental traditionalism inculcated at the Slade is largely responsible' for the kind of English painting he was describing.

44. Although Bomberg stated in some notes written in 1957 that *Jewish Theatre* was 'completed in 1912 for the Slade January composition competition', the drawing is clearly dated 1913 (cf. *David Bomberg 1890–1957* (London, Arts Council, 1967), p.22).

45. Moore, *Conservations in Ebury Street*, Joseph Hone, *The Life of Henry Tonks* (London, 1939), p.103.

46. Roberts, *A Press View at the Tate Gallery*, p. unnumbered.

47. Sir Cyril Butler, one of Roberts' earliest patrons, asked him to execute six drawings of street market scenes, but he finished only two.

48. Roberts, *Abstract & Cubist Paintings & Drawings*, p.4.

49. Roberts himself identified the *Holy Child* drawing with his work for the 1913 Prix de Rome. (Information relayed to the author by Rodney Capstick-Dale.)

50. The painting was simply called *Ulysses* in the catalogue of the NEAC's December 1913 exhibition. It was subsequently entitled *The Return of Ulysses* in the catalogue of a Chenil Galleries exhibition, November 1923. The listing

in the catalogue of Bomberg's July 1914 one-man show at the Chenil Gallery of a lost *Study for Ulysses in the Court of Alcinus* proves that he shared themes with Roberts at this time.

51. Alice Mayes, *The Young Bomberg 1914–1925* (1972), pp.11–12. Unpublished memoir, Tate Gallery Archives.

52. Photograph taken during a recent trip to the old baths buildings with Mrs Lilian Bomberg.

53. *The Jewish World*, 18 March 1914, p.11, claims that *Ju-Jitsu* was finished while Bomberg was at the Slade. In the first London Group exhibition at the Goupil Gallery in March 1914 and in the Whitechapel Art Galley exhibition of *Twentieth Century Art*, May–June 1914, it was listed as *Japanese Play*. But at Bomberg's Chenil Gallery one-man show in July 1914, it had acquired its final name, *Ju-Jitsu* – although only the study for the painting was shown at the Chenil exhibition, as Hulme's review makes clear (*The New Age*, 9 July 1914). Both alternative titles receive confirmation in a label on the back of the painting itself which reads: 'Ju-Jitsu, Japanese Play in the Integration of the Parts in the Mass, 1910'. Another label on the back, however, cites the date 1912–13, which is undoubtedly more correct. (See *The Tate Gallery: The Modern British Paintings, Drawings and Sculpture*, Vol. 1, p.64.)

54. See, for instance, the way in which Gris organizes the structure of 1912 paintings like *Portrait of Picasso* (Art Institute of Chicago) and *Still Life with Bottle and Watch* (Hans Grether Collection, Basel).

55. Bomberg, unpublished writings, 1957, owned by Mrs Lilian Bomberg.

56. Lewis's *Danse* was his only work in this exhibition.

57. *The Athenaeum*, 14 December 1912. The reviewer was anonymous.

**Chapter Four**

1. Fry to Lewis, 21 February 1912, *Letters*, p.355. This letter could, however, equally well refer to the formation of the Grafton Group, which first exhibited in March 1913 at the Alpine Club Gallery.

2. Aldington, *Life for Life's Sake*, p.119.

3. Nash, *Outline*, p.166.

4. Gertler to Carrington, 24 September 1912, *Mark Gertler. Selected Letters*, ed. Noel Carrington (London, 1965), p.47.

5. Fry to Lewis, 7 December 1912, *Letters*, p.361.

6. Robert Speaight, *The Life of Eric Gill* (London, 1966), p.66.

7. *Art Chronicle*, 26 April 1913.

8. Fry to Lewis, 5 April 1913, *Letters*, p.367.

9. Fry, *The Nation*, 2 August 1913.

10. Lewis, *Rude Assignment*, p.125.

11. Rothenstein, *Modern English Painters. Vol. II. Innes to Moore* (London, 1956), pp.121–2.

12. Prospectus (n.d.), *Omega Workshops, Ltd., Artists Decorators*, Tate Gallery Library.

13. Lewis, *Rude Assignment*, p.124.

14. This drawing, which is obviously by Lewis but is not included in Walter Michel's *Wyndham Lewis. Paintings and Drawings* catalogue (London, 1971), formed part of the Roger Fry Collection.

15. Grant's screen is still in his own collection.

16. From a note attached to *Design Representing a Couple Dancing*.

17. Fry, preface to an Omega Workshops prospectus (n.d.), Fitzwilliam Museum Library, Cambridge.

18. Winifred Gill to Duncan Grant, June 1966, unpublished, copy in Tate Gallery Archives.

19. Etchells, interview.

20. Hamnett, *Laughing Torso* (London, 1932), p.103.

21. Fry to Lowes Dickinson, 18 February 1913, *Letters*, p.362.

22. Winifred Gill to Grant, 4 July 1966, unpublished, copy in Tate Archives.

23. Fry, brochure (n.d.), for *Omega Workshops Ltd., Artists Decorators*, Tate Gallery Library.

24. Lewis, *Rude Assignment*, p.124.

25. Fry (?) Editorial, *Burlington Magazine*, March 1903.

26. Woolf, *Beginning Again*, p.95.

27. Lewis to Fry, August–September 1913, *Letters*, pp.46–7.

28. See Gore to Fry, 7 October 1913, Quentin Bell and Stephen Chaplin, 'The Ideal Home Rumpus', *Apollo*, October 1964, p.289.

29. Recalled by Winifred Gill, 'The Ideal Home Rumpus', p.289.

30. For the full text of the 'Round Robin' see 'The Ideal Home Rumpus', pp.284–5 and Lewis, *Letters*, pp.47–50.

31. Madame Strindberg to Gore, undated, but *c.* summer 1913, 'The Ideal Home Rumpus', p.291.

32. Etchells, interview.

33. Recorded in Vanessa Bell's letter to Fry written on 16 October 1913. Reprinted in 'The Ideal Home Rumpus', p.290.

34. Marsh to Sadleir, *c.*1913, Christopher Hassall, *Edward Marsh, Patron of the Arts. A Biography* (London, 1959), p.256.

35. See footnote 28.

36. Fry to Gore, 9 October 1913, ibid., p.289.

37. Grant, interview.

38. Bussy to Vanessa Bell, 22 October 1913, 'The Ideal Home Rumpus', p.290.

39. Lewis to Bell (probably not sent), October 1913, *Letters*, p.51; Lewis to Bell, October 1913, ibid., p.53.

40. Fry to Gore, 5 October 1913, 'The Ideal Home Rumpus', p.289.

41. Lewis, etc., letter to the press now preserved in the Fry Collection, King's

College Library, Cambridge.

42. *The Omega Workshops Ltd.*, official catalogue of *The Ideal Home Exhibition Organized by the Daily Mail* (London, 1913).

43. Fry to Lewis, 10 October 1913, Cornell University.

44. Vanessa Bell to Fry, *c.*12 October 1913, 'The Ideal Home Rumpus', p.290.

45. Nash, *Outline*, p.162.

46. Bell to Lewis, October 1913, *Apollo*, January 1966, p.75.

47. Vanessa Bell to Fry, 13 October 1913, 'The Ideal Home Rumpus', p.290.

48. Grant to Fry, 20 October 1913, 'The Ideal Home Rumpus', p.291.

49. Fry to Grant, October 1913, *Letters*, p.373.

50. Etchells, interview.

51. Wadsworth to Lewis, 22 December 1913, Lipke, 'The Omega Workshops and Vorticism', *Apollo*, March 1970.

52. Roberts, *Abstract & Cubist Paintings & Drawings*, p.7.

53. Winifred Gill to Duncan Grant, 29 August 1966, unpublished, copy in Tate Archives.

54. Nevinson, *Paint and Prejudice*, p.56.

55. Grant, interview.

56. Nevinson, *Paint and Prejudice*, p.57.

57. Monro, 'Varia', *Poetry and Drama*, September 1913.

58. Ibid.

59. Fanny Wadsworth to Lewis, 4 November 1913, Department of Rare Books, Cornell University.

60. Details of the dinner's date, etc., are specified in a letter from Nevinson to Lewis, 14 November 1913, now in Cornell University – which also preserves a copy of the letter of invitation.

61. Nevinson, *Paint and Prejudice*, p.57.

62. Nevinson to Lewis, 19 November 1913, Cornell University.

63. Lewis to Mrs Percy Harris, November 1913, *Letters*, p.53.

64. Lewis, *Blasting and Bombardiering*, p.37.

65. Epstein, *Let There Be Sculpture*, p.73.

66. Marinetti, *Zang Tumb Tuuum, Adrianopoli Ottobre 1912, Parole in Libertà*, (Milan, 1914), p.145.

67. Lewis, *Blasting and Bombardiering*, p.37.

**Chapter Five**

1. Apart from the English rebels, the exhibition also included examples of Cézanne, Matisse, Robert Delaunay, Picasso, Fergusson, Sickert, Gore, Ginner, Gilman, Bevan and Severini.

2. Rutter, foreword to the catalogue, *Post-Impressionist and Futurist Exhibition*, the Doré Galleries, London, October 1913.

3. *The Graphic*, 25 October 1913.

4. *Daily Sketch*, 18 October 1913.

5. In the revised edition of the Grafton Galleries' Post-Impressionist Exhibition catalogue, which states in the foreword that there has been a 're-arrangement', the precise dates of the extended period are recorded: 4–31 January, 1913. Wadsworth's two exhibits were: *Flowers* (No. 69) and *The Viaduct* (No. 182). The latter painting may well have been based on the same motif as Nevinson's *The Viaduct, Issy les Moulineaux* (page 108), which suggests that Wadsworth worked with Nevinson in Paris during 1912.

6. *The Times*, 8 January 1913.

7. Wadsworth to *The Nation*, 9 February 1913, published 15 February. Fry's review had appeared in *The Nation* on 18 January 1913.

8. Information supplied by Wadsworth's daughter, Mrs Barbara von Bethmann-Hollweg.

9. The untitled photograph of this dated watercolour is preserved in Wadsworth's own album.

10. According to the Walker Art Gallery, Liverpool, the picture was 'up until 1956 wrongly named *Reflections in Water*' (letter to the author, 28 July 1970). It could be identified as any of three Wadsworth contributions to Rutter's exhibition: *The River* (No. 70), *Watercolour* (No. 71), or *Watercolour* (No. 198).

11. *Trees Beside River* can likewise be identified as one of the three Wadsworth exhibits listed in the previous footnote.

12. The only record of *The Farmyard* is a reproduction illustrated in *The New Age*, 30 April 1914. T. E. Hulme's comments on *The Farmyard* in this issue of *The New Age* therefore serve as a valuable description of its appearance: 'Mr Wadsworth's drawing this week suffers somewhat in reproduction, as in the original it is coloured; the light background being yellow and grey, and the dark parts a very dark blue. The lighter parts of the drawing represent three farm buildings grouped around a pool. The space they enclose is concave to the spectator, the middle building being farther back than the two side ones. The darker parts represent the trunk and foliage of a tree standing on a slight mound.'

13. Hulme, ibid.

14. The only photograph of this painting, which bears no date or title other than those assigned to it by the author, is preserved in Wadsworth's own album. The date 1911 is pencilled below it in the album, but this seems far too early in view of the 1912 paintings *Nature-Morte* and *Landscape, Grand Canary*, neither of which shows any interest in Cubism. The picture can be tentatively connected with Wadsworth's *Sussex Farm*, exhibited as No. 159 in the December 1913 'Cubist Room' show at Brighton.

15. *The Sandpit* exists now only as a poor reproduction in *Dial Monthly*, May 1914, p.185. It was exhibited as No. 162 in the December 1913 'Cubist Room' show, which therefore definitely places it as a 1913 painting.

16. Wadsworth's *Adam and Eve* was listed as No. 196 in the Doré Galleries exhibition catalogue.

17. *L'Omnibus* was listed as No. 66 in the exhibition catalogue.

18. Severini, 'Get Inside the Picture: Futurism as the Artist Sees It by Gino Severini', interview with Severini, *Daily Express*, 11 April 1913.

19. Carrà's painting is now known as *What the Streetcar Said to Me*, but it was entitled *What I was Told by the Tramcar* in the 1912 Sackville Gallery catalogue, which listed it as exhibit No. 14.

20. 'Futurist Painting: Technical Manifesto', trans. Sackville Gallery catalogue.

21. Cf. Rothenstein, *Modern British Painters*, Vol. 2, pp.96–7.

22. Nevinson, *Paint and Prejudice*, p.46.

23. Ibid., p.47.

24. Ibid., p.51.

25. Ibid., p.43.

26. Ibid., pp.43–4.

27. Illustrated in Osbert Sitwell's *C. R. W. Nevinson* (London, 1925), which gives it a 1913 date. But *The Viaduct, Issy les Moulineaux* (page 108), which it would seem to antedate, was exhibited in the January–February 1913 Friday Club exhibition (No. 33).

28. Nevinson, *Paint and Prejudice*, p.34.

29. Ibid., pp.42–3.

30. Nevinson, *Paint and Prejudice*, p.35.

31. Ibid., p.44.

32. Ibid., p.40.

33. *The Viaduct, Issy les Moulineaux* (see footnotes 27 and 5) may well have been exhibited in Rutter's show as *Issy-les-Moulineaux* (No. 201).

34. Boccioni's painting is now commonly known as *The City Rises*.

35. Severini, explanatory note in the catalogue of his Marlborough Gallery exhibition.

36. 'Our Irreverent Critic', reviewing the Doré Galleries exhibition. Newspaper and precise date unknown: included in Vol. I of Nevinson's Cuttings, Tate Gallery Library.

37. *The Departure of the Train de Luxe* was listed as No. 67 in Rutter's show.

38. Rutter, *Art in my Time*, p.150.

39. Nevinson, *Paint and Prejudice*, p.7.

40. Nevinson's two *Gare St. Lazare* pictures were listed as Nos. 174 and 176 in the catalogue of the December 1913 'Cubist Room' exhibition.

41. Nevinson, *Paint and Prejudice*, pp.54–5.

42. Nevinson to Severini, 26 December 1913, published in *Critica d'Arte*, May–June 1970 (*Ommagio A Severini*), p.25.

43. Nevinson, *Paint and Prejudice*, p.56.

44. Grant, interview.

45. *Woman at a Mirror* might possibly be connected with the *Sketch of a Woman (in Tempera)* listed as No. 113 in the Doré Galleries catalogue.

46. *The Athenaeum*, 25 October 1913. The

anonymous reviewer specifically referred in his remarks on Etchells to exhibit No. 113 (see previous footnote).

47. Etchells, interview.
48. Etchells' two *Head* drawings could be identified with any of his following three Doré Galleries exhibits: *Head of a Man* (No. 116); *Drawing of a Head* (No. 146); or *Drawing of a Head* (No. 147).
49. This *Head* is in fact smoking a pipe, which makes it readily identifiable as the Etchells *Study of a Head* included in the 1927 Quinn Sale Catalogue (No. 437). Its size and medium are recorded there.
50. The only record which now exists of *Patchopolis* is the reproduction published in *Blast No. 1* (plate xi).
51. Etchells exhibited a picture called *Houses at Dieppe* as No. 79 in the first London Group exhibition, March 1914.
52. Etchells, interview.
53. Holroyd, *Lytton Strachey*, Vol. 2, p.96.
54. Hamilton's exhibits in Fry's show (Nos. 217–20) were listed only in the 're-arrangement' version of the catalogue, 4–31 January 1913.
55. Hamilton had three exhibits listed in the Doré Galleries catalogue: *Portrait* (No. 68); *Head (Watercolour)* (No. 111); *Two Figures* (No. 114).
56. Bell, *The Nation*, 25 October 1913.
57. Epstein, *Let There Be Sculpture*, p.32.
58. Ibid.
59. Ibid. There seems to be no documentary proof of *Sunflower's* extraordinarily early date, beyond the fact that Epstein himself appears to have remembered executing it in 1910, and he was never guilty of pre-dating.
60. Ibid., p.23.
61. Gill to William Rothenstein, 25 September 1910, Robert Speaight, *The Life of Eric Gill* (London, 1966), p.51. Gill and Epstein got as far as interviewing the owner of Asheham House, visiting Stonehenge and going to quarries at Portland and Wirksworth for suitable stone.
62. John to Gill, n.d., published ibid., p.49.
63. T. E. Hulme captioned his photograph of the sculpture *Garden Carving*, which suggests a specific commission (photograph now owned by Hull University Library).
64. Pound, *The New Age*, 21 January 1915.
65. *Evening Standard*, 3 June 1912.
66. *Pall Mall Gazette*, 6 June 1912.
67. Epstein, *Let There Be Sculpture*, p.60.
68. Ibid., p.61.
69. Ibid., p.63.
70. Ibid., pp.63–4.
71. Ibid., p.64.
72. Pound to Quinn, 10 March 1916, *Letters*, p.122.
73. Epstein, *Let There Be Sculpture*, p.64. It is only later on in his autobiography that Epstein firmly dates the Pett Level period, proving that he first settled there in 1913: 'My three years, 1913–1916, at Pett Level, near Hastings, were

productive of many carvings', he writes on p.126.
74. Epstein, *Let There Be Sculpture*, p.64. Although it has always been assumed that the word 'flenite' refers to the kind of stone used in these carvings, a geological expert recently examined *Female Figure in Flenite* at the Tate Gallery and realised that it was made of serpentine, a soft and fairly common stone (information supplied to the author by Penny Marcus).
75. Pound reported in 'The New Sculpture', *The Egoist*, 16 February 1914, that *Figure in Flenite* was executed after *Female Figure in Flenite*: 'I do not precisely know why I admire a green granite, female, apparently pregnant monster with one eye going around a square corner. When I say that I admire this representation more than an earlier portrait of the same monster (in the shape of a question mark) I am told "It is more monumental".' It is also worth comparing the two *Flenite* women with related carvings by Eric Gill reproduced on plate 4 of Joseph Thorp's *Eric Gill* (London, 1929).
76. This catalogue, with its sketch of *Female Figure in Flenite*, is owned by the Tate Gallery Library.
77. This legend originates in the Epstein family. Research suggests that Quinn disposed of the carving between 1924 and 1927. The *Granite Mother and Child* is listed as No. 23 in the *Catalogue of an Exhibition of the Sculpture of Jacob Epstein*, the Leicester Galleries, London, February–March 1917. It is described there as *Carving in Granite. 'Mother and Child'. Unfinished.*
78. The exact date of Brancusi's *Three Penguins* (version now in the Philadelphia Museum of Art) has always been a matter of controversy. But the latest and most authoritative theory, advanced by Sidney Geist in his catalogue of *Constantin Brancusi, 1876 to 1957. A Retrospective Exhibition* (New York, 1969), p.61, attributes its execution to *c*.1912.
79. Lady Epstein, writing in the catalogue of Buckle's *Epstein Drawings* (London, 1962), p.17, states: 'At this time the artist lived on the Sussex coast where he kept birds to work from.'
80. Possibly the *Group of Birds*, marble, listed as No. 5 in the 'Sculpture' section of Epstein's 1913–14 one-man show. The present titles of all three surviving *Dove* carvings should not be taken as an authoritative comment on their order of execution.
81. Pound to Quinn, 8 March 1915, *Letters*, p.95.
82. Epstein to Quinn, 28 April 1915, paraphrased by Reid, p.203.
83. Preserved in Nevinson's cuttings, Vol.1, Tate Gallery Library.
84. 'Our Irreverent Critic', in his review of the Doré Galleries exhibition, ibid.

85. Kate Lechmere, interview with the author, November 1969.
86. Pound, 'Exhibition at the Goupil Gallery', *The Egoist*, 16 March 1914. Epstein showed there: *Group of Birds* (No. 109); *Bird Pluming Itself* (No. 110); *Carving in Flenite* (No. 116).
87. Pound to Isabel Pound, November 1913, *Letters*, p.63.
88. Pound, 'Affirmations, III'. *The New Age*, 21 January 1915.
89. Pound, *The Egoist*, 16 March 1914.
90. Bell, *The Nation*, 25 October 1913.
91. Lewis's *Composition* was afterwards exhibited at the Redfern Gallery in May 1949 (No. 10) where Lewis himself subtitled it *Later Drawing of the 'Timon' Series.*
92. *Portrait of an Englishwoman* was reproduced in *Blast No. 1*, and it is likely that *The Archer*, basically a miscellany of Futurist verse and prose, took its illustration from this source.
93. The dating of Malevich's early Suprematist paintings is still a matter of controversy: the date of *House Under Construction* is here taken from Camilla Gray's *The Great Experiment: Russian Art 1863 to 1922* (London 1962), plate 106.
94. Malevich published his theory of Suprematism in a small 1916 brochure entitled *Ot Kubizma i Futurizma k Suprematizmu.*
95. Malevich's *Black Square* painting, now in the Tretyakov Gallery, Moscow, is inscribed: 'This initial element first appeared with *Victory over the Sun*', the name of the Futurist opera produced in St Petersburg in December 1913.
96. Severini, catalogue of Marlborough Gallery exhibition.
97. Ibid.
98. Lewis, *Blast No. 1*, p.143.
99. Sir Claude Phillips, review of the Doré Galleries exhibition, *Daily Telegraph*, October 1913.
100. Bell, *The Nation*, 25 October 1913.

**Chapter Six**

1. Nevinson, *Paint and Prejudice*, p.60.
2. Lewis, *Letters*, p.53, footnote 1.
3. Marsh to Elliott Seabrooke, November 1913, Hassall, *Edward Marsh*, p.258.
4. Nevinson, *Paint and Prejudice*, p.58.
5. Lady Drogheda to Lewis, undated, but probably *c*.30 November 1913, Cornell University.
6. Nevinson, *Paint and Prejudice*, p.60. No record remains of the commission which Nevinson here claims Lady Cunard 'arranged'.
7. Kate Lechmere, interview.
8. *The Sketch*, 24 March 1914. Four photographs of the decorations were reproduced there. The present Lord Drogheda told the author that no photographs, correspondence or relics connected with the dining-room scheme

survive in the family's archives. But the room itself still exists. It is the front room on the ground floor overlooking the street. Tests have recently been made to discover whether the decorations survive beneath the later additions, but with negative results.

9. Photograph taken from *The Sketch*. According to measurements taken by the author, the painting could not have been more than 86·5 cm high × 145 cm wide.

10. L. G. Redmond-Howard, 'The Futurist Note in Interior Decoration', *Vanity Fair*, 25 June 1914.

11. This photograph shows the dining-room's back wall, which faced the front window overlooking the street. This wall is now demolished. The painted frieze above was 20·3 cm high, in common with the frieze running round the rest of the room.

12. See footnote 10.

13. Kate Lechmere, interview.

14. According to measurements by the author, the side panels were each 235·5 cm high × 37 cm wide. The mirror itself was 170 cm high × 155 cm wide.

15. A copy of Lady Drogheda's invitation card is preserved by Cornell University, providing an exact date for the unveiling of the decorations.

16. John, *Finishing Touches*, p.118.

17. Pound to Harriet Monroe, 9 November 1914, *Letters*, p.87.

18. Pound, *The Egoist*, 16 March 1914.

19. Executed in 1916, illustrated in an Omega brochure, Tate Gallery Library.

20. *The Athenaeum*, 7 March 1914.

21. Nevinson, *Paint and Prejudice*, pp.63–4.

22. Bomberg, unpublished writings, 21 April 1957, owned by Mrs Lilian Bomberg.

23. Bomberg, unpublished writings, 14 April 1957, owned by Mrs Lilian Bomberg.

24. Lilian Bomberg, interview with the author, May 1970.

25. Kate Lechmere told the author that Lewis executed *The Enemy of the Stars* in direct emulation of Epstein's *Female Figure in Flenite*. And Lewis listed it in the catalogue of the first London Group show, March 1914, as a 'drawing for sculpture' (No. 43).

26. Lewis, 'Room III. (The Cubist Room)', introduction to the catalogue of *The Camden Town Group and Others* exhibition.

27. J. C. Squire, *The Honeysuckle and the Bee* (London, 1937), p.157.

28. Alun R. Jones, *The Life and Opinions of T. E. Hulme* (London, 1960), p.21.

29. Hulme, *Lecture on Modern Poetry*, delivered at the Poet's Club either at the end of 1908 or early in 1909, reprinted in Michael Roberts' *T. E. Hulme* (London, 1938).

30. Hulme, *The New Age*, 19 August 1909.

31. Pound, essay on *Guido Cavalcanti*.

32. Hulme, 'Modern Art. II. – A Preface

Note and Neo-Realism', *The New Age*, 12 February 1914.

33. Hulme, *Speculations. Essays on Humanism and the Philosophy of Art*, ed. Herbert Read (London, 1924), p.82.

34. Hulme, 'Modern Art. II. –'.

35. Ibid.

36. Ibid.

37. Reprinted in *Speculations*, pp.73–109. It is prefaced there by the quotation: 'The fright of the mind before the unknown created not only the first gods, but also the first art.'

38. Ibid., p.82.

39. Ibid., pp.91, 93, 94.

40. Ibid., pp.97, 104–7. Hulme specifically refers to Epstein's 'drawings for sculpture in the first room of his exhibition'. Epstein held the show at the Twenty-One Gallery, York Buildings, Adelphi, London, from 3 December 1913 to 17 January 1914. In the catalogue, his drawings included two *Rock Drill* studies (Nos. 1 and 2) and a *Drawing for Flenite* (No. 7).

41. Hulme, *Speculations*, pp.87, 105, 108–9.

42. Pound, 'The New Sculpture', *The Egoist*, 16 February 1914.

43. Bomberg to Alun R. Jones, 23 December 1953, Jones, p.116.

44. Epstein, *Let There Be Sculpture*, p.74.

45. Hulme, 'Modern Art. IV. – Mr David Bomberg's Show', *The New Age*, 9 July 1914.

46. Kate Lechmere, interview.

47. D. L. Murray, Alun R. Jones, p.92.

48. Nevinson, *Paint and Prejudice*, p.63.

49. Garnett, *The Golden Echo*, p.239.

50. Epstein, *Let There Be Sculpture*, p.75.

51. Lewis, *Blasting and Bombardiering*, p.106.

52. Hulme, *Speculations*, p.81.

53. Hulme, 'Appendix A. Reflections on Violence', *Speculations*.

54. Garnett, *The Golden Echo*, p.237.

**Chapter Seven**

1. Emmons, *The Life and Opinions of Walter Richard Sickert*, p.147.

2. Sickert to Nan Hudson, before March 1914. Unpublished, private collection.

3. Sickert, 'Democracy in Ease at Holland Park', *The New Age*, 25 June 1914.

4. Hone, *The Life of Henry Tonks*, p.101.

5. Lewis, note scribbled on a catalogue of the January 1914 Grafton Group exhibition, Walter Michel, 'Tyros and Portraits. The Early 'Twenties and Wyndham Lewis', *Apollo*, August 1965, p.131.

6. Fry to Simon Bussy, 28 December 1913, *Letters*, pp.375–6.

7. Fry to Grant, 6 March 1914, *Letters*, p.379.

8. Lechmere, interview.

9. From a note scribbled in the margin of the Tate Gallery Library's copy of the 1913 AAA catalogue. Lechmere's exhibits were listed as Nos. 467, 468 and

469 respectively.

10. Lechmere, interview. Etchells told the author that he could not remember suggesting the site of the Rebel Art Centre to Lewis, but he confirmed that he did then rent a first-floor flat opposite the house selected.

11. The letterhead reproduced here appears on a copy of the famous letter written by the Vorticists in repudiation of Marinetti and Nevinson's 'Futurist Manifesto' (see Chapter Nine).

12. Lechmere, interview.

13. *Daily News and Leader*, 7 April 1914.

14. Lechmere, interview.

15. *Vanity Fair*, 25 June 1914.

16. Goldring, *South Lodge*, p.65.

17. The Wadsworth painting looks like a version of *Caprice*. Michel, in his *Wyndham Lewis. Paintings and Drawings* (p. 334), tentatively identifies the Lewis painting hanging above the mantelpiece with a picture called *Group* exhibited by Lewis in the 1913 AAA Salon (No. 998).

18. Lechmere, interview.

19. Rutter, 'Art and Artists', *New Weekly*, 4 April 1914.

20. Lechmere, interview.

21. Information supplied by Helen Peppin.

22. Fry, *The Nation*, 20 July 1912.

23. Bell, *The Athenaeum*, 27 July 1912.

24. *The Oast-House* was listed there as No. 511. Saunders also exhibited three works – *Figure Composition* (No. 458), *Portrait* (No. 459), and *Sketch* (No. 460) – at the 1912 AAA Salon. All these pictures are untraced.

25. From a comment written in the margin of the Tate Gallery Library's copy of the 1913 AAA catalogue.

26. The same Tate Gallery Library catalogue (see previous footnote) has the comment 'cubist' written beside Dismorr's three contributions to the 1913 AAA Salon: *Portrait Study. Girl* (No. 517), *Portrait Study. Woman* (No. 518), and *Portrait Study. Little Girl* (No. 519). Dismorr also displayed three lost pictures at the 1912 AAA Salon: *Italian Landscape* (No. 730), *Italian Landscape* (No. 731), and *Landscape* (No. 732).

27. Dismorr's contributions to the October 1912 Stafford Gallery exhibition were listed in the catalogue as: *Night Scene, Martiniques* (No. 37), *The School, Siena* (No. 38), *Sunlight, Martiques* (No. 39), *In the Garden* (No. 40), *The Steps, Avignon* (No. 41), and *Boat Building, Venice* (No. 42). Apart from the last exhibit, which was probably a sketch, the other five pictures were all oil-paintings; and several of these were rediscovered in 1973.

28. Dismorr to Lewis, n.d., Lewis Collection, Cornell University.

29. Lechmere, interview.

30. Bomberg, unpublished writings, 1957, owned by Mrs Lilian Bomberg.

31. Lechmere, interview.

32. Antony Guest, 'Malcolm Arbuthnot's

"Impressions at the A. P. Little Gallery"', *Amateur Photographer*, 9 March 1909.

33. Arbuthnot, 'A Plea for Simplification and Study in Pictorial Work', *Amateur Photographer*, 12 January 1909.

34. 'Photograms of the Year 1908. A Fragmentary Retrospect', *Photograms of the Year*, 1908.

35. Although *The River* is reproduced here from an illustration in the 1 February 1910 *Amateur Photographer*, it did in fact also appear in the 1908 *Photograms of the Year* in diagram form (p.25).

36. ' "Portrait Lens", Some Professional Picture Makers And Their Work', *Amateur Photographer*, 12 June 1916.

37. Arbuthnot's show, an *Exhibition of Camera Portraits*, was held between June and July.

38. In Arbuthnot's unpublished autobiography, *Random Recollections* (*c*.1956), p.267, he writes: 'My first introduction to "advanced" thought and practice in painting, came from a visit to Wyndham Lewis, who had a studio in Fitzroy Street. There I met Wadsworth, Etchells, and a number of other "modern" Artists. Lewis was engaged in the production of a most remarkable book entitled "Blast". I had been experimenting in painting what I called "Decorative Realism", and told Lewis of my efforts. He asked me to let him see some of them, so on my next visit, I brought a few with me. Lewis was interested in them, gave me some good advice and I was promptly enrolled as one of the signatories to "Blast".' Owned by Miss A. E. Wisdom, Jersey. The first time Lewis came across Arbuthnot's work may have been in the August 1910 issue of *The Tramp*, which reproduced his photograph of *Limehouse Point* showing suitably Vorticist factory chimneys smoking by the Thames. Lewis contributed a story to the same issue.

39. ' "Portrait Lens", Some Professional Picture Makers', *Amateur Photographer*, 12 June 1916.

40. Pound to Joyce, 2 July 1914, *Pound/Joyce. The Letters of Ezra Pound to James Joyce, with Pound's essays on Joyce*. Ed. and with a commentary by Forrest Read (London, 1968), p.31.

41. Shipp, *The New Art. A Study of the Principles of Non-Representational Art and Their Application in the Work of Lawrence Atkinson* (London, 1922), p.76.

42. Lechmere, interview.

43. Atkinson, *Aura* (London, 1915), poem XV, p.27.

44. Ibid., poem XXIII, p.40.

45. It should be emphasized that the almost total dearth of reliable documentary information about Atkinson's work makes the dating of these two pictures at best hypothetical.

46. *Il Piccolo della Sera*, Trieste, reprinted in the original Italian by Pound in his *Gaudier-Brzeska. A Memoir* (London, 1916), pp.53–4. Lechmere, however, seemed to remember that Hamilton designed the Rebel Art Centre curtains.

47. *Daily News and Leader*, 7 April 1914.

48. Rebel Art Centre brochure, private collection.

49. L. G. Redmond-Howard, *Vanity Fair*, 25 June 1914.

50. Lechmere, interview.

51. RAC prospectus, private collection.

52. Ibid.

53. Goldring, *South Lodge*, p.65.

54. Lechmere, interview.

55. Ibid. The advent of *Blast No. 1* was similarly announced on the back page of *The Egoist* on 15 April 1914, in an advertisement which proclaimed 'End of Christian Era'.

56. Roberts, *A Reply to my Biographer Sir John Rothenstein* (London, 1957), p.9.

57. Roberts, *A Press View at the Tate Gallery*, pp. unnumbered.

58. Roberts, 'Wyndham Lewis, the Vorticist', *The Listener*, 21 March 1957.

59. *The Athenaeum*, 10 January 1914. The anonymous critic was discussing the *Figure Composition* which Roberts exhibited as No. 29 in the Grafton Group show at the Alpine Club Gallery in January 1914.

60. Roberts, *Abstract & Cubist Paintings & Drawings*, p.9.

61. Roberts, 'Wyndham Lewis, the Vorticist'.

62. Henri Gaudier-Brzeska, 'The AAA Ltd., Holland Park Hall', *The Egoist*, 15 June 1914.

63. Etchells, interview.

64. Lewis, interview with 'M.M.B.', *Daily News and Leader*, 7 April 1914.

65. Lechmere, interview.

66. Dorothy Pound, interview with Noel Stock, *The Life of Ezra Pound*, p.159.

67. RAC prospectus, private collection.

68. Epstein, *Let There Be Sculpture*.

69. Lechmere, interview.

70. Lewis to Beatrice Hastings, *c*.1914, *Letters*, p.63.

71. Lewis, *Blasting and Bombardiering*, p.107.

72. Lechmere, interview.

73. Lewis, *Blasting and Bombardiering*, p.39.

74. *Observer*, 8 March 1914.

75. Fry, *The Nation*, 14 March 1914.

76. *Daily News and Leader*, 6 March 1914.

77. Bell, *Art*, p.207.

78. *Daily Telegraph*, 10 March 1914.

79. Quinn Sale catalogue, 1927 (No. 383).

80. Lewis, *Blasting and Bombardiering*, p.4.

81. Rutter, *Some Contemporary Artists* (London, 1922), pp.182–3; and *Evolution in Modern Art* (London, 1926), pp.115–16.

82. O. Raymond Drey, 'The Autumn Salon', *Rhythm*, December 1912.

83. *The New Weekly*, 20 June 1914.

84. Rutter, *Since I was Twenty-Five*, p.196.

85. *Slow Attack* now survives only as an illustration in *Blast No. 1* (plate vi). Its appearance coincides with Rutter's description of *Night Attack* as 'an abstract painting' which was 'plainly geometrical in appearance . . . based on the diagrams of battle dispositions which are seen in history books, and illustrating an outflanking movement in geometrical patterns and Cézannesque colour' (*Art in My Time*, p.163). *Slow Attack* was actually shown under its own title at the Whitechapel Art Gallery's *Twentieth Century Art* exhibition, May–June 1914, No. 25.

86. Gaudier, 'The AAA Ltd., Holland Park Hall', *The Egoist*, 15 June 1914.

87. Gaudier to Sophie, 17 November 1912, H. S. Ede, *A Life of Gaudier-Brzeska* (London, 1930), p.199.

88. Brodzky, *Henri Gaudier-Brzeska, 1891–1915* (London, 1933), p.123.

89. Gaudier to Uhlemeyer, 1 January 1910, Ede, p.16.

90. Gaudier to Sophie, May 1911, ibid., p.36.

91. The original plaster version of *Ornamental Mask*, reproduced here from a photograph kindly provided by the Musée du Petit Palais, Geneva, was painted in harsh, brilliant colours and partially gilded. It was executed for Claud Lovat Fraser.

92. Gaudier to Major Smythies, Ede, p.255.

93. Ibid., p.256.

94. Gaudier to Sophie, October 1912, ibid.

95. Gaudier to Sophie, inscribed 'Sunday, May, 1911', ibid., p.58.

96. Murry, 'Aims and Ideals', *Rhythm*, June 1911, p.36.

97. Sadleir, 'Fauvism and a Fauve', *Rhythm*, June 1911, pp.14–18.

98. Epstein, *Let There Be Sculpture*, p.58.

99. Ibid., p.59.

100. Gaudier to Sophie, 8 October 1913.

101. David Garnett, in *The Golden Echo*, p.238, remembered that 'I was able to see some of Gaudier's drawings and sculpture at Frith Street and was very much excited by them'.

102. Brodzky, p.67.

103. Ibid., pp.67–8.

104. Gaudier's contributions to the 1913 AAA Salon were listed in the catalogue as: *Oiseau de Feu* (No. 1212), *Wrestler* (No. 1213), *Madonna* (No. 1214), *Haldane MacFall* (No. 1215), *Horace Brodzky* (No. 1216), and *Alfred Wolmark* (No. 1217).

105. Brodzky, p.127.

106. Pound, *Gaudier-Brzeska. A Memoir*, p.51.

107. Brodzky, p.130.

108. Winifred Gill to Duncan Grant, 29 December 1966, unpublished, Tate Gallery archives.

109. Gaudier also executed a marble version of *Cat*, which was exhibited at the Whitechapel Art Gallery, May–June 1914, No. 188, as *Cat (Marble) Owned by Omega Workshops*.

110. Reproduced by Hulme in *The New Age*, 9 March 1914, as part of his

'Contemporary Drawings' series.

111. Gaudier to Sophie, 28 November 1912.
112. Pound, 'Prefaratory Note' to the catalogue of *A Memorial Exhibition of the Work of Henri Gaudier-Brzeska*, Leicester Galleries, May–June 1918.
113. Brodzky, p.94.
114. Brodzky, pp.90–1.
115. Ibid.
116. MacFall to Brodzky, 'various dates in' 1919, Brodzky, p.172.
117. Gaudier, *The Egoist*, 15 June 1914.
118. Pound, *Gaudier-Brzeska. A Memoir*, pp.45–6.
119. Pound to William Carlos Williams, 19 December 1913, *Letters*, p.65.
120. The drawing is still preserved in Pound's collection of Gaudier's work.
121. Pound's 'The Serious Artist', 'Rabindraneth Tagore' and 'The Divine Mystery' were published in *The New Freewoman* on 15 October, 1 November and 15 November 1913.
122. Pound, 'The New Sculpture', *The Egoist*, 16 February 1914.
123. Gaudier to *The Egoist*, 16 March 1914.
124. Pound, *Gaudier-Brzeska. A Memoir*, p.50.
125. Epstein, *Let There Be Sculpture*, p.59.
126. Brodzky, *Henri Gaudier-Brzeska*, pp.58–9.
127. Lewis, 'Early London Environment', *T. S. Eliot. A Symposium*, ed. Richard March and Tambimuttu (London, 1948).
128. Pound, *Gaudier-Brzeska. A Memoir*, p.52.
129. Gaudier, 'Vortex. Gaudier-Brzeska', *Blast No. 1*, p.157.
130. Goldring, *South Lodge*, p.xix.
131. Gaudier to Wadsworth, 18 November 1914, wrote: 'I knew "Flushing", it was hanging on Ezra's wall when I departed' (Pound, *Gaudier-Brzeska. A Memoir*, p.81). The woodcut, which seems stylistically to have been executed early in 1914, is actually listed as *Harbour of Flushing* in the March 1919 catalogue of Wadsworth's Adelphi Gallery one-man show (No. 3).
132. Goldring, *South Lodge*, p.47.
133. Hunt, *The Flurried Years*, p.108.
134. Aldington, *Life for Life's Sake*, p.92.
135. Ford to Lewis, 1913, W. K. Rose, 'Pound and Lewis: The Crucial Years', *Agenda*, Autumn–Winter 1969–70, p.122.
136. Goldring, *South Lodge*, p.65.
137. Ford, *Return to Yesterday*, p.419.
138. Ibid., p.418.

**Chapter Eight**

1. In the first edition of the Twenty-One Gallery catalogue of *Drawings and Sculpture by Jacob Epstein* (3–24 December 1913 and 1–17 January 1914) five sculptures are listed: *Carving in Flenite No. 1. 1913* (No. 1), *Carving in Flenite. No. 2. 1913* (No. 2), *Head of Romilly John, Bronze. 1907.* (No. 3), *Babe's Head, Bronze. 1907.* (No. 4), *Group of Birds, Marble. 1913* (No. 5). See also footnote 40, chapter six.
2. Hulme, 'Mr Epstein and the Critics', *The New Age*, 25 December 1913.
3. Lewis to *The New Age*, 8 January 1914.
4. Hulme, 'Modern Art. I. – The Grafton Group (at the Alpine Club)', *The New Age*, 15 January 1914.
5. Fry to Grant, 26 January 1914, *Letters*, p.378.
6. Hulme, 'Modern Art. II. – A Preface Note and Neo-Realism', *The New Age*, 12 February 1914.
7. Hulme, 'Modern Art. III. – The London Group', *The New Age*, 26 March 1914.
8. This painting was perhaps shown as *The Dance* (No. 22) at the May–June 1914 Whitechapel Art Gallery exhibition, *Twentieth Century Art*.
9. Altogether Hulme reproduced drawings by Epstein, Gaudier, Roberts, Wadsworth, Nevinson and Bomberg in *The New Age* – although he announced at the start of the series that Lewis, Etchells and Hamilton would be represented as well. 'Some of the drawings are Cubist, some are not', he wrote in his introduction to the series. 'Perhaps the only quality they possess in common is that they are all abstract in character. The series includes everyone in England who is doing interesting work of this character.' (*The New Age*, 2 April 1914.) Roberts' *Study for Dancers* may well have been the 'Drawing' called *Dancer* which he displayed as No. 59 in the 1917 New York Vorticist Exhibition.
10. Roberts, in *Abstract & Cubist Paintings & Drawings* (p.5), gives both the study and the painting of *Dancers* to 1913. But Lewis would have borrowed *Dancers* in the spring of 1914 as the most recent and radical example of Roberts' work, and the painting therefore probably dates from the winter of 1913–14.
11. Roberts, *A Reply to My Biographer*, p.9.
12. Hulme, note on Roberts' *Study for Dancers*, *The New Age*, 6 April 1914.
13. Roberts, *Abstract & Cubist Paintings & Drawings*, p.4.
14. It is not known whether the proportions of this painting were literally as monumental as the figures they contain.
15. Roberts, *Abstract & Cubist Paintings & Drawings*, p.5.
16. Ibid. *Religion* now survives only as a reproduction in *Blast No. 1* (plate xiv). Roberts himself states that it was a 'drawing', but the 1927 Quinn Sale Catalogue notes that Roberts' *Religion* (No. 442B) was a watercolour measuring 75·5 × 56 cm.
17. *Chinnereth* was exhibited at Bomberg's one-man show in the Chenil Gallery, July 1914, No. 16.
18. Trans. H. L. C. Jaffé, *De Stijl, 1917–31. The Dutch Contribution to Modern Art* (Amsterdam, 1956), p.62.
19. Bomberg to Siegfried Gideon, 27 July 1953, Lipke, *David Bomberg*, p.48.
20. The opinion of Denis Richardson, reported by his mother Alice Mayes in *The Young Bomberg, 1914–1925*, p.37.
21. See footnote 19.
22. Hulme, 'Modern Art. III.'
23. Fry, *The Nation*, 14 March 1914.
24. Bomberg's five exhibits at the first London Group show were: *Acrobats* (No. 47), *Men and Lads Scheme A* (No. 48), *Men and Lads Scheme B* (No. 49), *In the Hold* (No. 67), and *Japanese Play* (No. 47).
25. *The Athenaeum*, 14 March 1914.
26. Roberts, *A Press View at the Tate Gallery*, pp. unnumbered.
27. Bomberg, unpublished memoir, 1957, in the possession of Mrs Lilian Bomberg.
28. Sonia Joslen, interview with the author, December 1971.
29. Bomberg, foreword to the catalogue of his one-man show at the Chenil Gallery, July 1914. It was composed in a hurry: Bomberg later remembered that 'one minute was allowed to dictate a few words for insertion as an introduction to the exhibition before the typed copy of the catalogue went to the printers'. (Unpublished 1957 memoir in the possession of Mrs Lilian Bomberg.)
30. Clive Bell, *Art*, pp.8, 154, 24–5.
31. Ibid., p.199.
32. Ibid., pp.237–8.
33. Ibid., pp.275, 254, 272, 262, 25.
34. See footnote 19.
35. Alice Mayes, letter to the author, 17 July 1973.
36. *Daily Chronicle*, 25 June 1914.
37. The Borough Librarian of Tower Hamlets to the Tate Gallery, 19 June 1969, *The Tate Gallery. Acquisitions 1968–9* (London, 1969), p.6.
38. James Newmark to the Tate Gallery, 17 December 1968, ibid.
39. Reported by Alice Mayes' son, Denis Richardson, in a letter to the author, 23 September 1973.
40. Lilian Bomberg, interview.
41. Lipke, *David Bomberg*, p.37.
42. Alice Mayes, *The Young Bomberg, 1914–1925*, pp.2–3.
43. Bomberg, unpublished memoir, 1957, owned by Mrs Lilian Bomberg.
44. Bomberg, 'The Bomberg Papers', ed. D. Wright and P. Swift, *X, A Quarterly Review*, June 1960, p.109.
45. To link *Composition* with the lost painting of *Reading from Torah* (Chenil catalogue No. 5) is pure supposition on the part of the author; but the resemblances between *Composition* and the *Gouache Study for The Mud Bath II* are strong enough for it to be likely. Bomberg would probably not have developed a theme as far as *Composition* without executing a final painting, and at least one study for *Composition* survives to prove that he devoted a lot of attention to the design. (Reproduced in the catalogue of *Abstract Art in England*,

*1913–1915*, d'Offay Couper Gallery (London, 1970), No. 11.) There is also a very elaborate chalk study on the back of *Composition*, showing the design in an almost identical stage of development.

46. Bomberg to Alun R. Jones, 23 December 1953, Jones, *Hulme*, p.116.

47. All the preceding passages from Hulme's review of Bomberg's exhibition have been taken from 'Modern Art. IV'.

**Chapter Nine**

1. Hulme, 'Modern Art. III'.
2. *The Athenaeum*, 14 March 1914, recorded that *Radiation's* 'colour is gay and daring'.
3. Konody, *Observer*, 8 March 1914.
4. Pound, *The Egoist*, 16 March 1914.
5. Wadsworth's *March* was exhibited neither in the first London Group show nor in any other exhibition.
6. Pound, 'Vorticism', *The Fortnightly Review*.
7. Printed in *Blast No. 1*, pp.119–25.
8. Ibid., p.119.
9. Ibid., p.122.
10. Hulme, 'Modern Art. III'.
11. *Improvisation No. 30* was listed as No. 286 in the 1913 AAA Salon catalogue.
12. Fry, *The Nation*, 2 August 1913.
13. Bell, *Art*, p.180.
14. Arthur Jerome Eddy, *Cubists and Post-Impressionism* (Chicago, 1914), pp.125–6.
15. *The New Weekly*, 20 June 1914.
16. *Planners (A Happy Day)* was simply called *A Happy Day* in the 1927 Quinn Sale catalogue where it was listed as No. 188A. The prefix 'Planners' must therefore have been added later, perhaps – as Lewis's 1949 letter quoted in the text here seems to indicate – before exhibiting the drawing in the May 1949 Lewis exhibition at the Redfern Gallery (No. 17).
17. Lewis to Charles Handley-Read, September 1949. The text of this important letter is here taken from the original version published in Lewis's *Letters*, p.504. Handley-Read's transcription of the letter in his *The Art of Wyndham Lewis* (London, 1951), rephrases some passages; but his rearrangement of 'by this is meant subjective intellection, like magic or religion' has been retained here for the sake of clarity.
18. Lewis, *Blast No. 2*, p.40.
19. Nevinson, 'Vital English Art – A Lecture Delivered by Mr Nevinson at the Doré Galleries', *The New Age*, 18 June 1914.
20. Konody, *Observer*, 8 March 1914.
21. Rutter, *Some Contemporary Artists*, p.194.
22. The only satisfactory record of *Tum-Tiddly-Um-Tum-Pom-Pom* is a photograph in the *Western Mail*, 15 May 1914. A photograph in the *Daily Herald*, 22 January 1920, shows it hanging in

Desti's, a London nightclub, under the title of *Gaiety*.

23. *The New Weekly*, review of the 1914 AAA Salon, 20 July 1914. The critic was, however, describing exhibit No. 64, *Syncopation*, in the passage quoted here. So either the *Western Mail* confused its photograph with *Syncopation*, or else Nevinson himself changed the picture's title for the AAA Salon. He did, nevertheless, also exhibit a work in the Salon's Applied Art Section as *Tum-Tiddly-Tum [sic]-Tum-Pom-Pom* (No. 1411).
24. Gaudier, 'The AAA Ltd.' Gaudier, too, is describing *Syncopation*, and adds that 'the coloured relief (i.e. No. 1411) is at least free from this banality – yet there are cyphers and letters – and though the whole is in good movement I do not appreciate it'. His description of No. 1411 suggests a totally different work, unconnected either with Bank Holiday crowds or Hampstead Heath. (See previous footnote.)
25. 'Futurist Painting: Technical Manifesto', 11 April 1910. From the translation in the Sackville Gallery catalogue.
26. Severini painted his *Dynamic Hieroglyph* in Pienza during the summer of 1912, but he must have brought it back with him later that year to his Paris studio, where Nevinson would doubtless have seen it.
27. Konody, *Observer*, 8 March 1914. *Portrait of a Motorist* was listed as No. 84 in the exhibition catalogue. The only photograph of this missing painting which the author has been able to trace is not worth reproducing here: a mere glimpse of a canvas set at an angle on an easel in Nevinson's studio, pictured in the *Daily Sketch*, 29 March 1919. Judging by Nevinson's *Chauffeur* drawing, which it closely resembles, this badly blurred image must represent *Portrait of a Motorist*.
28. Hulme, 'Modern Art. III'.
29. *The New Age's* reproduction is now the only surviving record of the *Chauffeur* drawing.
30. Boccioni, 'Technical Manifesto of Futurist Sculpture', 11 April 1912.
31. *Automobilist* is untraced, and the only clear record of its appearance is a photograph discovered by the author in the Tate Gallery Library's Nevinson archive: this is reproduced here. The following information is printed on the back of the photograph: 'The exhibition of the National Society of Painters, Sculptors, Engravers and Potters, at the Royal Institute Galleries, London. 445688. "Machine Slave", a metallic, angular sculpture by Mr C. R. W. Nevinson. S. and G. – 9.2.33.' Definite proof that this sculpture was originally called *Automobilist* is supplied by a photograph reproduced in the *Daily Graphic*, 11 September 1915, where a plaster version is shown on view at a Royal Army Medical Corps exhibition.

Konody's review of this exhibition in the *Observer* (12 September 1915) describes it as 'Mr Nevinson's futurist bust of an "automobilist"'. The sculpture was also exhibited in the February 1915 Friday Club Show at the Alpine Club Gallery. Another sculpture by Nevinson, which may be connected with *Automobilist*, was listed as *The Mechanic* in the catalogue of his 1916 one-man show at the Leicester Galleries, London.

32. Nevinson, *Paint and Prejudice*, p.63.
33. *The Star's* description of *The Arrival* agrees in so many respects with the painting now in the Tate Gallery that the two works must be synonymous. However, when Nevinson exhibited it again at the second London Group show in March 1915 it was retitled with the topicality of war in mind as *My Arrival at Dunkirk*. A photograph of the latter in the *Daily Express*, 25 February 1915, proves that it was the same painting as *The Arrival* now in the Tate Gallery.
34. Aldington, *The New Freewoman*, 1 December 1913.
35. From a report in the *Daily Sketch*, 23 May 1914.
36. Nevinson, *Paint and Prejudice*, p.61.
37. Pound, 'Vorticism', *The Fortnightly Review*.
38. Nevinson, *Paint and Prejudice*, p.61.
39. *Daily Mirror*, 16 March 1914.
40. Nevinson to Lewis, 19 November 1913, Department of Rare Books, Cornell University.
41. Edward Storer, *The New Witness*, 11 March 1915.
42. Henry Wood Nevinson, Newark *Evening News*, 17 January 1914.
43. Lechmere, interview. Miss Lechmere was referring to the evening staged by Hulme, Pound and Lewis for the Quest Society at Kensington Town Hall, Spring 1914.
44. Goldring, *South Lodge*, p.64.
45. Lewis, *Blasting and Bombardiering*, pp.37–8.
46. Boccioni, *Pittura Scultura Futuriste* (Milan, 1914), p.203.
47. Nevinson, *Paint and Prejudice*, p.60.
48. The text of the manifesto was also published by *Lacerba* (15 July 1914) in English and Italian. It was later reprinted by Nevinson in *Paint and Prejudice*, pp.58–60, but the final paragraph, with its controversial list of names, was understandably omitted.
49. Roberts, *A Press View at the Tate Gallery*, pp. unnumbered.
50. Wadsworth to Lewis, 17 December 1913, Department of Rare Books, Cornell University.
51. 'R.H.C.' (pseudonym for A. R. Orage), *The New Age*, 8 January 1914.
52. Pound to Joyce, *c*. 1 April 1914, *Pound/Joyce*, p.26.
53. Wadsworth to Lewis, 4 February 1914, Department of Rare Books, Cornell University.

54. Rebel Art Centre prospectus, private collection.
55. Nevinson, *Paint and Prejudice*, p.60.
56. H. W. Nevinson to Blip (?) 28 January 1914, Department of Rare Books, Cornell University.
57. Lechmere, interview.
58. Lewis, *Blasting and Bombardiering*, pp.36–7. The *Manchester Guardian*, however, contradicted Lewis's perhaps biased memory: 'the Vorticists, who promised at the beginning to provide a belligerent opinion, dwindled into silence very early in the evening.' (13 June 1914).
59. *Evening News*, 8 August 1914; 'Charles Brookfarmer', *The New Age*, 18 June 1914.
60. *Manchester Guardian*, 13 June 1914.
61. The letter was also printed in *The New Weekly*, 13 June 1914, and *The Egoist*, 15 June 1914.
62. Nevinson to Lewis, 13 June 1914, Department of Rare Books, Cornell University.
63. Nevinson to *The New Weekly*, 20 June 1914.
64. Lewis, 'Automobilism', *The New Weekly*, 20 June 1914.
65. Pound, *The Egoist*, 15 June 1914.
66. *Yorkshire Observer*, 15 June 1914.
67. Lewis, interview with 'M.M.B.', *Daily News and Leader*, 7 April 1914.
68. *The Egoist*, 15 April 1914.
69. Lewis, unsigned paper with other notes, undated, Department of Rare Books, Cornell University.
70. Pound to William Carlos Williams, 19 December 1913, *Letters*, p.65.
71. Pound to Quinn, 10 March 1916, *Letters*, p.121.
72. Roberts, *Abstract & Cubist Paintings & Drawings*, p.8.
73. Ibid., p.7.
74. Pound to Gladys Hynes, 1956, Walter Michel, *Wyndham Lewis*, p.67.
75. Lewis, 'The Melodrama of Modernity', *Blast No. 1*, p.143.
76. *Il Piccolo della Sera*, Trieste, June 1914, Pound, *Memoir*, pp.53–4. 'James Joyce sent me the clipping', Pound explained, 'but how all this nonsense ever got to Trieste remains a mystery to this day. It was, however, one of our jokes for the season.'
77. Pound, *Memoir*, p.55. Corroboration of the exact date is provided by a letter which Pound wrote to Amy Lowell around 13 July, where he reminds her that '*Blast* dinner on the 15th as I phoned this P.M.' (*Letters*, p.77).
78. Goldring, *South Lodge*, p.70.
79. Pound, *Memoir*, p.55.
80. Lechmere, interview.
81. Pound, *The Egoist*, 15 June 1914.
82. Lewis, 'Kill John Bull With Art', *The Outlook*, 18 July 1914.
83. Lewis to John, *c*.1914, *Letters*, p.64.

**Chapter Ten**
1. *Blast No. 1*, p.11.
2. Lewis to Lord Carlow, enclosing a copy of *Blast No. 1*, *c*.July 1914, Geoffrey Wagner, *Wyndham Lewis*, p.141.
3. All the preceding quotations are taken from the editorial of *Blast No. 1*, 'Long live the Vortex', pp. unnumbered.
4. See footnote 2.
5. *Blast No. 1*, pp.11, 12, 11, 18–19, 13.
6. Ibid., pp.17, 15, 16.
7. Ibid., pp.21, 12, 19, 146.
8. Lewis, *Blasting and Bombardiering*, p.42.
9. *Blast No. 1*, pp.22, 23, 25, 26.
10. Ibid., p.27.
11. Ibid., p.28.
12. Goldring, *South Lodge*, pp.67–8.
13. Ford, *Return to Yesterday*, p.419.
14. Rebecca West, interview with the author, 8 February 1971.
15. *Blast No. 1*, p.48.
16. Lewis to the editor of *Partisan Review*, *c*.April 1949, *Letters*, p.492.
17. Lechmere, interview.
18. Saunders to Walter Michel, 1962, Michel, *Wyndham Lewis*, p.152, footnote 11.
19. Goldring, *South Lodge*, p.11.
20. *Blast No. 1*, pp.30–1.
21. Ibid., pp.32–3.
22. Ibid., pp.36–7, 34.
23. Ibid., pp.36–8.
24. Ibid., pp.34, 39.
25. Ibid., pp.40–1.
26. Ibid., p.43.
27. Aldington, *The Egoist*, 15 July 1914.
28. Roberts, *Cometism and Vorticism. A Tate Gallery Catalogue Revised* (London, 1956), pp. unnumbered.
29. Etchells, interview.
30. Lewis, *Blasting and Bombardiering*, pp.35–6.
31. Lilian Bomberg, interview.
32. See T. E. Hulme, *Further Speculations*, ed. Sam Hynes (Minneapolis, 1955), p.107.
33. Hulme, 'Modern Art. IV.'
34. Epstein, *Let There Be Sculpture*, p.75.
35. A proof copy of Lewis's 'Preface' to the catalogue of *Exhibition, Leeds*, dated 16 May 1914, is owned by Omar Pound.
36. Goldring, *South Lodge*, p.67.
37. *Blast No. 1*, pp.135, 132, 130.
38. Ibid., p.144; the second page of 'Long Live the Vortex' (pages unnumbered); p.144.
39. Ibid., pp.134–5.
40. Ibid., p.138.
41. Ibid., pp.136, 142.
42. Ibid., pp.139, 140.
43. Ibid., pp.147, 148.
44. Ibid., p.149.
45. Goldring, *South Lodge*, p.65.
46. Lewis, 'The Vorticists', *Vogue*, September 1956.
47. *Blast No. 1*, p.147.
48. Ibid., p.148.
49. Rutter, *Modern Masterpieces. An Outline of Modern Art* (London, 1940), p.220.

50. Boccioni, *Pittura Scultura Futuriste* (Milan, 1914), pp.263–4.
51. The only other reference to a vortex in *Pittura Scultura Futuriste* occurs when Boccioni discusses 'colour as emotion in itself', and predicts that 'pictorial works will perhaps be whirling [*vorticose*] architecture, sonorous and perfumed, formed of great volumes of coloured gas'. (pp.330–1).
52. According to Gambillo and Fiori's *Archivi del Futurismo*, Vol. 2, Balla executed fourteen pictures in the 1913–14 period which contain the word *Vortice* in their titles, and eight of these are actually called *Vortice* alone. Four other works executed by Balla later in his career also contain the word *Vortice* in their titles; one of them is a lost sculpture.
53. Lewis to Etchells, April–May 1914 (from the Rebel Art Centre), *Letters*, p.60.
54. *Blast No. 1*, p.144.
55. Pound to Harriet Monroe, 7 November 1913, *Letters*, pp.61–2.
56. Pound to Kate Buss, 9 March 1916, *Letters*, p.120.
57. See footnote 70, chapter nine.
58. Eustace Mullins, *This Difficult Individual, Ezra Pound* (New York, 1961), p.98.
59. Pound, *Memoir*, p.93.
60. Pound, 'Vorticism', *The Fortnightly Review*.
61. Pound, 'Wyndham Lewis'.
62. Pound, 'Exhibition at the Goupil Gallery'.
63. Lewis, *Time and Western Man* (London, 1927), p.55.
64. Lewis, *Rude Assignment*, pp.128–9.
65. *Blast No. 1*, p.45.
66. Aldington, *Life for Life's Sake*, p.124.
67. Ibid., pp.126–7.
68. *Oriad*, *Blast No. 1*, p.154.
69. Lewis to the editor of *Partisan Review*, *c*.April 1949, *Letters*, p.491.
70. Pound to Amy Lowell, 1 August 1914, *Letters*, p.78.
71. Aldington, *Life for Life's Sake*, p.127.
72. Pound, 'Vorticism'.
73. Lewis, *Rude Assignment*, p.129.
74. Pound, 'Vorticism'.
75. Lewis to the editor of *Partisan Review*.
76. Pound, *Blast No. 1*, p.153.
77. Ibid., p.154.
78. Ibid. Pater's actual dictum, which appeared in *The School of Giorgione*, reads: 'All art constantly aspires towards the condition of music.'
79. Ibid., p.158.
80. Konody, *Observer*, 5 July 1914.
81. *Blast No. 1*, pp.151–2.
82. Nevinson to the *Observer*, 12 July 1914.
83. Anonymous letter to the *Observer*, 5 July 1914.
84. Lewis, *Blasting and Bombardiering*, p.40. He is here referring to an article called 'Kill John Bull With Art' which he wrote for *The Outlook*, 18 July 1914. (See the last page of chapter nine.)

85. *Morning Post*, review of *Blast No. 1*, reprinted in *Blast No. 2*, p.104.
86. Aldington, *The Egoist*, 1 July 1914. In his second review of *Blast No. 1*, published in *The Egoist* on 15 July 1914, Aldington declared that although 'I am not an art critic, so I suppose I have no right to praise or dispraise these works', it nevertheless seemed to him, 'as an outsider, that these Vorticist painters have created something like a new form of art'.
87. *Truth*, review of *Blast No. 1*, reprinted in *Blast No. 2*, p.104.
88. G. W. Prothero to Pound, 22 October 1914, Noel Stock, *Life of Ezra Pound*, p.162.
89. Bottomley to Paul Nash, 2 October 1914, *Poet and Painter. Being the Correspondence between Gordon Bottomley and Paul Nash, 1910–46*, ed. C. C. Abbott and A. Bertram (Oxford, 1955), p.75.
90. Hunt, *I Have This to Say*, p.212.
91. *Blast No. 1*, pp. unnumbered.
92. Lewis, *Blasting and Bombardiering*, pp.50–1.
93. Ibid., p.35.
94. Ibid., p.50.
95. Ibid., p.55.
96. 'R.H.C.' (pseudonym for A. R. Orage), *The New Age*, 8 January 1914.
97. Waugh, *Vile Bodies* (London, 1930; Penguin edition, 1953), p.52.
98. Pound, *The New Age*, 4 February 1915.
99. Pound, *Blast No. 2*, p.85.


**Chapter Eleven**
1. Pound, *Memoir of Gaudier*, p.56.
2. Lipke, *David Bomberg*, p.51.
3. Guy Deghy and Keith Waterhouse, *Café Royal. Ninety Years of Bohemia* (London, 1955), p.135.
4. Goldring, *South Lodge*, p.71.
5. Lewis, *Blasting and Bombardiering*, p.4.
6. Lewis, *Blast No. 2*, p.14; *Blasting and Bombardiering*, p.39.
7. Roberts, *Memories of the War to End War 1914–18* (London, 1974), p.1.
8. *The Times*, 10 March 1915.
9. Lewis, *Blast No. 2*, pp.78–9.
10. Lewis revealed that the commission came from Violet Hunt, rather than Ford, in *Rude Assignment*, p.122.
11. Goldring, *South Lodge*, p.13. The front room on the first floor was the site of Lewis's scheme, and in July 1971 it still bore traces of red paint on its skirting-boards and built-in cupboards.
12. Rebecca West, interview.
13. Although Lewis himself remembered that he had been asked 'to do a mural' (*Rude Assignment*, p.122), close examination by the author of the wall over the fireplace revealed that no mural had ever been painted on it. Lewis's painting must therefore have been executed on a detachable surface which was presumably taken away or destroyed at the time

of Violet Hunt's departure from the house. This hypothesis is confirmed by Sir Richard Temple, who moved in to South Lodge after Violet Hunt's death. (Letter to the author, 27 July 1971.)
14. Pound to Harriet Monroe, 9 November 1914, *Letters*, p.87.
15. According to measurements of the space above the fireplace taken by the author in July 1971, Lewis's painting could not have been more than 150 cm high × 180·5 cm wide.
16. Roberts, 'Wyndham Lewis, the Vorticist', *The Listener*, 21 March 1957.
17. Roberts, *Abstract & Cubist Paintings & Drawings*, p.7.
18. Roberts, 'Wyndham Lewis, the Vorticist'.
19. Roberts, *Abstract & Cubist Paintings & Drawings*, p.7.
20. Lewis, *Blast No. 2*, p.11.
21. Aldington, *Life for Life's Sake*, pp.150–1.
22. Lewis to Pound, January 1915 (?), *Letters*, p.66.
23. Lewis, 'Preface', November 1928, to the revised edition of *Tarr*.
24. Lewis to Hugh Kenner, 23 November 1953, *Letters*, pp.552–3.
25. Lewis to Harriet Shaw Weaver, March 1916, *Letters*, p.76. Miss Weaver's letter quoted in the text is also to be found ibid.
26. Lewis, *Tarr* (New York, 1918), pp.356, 219, 221, 237, 41–2.
27. Ibid., pp.353–4.
28. Roberts, *Cometism and Vorticism*, pp. unnumbered.
29. Pound to Quinn, 8 March 1915, *Letters*, p.95. 'What the later quarrel with Jacob is, I do not know', Pound wrote to Quinn on 10 March 1916, 'save that Jacob is a fool when he hasn't got a chisel in his hand and a rock before him, and Lewis *can* at moments be extremely irritating. (But then, damn it all, he is quite apt to be in the right.)' *Letters*, p.122.
30. Epstein to Quinn, April 1915, John Quinn Memorial Collection, New York Public Library.
31. Konody, *Observer*, 4 July 1915.
32. Garnett, *The Flowers of the Forest* (London, 1955), p.35.
33. Konody, *Observer*, 4 July 1915. Duncan Grant told the author in an interview that he could not now remember what his contributions were like.
34. Information about the changes undergone by this painting was relayed to the author by Anthony d'Offay, who discussed the picture with Grant himself.
35. Konody, *Observer*, 4 July, 1915.
36. See Patrick Heron's introduction to the catalogue of the *Exhibition of the work of B. S. Turner*, Leeds City Art Gallery, October–November 1964, where he explains how Turner became interested in English avant-garde experiments through his circle of friends – including Orage, Rutter and Epstein – to whom

he was introduced by Heron's father, T. M. Heron.
37. Konody, *Observer*, 4 July 1915.
38. *Glasgow Herald*, 10 June 1915.
39. Hulme prophesied his imminent retirement from art criticism in his *New Age* review of Bomberg's Chenil Gallery one-man show, where he admitted that although 'I have great admiration for some of Mr Bomberg's work, that does not make it any easier for me to write an article about it. An article about one man's pictures is not a thing I should ever do naturally'.
40. *Punch*, 9 June 1915.
41. *The Athenaeum*, 19 June 1915.
42. Lewis, *Blast No. 2*, p.7.
43. All the preceeding extracts from Lewis's 'Note' have been taken from the catalogue of *The First Exhibition of the Vorticist Group, opening 10th June 1915, at the Doré Galleries, London*.
44. Lewis, *Blast No. 2*, pp.39, 47.
45. Ibid., p.39.
46. Ibid., p.40.
47. Ibid., p.42.
48. Ibid., p.43.
49. Ibid.
50. Ibid., pp.44, 45, 46.
51. Ibid., p.47.
52. Ibid., p.5.
53. Ibid., p.92.
54. Lewis, *Blast No. 1*, p.146.
55. *Blast No. 2*, pp.93, 77.
56. Shakespear, quoted in *Etruscan Gate* (Exeter, 1971), p.11.
57. The more finished version of these two landscapes is not inscribed, but the other one is: 'Devil's Cheese Ring. V of R. 1912'.
58. The version of Dorothy Pound's *Ripostes* design reproduced in *Blast No. 2* (p.103) does not contain the words 'Ripostes' or 'Ezra Pound'. It is also reproduced horizontally rather than vertically.
59. Lewis to Pound, January 1915 (?), *Letters*, p.67.
60. Lewis to Pound, 1915, ibid., p.68.
61. The date given to this watercolour is purely hypothetical, but it does seem to stand half-way between Vorticism and her later landscape style.
62. Pound, *The Egoist*, 11 February 1915.
63. Pound, *Blast No. 2*, p.22. The word 'may' printed in the 7th line of *Blast No. 2*'s version of the poem has here been corrected to 'my'.
64. *Poetry*, October 1914.
65. West, 'Indissoluble Matrimony', *Blast No. 1*, pp.110, 111, 112.
66. Lewis, 'Enemy of the Stars', *Blast No. 1*, pp.60, 64, 70.
67. Pound, *Blast No. 2*, p.19. The word 'contes' printed in the final line of *Blast No. 2*'s version of the poem is here corrected to 'contest'.
68. Pound to Harriet Monroe, 10 April 1915, K. K. Ruthven, *A Guide to Ezra Pound's Personae* (*1926*) (Berkeley and Los Angeles, 1969), p.75.

69. Lewis to Pound, January 1915 (?), *Letters*, pp.66–7.
70. See Eliot's obituary article on Lewis, 'The Importance of Wyndham Lewis', *Sunday Times*, 10 March 1957.
71. Lewis, *Blast No. 2*, p.7. The list of contents proposed for the 'next number' included contributions by Lewis, Pound, Dismorr, Etchells, Gaudier, Kramer, Roberts, Saunders and Wadsworth.
72. Pound, 'Vorticism', *Fortnightly Review*, 1 September 1914. For an earlier discussion of this edition of *The Archer*, see the end of Chapter Five, in particular footnote 92.
73. Lewis to Kate Lechmere, Summer 1915 (perhaps not sent), *Letters*, p.69.
74. Ford, *The Outlook*, 31 July 1915.
75. Konody, *Observer*, 1 August 1915.
76. Lewis, *Blast No. 2*, pp.26, 23.
77. Ibid., p.23.
78. John Cournos, *The Egoist*, January 1917.
79. This painting, which only came to light after the Hayward Gallery *Vorticism and its Allies* exhibition, has always been called *The Vortex* by its owner. But a reproduction of *A Bursting Shell* in the *Daily Graphic*, 26 November 1915, identifies it correctly. The painting was No. 66 in the third London Group show, November–December 1915, and probably No. 24 in Nevinson's Leicester Galleries one-man show, September–October 1916.

# Index